Pandeism:
An Anthology

Pandeism: An Anthology

Edited by Knujon Mapson

BOOKS

Winchester, UK
Washington, USA

First published by iff Books, 2017
iff Books is an imprint of John Hunt Publishing Ltd., Laurel House, Station Approach,
Alresford, Hants, SO24 9JH, UK
office1@jhpbooks.net
www.johnhuntpublishing.com
www.iff-books.com

For distributor details and how to order please visit the 'Ordering' section on our website.

ISBN: 978 1 78535 412 0
978 1 78535 413 7 (ebook)
Library of Congress Control Number: 2016943150

A CIP catalogue record for this book is available from the British Library.

Design: Stuart Davies

Printed and bound by CPI Group (UK) Ltd, Croydon, CR0 4YY, UK

CONTENTS

To all humankind:
Bless yourself, for Thou Art God.

Preface

This book is a labor of love—a love of humanity, and a love generated by many people at that. Not all agree with the theory which constitutes its central thesis: Pandeism. But all agree that it is a conception worthy of reasoned examination, and all have made the effort not only to engage in such examination, but to write eloquently of their determinations.

For as long as history has chronicled human thought, humankind has been both united and divided by religion, and most especially by the idea often called 'God.' Vast majorities of peoples in all ages of civilization have subscribed—almost instinctively—to the proposition that our genesis, and the meaning of our existence, lies within the intentional endeavors of a power beyond our immediate abilities of perception. Possibly—if the mystics are to be credited—this power will forever lie altogether beyond our comprehension. But if at last this mystery could be solved, such resolution would go far towards ending human strife, and may even usher in an age of conciliation and peace among the many warring tribes of humankind.

But we, collectively, have had an impossible time agreeing where even to begin. Some hew to the long journey of distant starlight and the breakdown of radioactive isotopes and mathematical models which fill multiple blackboards as clues to this event, and possibly as the only ones. Others point to stories of revelation in dreams, revelation by possession, revelation in the appearance of vastly powerful forces prevailing upon prophets with stories of a metaphorical date and sequence of Creation. Our assumptions as to the past having proved an inconstant barometer, we discard them, and begin again in the now. We work our way backwards; and once we reach the beginning, work our way forwards again, all the way to the distant destiny of our Universe, the end of time as we know it.

It is a sufficiently simple thing to expound upon the commonplace definition of Pandeism: a system of belief interweaving the most logical and defensible aspects of two other, and more ancient, belief systems—Pantheism and Deism—to the degree that these are coherently reconcilable. And yet, it is something else entirely to explicate the logic through which these arguments are brought together, in order to generate a synergy, a rational holistic approach to answering the four great mysteries of life: Is there a God? How did we get here? Why are we here? And, where are we going?

The oversimplified explanation of Pandeism tells the story of an inquisitive entity of inestimable power, one which carried on alone in its existence. This entity lacked the knowledge of experiencing interactions with any other beings; at the same time, it was without limit in its power over whatever matter or energy existed. And, as such, it paradoxically lacked some knowledge relating to the limitations on its own power; it was without limit in its knowledge of that which was, and, as such, it lacked the knowledge of experiencing ignorance and uncertainty. As an equally paradoxical extended consequence, it knew nothing of the myriad experiences which flow from existence in such a state, experiences such as anger, fear, restlessness, and sorrow, and so nothing again of overcoming such things and in their place experiencing peace, courage, fulfillment, and joy.

This entity, being all-powerful (at least, relatively) and all-knowing (again, at least, relatively), was, to the best of our traditions, a 'God.' And this 'God' took the only measure which would allow it to gain all of its missing knowledge—it ceased to be a God. Whatever it was which constituted this being became—for a certain time, though a lengthy one by our means of observation—a Cosmos, a physical Universe of energy and matter, wherein all of the experiences our Creator existing alone lacked would come to manifest, and would necessarily unfold naturally.

In order to guarantee that these experiences would be the unadulterated truth of a Universe imbued with limitations, this unfolding would need to be bereft of any sort of guidance or intervention on the part of our Creator.

Naturally, this view has a great variety of ramifications, and there are many directions from which to approach it. This is precisely why an anthology was needed to address this topic. The articles between these covers come, by design, from all different sorts of people, people living all over the world, with widely different perspectives and different levels of formal philosophical training and writing experience. Some have published dozens of books or articles in a wide array of fields. For others, their article in this book is their first formal publication. This is by design. The world is a diverse place and Pandeism is a philosophy with diverse ramifications; our authorship intently reflects that.

This diversity is likewise reflected in the styles of writing variously adopted by our authors. Some meticulously footnote every assertion; some simply set their thoughts out there with no reliance on outside authority. Some wax poetic with spontaneity, others are steeped deep in mathematical prose, and others still communicate in straightforwardly common talk, all of which ultimately makes for a lively anthology—almost an extended conversation between well-spoken champions of a wide range of viewpoints.

Acknowledgments

The list of encouragers and contributors to the creation of this book is beyond words. I would be remiss if I did not extend thanks to those who have inspired our efforts through years of inestimably well-thought discussion: Amy Perry, Harshita Pande, Paul Seabrook, Nicholas Dewey, and William Singourd, and our literary agent—and an indispensable taskmaster—Brian Abramson. Certain of our article authors have similarly been indispensable in their encouragement and editing assistance beyond simply submitting their pieces—especially Alan H. Dawe, Bernardo Kastrup, Poffo Ortiz, and Dan Dana. The publication of this book was greatly aided by the support we received through our Kickstarter effort, which ran from 12 January 2016 to 11 February 2016.

Our most generous donors (and early buyers of the book) through this effort are:

Individuals

Lisa Bostlund
Marwan Gazali
Heather L. Hoffman
Roger Holzberg
James Kelsey
Zbigniew Komala
Eileen Kravitz
Mary Levy
Susan Lyon
Patrick McGinty
Amber Otto
Ríanna Peck
Mary Peleti
PerturbSecular
Albertine Rubin
William Singourd
Sheila Smith
Matthew Luis G. Zapatero

Organizations

Bourgeois Mystics (http://bourgeoismystics.com/)
The Paradise Project (http://www.theparadiseproject.org/)

A Brief History of Pandeism

Knujon Mapson

Mr Mapson is a naturist and philosopher who has, for over a decade, beginning during his pursuit of the Bachelor of Arts in Religious Studies, been a constant voice advocating the examination of Pandeism as a philosophical system. To this end, he has been a primary contributor to the Pandeism YouTube channel, and the creator of the Everything2 Pandeism Index. Much material in this brief history of Pandeism is adapted from the Wikipedia page on Pandeism—of which Mr Mapson is a substantial contributor as well.

Pandeism is a theological theory proposing that instead of the traditional notion of an external God-entity creating our Universe wholesale and then observing it from the outside, our Universe is more logically explained as the product of a Creator wholly becoming it, with principles in place from this becoming which allow its structure—including life within it—to arise organically within it as part of its experience. The history of this idea reaches back to the earliest etchings of human history. The struggle to formally define and delineate it as a category of thought has been but the last few hundred years of that, and much of that was critical of the concept, even immediately dismissive of it without exploration of its implications. But, slowly and certainly, Pandeism has forced itself to be reckoned with, taking its place along the continuum of theological possibilities.

As noted, all of this begins very, very long ago. Karen Armstrong's groundbreaking *History of God* opens with Father Wilhelm Schmidt's description of African tribal speculation in his 1912 book, *The Origin of the Idea of God:*[1]

> In the beginning, human beings created a God who was the First Cause of all things and Ruler of heaven and Earth. He was not represented by images and had no temple or priests in his service. He was too exalted for an inadequate human cult. Gradually he faded from the consciousness of his people. He had become so remote that they decided that they did not want him any more. Eventually he was said to have disappeared.[2]

Armstrong observes this God to be "strangely absent from their daily lives," having "no special cult and...never depicted in effigy," described as "inexpressible" and unable to be "contaminated by the world of men."[3] And so it was replaced, Schmidt theorized, by "the more attractive gods of the pagan pantheons."[4]

Anthropologically, spirituality appears to begin nearer the ground, with the conception of a spirit-force carried within other living things, and even natural phenomena possessing a motive capacity. Primitive man found it intuitive that storm and sun are just as alive as leaping gazelles and creeping vines, different manifestations of the same thing. The assignment of capacities to discrete forces of nature and ancestral spirits leads to their aggrandizement into the first polytheistic deities.

The Pandeism of the Mythological World

Notions of beasts and trees and rivers and thunderclouds having a spiritual existence all their own, combined with the idea that people's own deceased ancestors had spirits that lingered on in this world—some more powerfully than others—led to the first progression of religion, the belief that the more powerful spirits had ultimate authority over some domain, such as one spirit with power over the flow of all rivers. Once human beings devised the notions of these earliest gods, they rewrote the older stories passed down from times beyond memory to claim that these gods had always been so, crediting them with all manner of creative enterprise.

In due time, ancient mythologies came to express the idea of a world created from the physical substance of a destroyed deity, a necessary predecessor idea to the philosophy of Pandeism. Armstrong describes the 5000-year-old Sumerian myth of young god Marduk slaying elder goddess Tiamat and creating the world from her body:

> Marduk stood over Tiamat's vast corpse and decided to create a new world: He split her body in two to form the arch of the sky and the world of men; next he devised the laws that would keep everything in its appointed place. Order must be achieved.[5]

Norse mythology similarly tells of Odin and brothers Vé and Vili defeating frost giant Ymir to create our world from Ymir's body, his flesh becoming the dirt, bones becoming the mountains, brains becoming the clouds, and skull serving as the heavens. Aztec myths recount how voracious Coatlique was torn to pieces by her grandchildren—Quetzalcoatl and Tezcatlipoca—with her body then being used to create the Earth and Sky.

Ancient Chinese mythology held that "the entire Universe was a single organism,"[6] and later Chinese mythology describes the creation of elements of the physical world (mountains, rivers, the Sun and Moon, etc.) from the body of a being: Pángŭ. Born from a Cosmic Egg Pángŭ held the pieces of this egg apart as he grew, ten feet per day for thousands of years, to create the Earth and the Sky. When Pángŭ died, his eyes became the Sun and Moon, his blood became the rivers, and so on.

Perhaps the most pandeistic of these early ideas comes from the Georgia and Society islands of the South Pacific, whose people provide the tale of Ta'aroa, "a primal idea of divine unity,"[7] a lone godhead, far above the other denizens of his polytheistic pantheon. A poem by those holding Ta'aroa as their

Creator expounds:

> He was; Ta'aroa was his name; he abode in the void. No Earth, no sky, no men. Ta'aroa calls, but nought answers; and alone existing, he became the universe. The props are Ta'aroa; the rocks are Ta'aroa; the sands are Ta'aroa; it is thus he himself is named.[8]

Each of these myths presents the god-made world in its most visceral, physical sense—in some, our globe is the flesh of a god, the stones and mountains are bones, rivers and seas are blood. These myths, developed by people unaware of the true scope of our Universe, may fairly be posited to describe the creation of the 'entire world' from the body of one being. Armstrong points out that such "dramatic and evocative stories of gods and goddesses helped people to articulate their sense of the powerful but unseen forces that surrounded them."[9]

Ancient Movements into Monotheistic/Pantheistic Thought

The first foray into the next progression, from these polytheistic ideas to monotheism, happened nearly three and a half millennia ago, in Egypt, under the reign of Pharaoh Amenhotep IV. Physicist and philosopher Max Bernhard Weinstein identified the idea of primary matter derived from an original spirit as found by the ancient Egyptians to be an early form of Pandeism.[10] And this pharaoh in particular believed there was but one true and supreme deity, of which all others were simply pale reflections—and this was Aton (or Aten), originally God of the Sun-Disk. In worship of this one true deity, Amenhotep changed his name to Akhenaton: 'beloved of Aton.'

Aton had previously occurred in the ancient Egyptian "Story of Sinuhe," as a servant or perhaps simply a face of Sun-God Re. Akhenaton not only changed his own name to incorporate Aton into it, but decreed that the names of other 'false' gods were to be scratched out, their images destroyed. The epic poem he commissioned in worship of Aton—the "Hymn to the Aton"—deemed Re (formerly recognized as chief God) as simply another aspect of Aton (declaring to Aton, "As thou art Re, thou reachest to the end of them").

Atonism was enforced for two decades by decree of the Pharaoh, but the whims of man denied this newfound cult life beyond that of its progenitor. After Akhenaton's death, those left in power quickly abandoned the belief, renaming Akhenaton's child heir from Tutankhaten to Tutankhamun (Amun being one of the banished gods), and smashing the temples built to Aton during Akhenaton's reign. But the influence of the cult of Aton may well have been preserved and passed on to other cultures in the region, as evidenced by the word *Adonai*—today a chief name of God in Judaism.

Before we fall into the common trap of assigning the origin of all thought to the Western world, we must be mindful that the Rig-Veda and its successor, the Upanishads, the divine texts underscoring Hinduism, may themselves have been hundreds, possibly thousands, of years old by this time. The Vedas were born from a clash of early civilizations some thirty-seven centuries ago. Inhabitants of the Indus valley, who had established themselves earlier than 2000 BC, encountered the Aryans, of what would later become Iran. The Aryans, Armstrong writes, had "concluded that nobody—not even the gods—could understand the mystery of existence."[11] But Armstrong observes that "the *Upanishads* did evolve a distinctive conception of godhood that transcends the gods but is found to be intimately present in all things."[12]

A somewhat more recent work of great importance in Hindu mythology, the Bhagavad Gita, described by some scholars as the deepest scripture in the world, is the most famous chapter of the Mahābhārata, one of the two major Sanskrit epics. Here, the great warrior Arjuna, accompanied by his charioteer Krishna, is engaged in an epic battle of the Kurukshetra War between the Kauravas and the heroic Pandavas for the throne of Hastinapur. A brilliant archer, Arjuna knows he will easily slaughter many of his evil cousins on the battlefield. But, tired of battle, he desires to give up violence altogether.

Krishna persuades Arjuna against retiring from the fight, for it is a predestined cleansing of evil. To persuade Arjuna, Krishna reveals his true self, Viśvarūpa—the unity of all things, all beings, in all times and places. All things are shown to Arjuna to be one, and to be part of the Creator, which has itself become a great and universal game played out through our lives. Arjuna is part of the Creator, and so he is the same as everybody whom he is fated to kill, and as everybody else who simply sits and observes, or who has no knowledge of this battle at all. This too, Weinstein finds, echoes the primary thrust of Pandeism,[13] the Creator of our Universe in fact becoming our Universe, rationally motivated by a need to share in the experiences of beings coming to exist therein.

The Ancient Greek Philosophers

Thirty-two centuries after Akhenaton, on the other side of the Mediterranean Sea, it was the polytheism of the Greek world which was under attack. Doubt had arisen among a distinctive and elite group of philosophers, known as the philosophers of nature: Thales of Miletos, born around 624 BC; Anaximander, born around 610 BC; Xenophanes of Colophon, born around 570 BC—remembered now only through surviving fragments of his poetry; Heraclitus of Ephesus, born around 535 BC; Parmenides, likely born in 520 BC; and their later followers among cohorts such as the Eleatics and the Stoics.

These thinkers sought a rational and scientific reduction of the mysteries of the world to mundane knowledge. Thales, the first chronicled to have attempted to explain the nature of our

Universe by natural means alone, discounted supernatural influences. Indeed, classical German scholar August Heinrich Matthiae later declared that "Philosophy begins with Thales."[14] Thales was revered by his contemporaries among the Milesian philosophers who followed his efforts, and it is this which launched the philosophical direction which twentieth-century philosopher F. E. Peters would later credit in this way: "Pandeism...is the legacy of the Milesians."[15]

Another Milesian, Anaximander, was even more pandeistic, having similarly concluded that the fundamental element was air. Anaximander thought the substance to be a rarified element unlike the essential elements of the world, one called *apeiron*. This apeiron, Anaximander thought, had been temporarily liberated from its primal state to form the world. Friedrich Nietzsche would later characterize Anaximander as viewing "all coming-to-be as though it were an illegitimate emancipation from eternal being, a wrong for which destruction is the only penance."[16] English historian of philosophy Andrew Gregory notes in particular that "some construction using pan-, whether it be pantheism, pandeism or pankubernism, describes Anaximander reasonably well," though he does go on to question whether Anaximander's view of the distinction between apeiron and cosmos makes these labels technically relevant at all.[17]

The possibility that our Universe might be made of yet another substance—'God'—was the proposition of Xenophanes. Openly disdaining the anthropomorphic nature of the gods of the Greeks, he wrote of how:

> mortals suppose that the gods are born (as they themselves are) / and that they wear man's clothing and have human voice and body / but if cattle or lions had hands / so as to paint with their hands and produce works of art as men do / they would paint their gods and give them bodies in form like

their own / horses like horses, cattle like cattle.[18]

Xenophanes envisioned a god unlike man or anything else, but encompassing everything: "One god greatest among gods and men, not at all like mortals in body or in thought."[19] Here we see the first glimmerings of a God with boundaries far removed from the deities previously conceived in this corner of the world. Xenophanes' declaration suggests his belief in a single, overarching, conscious divine power. He characterizes this highest god as "conscious and perceiving with the whole of itself, capable of moving all things by exercise of mind and thought, able to accomplish all things while remaining itself unmoving."[20] For this, Weinstein wrote that Xenophanes spoke as a Pandeist in stating that there was one god which "abideth ever in the selfsame place, moving not at all" and yet "sees all over, thinks all over, and hears all over."[21]

Xenophanes influenced the pandeistic bent of other great thinkers of later generations, including Heraclitus, a philosopher known for the complexity and intricacy of his views. Seeking an understanding of our Universe which was rational, logical, and isolated from myth and legend, Heraclitus developed a unique conception: the Cosmos as a divine and ever-changing energy. This profound thought of Heraclitus is startlingly relevant when seen through the lens of the hard-won scientific discovery of forces driving our Universe in the age of physics, astrophysics, and organic chemistry. His cosmology contains four remarkable and prescient observations:

1. That the Cosmos is itself not an illusion;
2. The "flux doctrine": reality is not *being* but *becoming;*
3. That "fire is the ultimate reality; all things are just manifestations of fire";[22]
4. And, at last, the fire itself is the thing called the *Logos*.

The ancients had no conception of the modernly known 'Big Bang.' That fire, of sorts, might have offered a sufficient beginning and end of the divine, the logos which contained all which was necessary to the plan of our Universe—that would suffice for Pandeism, for in one fundamental allegorical sense the Pandeist god is the salmon god—it spawns and it dies. But the logos of Heraclitus was eternal—undying in its unstableness.

Xenophanes and Heraclitus would influence two further groups of followers, the Stoics and the Eleatics. Notably, Weinstein found Pandeism reflected in the ideas of Heraclitus, and of the Stoics,[23] who were immanentistic pantheists as well. Their natural fondness for Heraclitus and his fiery logos matched their estimation that it was reason—the logos—pervading our Universe as divine fire.

The Eleatics echoed the explanation of Heraclitus, viewing existence as unending change, but they used primary matter, as well, as the framework for describing the nature of our Universe. They maintained that a universal unity of being was the idea underlying any accurate explanation of the nature of our Universe. Because human sensory perception is easily fooled as to the nature of things presented to it, man may not experience this unity through investigation of the physical world. To overcome this deception, man must instead turn inwards, seeking fundamental truth in thought alone. In this way, thought the Eleatics, we arrive at the knowledge of being, at the All is One.

The Stoics and the Eleatics alike rejected the notion of Creation. The precipitating Big Bang of which we are now fairly well assured was simply not part of their knowledge. Having no conception of a growing Universe, traceable to a moment of origin, they rejected any idea of a Creator-God. Neither group believed that being could arise either from non-being, or from a radically different form. But even as the Stoics denied a transcendent God, they did believe the rational logos to be a benevolent cosmic mind.

These ideas continued to influence later students of the 'Platonic Pythagoreans' and the 'Pythagorean Platonists,'[24] whom Weinstein identified as Pandeists as well, and among them specifically, third century BC philosopher Chrysippus, who affirmed that "the universe itself is God and the universal outpouring of its soul."[25] But religious studies professor F. E. Peters found by contrast that "[w]hat appeared…at the center of the Pythagorean tradition in philosophy, is another view of psyche that seems to owe little or nothing to…pan-vitalism or *Pan-deism*."[26] And a few centuries further on, in AD 23, was born Pliny the Elder, a natural philosopher who was the first person ever to be described by the word 'Pandeist' in German bookseller Gottfried Große's 1787 annotations to his interpretation of Pliny's *Natural History*.

For Pliny, Große intones, the envisioned spiritual motivator makes him not a Spinozist, but "possibly a Pandeist" for whom Nature is not a being divided off or separated from the world. Nature is the whole of creation, solidified, and such seems, as well, to be true of divinity.[27] But Pliny's way of thinking was on the precipice of an overwhelming new force in the direction of philosophical discourse: Christianity.

Pandeistic Ideas in the Christian Era

Christianity forcefully, often violently, displaced nontheistic theological discourse in a great swath of the world for many centuries. Still, unmistakably pantheistic and pandeistic concepts are conveyed in the New Testament, especially in the Gospel of Matthew 25:31–46, popularly known as the 'Parable of the Sheep and the Goats.' In declaring to the blessed, "Inasmuch as ye have done it unto one of the least of these my brethren, ye have done it unto me,"[28] and to the cursed, "Inasmuch as ye did it not to one of the least of these, ye did it not to me,"[29] Jesus presents a vision of God which conforms to the view that God has become our

Universe, and wherein all things—including all people—are part of God. And so, Jesus tells us, everything which one person does for the benefit of another is in actuality done to God, as it is directly experienced by God. And in the same vein, whatever one person fails to do for another (or even whatever harm one person does to another) is directly experienced by God.

Again in Matthew, Jesus responds to a prodding Pharisee's inquiry as to which is the greatest commandment: "Thou shalt love the Lord thy God with all thy heart, and with all thy soul, and with all thy mind. This is the first and great commandment. And the second is *like unto it*, Thou shalt love thy neighbour as thyself." In identifying the second arm as 'like unto'—the same as—the first, Jesus demonstrates that there is, upon piercing the veil of distinctness, no difference between loving God and loving one's neighbors, or truly even one's self. This is best explained by finding that the neighbours *are* God, the self *is* God.

And in the very same sense, in 1 John 4:20, John teaches that "If somebody says, 'I love God,' and hates his brother, he is a liar." And how better than if God *is* every man's brother, as well as every man himself? Colossians 1:17 may be read somewhat more or less pandeistically depending on the particular translation used, but the New International Version reports it as, "He is before all things, and in him all things hold together"—a sentiment so expressly pandeistic as to almost shock.

Nevertheless, attempts to discuss ideas which would conventionally be considered pantheistic or deistic were effectively aborted throughout Europe during the early reign of Christianity. One notable exception may be found in the ninth-century works of Johannes Scotus Erigena, who derived a pandeistic formula which answered some of the riddles surrounding the Christian God. Weinstein examined with particularity Erigena's philosophy, identifying this as a form of Pandeism and noting that Erigena's vision of God was of one which does not know what it is, and learns this through the process of existing as its creation.[30]

Erigena was among the first to propose not only that God became our Universe, but—in an even more revolutionary arc—that God did so intently in order to attain knowledge which otherwise remained beyond its grasp. In his greatest work, *De divisione naturae* (The Division of Nature, alternately called *Periphyseon,* and probably completed around AD 867), Erigena wrote:

> When we hear that God makes all things, we should understand nothing else but that God is in all things, i.e. is the essence of all things. For He alone truly is, and everything which is truly said to be in those things which are, is God alone.[31]

The nature of the Erigenan Universe is divisible into four distinct classes:

1. That which creates and is not created;
2. That which is created and creates;
3. That which is created and does not create;
4. That which neither is created nor creates.

Erigena depicts God as an evolving being, developing through the four forms of existence which he outlines. In the first, we see God in its existence prior to the creation of anything; God in its natural state as the ground or origin of all things. The final form is the converse of this, God as the end result of all things, the point to which everything which has been created returns from whence it came. In the end, God is content and static, having fulfilled its needs through the passage of the interim steps.

Throughout all of this, it must be observed, Erigena takes the contentious stance that God is 'nothing.' God falls into no earthly classification. Here Erigena shows the influence of Pseudo-

Denys, who discussed God as the *theurgy*, to avoid using the name 'God,' weighed down as it was with connotation. Armstrong writes of Denys that he thought, "In fact, it is more accurate to call God 'Nothing': we should not even call him a Trinity since he is 'neither a unity nor a trinity in the sense in which we know them.'"[32] And so, she relates, "we must say that he is both 'God' and 'not-God,' 'good' and 'not good.'" So Denys finds of God, "he is not understood, nothing can be said of him, he cannot be named. He is not one of the things that are."[33] From this basis, Erigena found the inspiration to conclude that as God surpassed Being, so God was not *a* being:

> So supremely perfect is the essence of the Divinity that God is incomprehensible not only to us but also to Himself. For if He knew Himself in any adequate sense He should place Himself in some category of thought, which would be to limit Himself.[34]

A more contemporary interpretation of this statement is: "Since God is not a being, he is therefore not intelligible...This means not only that we cannot understand him, but that he cannot understand himself, as well. Creation is a kind of divine effort by God to understand himself, to see himself in a mirror."[35]

Returning to Erigena's four classes of God's experience of our Universe, the first and last are God alone, but the second and third classes together compose the created universe, which is the manifestation of God, God in process, Theophania. The second is the world of Platonic ideas or forms, of pure mathematics and mathematical knowledge. But it is the third class of being which is revolutionary, for there, for the first time in any explicit expression of philosophy, the world is pandeistic; it is the physical manifestation of God, having evolved through the realm of ideas and having made those ideas take on the characteristics of energy and matter:

> Erigena's view of God is revolutionary in two ways, one obvious and one subtle. First, in the broad physical sense, God is changeable, able to undergo a complete transformation through which one form is utterly (if temporarily) abandoned in favor of another. God begins as nothing we would recognize, and proceeds through stages to become the very Universe before our eyes. But at a more discreet level, God is making a more permanent transition as well, through this process. It begins as an entity incapable of comprehending itself. As perfect as its knowledge must be, it is nevertheless incomplete, and may not become complete without undergoing each step in the transformative experience Erigena defines.

There is a single essence to the arc of this divine progression; like all good narratives, it has a prologue, a period of exposition in the organization of the elements, a period of rising action leading to a climactic triumph of the spirit, and at last a dénouement. For Erigena's God, living out the story allows for its own character development. Existing as our Universe and all which inhabits it permits God to become something different, better than it was before, for it has gained the knowledge of what encompasses 'everything that is *not* God,' and as such it may begin to get a handle on understanding itself.[36]

> Erigena concludes this work with another controversial argument, and one which had already been scathingly rejected by Augustine of Hippo, that "[n]ot only man, however, but everything else in nature is destined to return to God."[37]

Erigena's account of the God–world relation is ultimately ambiguous. The world is created by God and so is other than God. The world is also eternal, for it is not outside God: its logos and primordial causes are in God, it participates in God, and God participates in it, and it will ultimately be assumed back into God when God will be all in all.[38]

De divisione naturae has been called "the sole speculative system to be produced between the final collapse of the Roman Empire and the 11th century."[39] But far from being widely read, Erigena's brilliant insights were first ignored, and later actively suppressed. His work finally came to the attention of the Church of Rome—and was promptly deemed heretical. In 1225, Pope Honorius III—obsessed as he was with rooting out heresy—decried Erigena's innovations as "swarming with worms of heretical perversity." Again, in 1585, the work would be condemned and remain banned at the direction of Pope Gregory XIII. The threat which Erigena's exposition presented to Christian dogma ensured that it would forever feel the full weight of the Church of Rome against it.

The Formalization of Deism and Pantheism

Despite the oppression of the theistic order, nontheistic thought continued to push its way forward in the sharpest minds. Weinstein found that thirteenth-century Catholic thinker Bonaventure—who championed the Platonic doctrine that ideas do not exist in *rerum natura*, but as ideals exemplified by the Divine Being, according to which actual things were formed—showed strong pandeistic inclinations.[40] Of Nicholas of Cusa, who wrote in the fifteenth century of the enfolding of creation in God and the unfolding of the divine human mind in creation, Weinstein wrote that he was, to a certain extent, a Pandeist.[41]

Absent the lost, forgotten, restored and regained knowledge of the ancients, it is odd to realize that the resurgence of Pantheism preceded the ascendance of Deism. Surely it must be imagined that as the Europeans became more sophisticated in the technological arts, they would realize that God was absent from what had before been perceived as the set of miracles of everyday life, illness and healing and death followed by birth anew. For those with a stern belief in God, the intuitive response would be that God was absent, not immanent; but the awakening of a new era of liturgical questioning preceded this level of sophistication.

In the mid-1500s Swiss religionist Pierre Viret published his *Instruction Chrestienne,* wherein he identified a new heresy: a movement of persons who believed in the existence of a God, but denied the stories of the Bible, and

> that there are of this band those who call themselves Deists, an entirely new word, which they want to oppose to Atheist. For in that Atheist signifies a person who is without God, they want to make it understood that they are not at all without God, since they certainly believe there is some sort of God, whom they even recognize as creator of heaven and Earth...

We come, then, to Giordano Bruno. Born in 1548 in the forgotten Italian village of Nola, Bruno was not precisely a Deist (preceding the greater period of the ascendancy of that innovation by some centuries), but he was influenced by the writings of Erigena to become a Pantheist. Believing as he did in a "sort of Stoic God who was the soul, origin, and end of the universe,"[42] Weinstein found that Pandeism was strongly expressed in Bruno's teachings envisioning a deity which had no particular relation to one part of the infinite universe more than any other, and was immanent, as present on Earth as in the Heavens, subsuming in itself the multiplicity of existence.[43] This was reiterated by others, including *Discover* editor Corey S. Powell, who wrote that Bruno's cosmology was "a tool for advancing an animist or Pandeist theology."[44]

Bruno was followed by Franciscus Mercurius van Helmont, who had written *A Cabbalistical Dialogue* (Latin version first, 1677; in English 1682), placing matter and spirit on a continuum, and describing matter as a "coalition" of monads. Weinstein also found this to be a kind of Pandeism.[45] And a century after Bruno, Baruch Spinoza would take the argument the further step to explain that we were in the body of God, an immanent God, but that God had been existent when our Universe had not, and so God was transcendent as well as immanent—God was the logos, and at the same time maintained an existence beyond the logos, and since God was infinite, each existence was infinite.

The 'mind/body problem' is not a phrase Spinoza would have used to address this philosophical question, having come in vogue long after his time. But Spinoza did believe in an all-encompassing God, with infinite attributes. Humans are only aware of two of those attributes: mind and body, two aspects traditionally viewed as substances in themselves. But Spinoza's God was the only substance, and things which seemed to be substances were only attributes. Understanding the scholastic background puts the terms in perspective as well: while Spinoza was a great believer in God, his pantheistic notion of God was classified as atheism by many.

Because mind and body were just separate attributes of a single substance, they were not causally linked. Mental events didn't create physical events, or vice versa. All events were just the one substance behaving in a perfect, predetermined manner, as manifested by two attributes of that substance. Spinoza's view of physical and mental processes was extremely sophisticated, and seems to be beyond the reach of many who seek to figure out the matter today.

In Spinoza's view, physical and mental processes might be analogized to the sides and angles of a triangle. Increasing one side of the triangle changes all the angles. But in this atemporal relationship, it is not as if the increasing side increases in size, and then taps the shoulders of the angles and tells them they have to change. Though the lines and the angles seem separate, they are actually just attributes of the one triangle.

And so in Spinoza's view, the physical substances of our brain did not somehow tap the shoulders of our emotions and tell them to change, which they were then obliged to do. No mental homunculus is responding to physical events, either with free will or in a predetermined way. No molecule of octopamine is bumping our minds into feeling angry. What there is, is a molecule of octopamine bumping into a receptor, and this is just a complementary attribute to our feeling of anger. The two events are like the lines and angles of a triangle: seemingly different, but determined by the overall shape of the phenomena.

Spinoza fared better than Bruno for his efforts. Bruno was burnt at the stake, his tongue nailed to the roof of his mouth to prevent him from uttering further heresies. Spinoza was only excommunicated, his death coming from a lung disease attributed to his work with glass, and the consequent inhaling of the dust generated by the grinding of lenses.

The Pantheists, some of whom found inspiration in Spinoza, were continental, but Deism arose in England. Sir Isaac Newton, contemplating the nature of our Universe, was concerned: "Was not space itself somehow divine, possessing as it did the attributes of eternity and infinity?"[46] Newton answered this question in an essay, *De Gravitatione et Aequipondio Fluidorum* (On the Gravity and Equilibrium of Fluids), likely produced around 1670. Armstrong explains:

> Since God is infinite, he must exist everywhere. Space is an effect of God's existence, emanating eternally from the divine omnipresence. It was not created by him in an act of will but existed as a necessary consequence or extension of his ubiquitous being. In the same way, because God himself is eternal, he emanates time. We can, therefore, say that God constitutes that space and time in which we live and move and have our being.[47]

The possibility that our Universe itself is both boundless and exclusive—that it fills up all that may exist—then gives rise to Pandeism. But the adjoinder of deistic to pantheistic conceptions would not be so swift in arising from philosophies which were, early on, perceived as irreconcilable and opposing competitors. Moses Mendelssohn, for example, attacked the pantheistic lines of Spinoza's thought while defending Deism, insisting "the deist affirms and the pantheist denies that finite things are distinct substances apart from God. What the deist sees as distinct substances, the pantheist regards as modes of a single substance."[48] And so could it be claimed of Mendelssohn that he perceived "the issue between the deist and the pantheist as a conflict between monism and pluralism."[49]

Europe was not alone in producing deistic and even pandeistic thought. As the reference, *American Philosophy: An Encyclopedia*, relates:

> Benjamin Franklin and the Deist political leaders and theorists of the American Revolution and Enlightenment believed in a Creator whose works were accessible by reason (rather than revelation) and a Creator who has not predetermined our world and does not intervene in it (thus rendering human action rather than prayer efficacious). Later Unitarian Christians (such as William Ellery Channing), transcendentalists (such as Ralph Waldo Emerson and Henry David Thoreau), writers (such as Walt Whitman) and some pragmatists (such as William James) took a more pantheist or pandeist approach by rejecting views of God as separate from the world.[50]

And note, again, that neither did the Western world exercise a monopoly on pandeistic thought. Weinstein asserted the presence of Pandeism in China, generally,[51] especially including in Lao-Tze's continually practiced Taoism,[52] and in the views of seventeenth-century Japanese Neo-Confucian philosopher Yamazaki Ansai, who espoused a cosmology of universal mutual interconnectedness.[53] Likewise, the untitled seventieth passage in Edward Vaughan Kenealy's 1872 book, *Enoch, the Second Messenger of God,* indexes the beliefs of Native Americans as "Pandeism, or Pantheism of the Red race."[54]

German and Italian Reflections on Pandeism

Even as the aforementioned American Revolutionary leaders flourished and, in America, drafted a new Constitution to govern their liberty, a separate discipline of Pandeism was formally conceived—though confessedly not well explored—in 1787, with Gottfried Große's aforementioned identification of Pliny the Elder as "wo nicht Spinozisten, doch einen Pandeisten."[55] And so was '*Pandeism*' born, in German, as a hybrid word, with blended roots coming from two other languages—Greek *pan* meaning 'all' and Latin *deus*, 'God.'

It has been postulated that Große made a simple spelling error, instead of a linguistic innovation, for his discussion is not inconsonant with Pantheism; the God thus described is synonymous with nature, there being no certain allusion to a God pre-existing its Creation. But an examination of the historical trends of philosophy makes it unsurprising that the sentiment of 'Pandeism' would be first expressed in German. German poet and scientist Johann Wolfgang von Goethe, who flourished at the same time as Große, is asserted to have described himself as a Pandeist in a letter to poet Johann Georg Jacobi dated 6 January 1813. Goethe wrote, "als Dichter und Künstler bin ich Polytheist, Pantheist hingegen als Naturforscher"—"as a poet and artist I am a Polytheist; on the contrary, as a searcher into Nature I am a Pantheist."[56] One of Goethe's compilers, Hermann Böhlau, identified this phrase as Goethe's own self-identification as a Pandeist.

Not long after this, the first invectives expressly condemning

Pandeism came forth in the Italian Cluster, a coincidental conglomeration of commentaries in the 1820s to 1830s.[57] In 1834, publisher Giovanni Silvestri posthumously published a volume of sermons delivered by Padre Filippo Nannetti di Bibulano (aka il Filippo Nani, Padre da Lojano) who had died five years earlier in 1829. In one of these sermons, specifically Sermon XVIII on Miracles, Nannetti had railed against "Jews, Muslims, Gentiles, Schismatics, Heretics, Pandeists, Deists, and troubled, restless spirits."[58] Nannetti went further in specifically criticizing Pandeism, declaring, "To you, fatal Pandeist! the laws that create nature are contingent and mutable, not another being in substance with forces driven by motions and developments."[59]

Four years after this publication came a learned anonymous treatise whose author, discussing the theory of religion presented by Giambattista Vico a century earlier, mused that when man first saw meteor showers, "his robust imagination recognized the effects as a cause, then deifying natural phenomena, he became a Pandeist, an instructor of Mythology, a priest, an Augur."[60] Neither Nannetti nor the anonymous 1838 scholar defines Pandeism distinctly enough to clearly distinguish it from Pantheism, or possibly Polytheism; nor do we learn from them where they had come across the concept, or whether the 1838 author knew of Nannetti's sermon addressing the subject.

But, again in 1838, another Italian—a phrenologist named Luigi Ferrarese—described Pandeism while critiquing French philosopher Victor Cousin. For Cousin, the solutions to all philosophical problems, or routes to them, had already been found by earlier philosophers—the task, then, was to set all those old ideas up against each other to wring out the best, and so to at last establish the 'true' philosophy. This method, he called 'eclecticism.' But this refinement of thought must be accomplished methodically, not haphazardly. Simple abstractions would not do. Our Universe contains man within it, reflected Cousin, and so man expresses a universal consciousness, as well as a reflection of our Universe. Man, then, may turn inwards through analysis of our own observations, and apply psychology phenomenologically (at the time, psychology itself was a discipline in its infancy), ultimately realizing that dispassionate reason is the summit of conceptual gifts, and the direction to be pursued in examining the world.

Theologically, Cousin was to a great degree an heir to the less fortunate Giordano Bruno (whose doctrines Cousin openly admired). Of all of his philosophical proposals, this engendered the greatest controversy. Though he perceived duality in the Universe, between 'the self' and everything else which was not of the self, he contended that our sense of self must proceed from some source outside the self acting both upon us and within us. And so he determined that these senses were absolutes, joined together creating the greater absolute of a God which was both the cause and result of all which was. For this, Ferrarese described Cousin's doctrine as one which "locates reason outside the human person, declaring man a fragment of God, introducing a sort of spiritual Pandeism, absurd for us, and injurious to the Supreme Being."[61]

An early proponent of pandeistic views was the German botanist Friedrich Franz Wilhelm Junghuhn. Junghuhn studied medicine in Halle and in Berlin, but fled Germany after being condemned to a decade in prison for his involvement in a duel. He entered the Dutch colonial service, arriving in Jakarta in 1835. He settled in Java, studying and writing on the land and its people. Ill health forced his return to Holland in 1849, and he set to work on his treatise, *Images of Light and Shadow from Java's Interior*. There, Junghuhn fiercely criticized Christian and Islamic proselytization of the Javanese people. He expressly abandoned Christianity, favoring a form of Pandeism: God was indeed in everything, was the sum of all things, he contended, but was inactive in our Universe, and could be determined only through reason. Like Erigena before him, Junghuhn's views met with censorship. Banned in Austria and parts of Germany for their "denigrations and vilifications of Christianity," and facing opposition from the Dutch Christian Church, they were nevertheless popular in Holland and colonial Indonesia.

Despite the poor reception of Junghuhn's work in Germany, in 1859 collaborators Moritz Lazarus and Heymann Steinthal penned in their *Zeitschrift für Völkerpsychologie und Sprachwissenschaft*:

> Man stelle es also den Denkern frei, ob sie Theisten, Pantheisten, Atheisten, Deisten (und warum nicht auch Pandeisten?) sein wollen: dem Volke aber predigt nichts von Gott und ja nichts von Unsterblichkeit.[62]

Roughly translated, this reads:

> Man leaves it to the philosophers, whether they want to be Theists, Pan-theists, Atheists, Deists (and why not also Pandeists?); but the people are preached nothing of God, and nothing of an all-encompassing immortality.

Here, then, is the first unhesitating advocacy of a philosophy of Pandeism, expressly distinguished from the Pantheism and Deism acknowledged to have come before it. Yet another German philosopher, Max Bernhard Weinstein, presented a broad and far-reaching examination of Pandeism in 1910, noting the distinction between Pantheism and Pandeism in stating "even if only by a letter (*d* in place of *th*), we fundamentally differ Pandeism from Pantheism."[63] Yet another German philosopher, Paul Friedrich Köhler, countered later in that decade: "Pantheism and Pandeism, Monism and Dualism: all of these are in reality only different forms of God, different ways of illuminating the fundamental idea."[64] Köhler ultimately characterizes God as the highest one from which all radiations project, to form our souls; our mirror image.[65]

The name of the concept remained in doubt. In 1900, Moncure Daniel Conway penned an essay titled "The Pilgrimage from Deism to Agnosticism," for John Mackinnon Robertson and G. Astor Singer's edition of *The University Magazine and Free Review*, elucidating the popular spiritual views of the day. Conway wrote that "Theologically Unitarianism has always been weak and timid, but on the moral and human side its strength has been repeatedly proved,"[66] recounting the involvement of Unitarians in ending the American institution of slavery.

Conway noted that "speculative religious thought...after leaving Deism, found its next station in Pantheism," noting that English Pantheism in particular "was never the exact and reasoned-out philosophy of Spinoza; it was Deism with a poetical aureole around it."[67] To his spiritual brethren of the time, Conway explained that "'Pandeism' would have been an unscholarly combination, and 'Pantheism,' in addition to its more euphonious sound, had the advantage of evading the arrows of Butler's '*Analogy*,'—for a time."[68] Indeed, a similar critique of Pandeism as an 'unsightly' combination of Greek and Latin was made in a review of Weinstein's own discussion of Pandeism.[69]

Interestingly, Conway further declares that "Pantheism wrote most English poetry from Shelley to Tennyson"[70]—though Tennyson himself has been described as having "left the faith wherein he was raised and near the end of his life said that his 'religious beliefs also defied convention, leaning towards agnosticism and Pandeism.'"[71] Other literary influences are noted; renowned literary critic Hayden Carruth commented on Alexander Pope that it was "Pope's rationalism and Pandeism...with which he wrote the greatest mock-epic in English literature,"[72] and Belgian poet Robert Vivier wrote of the Pandeism to be found in the works of novelist and poet Victor Hugo.[73]

Imperfect Perfection

Among the many innovations reached by process philosopher Charles Hartshorne was the conception of a God which was not perfect in all ways precisely because there are some ways wherein perfection is meaningless. Can God paint a perfect painting? (The question assumes that the people who see the painting do not know it is by God, and God does not alter their thoughts to make them think it perfect if they would not be so inclined.) Well, no, because different people possess different tastes, so even if some thought it was perfect, others might think it lacked something, or had too much of something, though a truly 'perfect' painting would be one which everybody would agree was perfect. Is it within God's power to commit a perfect sin? Can God be perfectly evil? If God is perfectly good, then it would seem these things exceed its power.

Hartshorne conceptualized a complex schematic for evaluating the nature of God, from which he reviewed all theological variations up to his day—including Pandeism. He coined a model called 'AR'—"absolute perfection in some respects, relative perfection in all others"—to convey the idea that God is indeed perfect, but to acknowledge that there are many characteristics not amenable to such a description.

Hartshorne determined that God expresses absolute perfection along some dimensions, relative perfection along others. God may not possess the power to create a 'perfect' painting, but his ability to create a painting would surpass that of any human who could ever lift a brush. So it is with power and, most importantly, knowledge. God is relatively all-powerful, in that God has complete power over everything which exists in our Universe (or over everything which was to become our Universe before our Universe existed); and similarly God has complete knowledge of everything which exists in our Universe (or, again, over everything which was to become our Universe before our Universe existed).

But Hartshorne rejected Pandeism in favor of Panentheism, for though he accepted that our Universe was a manifestation of God, he was not prepared to accept a God which was not separate from and above our Universe as well. He wrote:

> Just as AR is the whole positive content of perfection, so CW, or the conception of the Creator-and-the-Whole-of-what-he-has-created as constituting one life, the super-whole which in its everlasting essence is uncreated (and does not necessitate just the parts which the whole has) but in its de facto concreteness is created—*this panentheistic doctrine contains all of deism and pandeism except their arbitrary negations.*[74]

Hartshorne's rejection of Pandeism is conditional, applicable only if the 'negations' contained in Pandeism are indeed arbitrary. It is, naturally, possible to articulate such a theory of Pandeism, but in the most powerful conceptions of Pandeism these negations are not arbitrary at all, but are instead absolutely necessary to account for the nature of our Universe, and the motivation of its Creator.

Naturally, not all theological estimations of Pandeism are even this positive, especially those coming from theistic models which Pandeism would challenge. For example, in 1991, theologian J. Sidlow Baxter wrote: "If the Bible is only human lore, and not divine truth, then we have no real answer to those who say, 'Let's pick the best out of all religions and blend it all into Pan-Deism.'"[75] In 1996, Pastor Bob Burridge of the Genevan Institute for Reformed Studies, wrote in his *Survey Studies in Reformed Theology* an essay on 'The Decrees of God': "If God was the proximate cause of every act it would make all events to be 'God in motion.' That is nothing less than pantheism, or more exactly, pandeism."[76] Noted Christian apologist John Oakes calls Pandeism "ad hoc and a weak marriage" of Deism and Pantheism, and "a patch-up to save pantheism in a world in which creation is clearly implied by the data."[77] Christian website GotQuestions.org complains that: "The pandeistic god has no more concern for you than the chair has."[78] And Christian theologian Graham Ward insists that: "Attention to Christ and the Spirit delivers us from pantheism, pandeism, and process theology."[79]

The Era of God's Debris

In the latter half of the twentieth century, Pandeism showed continued influence in the arts. Literary critic Martin Lüdke noted it as a philosophy expressed by early twentieth-century Portuguese poet Fernando Pessoa, especially so in those writings made under the pseudonym of Alberto Caeiro.[80] Pandeism was likewise noted by authors like Brazilian journalist and writer Otávio de Faria, and British scholar and translator of Portuguese fiction Giovanni Pontiero, among others, to be an influence on the writings of noted mid-twentieth-century Brazilian poet Carlos Nejar,[81] of whom de Faria wrote that "the Pandeism of Nejar is one of the strongest poetic ideas that we have reached in the world of poetry."[82]

One of the most interesting—and perhaps unlikely—applications of principles of Pandeism was set forth in 2001 by Scott Adams, then best known as a comic strip author. But in 2001 Adams produced something in a very different vein, publishing *God's Debris: A Thought Experiment*. There, Adams surmised that an omnipotent God annihilated itself via the Big Bang, because such an entity would already know everything possible except his own lack of existence, and paradoxically would need to end its existence in order to complete its knowledge. Wondering whether such omnipotence would include "knowing what happens after he loses his omnipotence,"[83] Adams proceeds to the following analysis:

A God who knew the answer to that question would indeed

> know everything and have everything. For that reason he would be unmotivated to do anything or create anything. There would be no purpose to act in any way whatsoever. But a God who had one nagging question—what happens if I cease to exist?—might be motivated to find the answer in order to complete his knowledge...The fact that we exist is proof that God is motivated to act in some way. And since only the challenge of self-destruction could interest an omnipotent God, it stands to reason that we...are God's debris.[84]

Adams' fictionalized God-idea exists now as a combination of the smallest units of energy of which our Universe is made (many levels smaller than quarks), which Adams called 'God Dust,' and the law of probability, or 'God's debris,' hence the title. An unconventional twist introduced by Adams proposes that God is in the process of being restored not through some process such as a cosmological Big Crunch, but because humankind itself is becoming God, with advances such as the Internet being developed, as if by an instinctive compulsion.[85]

This technological connection was echoed in 2016, with German professor Walter Hehl writing of philosopher Karl Popper's three worlds:

> Identifying evolution as a grand software system development raises human questions, such as "who made the specifications?", "who developed the code" and "who runs the system?" This evokes new philosophical, religious and human versions of panpsychism, pantheism, panentheism, respectively panendeism and pandeism.[86]

To go further than this would bring us out of 'history' and into the work of some of the very authors included in the remainder of this book.

Notes

1 Armstrong, Karen, *A History of God* (Ballantine Books, 1993), p. 3.

2 Armstrong, *A History of God*, p. 3.

3 Armstrong, *A History of God*, p. 3.

4 Armstrong, *A History of God*, p. 3.

5 Armstrong, *A History of God*, p. 8.

6 Needham, Joseph, and Roman, Colin, "Chinese Cosmology," in Hetherington, Norriss S., *Cosmology* (Garland, 1993), p. 25.

7 Tylor, Edward Burnett, *Primitive Culture: Researches into the Development of Mythology, Philosophy, Religion, Art, and Custom* (1871), pp. 312–13.

8 Tylor, *Primitive Culture*, pp. 312–13.

9 Armstrong, *A History of God*, p. 5.

10 Max Bernhard Weinstein, *Welt- und Lebensanschauungen, Hervorgegangen aus Religion, Philosophie und Naturerkenntnis* (World and Life Views, Emerging from Religion, Philosophy and Nature) (1910), p. 155.

11 Armstrong, *A History of God*, p. 28.

12 Armstrong, *A History of God*, p. 29.

13 Weinstein, *Welt- und Lebensanschauungen*, p. 213.

14 Matthiae, August Heinrich, *Grundriss der Geschichte der griechischen und römischen Litteratur* (3rd ed., 1834; English trans., 1841), p. 30.

15 Peters, Francis E., *Greek Philosophical Terms: A Historical Lexicon* (NYU Press, 1967), p. 169.

16 Nietzsche, Friedrich, *Philosophy in the Tragic Age of the Greeks* (1873), § 4.

17 Gregory, Andrew, *Anaximander: A Re-assessment* (Bloomsbury, 2016), p. 100. Gregory defines a 'pankubernist' as "someone who believes that everything steers."

18 Fairbanks, Arthur, ed. and trans., *The First Philosophers of Greece* (1898), p. 67.

19 Xenophanes, fragment B23.

20 Xenophanes, fragments B24–6.

21 Weinstein, *Welt- und Lebensanschauungen*, p. 231.

22 *The Stanford Encyclopedia of Philosophy.*

23 Weinstein, *Welt- und Lebensanschauungen*, p. 303.

24 Weinstein, *Welt- und Lebensanschauungen*, p. 306.

25 Weinstein, *Welt- und Lebensanschauungen*, p. 338.

26 Peters, *Greek Philosophical Terms*, p. 169.

27 Große, Gottfried, *Naturgeschichte: mit erläuternden Anmerkungen* (1787), vol. 11, p. 165.

28 Matthew 25:40.

29 Matthew 25:45.

30 Weinstein, *Welt- und Lebensanschauungen*, pp. 283–4.

31 Eriugena, John Scottus, *De divisione naturae*, vol. I, p. 72, in Copleston, Charles, *A History of Philosophy, Bk. I, vol. II: Augustine to Scotus* (Image Books/Doubleday, 1985), p. 120.

32 Armstrong, *A History of God*, p. 127, quoting Denys the Areopagite, *The Divine Names*, II, 7.

33 Armstrong, *A History of God*, p. 127, quoting Denys the Areopagite, *The Divine Names*, VII, 3.

34 Turner, William, *The Catholic Encyclopedia: John Scotus Eriugena* (1909).

35 Genest, Jeremiah, "Duns Scotus Erigena: Life and Works" (1998).

36 One might with equal logic suggest that 'living out' the experience of our Universe enables the Creator to gain a knowledge of more [but not everything] of what the Creator is, instead of what it is not.

37 Turner, *The Catholic Encyclopedia.*

38 Irvine, Andrew, "Notes on John Scotus Eriugena" (1998).

39 Irvine, "Notes on John Scotus Eriugena."

40 Weinstein, *Welt- und Lebensanschauungen*, p. 303.

41 Weinstein, *Welt- und Lebensanschauungen*, p. 306.

42 Armstrong, *A History of God*, p. 287.

43 Weinstein, *Welt- und Lebensanschauungen*, p. 321.

44 Powell, Corey S., "Defending Giordano Bruno: A Response from the CoWriter of 'Cosmos,'" *Discover* (13 March 2014).

45 Weinstein, *Welt- und Lebensanschauungen*, p. 338.

46 Armstrong, *A History of God*, p. 304.

47 Armstrong, *A History of God*, p. 304.

48 Beiser, Frederick C., *The Fate of Reason: German Philosophy from Kant to Fichte* (Harvard University Press, 1993), p. 103.

49 Beiser, *The Fate of Reason*, p. 103.

50 Lachs, John, and Talisse, Robert, *American Philosophy: An Encyclopedia* (Routledge, 2007), pp. 309–10.

51 Weinstein, *Welt- und Lebensanschauungen*, p. 121.

52 Weinstein, *Welt- und Lebensanschauungen*, pp. 234–5.

53 Weinstein, *Welt- und Lebensanschauungen*, p. 235.

54 See Kenealy, Edward Vaughan, *Enoch, the Second Messenger of God*, vol. 1, pp. 300–2.

55 Große, *Naturgeschichte: mit erläuternden Anmerkungen*, p. 165.

56 Pelikan, Jaroslav, *Faust the Theologian* (Yale University Press, 1995), p. 19.

57 At almost the same point in the 1830s, occultist Godfrey Higgins used the word 'Pandeism' in his *Anacalypsis* to describe what may have been a different philosophy indeed, but that is largely a fluke of history—and indeed perhaps something of a clever twisting of the roots and branches of etymology by Higgins, whose writings show how ably he knew of Pantheism and Deism.

58 Padre Filippo Nannetti di Bibulano (aka il Filippo Nani, Padre da Lojano), "Sermon XVIII: Miracles," in *Sermons and Panegyrics of the Father Filippo Nani of Lojana* (Giovanni Silvestri, publisher, 1834), p. 284.

59 Nannetti, "Sermon XVIII: Miracles," p. 286.

60 *Il legato di un vecchio ai giovani della sua patria* (The Legacy of an Old Man to the Young People of His Country) (1838).

61 Ferrarese, Luigi, *Memorie risguardanti la dottrina frenologica* (1838), p. 15.

62 Lazarus, Moritz, and Steinthal, Heymann, *Zeitschrift für Völkerpsychologie und Sprachwissenschaft* (1859), pp. 262–3.

63 Weinstein, *Welt- und Lebensanschauungen*, p. 227.

64 Köhler, Paul Friedrich, *Kulturwege und Erkenntnisse: Eine kritische Umschau in den Problemen des religiösen und geistigen Lebens* (1916), p.

193.

65 Köhler, *Kulturwege und Erkenntnisse*, p. 193.

66 Conway, Moncure Daniel, "The Pilgrimage from Deism to Agnosticism" in Robertson, John Mackinnon and Singer, G. Astor, *The University Magazine and Free Review* (1900), p. 12.

67 Conway, "The Pilgrimage from Deism to Agnosticism," p. 13.

68 Conway, "The Pilgrimage from Deism to Agnosticism," p. 13.

69 Otto Kirn, reviewer, *Welt- und Lebensanschauungen, Hervorgegangen aus Religion, Philosophie und Naturerkenntnis* (World and Life Views, Emerging from Religion, Philosophy and Nature), in Emil Schürer, Adolf von Harnack, eds, *Theologische Literaturzeitung* (Theological Literature Journal), vol. 35, column 827 (1910).

70 Conway, "The Pilgrimage from Deism to Agnosticism," p. 13.

71 Veith, Gene Edward, Wilson, Douglas, and Fischer, G. Tyler, *Omnibus IV: The Ancient World* (Veritas Press, 2009), p. 49.

72 Carruth, Hayden, *Suicides and Jazzers* (University of Michigan Press, 1993), p. 161.

73 Vivier, Robert, "La Poésie de Victor Hugo," *Académie Royale de Langue et de Littérature Françaises*, Bulletin Tome XXX, No. 3 (Décembre 1952), p. 211.

74 Hartshorne, Charles, *Man's Vision of God and the Logic of Theism* (Archon Books, 1964), p. 348.

75 Baxter, J. Sidlow, *Our Bible: The Most Critical Issue* (1991).

76 Burridge, Bob, "Theology Proper: Lesson 4—The Decrees of God," *Survey Studies in Reformed Theology* (Genevan Institute for Reformed Studies, 1996).

77 John Oakes, "What Is Your Response to Pandeism?" *Evidence for Christianity* (25 May 2013).

78 "Question: 'What Is Pandeism?'" GotQuestions.org (March 2014).

79 Graham Ward, *How the Light Gets In: Ethical Life I* (Oxford University Press, 2016), p. 313.

80 Lüdke, Martin, *Frankfurter Rundschau* (18 August 2004).

81 Pontiero, Giovanni, *Carlos Nejar, poeta e pensador* (1983), p. 349.

82 de Faria, Otávio, "Pandeísmo em Carlos Nejar," *Última Hora*, Rio de

Janeiro (17 May 1978).

83 Adams, Scott, *God's Debris: A Thought Experiment* (Andrews McMeel Publishing, 2001), p. 43.

84 Adams, *God's Debris* (2001), pp. 43–4.

85 Adams, *God's Debris* (2001), p. 52.

86 Hehl, Walter, "A General World Model with Poïesis: Popper's 'Three Worlds' Updated with Software" (2016).

Section I

Fundamentals of Pandeism

What is the essence of Pandeism? This section contains articles broadly examining the heart of the proposition. It is logic-based, friendly to science and scientific discovery, and yet accounts for spirituality, and for characteristics of the human experience that defy quantification.

First, in "The Idealist Interpretation of Pandeism," Bernardo Kastrup PhD argues "for an interpretation of the facts of reality that renders Pandeism both *genuine* as a theology and metaphysically *sound*."

Next, in "A Theorem Concerning God," Robert G. Brown PhD sets forth a logical proof, effectively a mathematical argument demonstrating that any entity which could properly be called "God" in fact *must* be either pandeistic or panendeistic.

Alan H. Dawe then examines a divine reality, in "God, the Universe and Pandeism," outlining broadly the capacities of what he terms God-Consciousness, the operative force which undergirds both the pandeistic Creator, and the more expansive theological model of Dawe's own *The God Franchise*.

After a poetic interlude, we find "God Without Religion," wherein Dr Michael Arnheim sets forth the particular case for Deism as against both Atheism and Theism, and makes an especial plea for unity among those holding to variations of this middle view, including proponents of Pandeism.

In "Pantheistic God-Concepts: Ancient, Contemporary, Popular, and Plausible Alternatives to Classical Theism," Raphael Lataster argues for an end to the myopic focus of religious studies on the dichotomy between Theism and Naturalism, pointing to the often-ignored expansive history of pantheistic, panentheistic, and pandeistic theological options.

Lastly, in "Why Pandeism Is Better Than Theism," Knujon Mapson argues for the logical superiority of Pandeism as a theological model accounting for everything that theistic models claim, but doing so with fewer assumptions.

Sunflower Galaxy

Amy Perry

Miss Perry is a poet living in Southern California, amidst palm trees, pink and orange sunsets, and hummingbirds. Her poetry examines macro- and microcosmic elements of existence. She allows her intuition to be her flame guiding her onward with her spiraling Spiritual path. Please research reasons to go vegan!

The sunflower communicates with the galaxy.
Perfectly symmetrical,
Mathematically identical.

•

They speak the tongue of Fibonacci spiral,
Licking up wisdom and light.
One and the same. A spaceship for Life.

The Idealist Interpretation of Pandeism

Bernardo Kastrup PhD

Dr Kastrup has a PhD in Computer Engineering with specializations in artificial intelligence and reconfigurable computing. He has worked as a scientist in some of the world's foremost research laboratories, including the European Organization for Nuclear Research (CERN) and the Philips Research Laboratories (where the 'Casimir Effect' of Quantum Field Theory was discovered). Bernardo has authored many scientific papers and philosophy books. His three latest books are: More Than Allegory, Brief Peeks Beyond, *and* Why Materialism Is Baloney. *Alongside a managerial position in the high-tech industry, Bernardo maintains a philosophy blog and a video interview series, and continues to develop his ideas about the nature of reality. He has lived and worked in four different countries across continents, currently residing in the Netherlands.*

The theology of Pandeism, in a nutshell, posits that God created the universe by *becoming* the universe. It is elegantly parsimonious in that it avoids the notion of a Creator separate from Its[1] Creation. It also eliminates the distinction between God's will and the operation of the laws of nature: the latter is seen as the very *expression* of the former. The idea of a personal God interfering with nature from the outside finds no place under this view. As such, Pandeism is one of the most naturalistic theological formulations ever proposed.

It is so naturalistic, in fact, that one may wonder if it can still be considered a *theology*—that is, a discourse (*logia*) about God (*theos*). By equating the present state of God with nature itself, and the expression of God's will with the operation of the laws of nature, doesn't Pandeism actually negate the spirit of the word 'God'? Doesn't it effectively do away with God under a linguistic smokescreen? Isn't it, at bottom, just a version of atheism cleverly disguised by a pseudo-religious cloak?

As will later become clear, my answer to these questions is a categorical 'No.' But before we get there, we will need to critically reassess some of our least-examined assumptions about the nature of reality.

My project with this essay is to rigorously articulate a metaphysics that is both consistent with Pandeism and preserves ontological space for what the spirit of the word 'God' denotes. In other words, I intend to argue for an interpretation of the facts of reality that renders Pandeism both *genuine* as a theology and metaphysically *sound*.

Before I begin, though, a quick observation is in order. Pandeism has a sister theology called Panendeism. It's identical to Pandeism except in that Panendeism posits that only *a part* of God became the *known* universe, while another part transcends it. In my view, Pandeism and Panendeism imply nonetheless the same ontology. In both cases, there is only God and God is only cognizable to us in the form of the universe. The difference is merely epistemic: Panendeism suggests more explicitly that we, humans, cannot *know* everything about God; that there is always a part of God fundamentally beyond our cognitive capacities.

Indeed, this is eminently reasonable, for there can clearly be much more to the universe than what we humans can apprehend. Earth-based primates didn't evolve to perceive or understand the entirety of the cosmos. Notice, however, that what the universe is or isn't doesn't depend on what we humans can or cannot know about it. It simply is. God's being doesn't depend on our capacity to cognize it fully. As such, from the ontological angle that is the focus of this essay, Pandeism and Panendeism boil down to the same theology. The argument that follows endorses Panendeism as much as it endorses Pandeism.

The Meaning of the Word 'God'

For Pandeism to be a genuine theology, it must grant that God exists today—not only in a remote past—in a manner that honors the *spirit* of what theologians mean by the word 'God.' But just what do they mean by it? Obviously, there is no consensus at the level of details and nuances. But if one drills down into the semantic core of the word, I believe there would be broad agreement that the following four attributes are both necessary and sufficient to characterize God:

Attribute 1: God is the primary cause.
Attribute 2: God is omnipotent.
Attribute 3: God is omnipresent.
Attribute 4: God is omniscient.

Attribute 1 means that God is the ultimate cause of everything, but is Itself uncaused. In other words, everything in the universe must be ultimately explainable in terms of God, but God Itself cannot be explained in terms of anything else. Attribute 1 holds intact under Pandeism: since God created the whole universe by becoming it, it follows trivially that God is the ultimate cause of everything in the universe, while remaining Itself uncaused by anything in the universe.

Along similar lines of reasoning, it is straightforward to assert that Attribute 2 also holds under Pandeism: since all causal powers pertaining to the unfolding and evolution of the universe are comprised in the laws of nature, and since the laws of nature, under Pandeism, are the expression of God's will, it follows that everything that happens in the universe does so by the will of God. God is thus omnipotent under Pandeism.

Unlike the previous two cases, however, whether Attribute 3 holds is less straightforward to assert: since God *becomes* the universe, to what extent can we say that God is *still* present after the completion of the process of becoming? Is the caterpillar still present in the butterfly after the latter emerges from the cocoon? If we could coherently assert under Pandeism that the universe *is still essentially the same* as its Creator, then the omnipresence of God would follow trivially. But can we make such an assertion without violating the internal logic of Pandeism? In what sense can we say that something is still the same after it has become something else? It gets even less straightforward: for Attribute 4 to hold under Pandeism, we must grant that the universe as a whole is sentient. After all, since Pandeism posits that God can now only exist *as the universe itself* (for It became the universe), unless the universe *as a whole* is sentient there cannot be an *omni*scient God today. From a mainstream perspective, however, asserting that the universe as a whole is sentient is seen as metaphysically problematic.

In the next sections, we will explore how Pandeism, as well as the universe itself, must be interpreted so that Attributes 3 and 4 hold.

The Nature of Becoming

When the caterpillar weaves its cocoon, it encloses itself in an isolated environment. Nothing goes in or out. Within this self-contained system, what used to be the caterpillar then turns into a butterfly. In other words, the *essence* of the caterpillar *reconfigures itself* into the butterfly. No new or foreign elements come from outside the cocoon, for the caterpillar doesn't eat or drink during metamorphosis. It is the very organic building blocks of the caterpillar, as they entered the cocoon, which rearrange themselves into the form and function of the butterfly. Therefore, the difference between what enters and what leaves the cocoon is purely one of *configuration*, not of *essence*: the latter remains the same. What we call a butterfly is simply a different *configuration* of the original essence. If we had a designation for this essence—say, *S*—we would say that *S* entered the cocoon and the same *S* left it, unchanged.

Cut to Pandeism: since, by hypothesis, in the beginning there was nothing but God, no new or foreign elements could have come from outside God to take part in Its transformation into the universe. Like the caterpillar's cocoon, the system was self-contained. Whatever *essence* started the process of becoming was the same essence that emerged from the process in the form of the universe. The difference between what started the process and what emerged from it is, necessarily, one of *configuration* alone.

Therefore, by interpreting the word 'God' to mean the divine *essence* itself—as opposed to just one of its possible configurations—we allow Attribute 3 to hold intact under Pandeism: it was God-the-essence that started the process and God-the-essence that emerged from it. The universe *is still God* because it is made entirely of the essence of that which created it, just as the butterfly is made entirely of *S*. Therefore, God is omnipresent in the universe *today*.

Notice that taking the word 'God' to mean the essence, instead of one of its particular configurations, is the only interpretation that does justice to the spirit of the word. For the same reason that the spirit of the word 'man' applies to a male human whether he is sitting down or standing up, the spirit of the word 'God' applies, under Pandeism, both to the universe and its Creator. As such, what I am proposing here isn't an arbitrary semantic game, but an invocation of the very spirit of the word 'God': if this spirit is honored, Attribute 3 holds under Pandeism.

Notice that the hypothesis that the universe is made of a different essence than its Creator would, under Pandeism, entail an arbitrary, magical transmutation. Technically speaking, if the universe were of a fundamentally different ontological class than the Creator, there would be nothing about the Creator in virtue of which the universe could have been created from It. An unbridgeable causal gap would appear, contradicting the core claim of Pandeism and violating Attribute 1.

Therefore, the interpretation of Pandeism under which God is the essence whose mere configuration changes during Creation is the only one that is both technically coherent and does justice to the spirit of the word 'God.' A direct implication of this interpretation, of course, is that the world we see around us *is* God in one of Its possible configurations. "When you see the world you see God. There is no seeing God apart from the world," said Nisargadatta Maharaj.[2] "Holy art Thou, O God...of whom All-nature hath been made an image," proclaims *The Corpus Hermeticum*.[3] We will return to this point later, so as to make explicit what this change in configuration consists of.

The Facts of Nature

Having shown that Attributes 1, 2 and 3 hold coherently under Pandeism, we are left with Attribute 4. As we've seen earlier, for this last attribute to also hold the universe *as a whole* must be sentient. Naturally, whether this is the case or not is a question of metaphysics, not of science. The allegedly objective methods of science allow us to model the formal and structural aspects of the universe—how its various observable elements relate to one another—but can give us no access to what, if anything, it is like to *be* the universe as a whole.[4] This *intrinsic* view escapes the *extrinsic* methods of science.

As such, any ontological interpretation of nature entailing or implying that there is *nothing* it is like to be the universe as a whole—such as mainstream physicalism—is *metaphysics*, not scientific theory. The physicalist metaphysics cannot claim rational or empirical high ground based on the success of science, for it isn't—and couldn't, *even in principle*, be—derived from the application of scientific methods. Therefore, the key metaphysical question we need to answer in this section is wide open today, despite science's indisputable success as enabler of engineering.

To address this open question, I will ground myself on basic empirical facts available to observation, making no *a priori* metaphysical assumptions. My criteria for making inferences will be empirical honesty, logical consistency and ontological parsimony. I will allow the available evidence to lead me wherever it goes. As such, I will not aim *per se* at a metaphysics that validates Pandeism. That we will ultimately arrive at a conclusion that *happens* to be consistent with Pandeism is helpful for the purposes of this essay, but not at all derived by construction. For clarity, I will elaborate on my argument on a point-by-point basis.

I start by asserting nine things we *know* about the universe, irrespective of theory or metaphysics. These are empirical *facts* accessible to anyone through simple observation:

Fact 1: There is subjective experience. This is the primary and incontrovertible datum of existence.

Fact 2: From Fact 1, we know that there is *that* which experiences, since experience entails an experienc*er*. Notice that I am not, at least for now, passing any judgment or making any assumption about the fundamental nature or boundaries of that which experiences. I am not saying, for instance, that it is or isn't human, or physical, or spiritual, or informational, etc. I am simply asserting that it inevitably exists, whatever it may or may not be, and wherever its boundaries may lie. For ease of reference, I will henceforth refer to 'That Which Experiences' simply as 'TWE.'

Fact 3: A person's experiences are at least largely private, in the sense that other people do not have direct access to them at least ordinarily.

Fact 4: There is at least a partial correlation between measurable electrochemical activity in a person's nervous system and the person's private experiences.

Fact 5: Measurements of the activity of a person's nervous system can only be known insofar as they are themselves *experienced* in the form of perceptions. For instance, if a neurologist performs a functional scan or an electroencephalogram (EEG) of your brain, the results are only known insofar as the neurologist—or someone else—*sees* them consciously.

Fact 6: From Facts 4 and 5, we know that there is at least a partial correspondence between two types of experience: conscious perceptions of activity in a person's nervous system on the one hand, and the private thoughts, emotions and perceptions of that person on the other. Let us call these the *extrinsic* and *intrinsic views,* respectively. Both views, of course, are still experiences insofar as they can be known.

Fact 7: A nervous system has the same essential nature—that is, it belongs to the same ontological class—as the rest of the physical universe. After all, nervous systems are *physical* systems. They are composed of the same types of basic subatomic particles that make up the universe as a whole.

Fact 8: We all inhabit the same universe, despite the different points of view from which each person observes it and the different ways in which each person interacts with it.

Fact 9: The universe unfolds according to patterns and regularities that are at least largely independent of our personal volition. Human beings cannot change the laws of nature.

An Idealist Metaphysics

The question that presents itself to us now is this: What is the most parsimonious metaphysical explanation for these nine facts? Here I use the qualifier 'parsimonious' in the sense of Occam's Razor: the most parsimonious metaphysics is that which requires the lowest number of postulates while maintaining sufficient explanatory power to make sense of all known facts. In what follows, I offer nine inferences that, together, aim to answer this question.

Inference 1: The most parsimonious ontological underpinning for Facts 1 and 2 is that experiences are *patterns of excitation* of TWE. This avoids the need to postulate two different ontological classes for TWE and experiences, respectively.

As excitations of TWE, experiences aren't distinct from it in exactly the same way that ripples aren't distinct from water, or that a dance isn't distinct from the dancer. There is nothing to ripples but water in motion. There is nothing to a dance but the dancer in motion. In exactly the same way, *there is nothing to experience but TWE* 'in motion.' Ripples, dances and experiences are merely patterns of excitation of water, dancers and TWE, respectively.

Inference 2: From Fact 4, we know that a nervous system is *sentient*. In other words, there is something it is like to *be* a nervous system. Somehow, the activity of these systems is accompanied by inner experience. One possibility is that there is something about the particular structure or function of nervous systems that constitutes sentience. However, it is impossible to conceive—even *in principle*—of how or why any particular structural or functional arrangement of physical elements would constitute sentience.[5] This is a well-known problem in neuroscience and philosophy of mind, often referred to as the 'hard problem of consciousness.' The *qualities* of experience are irreducible to the observable *parameters* of physical arrangements—whatever the arrangement is—in the sense that it is impossible to deduce those qualities—even in principle—from these parameters.[6] It remains conceivable that physical arrangements could still *modulate* experience, without constituting it, if one postulates some form of dualism. But even if this hypothesis turns out to be coherent, it would still leave That Which Experiences entirely unexplained, since TWE would be that which is modulated (Inference 1). From all this we must conclude that

TWE is uncaused, irreducible. It simply *is*. Technically, we say that *TWE is an ontological primitive.*

Inference 3: From Facts 4 and 7 and Inference 2, we must also conclude that *TWE is coextensive with the universe as a whole.* After all, since That Which Experiences cannot be caused by local physical arrangements (Inference 2), and since nervous systems—which *do* experience (Fact 4)—are of the same essential nature as the universe as a whole (Fact 7), it follows that the latter must also experience. Rejecting this conclusion entails accepting a completely arbitrary discontinuity in nature. As such, the physical universe must be akin to a cosmic nervous system, at least in the specific sense that its activity must be accompanied by cosmic-level inner experiences.[7] Is there any circumstantial empirical evidence for this kinship? As it turns out, there is: a study has shown unexplained structural similarities—not necessarily *functional* ones, mind you—between the cosmos and biological nervous systems.[8]

Inference 3 is already sufficient to establish that Attribute 4 holds. But the metaphysics being constructed here doesn't yet explain Facts 1 to 9. So let us continue:

Inference 4: Inference 3 asserts that TWE is coextensive with the entire universe. However, from Fact 3 we know that people have at least largely separate, private inner experiences. Many of my personal inner experiences are surely not the same as yours. Moreover, I am not aware of what is going on in the universe as a whole and, presumably, neither are you. To reconcile these facts with Inference 3, we need to consider a common mental phenomenon called *dissociation*. For instance, a person suffering from Dissociative Identity Disorder (DID) exhibits multiple, disjoint centers of

> experience called *alters*. Each alter experiences the world as a separate subject, remaining largely unaware of—that is, *dissociated* from—the inner experiences of other alters.[9] So even while granting that TWE is coextensive with the universe as a whole, we can still coherently explain the seemingly private character of our inner experiences by inferring that there is a sense in which *we are dissociated alters of TWE*. Indeed, dissociation elegantly explains Fact 3 while reconciling it with Inference 3.

There has been debate about the authenticity of DID as a psychiatric phenomenon. After all, it is conceivable that patients could fake it. Recent research, however, confirms DID's legitimacy. For instance, in 2015 doctors reported on the case of a German woman who exhibited a variety of alters. Peculiarly, some of her alters claimed to be blind while others could see normally. Through EEGs, the doctors were able to ascertain that the brain activity normally associated with sight wasn't present while a blind alter was in control of the woman's body, even though her eyes were open. When a sighted alter assumed control, the usual brain activity returned.[10] This is a sobering result that shows the literally *blinding* power of dissociation. In another study, doctors performed functional brain scans on both DID patients and actors simulating DID. The scans of the actual patients displayed clear and significant differences when compared to those of the actors.[11] This study is interesting not only for confirming the authenticity of DID, but also for showing that *dissociation has an extrinsic view*. In other words, there is something dissociation *looks like* when observed from the outside, through a brain scanner. The significance I see in this will become clear shortly. For now, the point is that dissociation is an empirically established phenomenon known to occur in mental space. And since TWE is universal mental space (Inference 3), it is empirically coherent to infer that dissociation can happen at a universal level as well.

Inference 4 allows discrete centers of experience to form within the all-encompassing and otherwise unitary TWE, through top-down dissociation. The challenge we must now tackle is the so-called "boundary problem for experiencing subjects":[12] What physical arrangements in nature correspond to dissociated alters of TWE? We know that we, human beings, do. Do animals too? What about plants? Rocks? Atoms? Subatomic particles?

Inference 5: As Gregg Rosenberg put it, "we must find something in nature to ground [the boundaries of] an experiencing subject"[13]—that is, the boundaries of a dissociated alter of TWE. This 'something in nature' must be a physical arrangement whose structural and functional characteristics allow us to differentiate it from everything else. After all, only on the basis of this differentiation can we delineate the boundaries of dissociated alters from an extrinsic perspective. But just what is the physical arrangement Rosenberg was looking for? The answer seems empirically obvious to me: *metabolizing life*. My reasoning is simple: since we only have intrinsic access to ourselves, *we* are the only physical arrangements *known* to have dissociated streams of inner experiences. We also know that our metabolism is essential for the maintenance of this dissociation, for when it slows down or stops the dissociation seems to reduce or end.[14] These observations alone suggest strongly that metabolizing life is the physical arrangement corresponding to alters of TWE. But there is more: insofar as it resembles our own, the extrinsic behavior of *all* metabolizing organisms is also suggestive of their having dissociated streams of inner experiences analogous to ours in some sense. This is obvious enough for cats and dogs, but—you might ask—what about single-celled organisms such as amoebae? Well, consider this: "many types of amoeba construct glassy shells by picking up sand grains from the mud in which they live. The typical *Difflugia* shell, for example, is shaped like a vase, and has a remarkable symmetry."[15] Clearly, thus, even single-celled organisms exhibit extrinsic behavior somewhat analogous to our own, further suggesting that they, too, have dissociated streams of inner experiences. Of course, the same *cannot* be said of any inanimate object or phenomenon that hasn't been engineered by humans. Finally, there is no doubt that metabolism is a highly differentiated process. Consider DNA, morphogenesis, transcription, protein folding, mitosis, etc.: nothing else in nature exhibits structural and functional characteristics such as these. And it is these characteristics that unify all metabolizing life into a unique, clearly distinct natural category, despite the widely different forms organisms can take. This category is the unambiguously demarcated 'something in nature' that Rosenberg was looking for. *Metabolizing organisms are the extrinsic view of dissociated alters of TWE.*

The essence of Inference 5 is that there is something a dissociated alter of TWE looks like—namely, a metabolizing body. By now this shouldn't come as a surprise: recall that, in Inference 3, we concluded that the universe as a whole is, at least in a certain sense, akin to a cosmic nervous system. Recall also that a study has shown that dissociative processes in the nervous systems of DID patients have a distinct extrinsic view, detectable by brain scans. Therefore, it is only natural that dissociation in the cosmic nervous system should *also* have a distinct extrinsic view. It so happens that this view is what we call metabolizing organisms. As such, living bodies are to cosmic-level dissociation in TWE as certain patterns of brain activity are to DID patients. In the case of the cosmic nervous system, however, we don't need brain scanners, for we are already *inside* the nervous system. To see the extrinsic views of dissociated alters within it we just need to look around: the people, cats, dogs, insects, plants, amoebae and all other life forms we see around are the diagnostic images of cosmic 'DID.' Each corresponds to at least one alter.

For emphasis: there are two ways in which a dissociated alter of TWE can be experienced. One is the *extrinsic view*—that is, the metabolizing organisms we can *perceive* around us. The other is the *intrinsic view*, an example of which is your own stream of inner experiences as a dissociated alter yourself. Moreover, unless we are prepared to accept an arbitrary discontinuity in nature, the same must apply to the universe as a whole: its *extrinsic view* is the cosmos we can perceive around us, while its *intrinsic view* is the stream of inner experiences of God Itself—that is, TWE. As such, it is literally correct to say that "the universe is God's body,"[16] an assertion often made by Pandeists and Pantheists alike.

One may feel tempted to conclude that this implies some form of dual-aspect monism, *à la* Spinoza,[17] whereby intrinsic and extrinsic views are irreducible to one another. What I will attempt to show next is that this isn't so: *extrinsic views can in fact be reduced to intrinsic views*.

Before I continue, however, notice that it is *perceptions* that carry the extrinsic views, not thoughts or emotions. If all you experienced were thoughts and emotions, you would have no extrinsic point of view at all, only an intrinsic one. Therefore, if I can coherently reduce perceptions to thoughts and emotions—that is, explain perceptions *in terms of* thoughts and emotions—I will have shown that nature, at its most fundamental level, consists of purely intrinsic views.

Inference 6: Before its first alter formed, I submit that TWE experienced *only* abstract thoughts and emotions. There were no perceptions. The formation of the first alter then demarcated a *boundary* separating the experiences *within* the alter from those *outside* the alter (all of which were, of course, still

> within TWE). This newly formed boundary is what enabled perceptions to arise: the abstract thoughts and emotions surrounding the alter *stimulated* its boundary from the outside, which in turn impinged on the alter's internal dynamics. What we call perception is the experience of this impingement. More generally, *the perceptions of an alter can be reduced to the cognitive activity of TWE that impinges on the alter from the outside.*

You can easily visualize this by imagining the alter as an air balloon. Air pressure oscillations within the balloon represent the alter's private, dissociated stream of experiences. Air pressure oscillations surrounding the balloon represent the cognitive activity of TWE unfolding in the vicinity of the alter. These latter oscillations push and pull on the balloon's membrane—the alter's boundary—from the outside, thereby inducing *a particular type* of pressure oscillations inside the balloon, which is experienced by the alter as *perceptions*. Perceptions are thus the result of cognitive activity surrounding the alter impinging on its internal dynamics by stimulation of its boundary.

The actual extrinsic view of an alter's boundary is, of course, an organism's sense organs. In our case, these are our skin, eyes, ears, nose and tongue. They correspond to the balloon's membrane, which is stimulated from the outside. Therefore, even if the outside stimulation is very faint and subtle, evolution has had billions of years to optimize the sensitivity of our sense organs—our alters' boundaries—to pick up on these hypothetically faint signals.

Two questions can be raised at this point: First, how can a mere dissociative boundary give rise to a *qualitatively different* type of experience? After all, perceptions *feel* very distinct from thoughts and emotions. Second, how can outside experiences, which are by definition *dissociated* from the alter, cause experiences inside the alter? This seems contradictory at first sight.

Let us start from the second question. Contrary to the question's premise, we are all, in fact, familiar with dissociated experiences that causally affect each other while *remaining* dissociated from each other. Imagine, for instance, that you are having relationship problems at home. When you go to work, you successfully 'park' your problems—that is, repress your emotional life—in order to perform your tasks. Your emotions then become temporarily dissociated from your ego, in the sense that they are no longer in your awareness while you work. *But they do still impinge on it*: they may, for instance, cause your imagination to flow in a somber direction, lead you to misunderstand comments received from colleagues, lock your intellect into repetitive patterns of reasoning, etc. All the while, your ego doesn't directly experience the emotions themselves. They remain dissociated from it. But from across the dissociative boundary they, somehow, still causally influence what arises in your awareness. My claim is that something analogous to this happens across the boundaries of dissociated alters of TWE, causing perceptions.

I acknowledge that such causal influences operating across a dissociative boundary seem rather faint and subtle. But then again, evolution favors the sensitization of sense organs—the extrinsic view of an alter's boundary—for picking up on very faint signals. And evolution has had a lot of time to do its job.

Let's now tackle the first question. Still with reference to the example above, notice that your dissociated emotions at work have an impact on *qualitatively different* types of experience: they interfere with your imagination, understanding and reasoning, none of which *feels* like emotions. This shows empirically that, not only can there be a causal link across a dissociative boundary, *this causal link can also connect qualitatively dissimilar experiences.* A dissociated emotion can cause a thought; a dissociated belief can distort a perception or even generate one through hallucinatory mechanisms; etc. Therefore, it is empirically coherent to infer that cognitive activity outside an alter can cause experiences in the alter that are qualitatively dissimilar from such cognitive activity. It is reasonable to postulate even that evolution would have *emphasized* this kind of qualitative transition, if it helped enhance the sensitivity of the alter to external stimuli. I posit that the more sophisticated perceptual apparatuses in nature are the result of just such evolutionary emphasis on a qualitative transition.

Before taking the final steps to complete this metaphysics, we must briefly review the underpinnings of today's mainstream physicalism, which posits that physical reality is fundamentally independent of experience and that experience is somehow generated by particular physical arrangements.

To begin with, notice that our only access to a world allegedly independent of experience takes the form of perceptions, *which are themselves experiences*. Therefore, physicalism is a *tentative explanatory model* produced by thought, not an observable empirical fact. Its motivation is to provide a tentative explanation for Facts 6 (which comprises Facts 4 and 5), 8 and 9. After all, if the physical brain doesn't somehow generate experience, how can there be such tight correlations between observable brain activity and inner experience (Fact 6)? Moreover, if the physical world isn't fundamentally independent of experience, it can only be a kind of mentally generated dream. But in such a case, how can we all be having the same dream (Fact 8)? Finally, if the world is mentally generated, how can it unfold according to patterns and regularities independent of our volition (Fact 9)?

Physicalism is inflationary: in addition to experience itself—the one undeniable ontological class—it postulates the existence of unprovable physical stuff independent of experience. This step would only be justifiable if we could not make sense of Facts 6, 8 and 9 without it. Moreover, physicalism is severely limited in its explanatory power, for it fails to explain experience itself (recall the 'hard problem of consciousness').

Therefore, if we can explain Facts 6, 8 and 9 *without* postulating anything fundamentally independent of experience, physicalism must be rejected on grounds of parsimony. Furthermore, if we can circumvent the 'hard problem of consciousness' in the process of doing so, physicalism must be further rejected on grounds of explanatory power. As it turns out, this is precisely what we can now do:

Inference 7: Our inferences thus far allow us to elegantly explain Fact 8 based on excitations of TWE alone. Since TWE is coextensive with the universe as a whole (Inference 3), it follows that all dissociated alters of TWE—that is, metabolizing organisms such as ourselves (Inferences 4 and 5)—are immersed, like islands in a single ocean, in the thoughts and emotions that constitute the intrinsic view of the inanimate universe. These universal thoughts and emotions surround all alters and cause their perceptions by stimulating their respective dissociative boundaries (Inference 6). This explains the fact that we all perceive the same universe around us (Fact 8). Moreover, since the thoughts and emotions of TWE are excitations of TWE itself (Inference 1), it follows trivially that *we can explain our shared universe based on excitations of TWE alone.*

Inference 8: We can also explain Fact 9 on the same basis. Since volition is innately experiential, the volition of each and every alter of TWE is also dissociated from the rest of TWE (Inference 4). This explains why we do not have personal volitional control over the laws of nature (Fact 9). *The unfolding of the empirical universe reflects excitations of TWE from which we are dissociated.*

Inference 9: Finally, the explanation for Fact 6. As we've seen in Inference 6, for any given alter *A1* of TWE, it is the

> cognitive activity surrounding *A1* that causes its perceptions of the world around it. Naturally, dissociated activity corresponding to an alter *A2* can be part of the cognitive activity surrounding *A1*. As such, the inner experiences of *A2* can stimulate *A1*'s boundary and cause *A1*'s perceptions of *A2*. This is what gives *A1* an *extrinsic view* of the inner experiences of *A2* in the form of *A2*'s metabolizing body (Inference 5). And since *A2*'s nervous system is an integral part of its body, it follows that *A2*'s inner experiences *cause* the perception by *A1* of the electrochemical activity in *A2*'s nervous system. This causal link explains Fact 6. Putting it more generally, *the extrinsic and intrinsic views of an organism correlate tightly with one another because the intrinsic view causes the extrinsic view*—not the other way around. Contrary to physicalism, thus, it is the inner experiences of an organism—both self-reflective and obfuscated, so-called 'unconscious' experiences[18]—that cause its body, insofar as the body is no more than a set of perceptions. (It goes without saying that *A1* and *A2* can also be the *same* alter, since an organism can perceive its own body.)

This is it; this completes the proposed metaphysics. Facts 1 to 9 are now explained *in terms of* TWE. Naturally, from Inference 2 we know that we don't need to explain TWE itself: *it is an ontological primitive*. Indeed, every theory of nature needs to identify at least one ontological primitive, since we cannot keep on explaining one thing in terms of another forever. At some point we have to stop and say: at this level, nature simply is. So TWE *simply is*. The fact that I don't reduce it to something else is in no way a shortcoming. Physicalism itself, depending on its specific formulation, postulates a slew of abstract subatomic particles, the quantum vacuum, superstrings, hyper-dimensional 'branes' and whatnot as primitives, all of which also remain fundamentally unexplainable. If anything, my formulation has the advantages of both parsimony—for making do with a single primitive—and empirical honesty—for choosing an indisputable empirical fact as primitive, as opposed to abstractions of thought.

The proposed metaphysics thus reduces everything to TWE, its sole ontological primitive. And as you've probably already noticed, 'consciousness' is the ordinary English word that best fits what I mean by 'TWE':

TWE = universal consciousness = God

This way, the proposed metaphysics reduces everything to an uncaused (Inference 2), omnipresent (Inference 3), omnipotent (Inference 6) and omniscient (Inferences 1 and 3) God. Clearly, this validates Attributes 1 to 4, respectively. Moreover, the proposed metaphysics is idealist, in the sense that it explains reality purely in terms of *ideas*—thoughts and emotions—in universal consciousness. Finally, *the proposed metaphysics circumvents the 'hard problem of consciousness' altogether*: since consciousness is taken to be the ontological primitive, it doesn't need to be reduced to begin with. As a matter of fact, the 'hard problem' has never been more than a purely conceptual invention of confused human thinking; confused because it tries—absurdly—to turn abstractions of consciousness into concrete ontological primitives, and then finds it puzzling that it can't reduce consciousness to consciousness's own abstractions. Duh.

One final point: in an earlier work, I've rebutted the sixteen best physicalist criticisms of my proposed metaphysics.[19] It's not in the scope of this essay to repeat those rebuttals, but I do feel the need to anticipate and answer one particularly pervasive criticism related to Inference 9. It goes like this: I've stated that an organism's inner experiences—both self-reflective and obfuscated, so-called 'unconscious' experiences[20]—cause its body, not the other way around. However, it's a well-established fact that physical interference with our brain—through psychoactive drugs, trauma to the head, exposure to electromagnetic fields, etc.—affects our inner experiences. So the arrow of causation must point the other way: from the body to inner experiences. Or so the criticism goes.

Although this may sound persuasive at first, it's based on an unexamined, pervasive and highly pernicious dualist assumption: that the physical is in some sense distinct from, yet causally effective upon, the mental. *This is precisely what I am denying*. I am saying precisely that, in essence, there is *only* the mental, since there is *only* That Which Experiences. The physical is simply the contents of perception, a particular type of experience. As such, everything is essentially mental, including the physical. 'Physical interference with the brain' is simply the extrinsic view of *mental* activity in TWE that disrupts the inner experiences of an alter from across its dissociative boundary. This disruption, in turn, is simultaneously reflected on the extrinsic view of the alter—namely, the body—just as the proposed metaphysics explains. That certain types of mental activity disrupt other types of mental activity is not only *entailed* by the proposed metaphysics, but also empirically trivial. After all, our thoughts disrupt our emotions—and vice versa—every day. For exactly the same reason that thoughts disrupt emotions, 'physical interference with the brain' disrupts an organism's inner experiences. None of this contradicts the proposed metaphysics; on the contrary.

The Metaphysical Validity of Pandeism

We can summarize the proposed metaphysics as follows: there is only God and God *is* universal consciousness. We, as well as all other living creatures, are but dissociated alters of God, surrounded like islands by the ocean of God's mentation. The inanimate universe we see around us is the extrinsic view of God's thoughts and emotions. The living creatures we share the world with are the extrinsic views of other dissociated alters of God. A physical world independent of consciousness is a mistaken intellectual abstraction. Everything in nature can be reduced to the cognitive activity of universal consciousness. There is God and *only* God in the universe, for the universe *is* God.

This clearly echoes Pandeism, which posits that God exists today only *as* the universe itself. It is also fully consistent with the Pandeist view that the laws of nature are the expression of God's will, for according to the proposed metaphysics nature is simply the extrinsic view of God's ideas. Finally, the proposed metaphysics legitimizes Pandeism as a *genuine* theology, for it shows that God, as universal consciousness, is omniscient.

But there's a crucial element still left: a key tenet of Pandeism, which distinguishes it from Pantheism, is that God *created* the universe by *becoming* it. This entails an *Act of Creation,* a divine *reconfiguration event* at some point in the remote cosmological past. Before this point, according to Pandeism, God wasn't the universe. What does the proposed metaphysics have to say about this?

I submit that *the divine reconfiguration event began with the formation of the first dissociated alter of God*—that is, the rise of life from non-life. As discussed in the previous section, before the first alter formed *no perceptions* existed, only abstract thoughts and emotions. And since our very idea of the cosmos—its textured planets, bright stars, swirling galaxies, colorful nebulae, etc.—comes to us in the form of perceptions, what we call the universe didn't exist back then. Before the first alter, there was nothing to be seen, heard, tasted, smelled or touched. The Act of Creation changed this, giving rise to living organisms that, for the first time, could experience the eternal divine essence through colors, shapes, melodies, aromas, flavors, warmth and textures. What we call the universe started coming into being at that seminal moment, the birth of perceptual experience.

Scott Adams wrote a Pandeist book—suitably titled *God's Debris*—in which he speculates that the Act of Creation was the disintegration of God in a primal explosion. "We are God's debris,"[21] he says, the remnants of that explosion. Adams' metaphor echoes the Pandeist intuition that God's transformation into the universe somehow involved God's own *fragmentation*. And isn't the dissociation of a psyche into multiple alters a form of fragmentation? God split Itself into countless alters in order to create the universe as we know it. We are, indeed, God's debris.

The thing to remember, however, is that dissociation isn't annihilation. It isn't a fragmentation of *essence* but one merely of *appearance*. The metaphysics proposed in this essay implies that we will all, in due time, be reintegrated back into God. There's nothing more certain than this and taxes.

Conclusions

I've elaborated on a complete, logically coherent metaphysics that makes sense of reality in a more parsimonious and empirically honest manner than mainstream physicalism. This metaphysics also offers more explanatory power than physicalism, in that it doesn't fall prey to the 'hard problem of consciousness.'

As it happens, the proposed metaphysics validates the logic of Pandeism, giving ontological substantiation to key Pandeist tenets. It also legitimizes Pandeism as a *genuine* theology, in that it shows that the key attributes of divinity are applicable to the Pandeist universe. Therefore, this essay has shown that, not only is Pandeism consistent with the spirit of the word 'God,' it is also metaphysically sound.

Notes

1 In this essay, I use the gender-neutral 'It' and 'Its' instead of 'He' and 'His' when referring to God. I do it purely for gender neutrality, not to imply that God isn't sentient.

2 Maharaj, Nisargadatta (1973). *I Am That*. Mumbai, India: Chetana Publishing, p. 58.

3 Mead, G. R. S. (translator) (2010). *The Corpus Hermeticum*. Whitefish, MT: Kessinger Publishing, p. 11.

4 See, for instance: Russell, B. (2007). *The Analysis of Matter*. Nottingham, UK: Spokesman Books, pp. 382–93.

5 See, for instance: Strawson, G. et al. (2006). *Consciousness and Its Place in Nature*. Exeter, UK: Imprint Academic, pp. 12–21; as well as: Rosenberg, G. (2004). *A Place for Consciousness*. New York, NY: Oxford University Press, pp. 2–30.

6 Chalmers, D. (2003). "Consciousness and Its Place in Nature." In: Stich, S. and Warfield, F. eds. *Blackwell Guide to the Philosophy of Mind*. Malden, MA: Blackwell, pp. 102–42.

7 This, of course, doesn't mean that the universe must *function* like a biological nervous system. Clearly, it doesn't. And neither should it: the cosmos did not evolve to survive in an external Earthly ecosystem, as biological nervous systems did.

8 Krioukov, D. et al. (2012). "Network Cosmology." In: *Scientific Reports 2*, 793, doi:10.1038/srep00793.

9 See, for instance: Braude, S. E. (1991). *First Person Plural: Multiple Personality and the Philosophy of Mind*. New York, NY: Routledge.

10 Strasburger, H. and Waldvogel, B. (2015). "Sight and Blindness in the Same Person: Gating in the Visual System." In: *Psych J.*, 4(4), doi: 10.1002/pchj.109, pp. 178–85.

11 Schlumpf, Y. R. et al. (2014). "Dissociative Part-Dependent Resting-State Activity in Dissociative Identity Disorder: A Controlled fMRI Perfusion Study." In: *PloS one*, 9(6), doi: 10.1371/journal .pone.0098795.

12 Rosenberg (2004), cited above, pp. 77–90.

13 Rosenberg (2004), cited above, p. 80.

14 Kastrup, B. (2014). *Why Materialism Is Baloney*. Winchester, UK: Iff Books, pp. 42–50.

15 Ford, B. J. (2010). "Secret Intelligence of the Living Cell." In: *New Scientist*, 24 April 2010, p. 26.

16 *Routledge Encyclopedia of Philosophy* (1998), p. 104.

17 See, for instance: Skrbina, D. (2007). *Panpsychism in the West*. Cambridge, MA: MIT Press, p. 88.

18 Kastrup, B. (2015). *Brief Peeks Beyond*. Winchester, UK: Iff Books, pp. 17–18, 189–90.

19 Kastrup. *Brief Peeks Beyond*, pp. 22–36.

20 Kastrup, *Brief Peeks Beyond*, pp. 17–18, 189–90.

21 Adams, S. (2004). *God's Debris: A Thought Experiment*. Kansas City, MO: Andrews McMeel Publishing, p. 44.

A Theorem Concerning God

Robert G. Brown PhD

Robert G. Brown (PhD) teaches physics full-time at Duke University, in Durham, NC. He has authored several (free) online textbooks of physics and supporting subjects that are in widespread international use, and also writes novels and poetry. As an undergraduate physics major en route to a BS (also at Duke) he was a closet philosophy major at a time when the University did not recognize a double BA/BS major, and took half of the courses for the non-major from George Roberts, a student and colleague of Bertrand Russell. He has also studied math, logic, statistics, and computing, including information theory, which is a major point of synthesis between axiomatic statistics and computer science. The theorem presented below has roots in all of these disciplines.

1. Introduction

It is rare in the history of mankind that an actual theorem has been stated, let alone proven in a satisfactory way, concerning God. This lack of any empirically or rationally provable results has been one of the major stumbling blocks to rational religion, and of course that which is not, or cannot, be made rational remains *ir*rational to the great dismay and mutual destruction of humanity.

This document proves, from simple premises and definitions consistent with the more or less standard model of God, an actual theorem concerning God and the Universe[1] that might be of interest in the eternal conflict between those that allege that God 'created' the Universe and those that allege that there is no God and that the Universe didn't require a creator. It does not resolve the question of whether or not there is a God, but it puts an end rather nicely to the question of whether or not any hypothesized God created a distinct and separate Universe. It is an *ontological* proof, but it avoids the fallacies associated with Anselm's Ontological Proof of God and doesn't require an axiom of infinity (although it can tolerate one) and thereby dodges some of the Gödelian Russell paradoxes of set theory as well.

It will become apparent as one studies and understands this theorem that it establishes *strict constraints* on theisms in order for them to be *reasonable* and hence *possible*. It does not address the deeper (and more difficult) issue as to whether or not any theistic religion is *plausible*, as that requires further assumptions to be made and (as will be described in my book-under-construction *Axioms*) these assumptions invariably prove that God exists only by begging the question, by directly or indirectly including the conclusion in the premises. The axioms and definitions used below to prove this theorem, however, are ones that are frankly difficult to disagree with and still use English words in their commonly accepted (and nevertheless carefully defined) way, and do *not* beg the question addressed as the proof requires genuine synthesis from all of the axioms as well as input from various well-founded mathematical theories.

Let me be blunt: *Most theistic religions of the world are not in accord with this theorem and hence are literally impossible.* Because the theorem is based on reason (and its axioms are such that they can hardly be challenged and end up with a system of rational knowledge at all) this is simply too bad for those religions. They are incorrect. There is not the slightest window left open for them to be correct and have God possess certain key properties that those religions themselves ascribe to God. Augustine, Aquinas and Anselm, ardent Christian theists that they were, would have to accept this conclusion even as all of their arguments for a Christian theistic 'Creator' deity (such as asserting that a God that is real is greater than any imaginary God so that somehow my imagination of God becomes a proof of God) have long since been shown to be fallacious and even somewhat silly as e.g.

General Semantics has carefully drawn lines between 'things in our imagination' (the map) and 'things that have objective existential being' (the territory) where the former is most certainly not identical to or in any sort of logically necessary one-to-one correspondence with the latter.

I can imagine a pink unicorn, and my *imagination* of a pink unicorn may be objectively real, but that does not mean reality contains a single *actual* pink unicorn, as a realization of my imagination. As with unicorns, so with God. Although maps themselves are often things one can pick up and put into your pocket and hence are real enough, their existence has no bearing whatsoever on the reality of the territory they appear to represent or, if there *is* such a territory, the accuracy of the representation. Otherwise the existence of a map (or story!) of Narnia would imply that an actual place existed in correspondence to the map, right down to the talking Fauns and White Witches. We understand perfectly well the nature of *fiction* and *error*, just two ways that a map can exist in our imagination of something that does not exist at all in reality.

As to *why* the theorem proven below has been missed by all of the world's philosophers, the answer is simple. First of all, it really hasn't; the assertion itself is the basis for a whole family of the world's religions[2] and a common heresy of many others. The assertion played an important role in the Enlightenment of Europe and in the establishment of the United States. It was the directly stated belief of Benjamin Franklin, Thomas Jefferson, Thomas Paine, George Washington, and many other of America's founding fathers and important philosophers around the globe.

The *assertion* has thus been around for a very long time—only the *proof* has been lacking. The proof given below is (as far as I know) unique and has only been possible for the last few decades, and then only accessible to someone with an interest in and knowledge of philosophy, religion, physics, mathematics, and computer science as elements are drawn from all of these disciplines to make the argument.

Second, most philosophical reasoning about God has focused on 'proving' or 'disproving' God's *existence* using reason, a process that has continued long after Hume's *correct and unassailable* observation that such a proof is impossible: God cannot be proven by (reasonable) inference as a finite set of observations can never suffice to prove an infinite conclusion concerning the real world, and God cannot be deduced without begging the question in the axioms used in the proof. We will leave moot the simple fact that we don't have a *single* actual, reliable, reproducible observation of God or a coherent theory of deity capable of being supported by observation.

In general, empirical arguments have proceeded according to the following paradigm: "We see phenomenon X in the real world. We do not understand X. We conclude that the *only way* X could occur is by the direct action of something beyond our understanding, God."[3] That is, God(s) have always been 'God(s) of the Gaps'—a glib way of ascribing a sentient, usually anthropomorphic cause to anything that is observed that defies explanation on the basis of our (then) current state of knowledge.

The inexorable progress of science in closing the gaps in human knowledge has systematically reduced the empirical plausibility of any model of a God that intervenes in the Universe in detectable ways—there is simply no reliable, systematic body of evidence that suggests that this occurs. On the contrary, the entire body of physical law and its enormous basis of empirical support suggest the exact opposite. At the same time, the mathematics and logic of 'infinity' have been substantially developed and now have much to say about proposed infinities supposedly present in a very much finite sphere of observations of reality. Finally, we have learned an enormous amount about information theory and 'intelligence' and are in a much better position to address the plausibility of the existence of physical law violating, immaterial, infinite, sentient beings.

This theorem treats the question of God's existence as being fundamentally:

- logically/rationally unprovable (without begging the question);
- implausible (in a specific statistical sense) and empirically unsupported;
- but possibly *true anyway*.

This possibility is allowed by and logically consistent with Gödel's theorems, wherein there exist true—or false—but unprovable theorems in any sufficiently complex system of *formal* reason, and of course empirically, absence of evidence is not necessary or sufficient evidence of absence; it merely reduces the *plausibility* of the assertion *given* the evidence in a purely Bayesian sense, especially given competing explanations that *are* well-supported and leave little room. One can therefore easily argue (and indeed, I myself would agree with the argument) that even if it isn't logically and mathematically impossible for at least one consistent model of God to exist, neither is it very likely for that model to be correct, given our observations and the plausible knowledge derived from them so far.

To deliberately avoid being bogged down in the mire or having the wrong conclusions drawn from the argument, then, the assertion proven below is a simple *conditional* statement—*if* (at least one) God exists, *then* certain conclusions can be drawn concerning Its nature. No attempt is made to use these conclusions in *reductio ad absurdum* to prove or disprove the condition because post-Hume we know *a priori* that this is impossible. The conditional theorem thus proven leaves the possibility of rational belief (in God) in perfect balance with rational disbelief as being one of the questions that cannot be answered with certainty by any finite being, while *strongly constraining* the set of admissible consistent theistic systems contingent upon axiomatically asserted belief.

Why should we bother to state and prove such an obviously 'dangerous' theorem in a world already pulled apart by religious conflict? On a daily basis individuals commit murder and acts of war in the name of their favorite brand of supposedly divinely inspired perfectly true theistic scripture. This theorem proves that the detailed descriptions of the properties assigned to God in these scriptures are not merely unlikely, not merely unsupported by positive evidence and contradicted by much negative evidence, but they are *a priori impossible*. They assert one property in particular—an essential dualism between a 'standard model' God and Everything Else—that is essentially self-contradictory.

One can prove *anything* from inconsistent axioms, from a contradiction, and so it has proven throughout human history where every possible variant of human faith has spoken of God's love and in the same breath asserted God's wrath, has spoken of God's perfect justice and followed it up with a description of God's supposed actions that *any child* could see are perfectly unjust, has spoken of God's desire for peace and goodwill and followed it with war, persecution, torture, murder, slavery, greed, all in the name of that God. While religion can be a source of good, it is all too often a source of *genuine evil* in the world as people fight over a vision of deity that is now *demonstrably false*.

It is a fundamental and empirically supported belief of the author of this work that the world is ill-served by unreason, by deliberate self-delusion on the part of each and every human alive. Humans cannot, through the empirical process or for that matter through pure logic, arrive at *perfect, unconditional* knowledge of *any* truth (defined to be an unconditionally true statement *concerning the real world*)—we simply build the best, most consistent web of *provisional* knowledge that the evidence of our senses and common sense can manage. We quite literally *should* believe that which it is *best* to self-consistently believe, *given the unbiased evidence and the rest of the interlocking network of beliefs*. This is precisely the basis of the scientific worldview, which is infinitely open-minded about non-contradictory assertions, but which requires *sound reasons* and *consistency with other soundly held beliefs* in order to assign any significant *probability* or *plausibility* to an assertion.

It is not the basis of scriptural theistic religions, which positively *thrive* on anecdotally reported *implausible* assertion after assertion in their myths, legends, creeds and tenets. Yet because these theisms admit *pure magic* as a causal agency in the Universe—basically anything at all can happen merely because God wills it so—*no possible contradiction between their myths, however absurd, and science will suffice to convince them that their core mythology and derived creed is false*! For that reason a proof that demonstrates a *logical* inconsistency is infinitely precious.

The world is just completing the first of the revolutions begun with the Enlightenment. The Age of Kings is over, and freedom from individual or hegemonic rule to a greater or lesser extent is now nearly universal around the world. Never before have the people of the world been more free to shape the mutual destiny of humanity in constructive ways, guided by human reason. The second revolution is well underway—the liberation of the human species from literal belief, enforced by threats and extortion, in complex Bronze Age mythologies that distort the worldview and judgment of all their adherents and that today are very nearly the *only* significant cause of large scale human misery outside of impersonal natural disasters and the equally natural accidents of life. Given all of the evidence of falsehoods in their theistic scriptures *plus* the proof that their core belief system isn't just contradicted by evidence but is *logically impossible*, perhaps the world can at last carry this revolution through to a bloodless conclusion, by simply convincing a single generation of children to *reject* the inconsistent and demonstrably false scriptural theisms of their parents and/or society in favor of any of the belief systems that are consistent with the theorem below:

pandeism, a modern secular Buddhism—or better still, empirical scientific rationalism and the *lack* of strong belief in implausible assertions unsupported by evidence (including pandeism) that is called atheism.

None of these worldviews have a *salvation* meme or a *damnation* meme. They leave humanity free to decide its own destiny without any threat but ourselves and nature. If anything, they obligate good and socially constructive behavior *more strongly* than any of the theisms, because *The Good* is no longer defined to be 'believing what this scripture tells you to believe because of its great divinely inspired, God given, authority,' it is 'believing what makes the most sense given reason and the evidence.' It is *pure common sense* for all enlightened secular humans to seek a peaceful and safe world, to engineer a world that maximizes fairness and personal human freedom, that provides challenges for those endowed with greater abilities and protections for those unfortunate enough to have lesser ones, to recognize that many of our ethical failures as human beings are the result of *failures and imperfections in our evolutionary sociobiology,* and are neither malicious, free moral choices nor the mythological curse of a malignant, selfish creator deity.

2. Axioms and Definitions

As I am endeavoring to communicate in unequivocal terms in the work-in-progress *Axioms* (and as is already well known by mathematicians and logicians[4]), there is very, very little that can be considered to be *a priori* truth in the entire realm of human intellectual endeavor. Most of what was once considered *a priori* truth from the time of the early Greek mathematicians and geometers has slowly, painfully been revealed to be *contingent* truth, truth that can only be derived from *unprovable axioms*—assumptions that are necessary to the development of logical arguments. Modern mathematics is developed from sets of propositions that are no longer advanced as self-evident *truth,* but rather as just that—propositions. If you change the propositions you get a different, but quite possibly *equally valid*, contingent theory.

When it comes to the real world (where I use the term 'world' in an all-embracing way to include the entire real *Universe*, everything that has objective existence) the situation is even worse. When even mathematics or geometry is only contingent truth that strongly depends on unprovable assertions, how much less certain is it that any logically consistent assertion concerning the real world is true? In most cases we cannot even sensibly limit the *number* of logically consistent assertions that *one might be able to make* about the real world that could explain any given observation without assumptions that both restrict the mathematics and logic used and that establish some criterion for choosing among competing explanations consistent with those assumptions.

For us to use reason in addressing questions about God, we therefore will require a *common* set of assumptions and a *consistent* set of definitions. Otherwise, with different assumptions or contradictory assumptions who could be surprised if one arrives at different conclusions (or any useful conclusion at all, given that one can prove *anything* from a contradiction)? This will not be sufficient in and of itself to support an argument that the logically reasoned conclusion is (probably) *true*. That requires the last, perhaps most important, of the elements of reasoning about the real world: some criterion for choosing among competing explanations that are all (in principle) capable of consistently explaining the real world.

Theorem proofs are not concerned with this last bit—they only show a consistent path from the axioms and definitions to the conclusion but are utterly inadequate as a proof that some assertion about the real world is *true*.

The theorem concerning God that this short work will state and prove therefore follows from a set of axioms and definitions, as any theorem must, but may or may not apply to the real world, may or may not be *true*. This you must judge using a different criterion than pure reason.

It is important to understand the difference between a proven theorem and a truth about the real world. It is straightforward to prove, from the axioms of Euclidean geometry, the many theorems of Euclidean geometry. Similarly, it is simple enough to prove from *different* axioms the theorems of *curved space geometries*. These proofs, however, are utterly incapable of demonstrating which geometry best describes empirical observations of space and time and physics in the real world. To establish that, you have to look to evidence drawn from the real world itself, not to pure, self-referential logic based on assertions that themselves cannot be proven to hold for the real world by any logical means.

To put it another way (and highlight the difference between having a theorem and having 'faith'): If we encounter a race of intelligent space aliens some day, as long as they are capable of using logic and reasoning mathematically and consistently, they would have to agree that the theorem below is a proven conclusion that follows from the assumptions, and that the assumptions themselves (outside of the assumption that God exists) are ones that actually apply remarkably successfully to many disciplines in the real world such as quantum field theory and physics in general as well as the fields of computation and probability theory. Indeed, there would be a very reasonable chance that they might have *independently* arrived at the same conclusion from the same premises, if they are of a religious bent at all.[5] Those same aliens would almost certainly not agree that Christianity or Hinduism or Islam are anything but primitive mythologies with nothing either proven or even particularly plausible in their descriptions.

This theorem concerns God and the Universe, so it seems suitable to start by precisely defining these two terms. Otherwise you could fail to understand (or agree with) the proof simply because the words used mean something *different* to *you* in your everyday discourse, perhaps because you speak a different language than English, perhaps because you simply never thought about their precise meaning, perhaps because that's just the way you learned them.

If these words *do* mean something different to you, then of course the argument may fail to convince you, but this is no more surprising than the simple *fact* that the famous Euclidean conclusion that the sum of the angles in a triangle is π is often false in non-Euclidean geometries. We have to *agree* on the axioms and definitions or else there is no point in using reason at all to address the question. I therefore ask that you grant me at least 'for the sake of argument' agreement with the definitions below.

The Universe: The Universe is defined to be *everything that exists*. This definition must be carefully qualified because we must not take the *narrow* viewpoint that everything that exists is the single space-time in which we appear to live or our even narrower observational knowledge of this space-time. We must allow for the possibility of multiple space-time continua, or larger spaces in which our space-time is *embedded*. This is not to allege that we *know* whether or not such a larger space exists, only that when we use the term *Universe* we are referring to the *union* of all dimensions that have objective existence, known or unknown, simply connected, multiply connected, or disjoint, together with all of their contents. It is time-independent (obviously so, given that what we call 'time' is a single dimension in *our* space-time continuum).

The point is that any assertion such as "*A* exists (or existed, or will exist) but is not a part of the Universe" is a direct contradiction of the term Universe for any *A*. If a thing has objective being, it is in the set of all things that have objective being. Note well that this existential definition of the set itself completely avoids all difficulties with, for example, Russell paradoxes (for those that know what they are) as 'sets' do not have objective being as anything but abstractions, thoughts, descriptive groupings generated by our imagination; they are merely figments of our imagination where the Universe is precisely that which is objectively real *whether or not* we can correctly or precisely imagine it or define it as a set. Nor does this 'existential set' have the problems associated with infinite Universal *abstract* sets for much the same reason—the Universe is precisely what it is: reality, infinite or not as it actually turns out to be, and our beliefs concerning it or symbolic definitions of it (all being maps) will not affect the reality of the territory in any way.

God: Our proof requires that we associate with the term 'God' only *four* of the various qualities often associated with Deity. There may be other properties one *wishes* to assert, but in order to build a consistent rational theory of God, one must begin somewhere with a *minimal* set that everybody can agree on and then see if the others *can* be consistently asserted or asserted in a way that agrees with experience. Even limiting ourselves to just four, we will find that we are already so restricted that it is almost impossible for a consistent realization of the term to exist.

The term 'God' *in this work* refers to 'something' that possesses (at least) the following qualities, properties that are commonly ascribed to God in nearly all monotheistic or monistic religious faiths:

- **Unitary Being.** God must have objective existence in order to be God, and not just 'be a myth' or 'be an idea.' If you like, God cannot 'just' be a map independent of all territory because even a map that exists only in our imagination exists in our imagination. God already can be said to 'exist' in my imagination, but if God 'only' exists in the imagination, that is just like not existing at all as far as this argument is concerned, just as is the case for pink unicorns or Narnia, with or without ordinal properties of ontological 'greatness.' Also, there can be just one (or One, if you prefer) God at least with a capital G that has all of the properties we require.

- **Omniscience.** God must be a sentient, reasoning being that possesses a complete knowledge of the state of the Universe, right down to the last electron in the last space-time continuum, the last hidden dimension. For the moment we defer a discussion of just what 'knowledge' is (let alone sentience), but even without it we can agree that if God's knowledge of the Universe is incomplete—if there are objective truths about the Universe some otherwise very large and powerful sentient being with objective existence doesn't know—then that being is not God, it is just a bigger and more powerful natural entity, existing within a partly unknown Universe, much like ourselves. We might well fear such a being. We might well obey it out of that fear. We would never worship it; indeed all free humans would be more likely to hate it to the precise extent that it imposed its will by fiat upon us.
- **Omnipresence.** God must be 'everywhere.' In general this has been associated with omniscience—in order to know everything one must observe everything. In order to observe everything, one must be spatially contiguous in order to perform the observation. Of course any physicist knows that this is all very sloppy and incorrect—observation-derived knowledge is only meaningful in terms of entropy, which is missing information. We've already agreed that God has no missing information and is in a zero-entropy state relative to the Universe, which of course has consequences, one of them being the theorem we seek to state and prove. Nevertheless, omnipresence will be retained as a harmless and natural adjunct of

omniscience and a reasonable property of God.

- **Omnipotence.** This is a tough one. It is usually interpreted as 'God can do anything God wants to,' but this is at once far too narrow and too broad (as was recognized even by the 'philosophers' of the Church, e.g. Thomas Aquinas). God cannot make π=3. God cannot possess contradictory properties or perform contradictory acts. God cannot make the impossible (defined as something that is logically contradictory) happen. However, this property is essentially irrelevant to my argument below—it is in fact a contingent corollary of the only valid basis for information-theoretic omniscience and not really a separate property.

We will stop here and resist the temptation to add, for example, moral properties. Most of the rest of the properties theistic religions ascribe to God—being the Creator of the Universe, omnibenificence, being perfectly just, perfectly merciful, perfectly jealous, perfectly cruel, perfectly loving—are either directly contradictory (a perfectly just being gives to each the punishment they deserve, while the perfectly merciful does the *opposite*) or are fairly obvious anthropomorphic projections of human traits onto the Godhead (and are even more contradictory in combination with each other, as we contemplate an all-loving God who consigns self-aware creations to eternal fiery torment or simply allows them to contract cancer and die in a state of physical and spiritual suffering). Perhaps we will in the end have some room for more properties, perhaps not, but we must not invite theodicy or introduce the distraction of avoidable, contentious contradictions from the beginning.

Finally, we need a single assertion each from *information theory* and *physics*. From physics we need the idea that things that exist have *properties*. Indeed, we might go farther and state that existence itself *is* the existence of properties—it is very difficult to imagine a real thing that exists in the absence of at least the property of its own identity.[6] In physics the *properties* we typically ascribe to things like quarks and electrons (elementary particles out of which larger objects are built) include things like:

- Position
- Momentum
- Time
- Mass-Energy
- Charge
- ...

Things that exist, at least insofar as our direct experience goes, seem to have *intrinsic* properties, and in the case of so-called elementary particles, they are *irreducible* intrinsic properties. Even *thoughts* or *imaginings* have properties, elements that make them unique in space and time and perception. It is *non*existence that is a lack of *any* property, a complete lack of ascribable information.

The theorem below doesn't rely on any particular set of these properties, the independence or relationships between the properties, or whether or not we *know* what a complete set of the properties *are*, only that things that exist have them, while nonexistence is concisely described as the utter lack of any properties at all. It is valid whether or not we know what they are; it is valid however they might be 'causally' intertwined and interrelated. It is valid whether or not they are classical or quantum properties or something else altogether.

I don't know what it would mean to say that a thing exists but has no properties at all—that it has no properties of its own and isn't made up of things that have properties of their own that it inherits in aggregate, that it cannot be correlated in any way with things that have properties (as that correlation would be a property). Such a thing would presumably 'exist' at no place and at no time (in any generalized sense) and would in no way affect anything that did exist at some place and some time. I'd be pretty comfortable redefining the meaning of the word 'exist' so that it *excluded* such a thing, if need be, but I don't think that it is.

We need to carefully bear in mind that *coordinates* we might use to symbolically represent those properties are not the properties themselves but rather our semantic or mathematical *description* of those properties. Given that the Universe is the set of all things that exist, and that things that exist have properties, those properties themselves are the territory itself, that which is its own perfect map. It is only when we wish to represent those properties in the abstract as *coordinates* on a separate map that we encounter the need to generate a *representation*. In this case we can use the success of physics to motivate the idea of a *coordinate description* of the Universe, the set of all of the coordinates corresponding to all of the properties of all of the things that actually exist.

This 'Universal set' of coordinates is at its most abstract *information*, and we can use information theory to deduce certain very important conclusions concerning it and the Universe of actual things with actual properties that this coordinate description represents. We will need only one of these deductions below. We begin by mentally *compressing* the coordinate description—eliminating all redundant information and retaining only essential coordinates. This leads us to an *irreducible* specification of the *state* of the Universe as a complete set of non-redundant coordinates (where a lot of the reduction will appear in the form of exact or approximate coordinate relationships, a.k.a. 'the laws of nature' that make it unnecessary to include distinct values that are uniquely derived from included values).

This information is *self-encoded* in the actual properties of actual things that exist in the actual Universe, the territory that we wish to represent with a perfect map. We now need precisely one critical result from information theory itself.

We cannot represent this fully reduced coordinate description (which might well be infinite in size) within any system with *less* information content (where if infinite, we would require no less cardinality, since compressed it might well still be infinite in size). If we could, it wouldn't be fully reduced! The actual information content of the Universe is by definition, then, *incompressible* on whatever abstract system that is being used to represent it, *even if that abstract system is the Universe itself encoding its own properties*!

Note that we are pretty safe in insisting on the existence of a maximum compression (or minimal representation of the information) because there is an information-theoretic strict lower bound of 'no information' that is insufficient to reconstruct any non-empty set of properties at all. There is no guarantee that any original, sufficient coordinatization of the properties that are the state of the Universe is minimal, but somewhere between it and zero there must be one (possibly even more than one) that *is* minimal, a state of maximum compression.

That's all we really need below. I'm sorry I went so tediously about arriving at this simple statement but I wanted to make sure that it was clear.

3. The Pandeist Theorem

Let us now (at last) state the basic theorem:

If God exists, then God is identical to the Universe.

That is, the theorem is a statement of *conditional pandeism*. If God exists at all, God must *be* absolutely everything that exists.

It is amusing to 'foolishly' compare this with Anselm's argument. If I (happy to play the role of 'the fool') am able to imagine a being so great that nothing could be conceivably greater, and at the same time imagine that this being is *not* the Universe (defined as everything that actually exists), then I have contradicted myself and played the fool indeed. That is because the union of two sets—'God' and 'the Universe'—is *greater than or equal to either set alone*!

If I imagine any being that is a strict subset of everything that actually exists, that being cannot be God defined to be the greatest being that could conceivably exist as I can *easily* imagine a greater being that is the now definitely larger *whole thing*.

If God is *not* part of the set of things that actually exist, well, problem solved. Note well that this in no way obligates the Universe itself to poof out of existence—it just means that the Universe is in no sense 'a being' with sentience and the other properties we would like to use to elevate Deity from just being another word for an *impersonal, uncaring, non-sentient* Universe.

A God that actually exists and is identical to the set of everything that actually exists (the entire Universe) is thus *quite literally* the greatest God one can conceive of in *precisely* the way Anselm argued. This doesn't prove the existence of God because (regardless of what Anselm asserted) *my imagination does not determine reality*, but it does prove, in a slightly different (and less rigorous) way than that given below, that if God exists at all, God is the Universe.

To make this general *approach* more rigorous, we start with what is really just an ontological or semantic observation, something that is immediately obvious from the meanings of the words themselves. We have carefully defined the Universe to be *everything that exists*, the set consisting of all that has objective existential reality, *in accord with common usage*. The word literally means 'turned to one,' the union of all that has being.

It is therefore quite obvious that *if* God exists (has the property of 'being'), God must be either a *part* of the Universe or the *whole* Universe.[7]

We will now deviate from the simple (but compelling!) argument above in favor of an argument founded on something other than an ill-defined property of ordinal 'greatness' that might allow one to argue that a God that *wasn't* everything that exists is 'greater' than one that is because such a God is, I dunno, 'cooler' or 'even more amazing' according to *some* subjective and arbitrary assertion of just what 'greatness' is. To avoid this, we will turn to information theory.

God by the property of omniscience must have precisely the irreducible information content of the entire Universe.

3.1 Proof 1

Suppose God is only part of the Universe. This means, specifically, that there are things with objective existence and hence distinct properties in the non-God part and that the properties are self-encoded and constitute irreducible information. Then:

> Let us call the irreducible information content of the non-God part of the Universe I_N, the irreducible information content of the God part of the Universe I_G, and the irreducible information content of the entire Universe I_U (where of course any of these quantities could be infinite).

It is obvious that:

$$I_U \equiv I_G + I_N \qquad (1)$$

as the irreducible information content of the whole must match the total irreducible information content of the disjoint parts.

Also,

$$I_N \not\equiv I_G \qquad (2)$$

as the non-God and God parts are disjoint and cannot be mutually reducible.

Clearly,

$$I_G \equiv I_U \qquad (3)$$

as that's the meaning of omniscience.

Therefore:

$$I_N \equiv \varnothing \qquad (4)$$

It is obvious that:

> The only way the irreducible information content of the non-God part of the irreducible information content of the entire Universe can be encoded in the irreducible information content of the God part is if the irreducible information content of the non-God part is null—no information at all.

Nothing that *exists* has null information content and something that exists *is* its own minimal encoding; existence itself is the existence of properties, of *information,* that we have already argued are their own irreducible, incompressible coordinatization (this is a very fundamental and successful property of physics itself) that our symbolic maps attempt to duplicate in the abstract. From this we conclude that *if* God exists at all, the non-God part of the Universe is (quite literally) *no-thing,* nothing. It does not exist.[8]

For readers already familiar with (information or physical) entropy, the proof is largely unnecessary. All that is required is to note that entropy is an *extensive* quantity, one that scales with system size, one that *is* the log of the missing information required to precisely 'know' the state of the system. Any disjunctive partitioning of an irreducible system therefore introduces entropy of the whole relative to any nonzero part.

There are numerous ways to illustrate this entropy. Some of these ways are quite literally 'ancient wisdom' of a sort; others are quite modern. Before we proceed to a *second* proof of this theorem that proceeds from very *different* grounds, let us look at a few of them as they may be more compelling to a lay person who doesn't have a good idea of what 'entropy' actually is.

3.2 Example: partitioning a finite binary string

If you are not at least a bit of a mathematician, you are probably not happy with the proof above because you don't understand it. The idea of 'information' or the 'state' of a system may seem very abstract. To illuminate the situation, let's consider a very, very simple 'Universe' where you can *count up* the difficulties that illustrate the point a case at a time, and then extrapolate this example to the general case, where without exception the difficulties we encounter will be *much, much worse*!

Information theory is often applied to the encoding of a message in *binary*, so let's consider a very small *binary Universe*. It has a very small number of *possible* states, only one of which we will consider to be 'existential reality' and hence 'the message' that we seek to know. The information in a *single* such string is incompressible and irreducible—every bit is necessary to communicate the message as there is no metric of 'closeness,' only identity or non-identity. In the case of Universes, of course, there can only be precisely one if there are any at all. Let's look, then, at what happens when we partition a simple, irreducible binary string with a handful of bits *as* a Universe into two pieces.

At first glance this example seems inadequate—what about processes, consciousness, free will, awareness, abstract knowledge, and all that? However, it turns out that we can use our imaginations to do away with all of them. All of them, note well, involve *time*, involve a sort of 'doing' in a system that changes from instant to instant. However, we can completely *ignore* time in our meditations, as the time that events occur in the real Universe is just more knowledge, more data. The Universe itself is 'timeless'—it is the union of all things that actually exist, not at any *particular* place and time but at *all* times and places that themselves actually exist. We can therefore completely ignore the dynamics of 'reason' in general—sequential operations performed on data—because the operations themselves will necessarily have a description to differentiate them from all other possible operations and sequential orderings and that description is still *more* data.

Ultimately, you can then think of the Universe in all of its dynamic glory—all places, times, dimensions hidden or otherwise, and 'stuff' therein that has objective being—as being a *really, really large* (possibly *infinitely* large) DVD recording: a binary string. Each sequentially ordered time instant is a *part* of the data on the DVD—the part that makes the movie 'happen' as the slices are sequentially presented, each at the recorded time—the DVD itself becomes an abstract timeless set of data, and God (if God exists) must *both* be only a part of that data *and* somehow encode on the part that is It the data that is all of the rest.[9]

Instead of 'information,' then—which seems rather abstract—we will consider data, as we have plenty of concrete experience with data in the context of computers, and every schoolchild with sufficient mental capacity learns about binary numbers by the time they are in high school. We don't need to think of a particularly *long* binary string, because we can always imagine making a quite short one longer, and longer, and longer (without bound) in one of the time-honored methods of imagining infinity, as long as we get some idea of how the other quantities we shall discuss scale up as we do so. Each bit has two possible mutually exclusive states (property values) plus some intrinsic properties such as the location of the bit in some global ordinal arrangement of the bits.

Let's let our Universe have only eight such bits—enough to illustrate the problems and yet easy to count. We can then write a possible state of this tiny Universe as: 01001001. Our representation is not unique, of course. This bitstring is perhaps more easily recognizable as the decimal integer 73. The point is that *all knowledge* of this teensy, finite Universe has to be self-encoded. There is no 'outside' we can use to store *additional* knowledge such as bit location or a rule connecting the value of the fifth bit to the value of the second bit—to encode that we would have to adjoin *more bits* onto our bit universe, and then we'd have to adjoin still more bits to specify how to *decode* the encoded information, and...all of this *can*, actually, be handled (and thinking about it and handling it is part of what theoretical computer scientists and number-theoretic mathematicians and mathematical philosophers *do*) but as I said, including it all simply makes things *worse* from the point of view of this theorem as the Universe will forever be chasing its own tail, trying to encode how it encodes its previous metaphysical level of encoding on the next one, and then discovering that now *that* is an abstract string of binary data with no *a priori necessary* secret decoder ring.

Now let us partition this bitstring into a small piece (the non-God part) and a larger piece (the God part): **01**001001 where I will boldface the non-God part just so that we can keep track of it below. For purposes of illustration we'll place the non-God part on the left, but bear in mind that we could have selected any two bits to be non-God, or equivalently there is already information being encoded outside of our system when I perform the partitioning in this way and we'll have to account for this information later.

In this particular case, from the outside (which we usually would like to call a God's-eye view, only there is no outside to the real Universe where God could perch to obtain such a look) we can easily point to a bitstring in the God part (which I will do with ()'s) such as **01**0(01)001 or **01**0010(01) and say "Aha! Look! God knows about non-God!" simply because we see the naked bitstring recapitulated in God somewhere. But this isn't quite right. Consider the following four possibilities:

00001001
01001001 (!)
10001001
11001001

If we consider separately what God knows:

001001

it certainly doesn't seem to contain any information that uniquely specifies which of the four possibilities listed is the actual one and only existentially unique Universe. It is just the number 00001001 = 9, after all. It is simply not a profound metaphysical truth that the number 9 uniquely implies the number **01** = 1 (or the more informative number **01000000** = 64) due to some self-encoded rule buried in the number 9!

All four of these seem to be possible Universes from the set of all data Universes that have eight bits of information. If we restrict our one actual existential Universe 01001001 to the smaller sub-Universe 001001, we introduce entropy into the reduced description. We have lost information—even though we can indeed identify fragments of the latter that correspond to the former, they are information about the latter in and of themselves and we need a higher-level set of rules to identify the particular bit fragments that we omitted. God cannot really be said to 'know' all of **01**001001 unless God is 01001001, as only in this case is all of the information required uniquely specified in God!

Even this isn't really correct (as noted above, it is worse). Each bit is unique with a single property pulled from a pair of possibilities, but arranging them in some particular order is an additional piece of information! Or rather, a huge amount of additional information. To the extent that each bit has its own identity a set of 8 bits thrown into a bag and pulled out in an arbitrary order is still the same self-representation of the state of the 8 bits, but as soon as we want the state of six of the bits to represent the state of two of the bits, order matters!

To be concrete, consider the bitstring 00010111 or, even worse, 10001011. These strings are simple permutations of the original string. If you imagine the bits to be pennies with heads or tails, I needn't have changed the value of a single penny, just arranged the same pennies with the same head or tail up on the same table, but in a different order! This is no problem at all in an existential self-representation of the many pennies, but it is a huge problem for the representation of the complete state of the set of all eight pennies using only half of them. How does any one penny know (in the sense of being able to represent) the identity, not the state, of another? Yet the encoding of this identity is required along with the state. The God part has to know that it is the God part and that its bit that supposedly represents the 1 in the non-God part represents not just the value, but also the identity of the non-God penny/bit. Is it the 7th or the 8th? And which bit was it that was the representation? In computation, there simply isn't a problem. One cannot represent the state of 8 binary bits *even* given a fixed bit order in only 6 binary bits. The whole idea is ridiculous. And yet that is what the assertion of omniscience in a disjoint subset of a larger entity with irreducible information content in the excluded part is, without even *worrying* about sentience or how to *interpret* a representation.

Obviously, our binary representation of a data Universe can be extended by adding as many bits as we like to both the God and non-God partitions without changing the conclusions of the argument. As long as the non-God part of the Universe possesses any *conceptual* variability, the God part certainly *can* contain data and *can* contain encoded rules that with a suitable *external* decoder and process *can* transform that data into a match for the non-God part, but the only way to know if the result matches is to *look,* because one can *always* imagine the same right-hand part conjoined to *any* of the possible left-hand parts, assuming that one has any possible way of constraining just what, or how big, the left-hand part really is!

'Looking to find out' here is impossible, as we've eliminated time and interaction and really the possibility of external data transformations using data-encoded rules. Only when the God and non-God parts of the system *and the decoder* are all part of a single static view of the Universe can that Universe be said to be 'perfectly known' (lack information entropy) and only if God *is* the whole Universe can it be said that God as an omniscient zero-entropy God, missing *no* information concerning the state of the Universe, exists. Partitioning is still possible, relative entropy can exist, 'process' can exist in the form of global patterns in the static Universe, but one cannot point to any strict subset of the Universe and say this part is God and still *perfectly knows all about* the irreducible Universal complement of that part—the properties of everything else.

3.3 Proof 2

In the first proof, we saw that when we consider the irreducible information content of any partitioning of the Universe (defined as everything that exists), it is not possible for that entire Universe to be partitioned into two (or, obviously, more) non-empty irreducible sets and have one contain a *necessary* and *perfect* representation of the other. This was because entropy is an *extensive* quantity—all of the information-carrying capacity of the 'God channel' is being consumed by irreducibly specifying the *God* state and there is none left over for specifying the *not*-God state. The God channel can irreducibly encode the Universe only if it *is* the irreducibly self-encoded Universe. One is led to a contradiction whether or not one begins with the fully reduced Universe and attempts to partition it or one begins with it partitioned, fully reduces each partition, and then attempts to 'identify' one part in the other, although this short work contents itself only with the simplest sufficient proof and doesn't examine all possible variants of partitioning on domains with various dimensionality and cardinality. The problem is in the partitioning itself—the moment the whole is broken up into two distinct parts, *at least one bit of entropy* is introduced that differentiates one part from the other even if the two sets are otherwise *identical*.

If God can perfectly visualize all non-God real existing things in Its real existing but distinct 'mind's eye' (anthropomorphizing, of course, but what else can one do when thinking about knowledge), then It knows that Its knowledge is *of* those things (in Its mind) and is *not* those things (outside of Its mind)—not to know this is to not know all things. The map, after all, is *not the territory*—God is as subject to this precept of General Semantics as any other informational system. God's knowledge is therefore not complete—It cannot know these things as they really are *outside* of Its mind; Its abstract knowledge is not the same as the territory itself any more than *your* abstract knowledge is. Furthermore God cannot, as we saw above, be certain that Its visualization is in fact correct, that Its secret decoder ring is giving It the right values for the non-God part as the mapping it defines is certainly not unique, the space of possibilities it selects from is large, and recall, in this *timeless* view of things there is no such thing as *looking*. There is only an enormous DVD, broken into two pieces, where even if one piece contains a complete redundant copy of the data on the other there is no way of *knowing* that from possession of the one piece only—even if it is large and complex enough to contain a complete language and encoding system that self-consistently says that it does: it could simply be mistaken.

However, there is another way to prove the same conclusion in an entirely different context. This proof similarly relies in part on the axioms and definitions used in the first proof but in a very different way. To them we add the axioms that support *Gödel's theorem*, as they appear manifestly true for the Universe itself.

Suppose then, as before, that the existential Universe has a self-encoded irreducible state that is capable of *symbolically encoded self-reference*. This is not a terrible stretch, since you *are* a part of the Universe and you *are* thinking about the Universe in symbolically encoded ways—it is therefore *empirically* self-evident that this is true for any mind thinking about itself and the Universe. The proof then follows as:

> In order for God to possess *complete* abstract/symbolic knowledge of the Universe, that knowledge must include an expression of arithmetic, as the abstract expression of arithmetic manifestly exists in human knowledge if nowhere else; God's knowledge could hardly be complete if God cannot add two and two to get four. This body of knowledge is therefore subject to Gödel's first (completeness) theorem; since it is capable of the expression of arithmetic (and is in any event intrinsically both complex and self-referential, containing all *human*-known examples of Gödelian knots of unknowable propositions or set-theoretic paradoxes as a simple subset) it can be *complete* or *consistent* but *not both*.

God's knowledge of the Universe cannot be symbolic (encoded in any way that has to be decoded by a deductive, interpretive process) and inconsistent with the *true* state of the Universe and still be arguably correct knowledge. The Universe itself is *real* and hence cannot be inconsistent by the simplest precepts of logic—that which is true cannot be inconsistent and contradict itself—the Universe simply is what it is (timelessly). Finally, God's symbolic knowledge of the Universe cannot be incomplete or God is not omniscient and hence is not God.

These three statements, plus Gödel's theorem, constitute a contradiction. God's knowledge of the Universe must be both consistent and complete in order not to violate the definition of God given above, but if that knowledge is indirect and symbolic, capable of self-reference and encoded upon itself with sufficient complexity that it can and *does* represent mere arithmetic as just *part* of its knowledge, Gödel's theorem tells us that it *can't* be both complete and consistent.

A hypothetical God's omniscient knowledge of the Universe cannot, therefore, be indirect, symbolic, and capable of self-reference. Symbolic reduction and projection of the existential reality (all state information) of the Universe into a subset of the Universe as code that is *necessarily* self-referential and capable of expressing arithmetic renders it incomplete, inconsistent, or (most likely) *both*. In order for God to be omniscient (and omnipresent and omnipotent), Its knowledge can only be *direct* knowledge *of* the Universe itself *as* the complete set of the properties of the Universe itself, which *must* be complete and consistent by the existential property of the Universe and mere logic.

Therefore: *If God exists, God is the Universe itself.*

Another amusing corollary comes from considering Gödel's second (consistency) theorem:

> If God can *prove* that its symbolic, encoded knowledge of the Universe is consistent, then it *isn't* consistent. God can therefore never be *certain* that any symbolic encoding of the knowledge of the Universe (including itself) is consistent and hence true.

Again, only existential, self-encoded information lacking any partitioning and the consequently necessary layer of projective abstraction is guaranteed to be complete and consistent when speaking of the Universe. Unfortunately, in the process one very likely *necessarily* gives up the very self-referentiality that is a critical part of sentience and self-awareness. It is difficult to see how an informationally complete self-encoded Universe could in any useful sense be self-aware of its own complete information.

We conclude that God's knowledge of the Universe (including itself) *cannot* therefore be a symbolic *map* or encoding of any sort, which is a result that is entirely consistent with the information-theoretic analysis above. In addition to the entropy problem, the self-referential symbolic representation suffices to trigger Gödel's theorems so that true omniscience is literally *impossible*. Again, let's try to illuminate the difficulty with a concrete example, this one familiar to all readers as they contemplate their *own* knowledge of the Universe.

3.4 Example: human knowledge

A *God* partition of the Universe, whatever its material or immaterial microscopic self-encoded nature, is in exactly the same boat as a *human* partition of the Universe as it attempts to 'know' both the outside Universe and itself on top of its irreducibly self-encoded brain that is itself merely a part—a very small part compared to the Universe itself—of what it wants to know.[11]

Of course *we* can and do acquire a high-level, coarse-grained, approximate overview, a symbolic map that neglects *most of the detail* of the territory being mapped just so that it will *fit* in our limited storage and processing capacity, but this sort of knowledge can hardly be called 'omniscience' whatever the scale of any real being that does the same. Furthermore, since any such map is *necessarily* self-referential, any being that relies on it can *never* make it into a complete and consistent system of knowledge, and cannot be certain that such knowledge as it thinks that it has is merely consistent, let alone complete. These are all *mathematical* results and are as close to *a priori* truths as it is possible to be in any system of symbolic reason, so I really don't think there is much chance that they will be refuted by any rational argument or empirical observation.

We are left with an inescapable conclusion:

> *If* God is real (and hence at least part of the Universe) and *if* God is omniscient and omnipresent, then God's knowledge cannot be any sort of *symbolic map* of the state of the Universe, it can only be the *irreducibly self-encoded territory* of the Universe itself.

or

> *If God exists, God is necessarily the Universe itself!*

Q.E.D. Twice, even!

Those who wish to (for example) take the manifest existence of a non-empty Universe *at all* as de facto evidence of God should be somewhat relieved by this theorem as it provides them with a single way in which their belief can be consistent, and that is if the non-empty Universe and God are equivalent.[12] There is nothing *logically or empirically inconsistent* about the utter equivalence of the Universe and God. Obviously the Universe is omnipresent, by definition. Obviously the Universe is omniscient (of its own self-encoded state), again by definition. The Universe may or may not be omnipotent in the naive sense of the word, but it is a simple identity of being that everything real is in some sense the 'will' of God if God is equivalent to the Universe. The only question that remains, then, is *whether or not the Universe is sentient*!

To answer this is beyond the scope of this article, although I have several times suggested avenues of exploration that so far make this proposition enormously implausible. It goes beyond not just knowing the right engineering—it is a consequence of information theory that such a thing is *impossible* at the symbolic level, and only possible at the self-representation level that makes the representation perfectly complete and correct and perfectly useless at the same time.

Still, the theorem above *per se* does not in and of itself *completely* exclude the possibility that God exists (and should not, as this is ultimately an empirical question about the real Universe and cannot be answered by logic and reason divorced from observation). It is up to each sentient being to make up their own mind concerning the extent to which sentient existence versus nonexistence plus their life experience constitutes 'evidence' that makes the equivalence *plausible*.[13]

The consequences of this theorem are profound. If God exists, then *everything* is God: you are (a part of) God, I am God, a telephone pole is God, a speck of interstellar dust floating in intergalactic space is God, any hidden dimensions or alternative Cosmi are God—God is all that has being. Jesus (if he existed at all outside of myth and legend) was no *more* (nor less) God than you are—and *said so* on several occasions in the New Testament and Gnostic literature, all studiously ignored. Miracles become enormously implausible as they suggest that God's mind is inconsistent, but the real is never inconsistent—to quote C. S. Lewis's Aslan (speaking as God): "Do you think that I would break the Laws that I made?" Physical Law *throughout* the visible and invisible Universe quite literally *is* the mind of God (where now 'mind' and 'matter' are indistinguishable—both are in the abstract and concrete merely *self-encoded state information*), and your actions, completely determined by the utterly mechanical operation of your component parts in that mind, are not *morally* good or bad any more than the Law of Universal Gravitation and consequent orbiting of the planets about the Sun is good or bad. We can immediately apply this theorem to most of the world religions and reject their theisms out of hand except to the extent that they capture this theorem (some do very much, in rare and beautiful parts interspersed with their extortionist threats of eternal torments for unbelievers and other nonsense).

4. Possible Models of God

We now can see beyond any doubt that *if* God exists (and has the standard properties ascribed to God), God is the Universe. There are a number of 'instant' corollaries to this theorem. The condition "If God exists at all, then" is a presumed preamble for all of the following:

- God did not create the Universe. The Universe of all that has objective being cannot have been created, as the creator would have to have objective being in order to do the creating.
- God did not create *part* of the Universe. Creation is an act with a presumed arrow *in time* and the Universal set is timeless (time is just a parameter of events in the set). Also, God is already the whole thing, no part of which could have been created.

The following are *empirical* corollaries or open questions conditioned in the same way, based on, for example, the evidence of our own objective existence and experience of information-entropic time:

- God (as the Universe) is *no less sentient* than the aggregate sentience of all sentient beings within the Universe. My own human mind is a lower bound on the sentience of God looking at the only thing that exists to be looked at, Itself. My ability to 'look' and 'appreciate' is contingent upon a *lack* of perfect knowledge and my existence as a subset with *high* information entropy relative to the whole, which permits me to experience the passing of time.
- The upper bound of sentience, where the entire Universe is self-aware and able to experience entropic time *in a high-level way* appears to be blocked by both the zero-entropy requirement and Gödel's theorem. However, if the

> Universe is *open* (especially if it possesses an open infinity of dimensionality) then for certain orderings of limits God could function as Its *own* source of information entropy for an infinite interior out of a larger infinite exterior.

This leaves this as an *open question*—perhaps *the* open question that separates an atheist, a pandeist, and a panendeist, and the one that permits all three to be considered choices that can be made differently and yet at least somewhat rationally. However, the theorem has implications for the *current* formulation of panendeism as the belief that God is a superset of the Universe—the correct formulation that is consistent with the theorem above would be God is the Universe that is an *open* superset of the *visible Cosmos*. This correction is itself a healthy one from the rational point of view, as at least some aspects of this as a theory are in principle capable of verification—development of consistent, evidence-backed theories in physics for additional dimensions connected to *this* Cosmos, development of consistent, evidence-backed theories in physics for additional/parallel or embedded Cosmi.

Personally, though, as noted above I find it difficult to construct a really plausible argument in favor of the Universe being globally sentient in any useful sense. The arguments associated with the information-theoretic impossibility of any network of neurons being able *even in principle* to represent its own component parts in some *other* way than just being what it is are compelling. We could not even *in principle* build a computer capable of representing its own microscopic state. For one to argue that 'a miracle' makes it possible for the Universe to be sentient and usefully self-aware and *omniscient* is more or less a confession that the arguer has no idea how to do it either, and cannot usefully argue that it is at all possible to do so.

In the end, it hardly matters. If God is real, God is the Universe, so the only sensible way to *look* for God is to *study* the

Universe, at least as much of the Universe as we can *see*, and look for evidence of true, interactive sentience. Cosmology and physics together, then, are the only possible natural, reason-based places where science and religion can meet at the metaphysical cusp between plausible knowledge based on evidence and the vast unknown that always lies beyond our current reach.

We thus see that although we do not, and cannot, address the question of whether or not the Universe (which we can certainly see and which appears to have concrete objective existence) *is* in fact God, this proof has many consequences for *conditional* models of God, and it can certainly guide any serious search for God, now that one knows what to look for: evidence that the *Universe itself* is sentient, since there is little doubt that *it* exists.

5. Conclusions

In this work, a very simple theorem linking the Universe and a conditionally postulated God has been proposed and proven from clearly stated premises that makes the process of 'creation' as described by nearly all scriptural mythologies literally impossible.

A consequence of this theorem is that there is no such thing as 'creation.' In this essentially timeless view, there is no birth, no death, only eternal being, an existence of self-encoded *information*. The foundations of this theorem incidentally *also* provide something of a resolution to a number of other philosophical conundrums from the ages, for example the issue of whether 'things' are mind or matter, material or ideal. The answer is neither or both—they are *self-encoded information*. This conclusion is entirely consistent with the empirical and theoretical foundations of physics.

Self-encoded information has been shown to be distinct from symbolically encoded information and is something that can equally well be viewed as being 'matter' or as 'mind,' although it can never be sufficiently emphasized that *in general* when one speaks of mind one speaks of an entropic-time driven awareness that is *quite distinct* from the kind of information or awareness attendant upon calling the intrinsic existential coordinates of an electron situated in and interacting, or not, with the rest of the Universe across space and time, 'mind.'

This theorem has the potential to substantially alter the human perspective in useful, beneficial ways. For one thing, it leaves the issue of whether or not the Universe itself can in any useful sense be said to be sentient and self-aware in a unitary way, the way we experience our own being, in dire straits if not completely rejected as impossible. Viewing the Universe as *all* places, *all* times eliminates altogether the dynamical perspective of entropy-driven experience in a mostly unknown externality that is our own perspective of sentience but which requires *incomplete* information (entropy) in order to learn, discover, and experience time as a continuing revelation of change in the properties of that which exists.

Only the possibility of an infinite system that somehow can be considered omniscient but yet function as its own entropy source in a Hilbert's Grand Hotel model may retain sufficient freedom for a kind of sentience, but it seems all too likely that this sentience is ultimately illusory.

The conditional conclusion therefore can substantially reduce the gap between idealism and materialism by making both in some sense irrelevant; at the same time it reduces the gap between atheist and theist. If one wishes to be a theist of any sort, one can no longer be anything but a pandeist unless one deliberately pretends that the argument given above doesn't exist in an act of profound denial driven by cognitive dissonance. But what then of the atheist and the pandeist? Both agree that the *Universe itself* has objective existential being. Both agree that it is awesomely complex and beautiful. Both agree that there isn't the slightest freedom for the *timeless* view of the Universe to *change,* and both—if they think about it rationally—have to agree that there is no way that the Universe itself could care about being 'worshiped' or 'obeyed' by some tiny fraction of its highly composite Self, any more than a DVD can be said to be worshiped by a single tiny bitstring self-encoded deep within the whole or a book can be 'obeyed' by the letters 'e' contained therein.

If they differ at all, they differ in precisely one way. The atheist has no good reason to think that the Universe is sentient or alive in any useful sense and so embraces the default view that it is not unless or until evidence emerges that suggests otherwise. The pandeist, faced with precisely the same lack of evidence, nevertheless prefers to imagine that the Universe is in some sense alive and aware. They would be hard pressed to describe *how* this could be so, to give one any sort of overview of the mechanism intrinsic to 'the mind of God' and why one should view the operation of this mechanism, which after all can be nothing more than the natural progression of the laws of physics, to be 'sentience.' But since the atheist agrees that there is a natural progression of the laws of physics across space and time, that this progression is marvelously ordered and quite amazing, and that it is extraordinary and wonderful that the atheist or pandeist alike is privileged to be experiencing it as the heart of their personal existential 'Now,' *is there anything left worth fighting for*?

I would argue that there is not. All that then remains is to accept the Universe for being what it is *whether or not it is sentient* and, as a *thinking, rational* part of the Universe, deliberately construct the best possible world for humanity, one based on *virtuous behavior*, not according to the direction of moth-eaten creationist God-of-the-Gaps mythologies, but according to common sense and compassion.

Notes

1 Lest there be any semantic confusion, let us make it clear from the beginning that the word 'Universe,' in English, means 'everything that exists.' To avoid temporal confusion, we will use the word in a strictly time-independent way, one consistent with the modern concepts of e.g. relativity theory. If any set of 'things' has objective real existence *anywhere, anywhen, anyhow,* it is a part of the Universe. A more complete definition will be given later in the section on the premises of the theorem but this will suffice to avoid misunderstandings in the preliminary sections.

2 In particular, the variants of Vedantic Hinduism and Buddhism, to the extent that Buddhism is a religion at all.

3 This argument has, of course, often been accompanied by the further argument that anyone caught publicly *disagreeing* with this argument will be killed in various creative and painful ways.

4 See e.g. *Mathematics, the Loss of Certainty* by Morris Kline (1980), who does a brilliant job of explaining this point.

5 The author is grateful to Knujon Mapson for pointing this out in private communications.

6 It is tempting to express this in the form of a riddle: What is it that exists at no place, at no time, and has no intrinsic properties? Give up? No *thing*! Or rather, nothing that actually exists at all, ever, anywhere, anyhow.

7 It is also immediately quite obvious that God cannot have created the Universe—if God existed to do any such thing, so did the Universe, as the set of everything that exists, existed, or will exist.

8 Note well that the exact same reasoning applied symmetrically the other way suggests that if there *is* a non-empty, non-God part of the Universe, then there is no God (that satisfies the standard model properties listed above). Believers in a dualist 'creator' would do well to contemplate this.

9 Or, worse yet, must be at once only part of the data that encodes both itself and the rest of the data and be the player of the data, a DVD that by merely existing as a trans-temporal static entity 'plays

itself'—to itself. One can imagine the recorded part that is God, bored to tears and munching on popcorn, as the observer in the recording because, well, It knows how it is all going to come out.

10 Although The Beatles *did* seem to suggest otherwise in the song "Revolution Number 9" off of the White Album, which I'm listening to as I type this. Cosmic!

11 It is quite certain, for example, that it takes *many many neurons* to encode just the *word* 'neuron,' and far more to encode the general *properties* of neurons, and still more to encode the *particular functional state* of one particular neuron out of the entire brain, and a truly vast number of neurons to encode the particular state of the molecules, atoms, electrons and quarks and photons and gluons at a single instant in time. Indeed, it probably is quite literally beyond our capacity to 'know' the full microscopic detail of a single instant in the history of a single neuron in the human brain *using the entire brain's high-level capacity to encode it*! Note that the same thing is simple engineering as far as information storage devices are concerned. A single bit in a computer memory chip requires many, many atoms, let alone elementary particles, to encode. The amount of *quantum* state information in the *projective subspace* of the Universe represented by the physical matter of the single-bit storage device is vast, and the large numbers are *necessary* to achieve macroscopic state stability and reproducibility in the face of inevitable and *unknowable* entanglements of its state with the state of the rest of the Universe, the inevitable bleed of entropy from whatever is *not* it into it.

12 It is worth noting that those that do *not* consider mere existence of something in contrast with complete and utter nonexistence as evidence of God shouldn't be particularly bothered by this theorem either, given that is a *conditional* theorem beginning with "*If* God exists…" The atheist and pandeist alike can agree that *whether or not* one *names* the Universe 'God' hardly matters. Either way, it is what it is, the foundation of our being, awesomely complex (and yet simple), and the source of individual awareness in the form of

ongoing discovery.

13 This is the one place where empirical probability estimates are very, very difficult as we lack even the *possibility* of formulating a sensible Bayesian prior. The mere fact of our existence is the moral equivalent of reaching our metaphysical hand into an even more metaphysical urn and pulling out a *physical* Cosmos, ourselves included. What can this tell us about the contents of the urn and the process that prepared it? Only that the urn was not empty—it contained at least one ball. Mind you, there is a truly staggering amount of *information* encoded in that one ball—and none of it has the slightest bearing on whether or not the urn is now empty, whether or not we will ever have the opportunity to draw another ball, whether or not the urn itself is in any sense *alive*, and whether or not it is possible to construct an even more strained metaphor given that there is no urn.

God, the Universe and Pandeism

Alan H. Dawe

Alan H. Dawe has been a student of life and spirituality for over five decades. He has always been interested in writing, and published his first book, The God Franchise: A Theory of Everything, *in 2012. This book won the prestigious Ashton Wylie Charitable Trust Book Award for 2012. Home for Alan is Auckland, New Zealand. The content of this article, "God, the Universe and Pandeism," is taken directly from* The God Franchise. *It has, however, been edited and rearranged by the author to suit the present purpose. For a full bibliography, plus quotes supporting many of the arguments made, please refer to* The God Franchise.

The Really Big Picture

Although this may seem difficult or even impossible, try to imagine what it might have been like before there was an Earth, before there was a universe. Then ask yourself, what was there before that? If you come up with an answer, accept it and ask, what was there before that? Keep going back until you can go back no further.

Now try the same exercise forward in time. What comes after this universe that we live in? What comes after that? Clear away whatever comes up and ask, what comes after that? Keep going until you come to a stop.

If you go back far enough, there are only two possible answers to this question: either there was nothing, absolutely nothing at all, or else this universe is eternal and had no beginning. Likewise, looking forward, either there will be nothing left, absolutely nothing at all, or else this universe is eternal and has no end.

If there was absolutely nothing, the question is where and

how did the universe spring into existence? If there was absolutely nothing, there was no need to do anything and there were no resources to make it happen. Nothing would just continue to be nothing. The only power that could possibly create something from nothing is Consciousness.

I use the word consciousness (and Consciousness) frequently in this article, so please accept consciousness as meaning an *awareness of self, environment, and mental activity, and the ability to determine choice of action.*[1] So, in saying that Consciousness is the only power that could create something from nothing, I am saying that awareness and an ability to determine choice of action were the prime qualities needed to precede the creation of something from nothing. Science has no credible explanation of how nothing could suddenly become something. Scientists start with the Big Bang,[2] not before it.

Just as an idea might be created out of nothing (although this seldom happens), so conceivably a powerful enough Consciousness might create the universe out of nothing. So, if there was nothing at all, there at least had to be Consciousness existent in order to create the universe of which we are now part. Man has decided to call this Consciousness, *God.*

The other possibility, that the universe is eternal, without beginning or end, also seems to imply some sort of eternal force that underlies the whole process. We know that nothing physical lasts forever, so there would need to be a non-physical force underlying the universe just to keep it maintained. This force is best described as *Consciousness* or *God.*

If we take the scientific standpoint about the origins of the universe, Edwin Hubble's Big Bang theory indicates that all atoms of matter in the universe were concentrated (as hydrogen) at a point in space,[3] and that since the Big Bang, it has been expanding outwards in all directions, over a period of about 14 billion years. This is fine, except for the question: How did all that hydrogen come to be concentrated in one place before the

Big Bang? Once again, Consciousness (God) would seem to be the only possible creator of all the initial matter.

Now, if we look into the future, either things go on eternally, or there will suddenly be nothing. Where will everything go unless it is dissolved back into Consciousness (God)? If God switches off and dies, there will be absolutely nothing, and no chance of a new start. It is very unlikely that if God started out eternally (in our past), He would not continue into the future eternally too. And if He didn't, and there was absolutely nothing left, it wouldn't matter, would it?

So, if there is eternity, there has to be something that is eternal. That something is Consciousness or God. That aside, as there is something, there has to be a Prime Cause of that something, and this is Consciousness or God.

There is an alternative to the universe we see around us today, and that is absolutely nothing. Think about it. There could easily be absolutely nothing. Why not? If there were nothing, no one would know that there was nothing. There would be no universe of any type and no God or Eternal Being. There would be no life of any description. There would be nothing. Nothing at all.

If there were nothing, then how would anything get started? Nothing has no qualities whatsoever and has no urge, consciousness, or footholds from which a God and/or a universe could arise. We obviously do have a very wonderful and complex universe around us today and we have life. This could not have started from nothing. That is impossible and illogical.

If there was no universe, and there was also *not* absolutely nothing, then there was something there before, which was powerful enough to set the whole ball rolling. That essential starting point was Consciousness.

God = Consciousness = God-Consciousness

I have used the word *Consciousness* to describe God in order to open up the definition of God and to help you break free of any preconceptions that you might have. Some people use the word Universe, and I have previously done so, but this almost hints of no God, just a universe—a Creation without a Creator. Consciousness is a concept we can all understand. It is allied to being aware, to being alive and being able to conceptualize. God is certainly Consciousness, so let's allow Consciousness to be God.

Throughout this work, I have generally used the words *God* or *God-Consciousness* to include everyone's concept of God, and to help free us all from any false associations we may be hanging onto. This God or God-Consciousness is central to our existence, whether we like it or not. Apart from using the terms God and God-Consciousness, I maintain the common usage of *He* and *His* as pronouns. There is no implication that God is male (or female). God is an ***It***, but it just does not read well to use that pronoun; so He It is!

God is Consciousness, and to help us to remember that fact and to drop all previous concepts of Him, we will also call Him *God-Consciousness*.

The Nature of God

We will discuss the qualities of God-Consciousness in more detail shortly, but for now I would like to propose that the following qualities can be expected of God-Consciousness, if He is worth His salt:

- God is conscious
- God is eternal
- God is omnipotent (all-powerful)
- God is omnipresent (present everywhere)
- God is omniscient (all-knowing)
- God is the Creator of the universe
- God is likely to have a purpose for His Creation
- God is likely to be absolutely good (omnibenevolent)
- God is likely to be immutable (unchanging through time).

You may not accept all these qualities for God right now; although you might agree that if a God who displayed these qualities existed, He would definitely be worthy of the name, *God*.

Pandeism

Pandeism is the belief that God created the universe, is now one with it, and so is no longer a separate conscious entity. This is a combination of pantheism (God is identical to the universe) and deism (God created the universe and then withdrew Himself).

There are terms for God being in His creation and/or out of it: God is seen as immanent (present within His Creation) and/or transcendent (distinct and separate from His Creation). The Christian view is typically that God is transcendent and that His Creation is separate from Him. His omnipresence is seen almost as an outside observer who is everywhere, an intelligence system that we hope somehow doesn't catch us when we are busy sinning or naked in bed.

By contrast, this article seeks to show that God pre-existed the universe and created it out of his own substance. There is absolutely nothing that exists that is separate from God. Pandeists agree with this. Pandeists do not see God being outside of the universe and interfering with His universe when necessary, for example with healing, responding to prayers, and the like. I agree totally with this line of thought.

However, my model differs subtly in that I will show God to be bigger than the universe. Thus if there is anything beyond the universe (conceptually or beyond concepts) then that is God (God-Consciousness) too. Also, if the physical universe was to dissolve for whatever reason, God-Consciousness would still continue to exist, rather than die with His universe.

In cosmic terms I see the universe as a current manifestation of God, but not necessarily eternal. God I see as eternal, and therefore would continue even if this universe ceased to exist. God could then choose to create another completely different universe.

Further I see the God-Consciousness prior to the Creation and the God-Consciousness after the Creation as essentially unchanged. It is like I remain the same in essence when I create a thought in my mind or feel an emotion. I do not become that thought or emotion and so cease to be what I was before.

In keeping with Pandeist thought, none of this makes God a Personal God, despite my choice of words in the article. God exists beyond words and concepts, so however descriptions of Him/It are phrased, they are completely inaccurate anyway.

Has God been conspicuous by His hiddenness as some people think? God-Consciousness is in everything and is everywhere—how can He be hidden? He is your inner soul, whether you believe it or not. He sits on the sidelines of your daily searches for Him and smiles, the glint of love and joy in His eyes. He will reveal Himself when you allow Him to do so. In the meantime, He greets you as your pet dog at the gate, the rainbow in the sky, the music in your ears, the bacteria in your petri dish, the stars in your telescope, and the mud in a landslide.

The Motivation for a Creation

Now that we have determined who God-Consciousness is, as far as is possible using words, let's now turn our attention to the Creation of the universe.

If God-Consciousness were not aware or conscious of His own Being, He would cease to exist. Since we have agreed that Consciousness needs to exist or there would be absolutely nothing, we can take it that God is aware of Himself, God-Consciousness, always, eternally.

> There is God-Consciousness and nothing else. There is God-Consciousness and nothing else. There is God-Consciousness and nothing else. There is God-Consciousness and nothing else. There is God-Consciousness and nothing else. Great isn't it?

So, there is God-Consciousness and nothing else. "What is the point?" you might ask. And no doubt God asked Himself the same question.

God needed to experience Himself; God-Consciousness needed to experience Itself. At this stage, God-Consciousness was no more than Potential, formless Potential. While we cannot even start to conceive of what that must be like, it would seem obvious there was not a lot for God to see or do.

Do you not think, in our terms, that God would be lonely and bored? His experience would be of...well, not a lot anyway. It would be like looking at a blank photograph. A photo of the inside of the lens cap. Looking at that eternally, that is, forever.

Now, I expect that an omniscient God would be smart enough to figure out that there would be some fun in experiencing more than this. He may have come up first with a black and white (or even sepia) photo. Boring. How about a color photo? No, still boring. How about a moving picture? God could watch movies all day. Well, how about a live action world that He could sit up here and watch? No, this is all still very superficial. He needed to *really experience* what He was seeing.

Therefore, I submit that God-Consciousness did just that. He did not create a world that He could watch voyeuristically from Heaven. No, He created a world that He could take part in and experience first-hand.

In Pandeism, the eternality of God is an open question, since He need only have preceded the universe. However I see God-Consciousness as eternal. This means that He had no beginning and will have no end. Does this mean that He experiences all time at once? That is beyond the knowable and understandable. It is, in truth, incomprehensible. Whether that is true or not, one imagines He might be interested in seeing how things progress sequentially. To see everything at once might seem to be an unholy mess, to use a word. When you have all time (and beyond), why not see some of what you can experience sequentially? See it develop. See it change. See evolution.

In Pandeism, God is proposed to be at least powerful enough to create our universe, and cannot be known as being more powerful than that. However if He continues beyond our universe in time or presence, He would naturally be as powerful as He needed to be in such circumstances, so I see God-Consciousness as omnipotent. This means that He can do anything, and there is nothing that is too big or too powerful for Him to achieve. Handling a Big Bang is not an issue.

God-Consciousness is omnipresent, and Pandeism agrees with this as well. It means He is everywhere: in every atom, and in every square inch of the universe. He experiences the universe from within.

From omnipotence and omnipresence flows omniscience, the knowledge of everything that can be known, so God-Consciousness is omniscient. If He needed to figure out the constants that govern the universe, that would not be a problem. If He had to figure out how evolution would work, that would not be a problem either. Neither would the Law of Gravity, the Laws of Mathematics, the Laws controlling the structure of matter, and so on. God can figure it out and set it all in motion ahead of time. Bearing in mind that He is outside time if He chooses to be, He can be sure that all the things that need to be in place for the future will be there when they are needed. The universe could be "like a well-oiled machine" as described by the philosopher and mathematician, Leibniz.[4]

Therefore, God-Consciousness had the motivation and the ability to create the universe, and that is what He did. He also did not create something out of nothing, as that is impossible. What He did create was the universe out of His very essence. He created the universe out of Consciousness.

To recap: Before the Creation, there was either nothing or there was God-Consciousness. Since there cannot have been nothing or we would never have got started, there had to be God-

Consciousness. God-Consciousness had no way of experiencing anything without a Creation, an active environment in which He could take part. He, therefore, created the universe.

God's Plan for a Creation

I agree with the philosopher Gottfried Leibniz that God would have created the best possible world. Remember, God-Consciousness is doing this for His own purposes, just as we always do the best that we can for our own purposes and with the resources available to us. Since God-Consciousness had all possible resources, He would have created the best possible universe.

Looking around us, the universe does work pretty well. I would say it would be the ultimate arrogance to suggest anyone could do better. Sure, I agree, there are things we are not happy about, but I genuinely believe there is a very *good* reason for everything that happens in this universe. I would never dream of questioning what has happened, and what is happening in the world. I believe *everything is in its right place*, and *everything is perfect just as it is*.

God-Consciousness had the purpose of creating a universe that allowed Him to experience Himself. He, therefore, had to create the universe within Himself. As there was nowhere He was not, it would have been impossible for Him to do otherwise (assuming I can use the word *impossible* with regard to God!).

God's Plan was the ultimate game. One could view it as a game where God-Consciousness split Himself into lots of tiny pieces, and chose to forget who or where He was, with the object of putting the jigsaw puzzle pieces back together again and then removing the blindfold and regaining His memory so He once more knew He was God-Consciousness. I realize that this sentence is complete nonsense as it sits here, but I suspect it does point to something like the Truth. These words may be written in a light and playful way, but there is real Truth behind them.

Instead of there being one point of God-Consciousness as there was before the Creation, He wanted there to be a universe where He would be able to experience things from every possible perspective:

He could feel how a rock feels warming in the Sun.
He could feel the rain on His petals, and His fruit being eaten by a bird; and He could taste the fruit like a bird.
He could make love as a badger and as an elephant; make love as a man and as a woman.
He could see the beauty of the sunrise, and be the power and light of the Sun.
He could swim as a fish in the sea, be pushed helplessly as seaweed in the currents, and be smashed on the rocks.
He could feel joy as a child, and feel the pain of a rejected lover.
He could drink the water and drink the wine.
He could die in the desert, and die on an executioner's cross.
He could experience the flight of the electron in the atom; He could mystify scientists, and be a mystified scientist.
He could make spells; He could make smells.
He could rot on the ground, and enrich the earth with His lifeblood.
He could break His leg and heal His leg; He could be without legs and slither on the ground.
He could be inside the mouth of a lion, and inside the stomach of a whale.
He could smile and He could cry.
He could live at the depths of the ocean; and be a molecule of water at those greatest depths. And He could be the next molecule of water to that, rubbing up against it.
He could fly through the air as a beam of light, or as a bird.
He could be the air, the trees, the earth, and the sky. He could live on Earth or on Mars or on Betelgeuse.

He could use a telephone; He could design a rocket ship.
He could be inside a turbojet at full power; He could fling Himself over a waterfall, as a drop of water and as a log.
He could experience the fullness of life in the universe.

You may have the idea by now. With these sorts of experiences and goals in mind, God-Consciousness set about creating the universe exactly as it needed to be to fulfill these ideals. While God-Consciousness would be able to interfere if He needed to, there was no challenge in constantly tweaking this universe when something went wrong. As He could see ahead in time how things would pan out, He could create the universe with a set of rules or Laws that would see it through.

I am certainly not able to list what is needed to create a universe; however, our scientists have figured out some of the requirements, for instance:

- A stable set of rules or laws
- Oxygen, water, and carbon to sustain life
- A particular range of temperatures to support life
- A particular set of universal constants (Martin Rees[5] describes six of these)
- A supply of energy to make the universe dynamic
- And so on…

And so it was that God-Consciousness created a universe that met His requirements. While complicated in its details, mind-boggling in fact, it is very simple in its concept. We, as humans, overcomplicate things as far as I can see. The real Truths are essentially very simple.

God-Consciousness created the universe in a Big Bang. He created the Laws that were needed and the building blocks of matter—namely the ninety-four natural elements in a very simple system we can see today in the Periodic Table of the

Elements. He watched through time as 14 billion years passed, developing the rich and bountiful world we have around us today.

Finally, the time came for Man to appear on the scene. Bearing in mind that God-Consciousness is within each person on this Earth—in fact, within each cell of the bodies of each person on this Earth, and is them—He played His trump card.

He introduced **The God Franchise**.

The Qualities of God-Consciousness

Before we discuss The God Franchise, I said we would take a look at the qualities of God-Consciousness in more detail. We need to be comfortable that these qualities are quite feasible and acceptable ones for God-Consciousness to have.

In what we have covered so far, I have stated that:

- God is conscious
- God is eternal
- God is omnipotent (all-powerful)
- God is omnipresent (present everywhere)
- God is omniscient (all-knowing)
- God is the Creator of the universe
- God is likely to have a purpose for His Creation
- God is likely to be absolutely good (omnibenevolent)
- God is likely to be immutable (unchanging through time).

So let's take each of the above attributes and deduce what we can about God-Consciousness.

God-Consciousness is conscious

It (He) is Being. It is alive. The definition of a Personal God is one "having the attributes of an individual conscious being."[6] Let us avoid thinking of God as a person in the way that you and I are persons, and think of It as a focused awareness and consciousness much as you might experience in the deepest meditation, or when all feelings of self are absent. God-Consciousness has no sense of separation from anything. It is totally aware and present in this moment. It has total experience. It has no need for doing—just being. It has no desires, no emotions, no human-like qualities—just pure consciousness. Having said that in the best way I can, now let's extend that sense of God-Consciousness into the realms of the Unknowable and just allow whatever is really there to be there as our unbiased, un-predetermined, unlimited, formless sense of God-Consciousness. This sense we now have is a tiny pointer to the true essence of God, which we can best simply call God-Consciousness.

God-Consciousness is eternal

This means that God-Consciousness has no beginning and no end. It is difficult for us to conceive of anything having no beginning and no end because in our experience there is nothing like that. Nevertheless, logically, it is possible there could be something outside time. Though Pandeism does not seek to answer the question either way, there is no reason whatsoever why consciousness cannot be eternal. Perhaps a good analogy is the Laws of Mathematics. They are eternal, would you not agree? No one invented 1+1=2. It just is, was, and always will be. We can use a diagram to describe the situation:

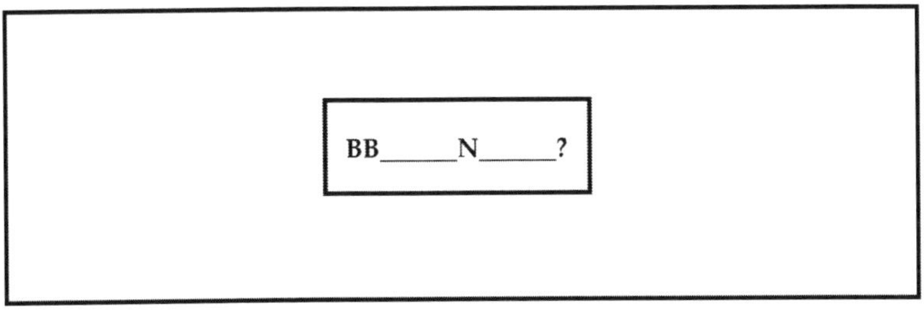

(Where BB = The Big Bang, N = Now, and ? = The end of our universe at some future time)

God's view is the whole of this larger rectangle (and of course beyond it) as the Eternal Now that He knows. In the midst of it, He has created a space-time bubble which has past, present, and future—and which is not eternal. The universe we know started with the Big Bang 14 billion years ago and, no doubt, will end one day in the distant future.

Our space-time bubble is held in God-Consciousness, and exists there. If He decided to discontinue our space-time bubble, He literally could just forget it. It would cease to exist. Now, do not be alarmed. There is no reason why God-Consciousness would do this—there would be no point. He has kept us going for 14 billion of our years so far, and long may the years continue. However, if He did decide to forget us, it would not matter one iota, as absolutely everything would be gone and only God Himself would be aware of its going, if He chose to. You and I wouldn't feel a thing.

God-Consciousness is omnipotent (all-powerful)

If absolutely everything is held in God-Consciousness, then anything that exists or could exist is within the power of God to create. If something like the square circle is logically impossible, then God cannot create it either. This does not reduce His power.

God-Consciousness can do whatever He can conceive of doing. Since there is nothing that can be conceived where God-Consciousness is not the one conceiving it, then nothing more powerful can exist. So, there is no need for any definition of what omnipotence means other than it is as powerful as it gets—however powerful that might be!

While you may be able to dream up some way in which God is not omnipotent, you are asking either for something which is intrinsically impossible and, therefore, nonsense, or something that is unreal and does not and cannot exist.

God-Consciousness is omnipresent (present everywhere)

If God-Consciousness is the very substance of every aspect of our universe, and of all other possible universes, as well as Himself, He is by definition omnipresent. He is everything that is. There is nothing else that exists.

There can be no place that exists where there is something that is not God-Consciousness. This also implies that He is immaterial in His essence, even if He is also present in all matter. God-Consciousness is present in every atom that exists—in every subatomic particle.

God-Consciousness is omniscient (all-knowing)

God-Consciousness could not have created something out of nothing. God used His own substance, which is Consciousness, to create our universe, and any others He might have created. Science knows that things get a bit strange when you go into the makeup of the atom, which can be seen as the fundamental unit for the existence of all physical matter. I am not a scientist, but I have read of the strange behavior of matter there, and that it starts to look less like matter and more like consciousness the deeper you go. Likewise, energy and matter are interchangeable and matter/energy cannot be created or lost, just transformed. When God wrote the Bible (i.e. God-Consciousness wrote the Bible as various human writers—just as with any other book), His omniscience knew nothing about the motorcar, the computer, the Internet or TV. Does this make Him less than omniscient? Of course not. God-Consciousness is aware that anything can be brought into being as it proves to be necessary or desirable, yet He has neither preordained nor forecast any specific inventions or developments. The potential for all inventions is, nonetheless, inherent in God-Consciousness. As He has developed the specific fundamentals of modern life through individual human inventors, His knowledge of these things has increased as the inventors' knowledge has increased, because they are identical (when looked at from God's viewpoint). So, if God-Consciousness is the very substance of every aspect of our universe, and of all other possible universes, as well as of Himself, He is by definition omniscient. He knows everything that is, because He is everything that is. There is nothing else.

God-Consciousness is the Creator of the universe

There is very little matter in matter, and what matter exists is derived from Consciousness. It is a denser form of the essence of God, which is Consciousness. God-Consciousness is the Prime Cause of everything, He is the only thing that is eternal, and therefore, He must be the ultimate Creator. Also, everything is made out of the essence of God-Consciousness. This is not to say what the mechanism is that He has chosen to use. For instance, He may have created the Archangels and Angels first and instructed them to create the universe we see. Of course, the Archangels and Angels are made of the substance of God-Consciousness too, so whatever we conjecture still comes back to the same thing. We can definitely accept that the Big Bang and evolution is part of the mechanism, as the evidence is there for us to see. The Prime Cause behind that provides the explanation science does not have. It is the only rational answer.

God-Consciousness does have a purpose for His Creation

Without His Creation, God-Consciousness is nothing but eternal nothing and some idle musings about nothing. As we said, with all due respect, this could get boring. So, God's first purpose in creating the universe was to add experience, expression, and enjoyment into His Life. God-Consciousness experiences what it is to be a grain of sand on the beach, to be the Sun that warms it, and the wave that cools it. He is the child who puts it into a bucket and He is the bucket. How much experience, expression, and enjoyment can God take? God-Consciousness added free will into the mix when He gave each individual the right to do whatever he or she wanted to do. This freedom quickly turned into Ego as one man thought he could be better than others. Another purpose is for God's Creation to learn to see through the futility of Ego and evil. From God's perspective, it is all experience, and at the same time it is illusion (*maya*); it would be wonderful to see all that has come out of Pandora's Box returned inside and locked up forever. It would be very rewarding to see His Creation, and humanity in particular, realize the Truth and then to voluntarily recapture and lock up Ego and duality in Pandora's Box for eternity. I described the universe as a Giant Jigsaw Puzzle that God-Consciousness created so He can put it together and show off the beauty of His perfect Creation. God's purpose is to put this puzzle together. Then, as with all great jigsaw puzzles, He can either frame it and look at it forever, or break it up into pieces and start again.

God-Consciousness is absolutely good (omnibenevolent)

This attribute has been very controversial, as one looks around at all the so-called evil in the world. So, let's take it slowly. Before Man discovered the knowledge of good and evil, there was neither. There was just whatever was, and that was not judged as being either good or bad. Likewise, plants and animals do not judge things as good or bad. If a tree gets its leaves eaten by a passing giraffe, this is not bad. Even if an elephant uproots the whole tree, this is not evil. Likewise, if a lion is able to bring down a zebra or baby wildebeest, this is not evil; it is the law of the wild. Plants and animals live in the Now and face whatever the conditions, experiences, and situations are now, and the fittest survive. So, God too is as He is, and that is it. Nothing He is or has created is either good or bad. It is just what it is. It is all in keeping with how things should be and how they are, as created by God, and as experienced by God-Consciousness through us. Therefore, we can say that God-Consciousness is omnibenevolent because He has not created anything for an evil purpose—everything is created for a positive purpose. He has not set out to torture, to destroy, to goad, to cause pain, or to cause sorrow. His Creation is perfect, and He is perfectly omnibenevolent. It is Man and his Ego, abusing free will, this gift from God, that has created the notion of good and evil. All the crime, wars, rape, pillage, and torture that men and women have imposed on others have come from Ego. If a true understanding of God and His universe were realized by everyone, then all evil would cease. Even natural disasters—floods, earthquakes, drought, eruptions, tsunamis, plagues—are merely part of the way things are. They are not intrinsically evil. We judge them so, particularly when we are caught in the midst of them. However, great good can come from these things too. In the end, it is all experience. The very worst thing that can happen is that we die and the earthly experience ends. From the perspective of God-Consciousness, who is our very being, this is acceptable and perfect in the moment.

God-Consciousness is immutable (unchanging through time)

God Himself is unchanging in that He has no need to change. Also, with His view of the Eternal Now, there is no need to change in essence. Nevertheless, as we have said above, within the confines of God's experience, within His creation, there is all that change, growth, evolution, experience, invention, and development offers. By putting on a blindfold and experiencing time as you and I experience it, God-Consciousness experiences movement, change, life, joy, and excitement. And this is within His overall immutability. God-Consciousness is and always will be God-Consciousness. God-Consciousness is outside time, is all-encompassing, and so is unchanging. Yes, within Himself He has created our universe as a source of experience. This experience does not change God-Consciousness in essence as He has no need to change. Experience is experience and that is all it is.

The God Franchise

Now to The God Franchise, and we start by describing a franchise as developed in the business world. A franchise agreement between a franchisor (the originator) and a franchisee (you) allows you to create and run a business under the franchise name, and market and sell the franchised product or service. For the privilege of being able to do this, you pay the franchisor a franchise fee, plus a percentage of the sales of your business. In return, the franchisor provides the systems you will need to run the business, as well as some marketing support, including group advertising.

The God Franchise takes this concept to the ultimate. It states that God-Consciousness can be seen as a Franchisor, and that you and I and every other person on this Earth individually is a Franchisee. By creating Mankind,[7] *God-Consciousness franchised His Creative Power to each and every man and woman on Earth.*[8] This is a *key* concept of The God Franchise. In addition, God-Consciousness gave us free will (as He naturally has), consciousness, and purpose. In fact, He gave us all His qualities to a greater or lesser extent, and we will discuss these in a moment. He franchised everything to each of us in what may be termed The God Franchise. Now, before you get too carried away with this concept, let's look at it more closely. It does not mean that you can rush off and create universes. We have many veils covering our Godhead (such as unconsciousness, Ego, self, separateness, and materialism), and there are other constraints as well.

Let's create a table comparing the key concepts of a franchise and The God Franchise (see table).

Business Franchise	**The God Franchise**
Franchisor: the originator of the franchise	God (or God-Consciousness)
Franchisee: you, the beneficiary of the franchise	You and me, individually
Franchise Agreement: the agreement between these two parties	Your birth certificate; also, the fundamental code by which you live your life (e.g. moral code, life's purpose, etc.) is your personal pact with God.
The Offering: the product, name, brand, and concepts that make this franchise valuable	The ability to create and be a creator; individual life and free will.
The Systems: the rules, procedures, and methods that enable this franchise to operate profitably	Universal Laws (God's Laws)
Franchise fee and royalties: any returns to be paid to the franchisor for these ongoing benefits	The experience of life, pain, and suffering until you learn the realities of creation and free will. For some it is a life of devotion, worship, and/or a commitment to help others. It is also enlightenment and/or conscious creation for universal evolution.
Nonexclusivity: except for a specific territory	Each of us, individually, is our own territory.
Ongoing support	We have constant support from God through His Universal Laws, and our Higher Self which is God-Consciousness incarnate—the ultimate support.
Business plan: your plan for making the franchise work	Both God's Plan and our own determination to follow a specific plan to achieve what we desire.
Brand recognition	Personal Creative Power; son/daughter of God.
Brand advertising and global marketing	Books like this one; all books, scriptures, teachers, gurus, courses, religions, sermons, and churches promoting the Power of God within each one of us.

Training	Life experience, study, and meditation, seeking the Truth, scientific work, spiritual work, opening to the Now, and being present.
A franchise is already a functioning business system.	Creative Power and the Universal Laws are already proven in the universe.
Turn-key business: everything is provided ready to operate.	Everything is provided.
All franchisees share responsibility for maintaining high standards for the brand.	We collectively share responsibility for keeping standards of personal creation high.
The ability to quit the franchise at some future time	We cannot quit. Only God-Consciousness could take that power away from us, and that would likely mean annihilation.

You and I are franchisees in the ability to create and to live our lives from a divine perspective. However, there is a vast difference between using The God Franchise consciously and using it unconsciously.

This is all very well, you say, but does that make me God? No, not quite. Just because God is you, this does not make you God. Just because you are a McDonald's franchise holder does not mean you are McDonald's! It means you have the right to run a store according to some very strict rules, and you are compensated for your efforts. However, you also need to pay dues to McDonald's Corporation, and you cannot claim to be the McDonald's Corporation.

As spiritual adepts know, it is possible to get close to God-Consciousness. In doing that, they usually, if not always, leave behind the trappings of the earthly experience. However, we have a lesser set of powers than God-Consciousness. All the powers and qualities of God-Consciousness are represented in each of us in a more manageable potency. We have all the powers and qualities we need and, frankly, all we can handle.

Nevertheless, whether we are a spiritual adept, a high-flying businessperson, or a beggar in the street, we have an equal stake as a God Franchisee. God is an equal-opportunity franchisor!

So Who Am I?

We now review the qualities we've identified as being God's qualities and see how each of us is able to use these as a God Franchisee. Making sense of these concepts is critical to your understanding of God as God-Consciousness and of you and your role in His Plan.

We look at every individual person on this planet, irrespective of what religion or what beliefs he or she has. We are all in this together, and more together than you might think. I will address you, the reader. However, you will know that at the same time we are discussing what is true for every other you in the world of 7 billion people.

Essentially, you are made up of two parts. Let's call them a Higher Self and a Lesser Self, but this is just for convenience. However, let me rush to add that the two parts are not quite so distinct, and, therefore, I ask you to give this description open-minded contemplation.

The Higher Self

In the first instance, you are a part of God-Consciousness. God-Consciousness is one whole (the One God we speak of) present in the Eternal Now, and within Himself he has differentiated a Creation in order to have experiences. As a child might play blind man's bluff,[9] God has blindfolded Himself and has taken on an individual form, many times over. Each one of us is a blindfolded subset of God-Consciousness.

To put things in perspective, it is not so much that you are God—it is that God is you. Does that make you (your Higher Self) conscious, eternal, omnipotent, omniscient, omnipresent, a creator, with a purpose, absolutely good and immutable? Let's take these questions one by one.

• **Are you a conscious being?** The answer is Yes. That is the importance of being present in the Now—the importance of the *Power of Now*[10] as presented by Eckhart Tolle. It is very easy to get caught up in the machinations of the Lesser Self, and in day-to-day affairs, so losing sight of our Higher Self Consciousness. However, God-Consciousness does not lose sight of Itself, thank God!

When we pray, it is to a Personal God—it is to our Higher Self, the personal form that God-Consciousness is taking. When we meditate, we are in communication with our Higher Self. When we sit quietly and receive inspiration or intuition, God-Consciousness is talking to us. Our Higher Self is talking to us. As Alfred, Lord Tennyson wrote, "Closer is He than breathing, and nearer than hands and feet."[11]

When we are focused and giving our whole being to a task in complete enthusiasm, honesty, and openness, we experience the consciousness of the Higher Self. However, much of the time we cover our consciousness under many veils, and, therefore, act unconsciously.

• **Are you an eternal being?** The answer is Yes. Your Higher Self is eternal because it is God-Consciousness. You were never born and will never die. However, we are talking here of the Higher Self, which we can compare to a splash of water from the Ocean of God-Consciousness that is briefly separated from the Ocean, and then falls back into the Ocean again.

The Lesser Self certainly dies as we realize the illusion it is, and we will discuss this in a minute. The physical body dies because it is not designed to live forever—it wears out over time, what we call a lifetime. The Higher Self is God-Consciousness with a blindfold on. We retain our individuality in this lifetime and possibly in further lifetimes (and I say this without prejudice either way), and one day the blindfold comes off, when God is ready, and we will recognize and be recognized for who we truly are: God-Consciousness Itself.

• **Are you an omnipotent being?** The answer is No, although you do have all the power you need. While God-Consciousness is omnipotent in the Eternal Now, He has put on a blindfold in coming to form as you. This has also reduced His power to a level that is appropriate to you. Imagine if He gave 7 billion people both free will and omnipotence! Yes, it is not a pretty thought.

So, for the purpose of experiencing life in form, God-Consciousness has reduced the power that is available to the individual. Remember, He does have the ability to do this, so this statement is not a cop-out. Nevertheless, the power that your Higher Self does have is phenomenal when measured against what you normally use. The fact that it is not omnipotence is really just academic.

You can achieve whatever you desire to achieve, and God's Laws (to be discussed shortly) are there to assist you with that. The Law of Manifestation attracts into our experience whatever it is that we want or need, either consciously or unconsciously.

• **Are you an omnipresent being?** The answer is No. Nevertheless, you can travel in thought to distant places, times, and concepts. By using modern technology, you have the ability to communicate with people in other places with ease. We can approach experiencing God-Consciousness in meditation and other spiritual practices. We can experience presence in this moment by being present in the Now, as described by Eckhart Tolle.

Your Higher Self, as God-Consciousness, is a part of God's overall omnipresence. In addition, every cell of our bodies, every molecule, even every atom, contains a spark of God-Consciousness because the whole universe is made from the substance of God-Consciousness. Omnipresence is thus the totality of these individual presences, if you like.

Any restrictions on where and when we are present are self-imposed.

• **Are you an omniscient being?** The answer is No, although you do have access to all the knowledge you need. Your Higher Self does not know everything, once again because of the blindfold. Carl Jung wrote of the collective unconscious, and we are told there are Akashic Records that purport to hold all the information of the universe. I am not saying these exist, although it does make sense that we have access to a vast amount of information and knowledge that is not normally available when one is restrained by the limitations of the Lesser Self. It may be easy to interpret this as accessing the Mind of God through your Higher Self.

If what I have just said sounds a little esoteric to you, that is fine. Let's look at it in a different way. When you go to your Higher Self, consciously or unconsciously, seeking inspiration or help with some particular problem, you are always able to get an answer. Sometimes you get the answer directly, and other times you are directed to a person who can help you or to a book that contains the information you need. No problem is too hard to solve, and using your Higher Self to find the answer is the best way to go. It is interesting that often scientists discover the same facts about the universe or develop the same ideas at roughly the same time as each other, without working together or even being aware of the other's work. Carl Jung called this synchronicity.

From a practical point of view, it is also sensible that you don't know everything. It would leave no room for the growth of knowledge and experience. Even God-

Consciousness is acquiring new information and knowledge as we individually add to that knowledge through our experiences of life. Your Higher Self is the medium of God's experience and knowledge accumulation.

In the search for information, we are assisted by modern tools such as the Internet. We are in the Information Age. Our biggest constraint is our own Ego that restricts us with preconceptions and limitations. We have the ability to shake off these shackles if we desire to.

• **Are you a creator?** The answer is Yes. This is an important and very practical part of The God Franchise. God-Consciousness created the universe out of His own substance. You create whatever you create in life out of the substance of the universe. Nothing can be created out of nothing—not even God can do that. As inventors have shown, there is no limit to the innovations that can be created. Science has no boundaries, certainly not in its own sphere, and all that work is creative work. The source of the inspiration is the Higher Self, God-Consciousness. The main tool we have is the Law of Manifestation, and with this, we create our lives and life experiences, whether we do it consciously or unconsciously. You could say we each create our own universe.

• **Are you a being with a purpose?** The answer is Yes. Firstly, you are fulfilling God's purpose, and after all, that really is the only significant purpose. We have already discussed God-Consciousness's purpose, so I will summarize: to add further experience, expression, and enjoyment to God's experience of Himself, to see through the futility of Ego and evil voluntarily, and to put the universal puzzle (the Giant Jigsaw Puzzle) together, so that He can then frame it, or break it up and start again. At an individual level, you can choose many other purposes in life, ones that suit your interests and your talents.

These purposes all add to the experience, expression, and enjoyment of God-Consciousness, and with them you make positive use of your free will.

• **Are you a being who is absolutely good?** The answer is Yes. This is true at a Higher Self level. Any evil, mistakes, or badness is the doing of the Ego in the Lesser Self. You look at any young child and you see good, not evil. Everything a person does is with a positive intention. If that positive intention is for evil, or is in some other way misguided, this is because it has been driven by the Ego, the Lesser Self. It has been driven by pain and ignorance. In essence, in your Higher Self, you are perfect and absolutely good.

• **Are you an immutable being?** The answer is No. Immutable means unchanging. As we have said, God-Consciousness has no need to change at the formless level. However, by putting on a blindfold and experiencing the Now that you experience, God-Consciousness experiences movement, change, life, joy, and excitement through your Higher Self.

However, you could say we are immutable in our essence as we are a splash in the Ocean of God-Consciousness; but, in the environment of time and space, and in terms of our Lesser Self, we do change.

In summary, we can say that the Higher Self, which every one of us is individually, is similar in quality to God-Consciousness Himself in five of the nine attributes that we have discussed. In the case of the other four—omnipotence, omniscience, omnipresence, and immutability—it is illogical for us individually to have those qualities. Nevertheless, we have access to all the power and all the knowledge we could possibly need. We collectively provide God's omnipresence and provide God with the experiences of Life that He needs, without compromising His immutability.

You may not realize that you experience your Higher Self directly quite frequently during the day. I would like to clarify what this feeling is so you can get a clear experiential sense of it. You might be surprised to find you do not have to be an overtly spiritual person to experience your Higher Self on a regular basis. By the same token, there will be some regular churchgoers (synagogue-, temple-, mosque-goers) who very seldom if ever experience their Higher Selves.

Your Higher Self is what you experience when you are at peace with yourself. Many people will experience their Higher Self as unconditional love for themselves, for all other people, and for the whole world (and universe). Others will experience great joy, bliss, or other heightened emotions or states of mind and/or being. You could be doing anything, and somehow you know it is going well. There is no sense of Ego or comparison with others. There is no fault-finding with the world or with yourself. Everything is just great in that moment. Perhaps you have just completed a task such as the ironing, or mowing the lawn, or washing the dog, and you just acknowledge that it is good. Just as God completed each day of the Creation and saw that it was good.[12]

Let me clarify that this feeling of good you are experiencing is not from a sense of duality. It is not the opposite of bad or evil. It is just an acknowledgment of what is, without any real connotations. You, therefore, do not feel pious, or special, or self-righteous, or even pleased with yourself. It is not an ego-type feeling; it is much higher than that. It is your Higher Self.

You might wish to remember to keep your attention open to this feeling whenever you get a chance, and acknowledge the feeling to yourself. It is worth keeping in touch with your Higher Self.

The Lesser Self

The other side of you is your Lesser Self. This is the side that developed from the misuse of free will, and has been passed down through the generations. Each child is taught, by commission or omission, to fit into the material world, the world of Ego, free will, limitation, evil, and pain.

First, let me say that God-Consciousness, through our Higher Self, is totally aware of all aspects of our Lesser Self. He does not approve or disapprove of what we do with our Lesser Selves. After all, the reason for it is free will, and God-Consciousness gave us free will so He could add to His experience, whatever form it takes. Most importantly, it is self-regulating, so the Lesser Self should never completely destroy itself. If it did get so bad that it did destroy itself, it still would not cause any significant problem for the Higher Self, God-Consciousness. Essentially the Lesser Self, in the grand scheme of things, can be seen as illusion (*maya*).

The Lesser Self is the Ego. While we need individuality to operate in this world effectively, that is provided by the Higher Self, which is God-Consciousness divided into individual beings with blindfolds on. There is differentiation and free will in the Higher Self, but not the egotistical, self-serving, and limited frame of reference of the Ego. The Ego is the source of our problems.

So what is this Ego? Think of someone who annoys you, someone who can't get it right and somehow causes you strife. Think how you could do whatever it is in a better way. Think how you might be better than they are. Think how maybe you should be paid more, have a better partner, live in a nicer house because you have earned it. Imagine how things would be better if a particular person was not in the way of your achieving it. Think what you could do if you had your own way.

Stop and get a sense of how this is different to how you felt with your Higher Self. Notice that with the Higher Self, you felt gently positive, but not in a way that was competitive. You did not feel that you were better than anyone—more spiritual, more relaxed, or more evolved—you just felt comfortable in yourself. However, when the Lesser Self is engaged, suddenly you are comparing yourself with others, and you are feeling emotions—and not necessarily very pleasant ones either. You may even feel tension about the state you are in. You do not feel at peace, but rather somewhat at odds with the world. You are more in your mind, more strategizing to get your own way, and more critical of others.

The Ego has a nasty streak, and has an ulterior motive for everything it does. It increases the feeling of separation. It engages with you quite easily, almost as if this was the real you. *You've got to look after yourself. Right? Or you'll just be walked over.* The Ego is very involved in the mind and in justification, self-pity, blame, and superiority. Sometimes it is a feeling of inferiority, but it is always with a feeling of the need to protect yourself.

Do you have a sense of this now? The Ego could be described as a false sense of self. It is one built on the fear of loss of self. It is a fear of annihilation. In contrast, the sense of individuality and free will are a part of the Higher Self, a self-blindfolded God-Consciousness who is having a bit of fun. That side of you is fine. Could you have a game of football without having eleven or so individuals on each side, with the free will to kick the ball when and where they wanted to? No. Free will and individuality is not the issue. The issue is the Ego. And the Ego's greatest ally is the mind.

This Is Who I Am

To answer the question asked in the previous section: "So Who Am I?," and to summarize the ideas above, I can say that each and every one of the 7 billion people on Earth is formed in the same way, whether we are good, bad, or indifferent. I will describe how I view myself, and then you can assess how you feel in contrast or similarity.

- I am in essence a Higher Self and a Lesser Self that together make up what I call *me*. There is no one else in the universe who is the same as me and I am unique in my expression in the universe.
- My Higher Self is God-Consciousness. This is God expressing Himself in the form of a human being on planet Earth. God is in everything and is everything in the universe (omnipresence) and is the only reality. Among all those things and creatures and plants and minerals, He is also in the form of Alan H. Dawe. In this, I am no better and no worse than any rock, plant, animal, or other person. I am 'just' God-Consciousness in expression (or form).
- My Lesser Self is an illusion, a very real illusion that I can't see through at this stage, but an illusion nevertheless. It hides my Higher Self and pretends to be *me*. Here resides my Ego and my mind. This is what I have created through expressing my free will. However, this Lesser Self is not separate from God—as it cannot be—it just lives in the illusion that it is separate from God.
- When I was born, I came into form as Alan H. Dawe. Whether I was a separate entity before that really doesn't matter. Maybe I am a separate spirit or soul who has incarnated many times before, or maybe this is the first (and only) time. Frankly, it does not matter, as I cannot remember the time before I was born, and I am happy with myself and understand why I am as I am with reference purely to this lifetime. I am not going to argue one way or the other on the question of whether I have lived before, because it is irrelevant to this life, and it is irrelevant to the eternal Now, which is the only reality.
- During this lifetime, I express myself as I feel at the time. I

do the best I can in every moment. Sometimes my best meets the standards I expect of myself and meets the expectations of others, and sometimes it doesn't. Whatever happens and whatever I do, my Higher Self (God-Consciousness) is right there and is experiencing it without judgment.

• All experience that my Lesser Self and Higher Self have is perfect. That is one of the major purposes of life—God experiencing Himself. There is no judgment from God—there is only the Lesser Self judging itself and judging others. It is the Ego that thinks it can judge. From God's perspective, the perspective of my Higher Self, what I *do* is experience.

• When I die, I may cease to exist as an individual and may be absorbed back into the Ocean of formless God-Consciousness. Alternatively, I might continue as a separate entity. Frankly, it doesn't concern me. It is only the Ego (Lesser Self) that needs to think it is special enough to continue separately. I am not going to argue one way or the other as to whether I continue as a separate individual in the afterlife, or whether I become One with God-Consciousness, which I am anyway. It is irrelevant to the eternal Now, which is the only reality.

• My body is an expression of consciousness. How things are with my body may influence the Lesser Self as to how it responds to that body. However, the greater influence is the other way around—my body will respond to what is in my mind and in the consciousness of my Lesser Self. If I am sick, it is my mind that is usually sick first, and the body is just reflecting that state of mind.

• If I need to heal my mind or body, I need to allow my Higher Self to come through, and then allow my Lesser Self to withdraw from its fixed attitudes or stance. Healing comes from God-Consciousness. Prayers to God are heard by the God-Consciousness of my Higher Self, and can be immediately answered if my Lesser Self is prepared to allow the healing in. God does not interfere from outside His Creation (including me); He *interferes* from within, and then upon invitation. Thus, the Lesser Self and free will are not compromised. They are healed by acceptance and surrender. Healing is always readily available through my Higher Self.

- My purpose in life is to express myself and experience. I can choose to do a lot in each minute of my life or I can choose to do very little. I have free will. I cannot complain about my excess or lack of life experience as it is in my own hands. My Lesser Self has the say as it has usurped the free will that I have been given as a God Franchisee. My Higher Self accepts what is presented to it, and will help my Lesser Self whenever it is truly asked for that help. This is my hotline to God.

This gives you an idea of how I see my place in the universe. I also see you and every other person in the universe in the same way. The effect of viewing people in this way may lead you to become much more empathetic to others, much less swayed by trivia driven by ignorance and illusion (or delusion), and much more understanding of why people do what they do. There have been many occasions when I have read or seen in the news a story of someone who has committed a serious crime and is described as evil. Based on the perspective stated above, I have come to realize they are not evil, but have acted from a place of pain, ignorance, and Ego. Forgiveness and understanding arise much more easily.

How God Experiences His Creation

God is present within each of His Creations—every person, every animal, every plant, every rock, and of course within every cell of every living thing, and in every atom of every molecule of every physical manifestation in the universe. This is what *omnipresence* means.

God-Consciousness experiences all the different aspects of your life from your perspective. He also experiences your interactions with all the other players, and therefore, experiences all interactions from all points of view simultaneously. God-Consciousness is and experiences each of the 7 billion people on Earth from an individual perspective, and the collective experience of all involved is God's total experience.

I used to hold the idea that God had created only the natural world of Earth, the Sun, the Moon, and the stars; God had created the humans, the animals, the plants, and the minerals; God had created the atom, the ninety-four chemical elements that make up the physical world, and so on. I also believed that Man had created the invented world that we see around us: the buildings, the cars, the space shuttles, the computers, the CDs, DVDs, iPods and iPads,[13] the clothes, the sculptured gardens, the genetic modifications, the hybrids, and essentially the whole modern world.

Of course, everything that Man has invented and *created* is made out of the materials that God has created: the minerals, the oil, the wood, the plants, and so on. It seemed to me that God gave us the ability to go out and create whatever we wanted to of our own right. I felt, and still feel, there is no limit to what can be invented, designed, and created. No limit whatsoever.

With my realization of The God Franchise came a subtle shift. What if it is not Man who creates all these new things? What if it is God who creates them through us instead? What if God is the Creator of everything, from the natural world and wonderful modern creations we have around us, to the atom bomb, the gun, the porn movie, and junk food?

God uses you and me as channels for His further creation. In reality, not even as channels. As I have said, God is you and me continuing His Creation through our forms. You and I have this false idea of self, which is effectively just Ego showing up. Ego says I created that or I designed this. Ego says I wrote this wonderful song or I painted this fantastic picture. If we remove Ego, all that is left is God creating.

Of course, many human *creators* have been humble enough to recognize that it is not themselves as individual Egos who should be credited with their creations. But what about you and me? How often do we think we have just done something marvelous? We don't need to know about how to create—that is not our job. Our job is to be the best channel we can be for the creation. By learning practical skills (art, music, design, writing, cooking, carpentry, welding, you name it), and by leaving the Ego out of it, we are creating the best channel we can for God's work. Our second job is to appreciate and enjoy what has been created for us, and through us.

The Ego is the illusion of the self as a creator. God-Consciousness is the Creator of everything, and He also is the substance of the whole of His Creation. So, why is there so much around us that appears to be the exact antithesis of what one would expect God to create? Why is there disease, poverty, war, corruption, danger, and death? Philosophers ask how God can be omnibenevolent in the face of all these dreadful occurrences if He is also omniscient and omnipotent. The argument is that if God knows about Evil, as He is omniscient, and is powerful enough to destroy all Evil as he is omnipotent, how can He be omnibenevolent if He allows Evil to occur? This is the so-called Problem of Evil.

Let me say that while God is the Creator, His creations are filtered through our physical being, including our Egos. If our Ego is so big that we want to interfere with the creation, or so big that we think we have greater skills than we really have, we are dumbing down the creation. Our Egos can even pervert the creative process so that what starts as a benign discovery (e.g. atomic power, motion pictures) is directed by Ego into being something we can view as being very evil (e.g. nuclear weapons, child pornography).

Nevertheless, the reality is that you are looked after by God-Consciousness just by being a perfectly open channel for His creation. All you need will flow to you as well, including money as the current common exchange unit. You are constantly in the presence of creation. It is happening all around you. Bow with me in awe to the whole Creation!

God's Laws

Now that we've discussed the Creation in great detail, it will be useful to discuss some of the Laws that God-Consciousness has set up to ensure the universe runs without any need for intervention.

Physical and Mathematical Laws are immutable facts, and we live within those constraints. In fact, we can say we would not be alive unless those constraints were in place. The universe only works as it does because of the physical and mathematical laws. These are Laws that cannot be broken, and, whether we have free will or not, these Laws apply.

Apart from the laws of science and physics, I list a group of six **Universal Laws**, which like the physical laws, cannot be broken. These are simply truths that exist. A great example is the Law of Manifestation, currently popularized as the Law of Attraction.

In addition there are the **Moral Laws** which some religions have set up as being God's Laws, but since they are able to be broken, they cannot be God's Laws but rather are moral guidelines. However, an effect comes into play if we do break these Moral Laws, for example, the Ten Commandments.

So, let's take a brief look at God's Laws, starting with the physical and mathematical laws, and see what we can make of them.

The Laws of Mathematics

There is 1+1=2, and all the other mathematical statements that remain true whatever you do. If you get a different answer, you have made an error. That is all there is to it. Mathematics is the foundation of all science. Due to the dependability of mathematics, science has been able to calculate and postulate many discoveries in the physical world, and in the universe. Such predictions go on to be proved in due course by observation.

Mathematics is also the foundation of all aspects of modern life. How would commerce run, how would appliances work, how would computers operate, or how would anything else we use in this modern world work, if it was not for the dependable Laws of Mathematics?

The Law of Gravity

Newton's Universal Law of Gravitation says that every object in the universe is attracted to every other object in the universe. Gravitational force is proportional to the product of the two masses involved and inversely proportional to the square of the distance between their centre points. Just as π (pi) is a constant (3.1416) for the relationship of the circumference of a circle to its diameter, so there is a Universal Gravitational Constant called G, as a constant of the proportionality. While gravity is obviously useful for holding the universe together, why there is this attraction between objects is not known.

Gravitation acts on all objects with mass, it has an infinite range, it cannot be modified or protected against, and it is always an attractive force, rather than a repelling one. Gravitation is one of four fundamental forces in nature.

It also enables us to walk on the surface of the planet and keeps our coffee from floating out of the cup.

The Laws of Electromagnetism

Electromagnetism is the second of four fundamental forces in nature; it acts between electrically charged particles and has an infinite range. Electricity, magnetism, and light are produced by this force. There are a number of laws related to it such as Faraday's Law, Coulomb's Law, and Ohm's Law. Magnetism and electricity are intrinsically linked as electricity produces a magnetic field, and magnets are used to produce electricity.

The modern world could not function without electricity. We take it for granted with our lighting, refrigerators, stoves, water heaters, electric motors, computers, communications, the Internet, heating, banking, factories, and many other applications. Electricity enters every facet of our lives, yet we barely give it a thought. It was only 150 years ago that scientists started to figure out how to generate and apply this powerful energy.

The Laws of Electromagnetism have applied since the Big Bang 14 billion years ago, yet we have only just come to realize what electromagnetism can do for us and how to apply it. One wonders what other universal secrets there are that we have yet to discover and apply to our lives.

The Strong (Nuclear) Force and the Weak Force

The other two of the four known fundamental forces in nature are of short range and operate at a subatomic level. Strong Force is the strongest force, followed sequentially by Electromagnetic Force, Weak Force, and Gravitational Force.

Newton's Laws of Motion

Sir Isaac Newton discovered three Laws of Motion and published them in his *Principia* in 1687. They are:

1. **The Law of Inertia:** Every body continues in its state of rest, or of uniform motion in a straight line, unless it is compelled to change that state by forces impressed upon it.
2. **The Law of Motion:** The acceleration of a body is directly proportional to the net force acting on the body and inversely proportional to the mass of the body.
3. **The Action–Reaction Law:** To every action force there is an equal and opposite reaction force.

These laws only start to break down at subatomic levels and nearing the speed of light. The principles of Albert Einstein's Special Theory of Relativity then apply.

The Laws of Thermodynamics

These have developed over time and have been modified and renumbered. The current Laws of Thermodynamics, which of course have continued through all time, however they came to be discovered or numbered, are:

1. Objects in thermodynamic equilibrium have the same temperature.
2. **The Law of Conservation of Energy:** Energy cannot be created or destroyed; it may be transformed from one form into another, but the total amount of energy never changes.
3. **The Law of Increased Entropy:** Energy flows naturally only from hot to cold, and tends to become dispersed as heat (entropy). Usable energy diminishes as it converts to unusable energy.
4. The entropy of a substance is zero if the absolute temperature is zero.

Absolute Zero

Absolute Zero temperature is the lowest possible temperature and is equal to minus 273.16°C. It is also known as 0°K (Kelvin).

We could, of course, go on, but the point I want to make is that science has not created these laws, nor are these laws new. The laws that rule the way the universe works are laws that have been in place for 14 billion years, dating back to when God-Consciousness set up the universe with a Big Bang. Just because we have only recently discovered these Laws does not mean they did not exist. Likewise, the fact that we have not codified other laws that have yet to be discovered does not mean that they do not exist and operate right now.

Now that we've covered some of the laws of the universe that science has discovered, let us take a look at the Laws of God as the Church has depicted them.

The Ten Commandments

The Ten Commandments[14] were given to Moses (c. 1500 BC) to give to the children of Israel. These were followed by sundry other laws and ordinances, which were coined in terms specific to the people then.

The Ten Commandments are:

1. Thou shalt have no other gods before me.
2. Thou shalt not make unto thee any graven image, or any likeness of any thing that is in heaven above, or that is in the earth beneath, or that is in the water under the earth: Thou shalt not bow down thyself to them, nor serve them.
3. Thou shalt not take the name of the Lord thy God in vain.
4. Remember the Sabbath day, to keep it holy. Six days shalt thou labor, and do all thy work: But the seventh day is the Sabbath of the Lord thy God.
5. Honor thy father and thy mother.
6. Thou shalt not kill.
7. Thou shalt not commit adultery.
8 Thou shalt not steal.
9. Thou shalt not bear false witness against thy neighbor.
10. Thou shalt not covet thy neighbor's house, thou shalt not covet thy neighbor's wife, nor his manservant, nor his maidservant, nor his ox, nor his ass, nor any thing that is thy neighbor's.

With the Commandments, which many people treat as God's Law, the 'laws' can in fact be broken. This is called sinning. We do not get punished directly by God for our sins, despite what the Church may say. We punish ourselves by believing in attitudes and actions that are incompatible with 'God's Law' and, therefore, with Truth. These attitudes and actions are created by the Ego, and the fruits of them are pain, suffering, and unhappiness that we experience directly.

The punishment we experience occurs through the workings of the third set of God's Laws, the Universal Laws. This punishment may even be delivered by the state, as in if we break the Sixth Commandment, "Thou shalt not kill," then it is codified in the law books of most if not all countries that the culprit will be punished, be it with a jail sentence or even execution.

Universal Laws

This is a group of laws that are always true and cannot be broken, just like the physical laws. Some of these laws are well known, although unfortunately, many people forget them or don't believe in them. This is unfortunate because it means such people are cutting themselves off from reaping the benefits the laws provide. The laws continue to operate whether you believe in them or not, just as with the physical laws. This will become clearer to you once we have discussed them.

Bruce McArthur defines a Universal Law as "an unbreakable, unchangeable principle of life that operates inevitably, all the time."[15] This means that each of us individually is in the same boat. The Universal Laws act impartially, justly, and equally for every single person. What could be fairer than that?

Universal Laws, by definition, cannot be transgressed. Thus the concept of sin in this sense would be a little out of place. If you do something that is harmful to another, the Universal Law that is invoked will bring the appropriate punishment (karma) on you. It is just a question of reaping what you sow.

There are many Universal Laws worded in many different ways. Here is my choice of the six most significant ones.

1. God is
2. The Law of Cause and Effect (including the Law of Karma)
3. Like creates like (including the Law of Manifestation)
4. The Law of Increase: Your attitude and intention determine the extent of your result
5. The Law of Balance: The universe remains constantly in a state of equilibrium
6. The Law of Self: You are a unique individual, and the fulfillment of your desires is of primary importance. The same is equally true of every other person.

1. God Is

We should say "God-Consciousness Is" of course, except that "God Is" is much snappier! The corollaries that apply to this law include:

- The Universal Laws are *created* by God-Consciousness and are, therefore, as infinite, inevitable, and unchanging as He is. The Laws are, in truth, the very nature of God-Consciousness.
- The universe is ultimately good. Evil (or other bad things) is purely the appearance of an absence of good.
- God loves His Creation, and Love is an essential force of the universe.

2. The Law of Cause and Effect

The essence of all causative factors, including your own intentions and the current conditions or way things are, results in the exact effect you will experience. This law has a number of corollaries:

- Nothing is by chance.
- There are no such things as accidents or bad luck.

- Life is the experience of your choices.
- You are responsible for everything that happens to you.

Naturally, the Law of Cause and Effect includes the Law of Karma—that you reap what you sow. The next law, Like Creates Like, can also be seen as related to the Law of Karma. You could say that if you look at the Universal Law of Cause and Effect as having either desirable effects (pleasure) or undesirable ones (pain), then sin would be those actions that cause undesirable effects.

3. Like Creates Like

While you may not have heard of the Like Creates Like law before, no doubt you will have heard of more colloquial renditions such as:

- What goes around comes around.
- You reap what you sow (the Law of Karma).
- The Law of Attraction.
- The Law of Manifestation.
- You must give in order to receive.
- As you believe, so it will come into reality for you.
- You attract what you expect.

4. The Law of Increase: Your attitude and intention determine the degree of your result

As we have said, what you sow, you reap. This law says your attitude and intention directly affect the extent of the result you get. There are three aspects to working with the Law of Increase: desire; intention and expectation; and attitude.

5. The Law of Balance: The universe remains constantly in a state of equilibrium

Just like water settling to find its lowest level, the universe as a whole always moves to maintain a state of equilibrium. Two of the corollaries are:

- All exchanges between you and others balance.
- You have to sacrifice one thing in order to receive something else.

6. The Law of Self

The Law of Self can be stated as follows: You are a unique individual, and the fulfillment of your desires is of primary importance. The same is equally true of every other person. This is not a sign of selfishness, but rather an acknowledgment of your unique role as a God Franchisee.

We have just touched on some of the more important of God's Laws. We can rest assured that whether we have identified all God's Laws or not, they are alive and well and operating in the universe. Some are laws that affect the physical operation and existence of the universe, and science has made an excellent job of uncovering these. No doubt, there are many more physical laws to be uncovered, or at least to be rephrased. Likewise, with the Universal Laws, there are many more that have not been listed here. This list is just a sample of the types of laws that exist.

Many scientists and mathematicians have worked on, and still work on, the problem of the elusive "theory of everything." One would imagine that such a unified theory is feasible, although scientists will need to allow their view of the world to widen to include consciousness. As we know by now, God-Consciousness is the source and the foundation of the universe, so by excluding Him/It, the theory of everything might well remain elusive. In a unified theory, all God's Laws need to be taken into account.

God's Grace

We hear of Grace or God's Grace, but what are we really talking about? The word grace means "the free and unmerited favor of God shown towards man; the divine assistance and power given to man in spiritual rebirth and sanctification; the condition of being favored or sanctified by God; an unmerited gift, favor, etc., granted by God."[16]

There are two main aspects that come out of these definitions. The first point is that the favor received from God is unmerited, that is, Man is blessed by God-Consciousness even though his own actions do not merit such blessings. The mere fact that we exist as God Franchisees and our whole being is God-Consciousness is indeed a huge blessing. We of ourselves, our Egos, can do nothing and, therefore, do not merit God's Grace. The Ego is built from the abuse of free will and has no real significance. It is a veil of illusion covering our Higher Self, our God-Consciousness.

Secondly, Grace is the condition of being favored or sanctified (made holy) by God. It is the assistance and power given to us in spiritual rebirth, that is, the recognition of our Higher Selves. As we come to understand our true spirituality, God's Grace will flow upon us and we will realize that we are truly blessed. It is not that God-Consciousness is withholding His Grace from anyone at any time. It is rather that if we believe we are the Ego, and cut ourselves off from our Higher Selves, we are cutting ourselves off from God's Grace.

Our birthright, in fact our very being, is God's Grace. All we (our Egos) have to do is open our hearts and minds and allow that Grace in. This is another way of saying we need to live as an expression of our Higher Selves and allow the Ego to dissolve into the mists of insignificance and irrelevance where it belongs.

Without God's Grace, we would not exist, either individually or collectively. We could even use the word *Grace* to describe God instead of the words *God* or *God-Consciousness*. Grace is that significant.

The Purpose of Life

So, what is the purpose of life?

- Some people say, "To worship God"
- Some people say, "To have a relationship with God"
- Some people say, "To be happy"
- Some people say, "To live your passion"
- Some people say, "To become enlightened"
- Some people say, "To clear your karma"
- Some people say, "To do God's will"
- And some people say, "Life has no purpose at all."

My view is that there is only one main purpose of life, and that is the purpose for which God created the universe. That purpose, as Pandeism also asserts, is to experience. Before He created the universe, God did not have anything to experience, and so He created the universe in order to experience the wind through His hair, the water through His fins, the beauty of His sunset, and the feeling of being entwined with His lover. God gave Man a God Franchise so we can be co-creators with Him. He gave us free will so we are not pre-programmed automatons.

God-Consciousness also blindfolded Himself so He would not know all the answers beforehand. He broke Himself (at one level) into billions and billions of pieces just like a Giant Jigsaw Puzzle. In this way, He could experience Himself from many, many different vantage points. He experiences Himself as an atom, as an element, as a tree, as a bug, as an albatross, as a lion, as a man, as a woman, as a beggar, and as a king. God-Consciousness is omnipresent in every single thing in the universe and He experiences what it is to be that thing.

Then, another experience that God-Consciousness wants to have is the experience of putting this Gigantic Jigsaw Puzzle back together again. You could say the purpose of life is to put this wonderful jigsaw puzzle back together, for everyone to realize the

Truth, and for them to close Pandora's Box of free will and Ego voluntarily. This is the ultimate purpose of life: the voluntary relinquishment of separation from God, of personal Ego and of free will gone bad. This is the climax of evolution. This is the Heaven or Paradise that the religious seek, and this is the "new heaven and…new earth"[17] written about by St John the Divine.

So, if we look at the purposes of life other people have identified, we will see they all are covered by this greater purpose of life. Those people who still think life has no purpose have not been following this article. If once there was nothing except God-Consciousness, and now there is a universe, I cannot imagine that God-Consciousness created it without some sort of purpose in mind, even if it is not the one I am proposing.

While we all have our individual purpose in life, whether or not we know what it is, we also have these more fundamental purposes people generally apply. Yes, one purpose of our lives is to worship God, but this does not mean we have to do so in a church, synagogue, mosque, or temple. It means that in our daily lives we are always aware, at the back of our minds, how wonderful life really is, despite any difficulties and challenges we might have. We can worship God as the *source* of our life, since without Him we would not exist.

Our purpose is also to have a relationship with God. As we have relationships with many different people on various levels, we should make a point of recognizing the God-Consciousness in each of these people. We can look into their eyes and see God there. We can be happy and we can live our passion. As we do this, we show our enthusiasm for life and, therefore, our enthusiasm for what we experience.

If we live a life of true clarity about the presence of God-Consciousness, and allow the veils of Ego to fall from our eyes, then we are truly enlightened. As we become enlightened and see the past deeds that lead to the creation of our karma, we will be able to clear all karma.

And, in experiencing life fully and consciously, we are doing God's will.

Benediction

What do I *know* about the nature of God anyway? Absolutely nothing. However, I am certain He is not a superhuman sitting in a place called Heaven, and ruling us from above. I am equally certain that God is our personal essence, and everything that exists anywhere in this universe—and any other universes—is made up of His Essence. All is God-Consciousness in some form or another, and that is all there is to it.

This benediction is for the invocation of God-Consciousness in your own being.

May God-Consciousness reveal Itself to your human consciousness as your Higher Self, so you can more easily pull aside the veils in your own life.

May your heart open and receive direct access to the Truth of your own Being.

May you appreciate that your Higher Self, your true Consciousness, is God-Consciousness Itself, and you are truly blessed.

May you come to realize that all that stands between you and Freedom, Heaven, and Absolute Bliss is your insistence on maintaining your Ego and your personal sense of free will. As you surrender to the reality of your Higher Self, the sheer ridiculousness of your previous life, your fears, your prejudices, and the protection of your personality and Ego, will become apparent.

Bless you. Bless you. Bless you.

Notes

1 Derived from the definition in *Collins English Dictionary*.

2 The Big Bang theory has been accepted as the most likely explanation of the beginning of the universe, and is the one I accept in the

context of this article.

3 Any location in the universe could be seen as being that central point, and so there is no specific location for the Big Bang.

4 Gottfried Leibniz (1646–1716)—German philosopher and mathematician, who invented the binary system and many other concepts.

5 Rees, M., *Just Six Numbers: The Deep Forces That Shape the Universe*, Basic Books, New York, 2001.

6 *Collins English Dictionary*.

7 "in his own image" according to Genesis 1:27.

8 There could be civilizations in other solar systems that have similar opportunities, but we will stick with planet Earth. I have generally avoided the issue of other inhabited planets, but this is for simplicity only.

9 Also called blind man's buff, this game is similar to the children's game Marco Polo.

10 Tolle, E., *The Power of Now*, Hodder Headline Australia, Sydney, 2004 (originally published by Namaste Publishing, Vancouver, 1997).

11 Alfred, Lord Tennyson (1809–92) in a short poem, "The Higher Pantheism."

12 Genesis 1:31. "And God saw every thing that he had made, and, behold it was very good."

13 iPod and iPad are trademarks of Apple Inc., registered in the US and other countries.

14 Exodus 20:3–17. Note that Neale Donald Walsch used the term Ten Commitments in *Conversations with God: An Uncommon Dialogue*, Book 1 (Hodder & Stoughton, 1996) to show that the Ten Commandments are not to be viewed as God's Laws.

15 McArthur, B., *Your Life: Why It Is the Way It Is and What You Can Do About It—Understanding the Universal Laws*, A.R.E. Press, Virginia Beach, 1993, p. 5.

16 *Collins English Dictionary*.

17 Revelation 21:1.

On Celebrating Life

Amy Perry

My thoughts are chemicals.
I am made of recycled cells
That I ingest, I take in what's best
For optimal health, active or at rest.
My DNA as mysterious as the Cosmos.
The Cosmos less of a mystery than Ocean floors.
I come from the Ocean, an awesome notion.
A family with all others, every Thing is a cousin.
My ancestors all made it to reproduction.
I am assembled, through history, through selection.

My traits have been crafted, positively reacted.
Nurtured by Nature, genes that have lasted.
I am made from the fire of expired stars,
Drink water that passed through dinosaurs.
I experience Life, though filled with a bounty of strife,
Through eyes of a Sapien, intelligence sharp as a knife.
And though my species feels more advanced
And in control of a world we craft with our own hands,
We are not self-efficient, resources increasingly deficient,
A virus to be easily shaken, in which the planet would not be missing.

I have a fleeting gift,
Amidst the destruction that here lives,
And that is my consciousness,
No fear of abyss, no promise of bliss,
But in my spark of a lifetime,
Seemingly insignificant, and that's fine,
I have inside endless thoughts with my mind,
No need of afterlife with a gift so divine.

God Without Religion

Dr Michael Arnheim

Dr Arnheim (also known as 'Doctor Mike') is an English barrister, sometime Fellow of St John's College, Cambridge, and author of eighteen books to date, including Is Christianity True? *and* The God Book. *His Wikipedia page is: https://en.wikipedia.org/wiki/Michael_Arnheim.*

This article is in two distinct parts:

A. This part offers a whole new take on the relationship between theism, deism and atheism. Theism and atheism are normally seen as at opposite ends of the spectrum of religious belief, with deism somewhere in between. This is undoubtedly correct in certain obvious respects, but not in a number of less obvious but equally important respects, in which deism stands out against both theism and atheism.
B. This part is a plea for unity among the various deism-related schools of thought, including deism itself, pandeism, panendeism, pantheism and panentheism.

A. Deism Opposed to Both Theism and Atheism

Let's start with some brief definitions:

- **Theism** is belief in a personal creator God, as found in most conventional religions.
- **Atheism** is rejection of belief in a God, deity or creator of any kind.
- **Deism** is belief in an impersonal creator God who does not become involved in the day-to-day affairs of the world. It must be emphasized, however, that deism is not a church or a religion and has no dogma, creed or single set of

beliefs. There are wide variations between the beliefs of individual deists.

The Conventional Alignment

It is easy to see why theism and atheism are normally regarded as diametric opposites, with deism somewhere between the two:

Creation

Theism or conventional religion believes that the universe was created by a supernatural being, an eternal God. Atheism completely rejects the concept of creation in favor of some sort of naturalistic explanation, commonly a 'Big Bang' bringing the universe into existence, followed after billions of years by the ill-explained appearance of life on earth, and then Darwinian evolution by natural selection. Some religions accept a similar pattern of development to that of the atheists, with the important difference that the 'Big Bang' and the further developments are seen as mechanisms controlled by a personal God. Pope Pius XII of the Roman Catholic Church waxed lyrical about the Big Bang as long ago as 1951. The current Pope, Francis, has similarly remarked that: "The Big Bang, which is today posited as the origin of the world, does not contradict the divine act of creation; rather, it requires it." And: "Evolution of nature is not inconsistent with the notion of creation because evolution presupposes the creation of beings which evolve" (*Catholic Herald*, 31 October 2014). Some Christians have rejected the Big Bang and evolution in favor of 'creationism,' the belief that the universe, life and all subsequent variations originated "from specific acts of divine creation" (https://en.wikipedia. org/wiki/Creationism). So, where does deism stand in this intellectual minefield? Slap in the middle—in favor of creation but against creationism and also against the atheists' belief in purely automatic development.

Divine power

Conventional religion believes that God is omnipotent and omniscient, although there is a long-recognized logical contradiction between these two qualities, which the 'new atheists' like Richard Dawkins gleefully exploit to the full. For, if God knows everything, then he must already know what he himself is going to do in the future, which ties his hands as far as his future actions are concerned. So he can't be omnipotent as well as omniscient. (See Arnheim, *The God Book*, 2015, p. 61.) Conventional religion nevertheless still tends to cling to a belief in these dual qualities of the godhead. Atheism of course rejects both, as it rejects the existence of any kind of God in the first place. Deism is again in a middle position, believing in a creator but eschewing a belief that that creator is involved in the day-to-day affairs of the world.

Afterlife

Belief in an afterlife gives conventional religion a more powerful hold over its adherents than anything else. Religion resorts to the afterlife to solve the otherwise intractable problem of reward and punishment. Most religions preach acceptance of a certain creed or set of beliefs coupled with a code of ethics and sometimes also elaborate rituals. Worshipers are taught that observance of and obedience to these norms will be rewarded and disobedience will be punished. But when? To the cynical observer who objects that good often goes unrewarded and evil unpunished religion has a ready answer: justice will be meted out in the afterlife—those deserving a reward will go to heaven, while those deserving punishment will go to hell. Islam promises *jannah* ('paradise,' literally 'garden') to the faithful after death, including the companionship of more than one *houri* (literally 'gazelle-eyed woman'). Atheism simply rejects the whole concept of an afterlife, which might disappoint some while providing relief probably to the majority of its adherents. Hence the slogan emblazoned on buses in the British and European Atheist Bus Campaign of 2009: "There's probably no God. Now stop worrying and enjoy your life" (https://humanism.org.uk/about/ atheist-bus-campaign/). The point here is of course to free people from the fear of fire and brimstone after death. Some deists adopt a similar position to atheism on this, while others believe in some sort of immanent but impersonal spirit surviving as part of nature after death. This kind of belief is well represented by the haunting poem "Do Not Stand at My Grave and Weep" composed in 1932 by Mary Elizabeth Frye:

> Do not stand at my grave and weep.
> I am not there; I do not sleep.
> I am a thousand winds that blow.
> I am the diamond glints on snow.
> I am the sunlight on ripened grain.
> I am the gentle autumn rain.
> When you awaken in the morning's hush
> I am the swift uplifting rush
> Of quiet birds in circled flight.
> I am the soft stars that shine at night.
> Do not stand at my grave and cry;
> I am not there; I did not die.
> (https://en.wikipedia.org/wiki/Do_Not_Stand_at_My_Grave_and_Weep)

The Revolutionary New Alignment

So much for the conventional view of deism as somewhere midway between theism and atheism, which holds good in regard to the areas covered above. Paradoxically, however, there are certain other important respects in which deism is quite distinct from both theism and atheism, which are bunched together. *This article is the first place that I know of to recognize this dichotomy.*

Proof of truth

Theism, atheism and deism all claim to be 'true.' However, belief in theism depends on a leap of faith and cannot actually be proved. This is a particular problem with Christianity, which stands or falls on the historicity of certain claims for Jesus, notably his virgin birth, his miracles, the claim that he rose from the dead and, above all, the claim that he was the 'Christ' (the Messiah), the 'Son of God,' and indeed part of a threefold godhead—for none of which is there any reliable historical evidence. (See Chapter 6 of *The God Book*.)

Islam is a lot easier to accept than Christianity in terms of its creed, which makes only two claims: that there is only one God and that Muhammad is his prophet. The problem here is the one that affects any belief in a personal God—the absence of any evidence that a supernatural being out there monitors and controls the day-to-day events on earth.

Atheism, on the other hand, prides itself on its rationality. Richard Dawkins, arguably the high priest of the new atheism, has established the so-called 'Richard Dawkins Foundation for Reason and Science.' Yet, as I show in *The God Book*, Dawkins's writings are tainted by error and logical fallacies. (See Chapter 2 of *The God Book*.) The subtitle of Dawkins's *Blind Watchmaker* is a good example, reading: "Why the evidence of evolution reveals a universe without design." In fact, however, the theory of evolution says nothing whatsoever about the coming into existence of the universe or the origin of life, only about variations that have occurred in living organisms, therefore *after* the emergence of life on earth. As Sir Fred Hoyle, the famous scientist (and, incidentally, a member of my Cambridge college), put it in characteristic style: "The Darwinian theory is correct in the small, but not in the large. Rabbits come from other slightly different rabbits, not from either soup or potatoes. Where they come from in the first place is a problem yet to be solved, like much else of a cosmic scale" (Hoyle, *The Mathematics of Evolution*,

1999. See Arnheim, *The God Book*, p. 71).

What about deism? Deism also lays claim to truth. Like atheism, deism prides itself on its rationality, but the difference is that its claim is far stronger and much less strident than that of the new atheism. I particularly like Einstein's simile between the universe and a vast library in answer to an interviewer's question about God:

> Your question [about God] is the most difficult in the world. It is not a question I can answer simply with yes or no. I am not an Atheist. I do not know if I can define myself as a Pantheist. The problem involved is too vast for our limited minds. May I not reply with a parable? The human mind, no matter how highly trained, cannot grasp the universe. We are in the position of a little child entering a huge library whose walls are covered to the ceiling with books in many different tongues. The child knows that someone must have written those books. It does not know who or how. It does not understand the languages in which they are written. The child notes a definite plan in the arrangement of the books, a mysterious order which it does not comprehend, but only dimly suspects. That, it seems to me, is the attitude of the human mind, even the greatest and most cultured, towards God. We see a universe marvelously arranged, obeying certain laws, but we understand the laws only dimly. Our limited minds cannot grasp the mysterious force that sways the constellations.
> (Quoted in George S. Viereck, *Glimpses of the Great*, 1930, p. 372f. See Arnheim, *The God Book*, p. 43)

The first thing to notice in this important passage is (*pace* Richard Dawkins) Einstein's categorical denial of being an atheist, but he is not sure what label to adopt. He tentatively suggests that he might be a pantheist, under the influence of Spinoza, whom he goes on to describe in the same interview as "the greatest of modern philosophers, because he is the first philosopher who deals with the soul and the body as one, not as two separate things." Yet, on the basis of his graphic library simile Einstein could equally well be a deist or a pandeist as a pantheist. (See Part B of this article.)

While vainly trying to claim Einstein as one of their own (see below), the new atheists sensibly stop short of defining Charles Darwin as an atheist—even while worshiping at his shrine and invoking his name at every opportunity. Darwin's rejection of atheism certainly comes through loud and clear, but, like Einstein, he was modest enough to admit puzzlement over the appropriate classification of his position on the big question. In an important letter written in 1860 to his friend Asa Gray, the leading American botanist of the day, Darwin, having rejected atheism, goes on to forswear theism as well:

> There seems to me too much misery in the world. I cannot persuade myself that a beneficent and omnipotent God would have designedly created the Ichneumonidae [wasps] with the express intention of their [larvae] feeding within the living bodies of caterpillars, or that a cat should play with mice. Not believing this, I see no necessity in the belief that the eye was expressly designed. On the other hand I cannot anyhow be contented to view this wonderful universe, and especially the nature of man, and to conclude that everything is the result of brute force. I am inclined to look at everything as resulting from designed laws, with the details, whether good or bad, left to the working out of what we may call chance. Not that this notion at all satisfies me. I feel most deeply that the whole subject is too profound for the human intellect. A dog might as well speculate on the mind of Newton.
> (Quoted in Arnheim, *The God Book*, p. 77)

Darwin's distress at cat-and-mouse play reads rather strangely coming from a believer in the survival of the fittest! Yet it was enough to knock on the head Darwin's belief in "a beneficent and omnipotent God"—or, in other words, the personal God of conventional religion. Although self-doubt made Darwin sometimes label himself as an agnostic, his position in the quoted passage and elsewhere is closer to that of deism: "I am inclined to look at everything as resulting from designed laws, with the details, whether good or bad, left to the working out of what we may call chance." Darwin's diffidence and genuine modesty, similar to that of Einstein, is encapsulated in the wonderful evocative phrase: "A dog might as well speculate on the mind of Newton."

We can only conclude that deism has a stronger basis of truth than either theism or atheism.

Authority

A tactic often used in order to bolster up a weak argument is to resort to authority. The trouble is that this type of argument is only as strong as the authority on which it rests, and trying to hang a weak argument on some big name is a common, but serious, fallacy, especially if there is a mismatch between the argument and the authority on which it purports to rely. (See *The God Book*, Chapter 2, "A Fistful of Fallacies".)

Theism depends almost entirely on unsubstantiated 'authority,' notably scripture. So strong is the traditional trust in these writings that to this day there are phrases in colloquial English such as 'Gospel truth'—not to mention the custom of taking oaths in court on the Bible, Qur'an or other supposedly sacred book. The reliability of the contents of these books cannot be verified by any outside sources. Much of what they contain is myth, legend or propaganda—or internal contradictions, like the two completely divergent genealogies for Jesus given in the Christian Bible, one in Matthew and the other in Luke. None of the authors of the Christian Bible ever met Jesus. The earliest of the Gospels, Mark, was only written about 40 years after Jesus' death, and even Paul's Epistles date from no earlier than about 20 years after Jesus' death. (See Chapter 6 of *The God Book*.)

Atheism of course rejects all scripture out of hand, but, surprisingly enough, relies on authority to bolster up its thin logical underpinnings (see above). Richard Dawkins provided a particularly amusing example of this by excitedly chasing after a misinterpreted Einstein letter in the desperate hope of posthumously recruiting the great man to the atheist cause—in the face of Einstein's categorical rejection of the atheist label. (See Arnheim, *The God Book*, p. 40ff.)

By contrast with theism and atheism, deism does not rely on authority at all and does not need to—although it can boast an impressive roll-call of adherents, including such prominent Americans as Benjamin Franklin, George Washington, Thomas Jefferson, James Madison and Mark Twain.

Here too, therefore, deism is on one side of the fence, not relying on any authority other than reason, while theism and atheism are both on the other side of the fence—theism being wholly dependent on 'authority' while atheism is anxious to latch on to some big name in order to bolster its weak claims to rationality.

Proselytism

Creed religions such as Christianity and Islam came into existence by dint of conversion, and they still depend on missionary zeal and proselytism to quite a large extent today. For example, the Mormons (or, more formally, the Church of Jesus Christ of Latter-day Saints) require their young members to go on an unpaid 'mission,' typically for two years for males and 18 months for females, in order to recruit new converts. And receiving a knock on the door from a couple of Jehovah's Witnesses on a recruiting spree is a common experience in many countries around the world. Not that the older Christian denominations can be accused of lagging behind in the race for converts. Hence, for example, the busy papal schedule of international trips. (It is worth noting that, by contrast with *creed* religions, *communal* religions like Judaism, Hinduism and Japanese Shinto do not actively seek, or even encourage, converts. See Chapter 4 of *The God Book* for this classification.)

Until the 'new atheism' reared its head in recent years atheism was not particularly vocal and was quite largely on the defensive. But that has all changed now, and the new atheism is not only more strident but also quite aggressive. In a 2007 talk titled "Militant Atheism" Richard Dawkins boldly declared that "evolution is fundamentally hostile to religion," adding that religious evolutionists like the Pope were "deluding themselves" by thinking otherwise. (See Arnheim, *The God Book*, p. 81.) The Richard Dawkins Foundation actually uses the word 'mission' in regard to its aim of "advancing secularism," or, in other words, combating religion.

Deism, together with its related beliefs, has never been in the missionary business. This is good as far as toleration is concerned (see below), but bad in terms of success!

So here again deism is on one side of the divide while most theistic religions together with the new atheism are on the other.

Religious toleration

Since the rise of Christianity religious toleration has been in short supply in the world. The litany of persecutions, burnings at the stake and religious wars is practically endless. Even the schism between the Roman Catholic and Eastern Orthodox Churches, dating from 1054, has still not been healed. The wordy "Joint Declaration" between Pope Francis and Russian Orthodox Patriarch Kirill of Moscow, signed in Cuba on 12 February 2016, gets no closer to reunification than the pious hope that it would occur "in God's own time" (en.radiovaticana.va/news/2016/02/12/joint_declaration_of_pope_francis_and_patriarch_kirill/1208117). Of course, this schism pales into insignificance in the face of the continuing or indeed escalating bloody conflict between Sunni and Shia Muslims.

The new atheism is not noted for its tolerance either. The late rabid atheist Christopher Hitchens in his book *God Is Not Great* screamed "Religion kills," not realizing that his hyperbole revealed him to be every bit as intolerant as the butt of his attacks. And Richard Dawkins has described religious faith as "one of the world's worst great evils, comparable to the smallpox virus but harder to eradicate." And: "I regard Islam as one of the great evils in the world." (See Arnheim, *The God Book*, pp. 3 and 40.)

It is wrong to blame religion for all the conflicts fought in its name. The 'troubles' in Northern Ireland are a case in point, which were finally ended by the so-called 'Good Friday Agreement' of 1998, a political settlement for what was essentially a political conflict. Underlying even the schism between Sunni and Shia Islam is an ethnic divide between Iranians and non-Iranians, Iranians being non-Arabs and non-Turks. Iran was deliberately switched from Sunni to Shia by Shah Ismail I (reigned 1501–24), who was intent on giving Iran a religious and national identity distinct from the Ottoman Turks and the Arabs, both of whom were Sunni. (See Arnheim, *The God Book*, p. 171.)

However, placing a religious label on a conflict tends to intensify it.

But deism stands above and apart from any kind of conflict or intolerance of any kind. Once again, therefore, deism and its related beliefs stand on one side of the divide, with both most theistic religions and atheism on the other side.

Conclusion

Tying the threads together, we can only conclude that deism and its related beliefs are superior to most theistic religions and atheism in these important respects: proof of truth, non-reliance on authority, and toleration. Deism and its related beliefs also stand apart from both theistic creed religions and the new atheism in not actively seeking converts, but this has also undoubtedly resulted in deism's weakness in terms of numbers and influence.

B. A Plea for Unity

Most people know the meaning of the word 'atheism' and many also understand the meaning of 'agnosticism,' but it is only comparatively few who would be able to define 'theism' or 'deism,' let alone 'pandeism,' 'panendeism,' 'pantheism' or 'panentheism.'

The definition of these terms is by no means uncontroversial, but it may help to at least attempt a simple differentiation between them. The first thing to note is that all these terms are based either on the word *deus* or the word *theos,* the former being the Latin word for 'God' and the latter the Greek equivalent. However, whether a belief is based on the one rather than the other provides no clue whatsoever as to its meaning.

- **Theism:** Belief in a 'personal' God—an omnipotent and omniscient creator God as found in most conventional religions, who metes out rewards and punishments, is responsive to prayer and supplications, controls the day-to-day affairs of the world and the afterlife, and (usually) is capable of working miracles.
- **Deism:** Belief in an 'impersonal' creator God who does not get involved in the day-to-day affairs of the world. Beyond this there is a wide variety of beliefs among people who regard themselves as deists.
- **Pandeism:** Belief "that the creator deity became the universe and ceased to exist as a separate and conscious entity...It is one of several subsets of deism" (https://en.wikipedia.org/wiki/ Pandeism).
- **Pantheism:** "The belief that the Universe (or nature as the totality of everything) is identical with divinity, or that every-

thing composes an all-encompassing, immanent god" (https:// en.wikipedia.org/wiki/Pantheism). Pantheism is often associated with the name of Spinoza, although he himself never used the term and actually specifically denied that he identified God with Nature (*Correspondence of Benedict de Spinoza*, 2009, letter 73).

- **Panentheism:** "A belief system which posits that the divine—whether as a single God, number of gods, or other form of 'cosmic animating force'—interpenetrates every part of the universe and extends, timelessly (and, presumably, spacelessly) beyond it. Unlike pantheism, which holds that the divine and the universe are identical, panentheism maintains a distinction between the divine and non-divine and the significance of both" (https://en.wikipedia.org/wiki/Panentheism). Spinoza is sometimes labelled a panentheist rather than a pantheist.
- **Panendeism:** "Panendeism combines deism with panentheism, the belief that the universe is part of God, but not all of God. A component of panendeism is 'experiential metaphysics'—the idea that a mystical component exists within the framework of panendeism, allowing the seeker to experience a relationship to Deity through meditation, prayer or some other type of communion. This is a major departure from classical deism" (https://en.wikipedia.org/wiki/Deism#Panendeism).

These are only basic definitions. Besides the differences *between* these belief systems, there also are many variations *within* each of them. Many ingenious and convoluted arguments have been advanced supporting one individual's interpretation of one of these belief systems as against others. Subtle, fine distinctions are drawn and sophisticated conclusions advanced.

But, at the end of the day, is it really possible to prove that, say, panendeism is superior to pantheism, or whether panentheism provides a more definitive solution than either? I am constantly struck by the modesty and genuine humility of those towering intellects, Darwin and Einstein, to mention but two. As we saw in Part A of this article, both rejected atheism but were uncertain about how to characterize their beliefs beyond that. Einstein's wonderment at the universe as a vast library is an abiding image in my mind, together with Darwin's similar view of "everything as resulting from designed laws, with the details, whether good or bad, left to the working out of what we may call chance."

Does this make Darwin or Einstein a deist, a pandeist, a pantheist, or what? I believe it would be a mistake to try to be too precise. For my own part, I could not swear hand on heart that one of these worthy concepts is truer or more correct than the others. The distinctions between them, though often overpowering in the eyes of their adherents, may appear to the objective observer to be distinctions without a difference.

Let us make sure that the differences between these various schools of thought do not come to resemble a debate about how many angels can dance on the head of a pin—and do not result in a schism like that between Roman Catholics and Orthodox Christians over the word 'filioque.'

Let the wonderment, modesty and genuine humility of the two towering intellects of Darwin and Einstein serve as our guide, recognizing always the puniness of man's mental powers against those of God. In Darwin's words: "A dog might as well speculate on the mind of Newton."

Pantheistic God-Concepts: Ancient, Contemporary, Popular, and Plausible Alternatives to Classical Theism

Raphael Lataster

Raphael Lataster is a professionally secular PhD researcher at the University of Sydney (Studies in Religion) and teaches on religion at various institutions. His main research interests include philosophy of religion, Christian origins, logic, Bayesian reasoning, sustainability, and alternative god-concepts such as pantheism and pandeism. He is also an avid rock climber, a card-carrying Discordian pope, and an officially ordained Dudeist priest. Raphael wrote his Master's thesis on Jesus ahistoricity theories, concluding that historical and Bayesian reasoning justifies a skeptical attitude towards the 'Historical Jesus'. For his doctoral work, Raphael is analyzing the major philosophical arguments for God's existence (as argued by William Lane Craig, Richard Swinburne and Thomas Aquinas), attempts to demonstrate the logical improbability of theism, explores the theological tendencies of philosophy of religion, and considers the plausibility of pantheistic worldviews. An earlier form of this chapter was published as an academic paper in Literature & Aesthetics *in 2015.*[1]

Introduction

Scholarly arguments for God's existence in Western academia tend to focus on the Judeo-Christian god, and unsurprisingly, are often proffered by those scholars who personally profess the Christian faith. Respected and influential Christian philosopher of religion Alvin Plantinga goes so far as to implore his fellow believing philosophers to use their skills in advocating and promoting the Judeo-Christian God.[2] However, the majority of philosophical arguments for God's existence, including

Plantinga's lauded ontological argument, do not successfully identify the hypothetical god in question as any particular god (for example, the god of theism or the god of deism), let alone the Judeo-Christian deity.[3] For example, William Lane Craig's *Kalam* cosmological argument merely indicates a creator (actually, it only indicates a cause); it does not identify the creator, or specify that the creator is itself uncreated.[4] Fine-tuning and moral arguments only indicate some sort of design in the universe. Plantinga's ontological argument indicates a maximally great being; again, the argument does not specify the identity of this being. Additionally, Plantinga acknowledges the grave error of those who wish to use his argument as a 'proof' of God, by acknowledging the difference between epistemic possibility and actual or physical possibility.[5]

This unspecific nature leaves open the possibility that even if such arguments were sound, they could 'prove' the existence of another god, even one that is a different type of god, and incompatible with the preferred god of these Christian theological philosophers. While theistic religions purport a separation between creator and created, pantheism provides a monistic view: all is one, and all is god. This leads to many important differences between the two mutually exclusive views, further leading to an intellectual conflict. There are a number of forms of pantheism, which can be found from antiquity to among contemporary sources, which shall be explored. Many New Age and contemporary Pagan religions are pantheistic to some extent. Furthermore, pantheism, as relative to classical theism (itself one of the many possible monotheisms), seems to fit many philosophical arguments for God's existence equally well, and may even be a logically superior possibility. Brief discussions on logical plausibility reveal many pantheisms to be relatively simple, and plausible, God-conceptions. In referring to God, gender neutrality has been considered.

Various Pantheisms, and Their Differences from Monotheisms

Etymologically, 'generic' pantheism merely asserts that God is everything and everything is God. There are also naturalistic forms of pantheism, in which God is essentially a redundant concept, reduced to a synonym for the natural world; in this view there are no supernatural entities.[6] One particularly interesting form of pantheism is pandeism, which involves a creative act that is somewhat similar to that in traditional monotheism. In pandeistic scenarios, there is a powerful deity who sacrificed itself in order to create the universe. In this case, one possibility is that the deity is not fully 'consumed' by the creative process, and some remnant remains which can be described by panendeism, a conflation of deism and panentheism. The latter is the view that the universe is and is in God, but that God is yet greater or more substantial. Despite the great variety of pantheisms, they tend to share one crucial element, which leads to numerous differences from monotheistic traditions: the Universe, and all that lies within, is God. That is, it consists of divine 'stuff.'

All these God-conceptions share the idea that God and the universe are of the same substance, or essence. Even in panentheism, a seeming attempt to continue positing a 'superior' and 'separate' god, the creation is of the same essence as the creator. This directly opposes traditionally theistic notions of transcendence, that the creation is separate from God.[7] One example of the incompatibility of these opposing views is demonstrated by the Judeo-Christian traditions' prohibitions on idolatry.[8] If all is God, it would be counter-intuitive to outlaw reverence towards trees, heroes, statues and other objects. And while the God of theism is personal, the pantheistic God is possibly impersonal; in fact, under pandeism, it may be considered that the God that did exist no longer exists as God, and humankind is largely left to its own devices (as in deism). Another significant difference is that theism generally implores adherents to seek and to please God. In many forms of pantheism such action is unnecessary and even fruitless. For God is within, and humankind's only 'requirement' would be to *be*; seemingly all a pantheistic God would desire of us, if anything.

Various forms of pantheism, such as naturalistic pantheism and pandeism, provide some measure of support to the skepticism of modern secularists who sometimes point to the lack of scientific evidence for God, with a strong focus on monotheistic gods and associated fundamentalisms.[9] The clear lack of dogmatic adherence to a particular god in many pantheisms may foster greater religious tolerance, and could lead to wider acceptance of non-theistic and possibly more open religions such as Buddhism, Daoism, or indigenous animisms. Pantheistic worldviews tend to be very inclusive, and could thus have positive societal impacts. Rather than teaching that there exists a special race of people, from a special species, chosen by the one true God, pantheists understand that 'all are one.' God does not choose one people/species, and command them to kill or subjugate other peoples/species who do not please him/her, as may be the case with certain incarnations of classical theism.[10] Rather, all people are God. All species are God. And all that is, is God. A worldview that encourages reverence for humanity and nature may increase the chances of cooperation, egalitarianism and unity, and could result in ecological benefits.[11]

Ancient Examples

While theism enjoys a rich history, which extends beyond the origins of Christianity, pantheistic concepts too are not without historical precedent. It is relatively easy to find pantheistic ideas among early indigenous, animistic and Pagan traditions; the identifying of divinity in animals, plants and even inanimate objects, and reverence for the natural world are found in many early religious traditions and are compatible with pantheism.

Certain (and early) streams of Indian religions (such as Advaita Vedanta), however, express unambiguous and clear pantheistic, or panentheistic, teachings via the concept of Brahman.[12] Brahman is reality; all that exists is incorporated into it. Brahman is indistinguishable from the natural world, leading some Hindus to assert *aham Brahmasmi*, "I am Brahman."[13] Panentheism, a pantheistic variant entailing a world contained within God rather than being necessarily equivalent to God, is commonly found among the ancient South Asian traditions.[14] The Chinese concept of the *Dao* also seems synonymous with the all-encompassing pantheistic 'divine' and may have influenced Zen Buddhism.[15] From the *Daodejing*, attributed to Laozi, we find that the Dao, apparently the essence of the pantheistic God, is eternal and all-encompassing; said to be older and greater than 'God' or the universe.[16] From another influential Daoist philosopher, Zhuangzi, "The universe and I exist together, and all things and I are one."[17] Zhuangzi further explained that the Dao is everywhere, even in the "excrement and urine."[18] Pantheistic elements can also be found among certain—often 'mystical'—streams of traditionally theistic religions, such as Judaism, Christianity and Islam.[19] There are also various Chinese folk myths about Pàngu, a primordial being who created the universe and simultaneously destroyed himself, with his body parts said to have formed many aspects of our world.[20] That this pandeistic concept of the god that became the universe could be a misinterpretation of the original texts, does not diminish the truth that the concept had taken root, perhaps as an elaborated myth, and in any case there is a clear indication of a divine, transformative process. The motif of the world being formed from the bodies of slain powerful beings can also be found among Babylonian, Scandinavian, and Polynesian myths, demonstrating the antiquity of these concepts.[21]

Modern Expressions

Pantheism is not merely an ancient God-model; it can also be found in contemporary contexts. New Religious Movements, for example New Age or contemporary Pagan religions, often contain many pantheistic elements, such as an all-pervading divinity, interconnectedness, tolerance, and reverence for nature.[22] In responding to physicist Leonard Mlodinow on the *Larry King Live* television program, New Age guru and best-selling author Deepak Chopra demonstrated his pantheistic, or specifically pandeistic, worldview:

> In fact, he says in the book that at least 10 to the power of 500 universes could possibly exist in super position of possibility at this level, which to me suggests an omniscient being. The only difference I have was God did not create the universe, God became the universe.[23]

Academics from varying fields have either noted modern pantheistic trends, or otherwise argued for pantheism. Religious Studies scholar Carole Cusack asserts that the West has gradually become 'Easternized,'[24] with a move from its more traditional values, such as monotheism, to foreign concepts such as deep ecology and pantheism.[25] Many scholars have identified the decline of theism in the West, particularly in Europe, and the increasing acceptance of religious plurality and alternative spiritualities.[26] In an earlier article, Cusack noted the pantheistic tendencies of the Pagan Church of All Worlds, particularly the concept that is so offensive to many monotheists, 'Thou art God,' as well as themes of unity. Cusack ends the article with a possibly hopeful idea: as early Christians, Buddhists, Zoroastrians and Daoists may have been unable to predict the degree of their respective creed's global penetration, so too might pantheistic new religious movements become influential in future.[27]

Theoretical physicist Paola Zizzi also seems to support a

pantheistic view, arguing that at the end of cosmic inflation (occurring almost simultaneously with the Big Bang), the universe could have had a "primordial conscious experience" in which the universe 'selected' one out of many possible universes.[28] Such a possibility should not be viewed as particularly irrational, given that many small parts of the universe actually are 'conscious.' There is no logical reason to dismiss the possibility that the universe itself is, or was at some point, conscious. This is further made plausible by various contemporary theories on consciousness, and eventually, on 'life.' Cognitive scientist Marvin Minsky, for example, theorizes that there is nothing particularly significant about consciousness; that thoughts and emotions are merely products of natural and physical processes.[29] In other words, human beings are not necessarily as significant as classical theologians might have us believe. We are merely machines, made of the same materials as mountains, oceans, stars, and recalling the humble Daoist thinkers, smegma and shit.

Astrophysicist Bernard Haisch recently espoused a pandeistic worldview, implying that it combines scientific knowledge with more inclusive religious ideas.[30] Physicist Albert Einstein personally held some sort of pantheistic worldview: "I believe in Spinoza's God who reveals himself in the orderly harmony of what exists, not in a God who concerns himself with fates and actions of human beings."[31] Historian Arnold Toynbee, who took special interest in the rise and fall of civilizations, went so far as to argue that if humankind did not move from monotheistic faith towards pantheistic ideals, self-destruction could result.[32] Astronomer and physical cosmologist Carl Sagan seemed to espouse a naturalistic pantheism in his popular book, *Pale Blue Dot* (which also alluded to the relative insignificance of humankind):

A religion old or new, that stressed the magnificence of the

> universe as revealed by modern science, might be able to draw forth reserves of reverence and awe hardly tapped by the conventional faiths. Sooner or later, such a religion will emerge.[33]

Pantheism has also been made accessible to modern audiences, through films and popular books. One example is the film *Avatar* (2009), which presents themes of interconnectedness, nature-worship, sustainability (balance), simplicity, and respect for all.[34] One interesting scene explains that, much like an impersonal pantheistic God (and as a not-so-subtle critique of theism), the Great Mother "does not take sides." *Avatar* has become the highest-grossing film of all time, which may have more to do with the West becoming increasingly receptive towards 'Eastern' and pantheistic ideals, and less to do with its award-winning special effects.[35] In his bestselling book, *The God Delusion*, biologist Richard Dawkins briefly mentions naturalistic pantheism, describing it as "sexed-up atheism," while philosopher Martin Yalcin somewhat similarly sees pantheism as "a version of theism that has been naturalized, but only half-heartedly."[36] While the term 'pantheism' may be unknown to most, its principles and unifying ideals seem to resonate deeply with those dissatisfied with a contemporary or consumerist lifestyle.

The Logical Plausibility of Pantheistic Models

Philosophical arguments for God's existence in the analytic tradition are often put forth by Christian philosophers of religion, in support of the theistic (and more specifically, the Judeo-Christian) God. Even a cursory glance over these arguments makes clear that not only do the majority of these arguments not identify the theistic god in question, but they do not necessitate that the god in question must be theistic (or even monotheistic) in the first place. In his apologetic *magnum opus*, William Lane Craig presents a clear and thorough cumulative case for God's existence.[37] He presents an argument from contingency, his noted *Kalam* cosmological argument, a teleological argument from fine-tuning, an axiomatic argument, an ontological argument, a quasi-argument from personal experience, and finally his Christological argument. Respectively, these arguments conclude that there exists at least one necessary being, the universe has a cause of its existence, the universe was designed, there is (or was) an absolute moral law-giver, a maximally great being exists, some supernatural entity speaks directly to believers like Craig, and that Jesus was resurrected. These arguments are typically unsound, but can be assumed sound in order to entertain the possibility of various gods and God-conceptions.

Apart from Craig's Christological argument (likewise Swinburne's supposedly Bayesian Christological argument), these arguments do not specify that the god in question must be Yahweh, the god of the Judeo-Christian religions.[38] Nor do these conclusions necessitate that the god in question must be of the theistic tradition. A pandeistic god, for example, could be a necessary and maximally great being, who created and designed (in terms of intelligent life and moral standards) the universe, and whose spiritual essence manifests itself as miracles and 'personal communications with the divine.' Even when considering Christological arguments, granting the resurrection of Jesus still leaves open the possibility that the god in question is Zeus, Odin, or some pantheistic god. In the pandeistic example above, Jesus may have been more in tune with his spiritual and ultimately divine essence than most, allowing him to overcome death. Another type of pantheistic and maximally great god could also have shown mercy towards Jesus and other great prophets, despite the great confusion that would result (that it was the lesser or even non-existing god, Yahweh, that raised Jesus from the dead).

Also, there is nothing in these arguments to suggest that all the conclusions must apply to the same entity. There may be a maximally great entity, for example, that created a Demiurge-like being, which then created the universe, while her 'sister-god' designed or refined it and provided moral instruction. There are all manner of possibilities with numbers and even numbers of 'levels' of gods, similar to the complex hierarchy of divine entities found in John Milton's *Paradise Lost*.[39] It can be concluded that the generic and specific arguments for God's existence leave open the possibility of a pantheistic-type god, as well as a theistic god. Furthermore, there may be a case to be made that pantheism, or some variant thereof, is the more plausible view. One way to demonstrate this may be through consistent application of Plantinga's (which Craig summarizes in *Reasonable Faith*) lauded ontological argument.

Would a Maximally Great Being Be Pantheistic?

The ontological argument is perhaps the only argument presented by Christian philosophers of religion that moves the discussion from merely some creator, designer or moral-lawgiver, to the greatest being that exists, or specifically, the greatest being imaginable and possible; what many believers and non-believers alike would consider to be God. Plantinga's version of the ontological argument essentially states that if it possible for a "maximally great being" (God) to exist, it must exist in some possible world and in every possible world, which therefore means that it exists in our actual world.[40] There are problems with this argument, such as the first premise being merely epistemically possible, in the sense that we do not know if such a being could/does exist or not, so the truth could be either, but it is not demonstrably physically or actually possible. Plantinga himself admits to this limitation, only noting that the concept does not seem irrational, and concedes that his argument is not a 'proof' of God, before alluding to his reformed epistemological notion that belief in God is rational and warranted, without the need for proof. If the argument were assumed to be sound, it would be interesting to identify what sort of God would exist, if such a maximally great God does exist.

Though Plantinga is of the opinion that this argument demonstrates the rationality of his belief in God, it does not specify the Judeo-Christian god, nor does it demonstrate the plausibility of classical theism. In fact, the subject of this argument may be a god who is greater than the Judeo-Christian god. For example, various passages in the Jewish Scriptures possibly point to the existence of other gods, and to at least one that may be superior to Yahweh, the god of Judeo-Christianity, if the antiquity and reliability of the Septuagint is upheld.[41] More interesting however, is the God-concept of pantheism. While a theistic god such as Yahweh could be conceived as the 'greatest possible being' (though it may contradict the Jewish Scriptures which espouse him), the all-inclusive God of pantheism can also be conceived. The question is whether this pantheistic God should or can be considered 'greater.'

According to Plantinga, 'maximal greatness' includes the properties of omniscience, omnipotence and moral perfection. While this is arbitrary, a pantheistic God could certainly demonstrate these properties. My assertion is that if the concept of 'omniessence' (not to be confused with omniscience, with *esse* being Latin for 'being') were included into this concept of 'maximal greatness,' then the traditional monotheistic God of Christianity becomes impossible, and pantheism is the only logically possible God-conception. Omniessence is a concept relating to being and existence. There is a clear separation or duality in the monotheistic worldview; there is God and there is the Creation, whether that is Earth, the known universe, or a hypothetical multiverse or 'complete description of reality.' If omniessence were a valid property of a maximally great entity, such a 'dualistic God' would not be considered maximally great.

The pantheistic God, however, incorporates the Creation, and is thus a much stronger candidate for being this maximally great entity. Interestingly, this concept of omniessence is compatible with the concept of omnipresence (which is not mentioned in Plantinga's argument) and omniscience. In fact, omniessence might be a requirement of omniscience.

Omniscience is a characteristic commonly attributed to God by philosophers of religion such as Plantinga, and also has Biblical precedent.[42] In order for an all-knowing God to know what a person feels when they burn their hand, it may not be enough for God to understand that intense heat causes pain to human beings; God might have to *be* that person, in order to acquire the experiential knowledge. If God were not that person, its experience is only theoretical and derived, rather than perceptual and immediate.[43] Philosopher William Mander (University of Oxford) agrees that on the basis of knowledge, only a pantheistic God could exist.[44] New Age theorist Neale Donald Walsch also describes his pantheistic God as creating the universe in order to experience his theoretical knowledge directly, or experientially.[45] In this case God would not merely be 'part' of the totality of all that exists; God would 'be' the totality of all that exists. And thus, omniscience could imply omniessence. Such a God seems intuitively and conceptually greater than the seemingly limited monotheistic God. And conception strikes at the very origins of the ontological argument.

One potentially critical flaw with such reasoning is that there is no established logical reason to demonstrate that an omniessent being would be necessarily greater than one that is not all-encompassing. The same could of course be said about other traditional aspects of God and maximally great beings, such as moral perfection. Of great relevance concerning Christian philosophers of religion, the concept that a 'bigger' or 'more substantial' god is a greater god may also have Biblical precedent, whereby the Judeo-Christian Scriptures equate size and/or substance with greatness, indicating that a smaller Temple or even the 'heavens' cannot contain God.[46] When 'more substance' or 'more essence' is clearly associated with greatness, it seems logical to deduce that maximal essence, or omniessence, could, if not should, be a characteristic of maximal greatness.

This point is perhaps unexpectedly conceded by contemporary theologian and philosopher LeRon Shults of the University of Agder, Norway, who claims that if God is not equivalent with the universe or the multiverse, then God and 'the world' would be parts of "the Whole."[47] God would be merely a part of the universe, as we all are; as is the humble tufted titmouse. Such a god may still exist, but may be more accurately described as a powerful extra-terrestrial, such as Lord Xenu, the intergalactic dictator of Scientology.[48] In Shults' scenario, there would be at *least one* entity that seems to be greater: the universe itself. To avoid the embarrassment that God is not the greatest being in existence, the believer would be compelled to accept the pantheistic conclusion that God is one with the Creation. A possible limitation with this view however, is the assumption that 'God plus the Creation' can be considered to be a single entity, and also the aforementioned issue that bigger is not necessarily better (such as a cake not being as sweet as the sugar that partly comprises it).

Certainly, a pantheistic god can be conceived (which lies at the heart of historical ontological arguments), and does not seem any less rational than a theistic god. Whether such a god is necessarily greater is open to discussion, largely hinging on the inclusion of 'omniessence' as a property of 'maximal greatness.' Recall that the elements that make up a 'maximally great being' were arbitrarily chosen. If the case can be made that a maximally great being must demonstrate omniessence (or even omnipresence), in addition to omnipotence, omniscience, and moral perfection, then monotheism is instantly rendered logically inferior to various forms of pantheism. Given that such ontological arguments are historically concerned with what can be imagined, logically proving that God should demonstrate omniessence may actually be unnecessary; though this would hardly be convincing to those whose beliefs do not hinge on ontological arguments.[49] Another way in which pantheism could possibly be presented as the more plausible worldview, hinges on levels of uncertainty.

Creatio Ex Nihilo

Dualistic theists, such as Swinburne and Craig, tend to accept the doctrine of *creatio ex nihilo*. If a God brought into existence the Creation (whether that be the known universe, or the totality of all that exists), it could have done this in three ways: from pre-existing material, *creatio ex materia*;[50] from God's own substance or essence, *creatio ex deo*; or from 'nothing,' *creatio ex nihilo*. Consider that *creatio ex materia* essentially serves the skeptic. If God created the cosmos from pre-existing material (actually a popular concept among process theologians), a further three possibilities are raised, with two of these being redundant. The first is that the material was produced by God, from God, leading to pantheism, and being equivalent to *creatio ex deo*. The second is that the material was produced by God from nothing, which is equivalent to *creatio ex nihilo*. These possibilities raise the same questions, albeit at another level. The third possibility presents the most interesting option. Perhaps this material is eternal, and existed independently of God; this 'material' could then serve as an 'alternative' to God. If this were the case, the precedent is set that the universe, like this pre-existing material (perhaps they are identical), could be eternal, uncaused, and independent of God. In this case, God simply is not necessary, making it difficult to 'force' God's existence by way of cosmological arguments. As this article briefly considers the relative (and not absolute) plausibility of pantheism and monotheism, *creatio ex materia* shall be ignored, with the focus being on *creatio ex nihilo* and *creatio ex deo*.

Many prominent and popular theistic and Christian philosophers of religion do hold to the concept of *creatio ex nihilo*, evidenced by Alvin Plantinga, Richard Swinburne, Paul Copan and William Lane Craig.[51] Regardless of whether certain theists accept the doctrine or not, without it, there is no rational reason to reject pantheism (or a godless and eternal reality). Indeed, there are pantheistic and even atheistic Christians, though they are typically few in number, and are not the focus of this article. There is no logical problem with the concept that an extremely powerful Creator-god created something from itself. It would certainly make content those who hold to laws of conservation (whether of matter, energy, aether, essence, or spirit), given that, pre-Creation, there is supposedly nought but God. Pantheism, or pandeism (assuming a creative act), asks us to assume that God can use part of his essence to fashion some other object. This certainly does not seem irrational, considering laws of conservation and precedent from the natural world. Many birds for example use part of themselves, their saliva, to construct nests. There is no logical reason to think that an all-powerful god could also not use part of its self to create another object.

There are, however, serious question marks over the validity of the traditional theistic and dualistic concept that God created the universe from 'nothing,' and is thus separated from it. Monotheisms that depend on *creatio ex nihilo* rely on greater uncertainty. There is no empirical precedent for anything having come from a state of absolute nothingness. Indeed, the very concept of 'nothing' is itself up for debate. When astrophysicists and cosmologists such as Lawrence Krauss discuss 'nothing,' they refer to 'something' that contains much potentiality, as noted by popular theological philosopher, William Lane Craig.[52] The scientists' view of nothing renders Creation a natural process, removing the need for a Creator-god. The theological concept of 'nothing' then seems to be merely a concept such as infinity (though that is arguable), with no obvious and tangible application in the real world. If such theologians wish to assert that God created the universe out of nothing, they must first establish that there is or was 'nothing.' This is admittedly a tough task, given that there is no philosophical or empirical evidence for the existence of 'nothing.' Indeed, proving the existence of some sort of 'absolute nothing' may be impossible, given the very existence of the person asking the question, and how 'nothing' is typically defined.

When both the existence of an incredibly powerful God and the Creation event are assumed, *creatio ex deo*, which leads to pantheism (specifically, a pandeism or a type of panentheism), requires the prospective believer to accept no more controversial premises. Not so with arguments revolving around *creatio ex nihilo* (leading to Plantinga's brand of theism), which asks the audience to accept the unproven premises that the theological concept of 'nothing' is sound, and that something can be made to arise from this 'nothing.' In a pre-Creation world, the substance dualist may believe that only God exists, prompting theologians to ponder on the location and scope of the 'nothing' and whether God, a supposedly maximally great entity, could possibly be constrained by it or a hypothetical God–nothing barrier.[53] In comparison with *creatio ex deo*, hypotheses revolving around *creatio ex nihilo* beg the question to a greater extent. Such philosophical theologians confidently assert that their unproven God created the cosmos out of unsubstantiated nothing, by way of unknown methods. The empirical and *a priori* proof for all this, including the very existence of 'nothing,' is of course, nothing. In this sense, based on current knowledge (in a quasi-Bayesian epistemological sense), pandeistic forms of pantheism could be considered to be more plausible than monotheism, and the most probable god-models, in general. I suspect that a benign form of pandeism, combining the probabilistic benefits of deism and pantheism, is the most probable god-concept or god-model of all.

However, the removal of more and more assumptions could potentially lead to the concept that there is no deity at all being the most logically plausible. Theism (at least those forms reliant on *creatio ex nihilo*), for example, relies on many assumptions, including the concept of nothing and the method by which something can come from nothing. When rejecting these unjustified assumptions, pandeism seems to be the more plausible view. For example, its lack of a personal god currently interested in human affairs coheres well with the lack of contemporary empirical evidence for such a god. And yet pandeism relies on the assumption of a creative act. Dismissing this controversial premise renders 'straight pantheism' a more plausible view still. And even this view relies on the assumption that the universe is somehow conscious or divine. Once that assumption is rejected, naturalistic pantheism or naturalism (or 'strong atheism' as some may prefer to call it) sits alone, atop the probability pyramid.

Conclusion

By surveying primary and secondary sources of ancient religions and mythologies, pantheism and its variants were shown to be ancient, and quite common, particularly in South Asia, East Asia, and among indigenous cultures. Shifting focus to the present, it became clear that our evolving modern society is becoming increasingly exposed to, and receptive of, Eastern, indigenous, and pantheistic views. Though the term 'pantheism' is not so widely disseminated, pantheistic concepts and ideals can be found in popular culture, academic writings, and New Religious Movements such as contemporary Paganism and the Church of All Worlds. The differences between pantheisms and classical theism were made obvious, with brief discussions on societal and environmental factors. It was also discovered that many influential philosophical arguments used to demonstrate the existence of a theistic god are actually generic in nature and do not necessarily imply theism; various forms of pantheism can also be deduced from these arguments' conclusions. It was further explained that more specific arguments, such as Christological arguments revolving around Jesus' alleged resurrection, could also be explained through pantheistic hypotheses.

Brief considerations of issues such as the biblically supported notion of a relation between God's size and her greatness, and also the crucial monotheistic and dualistic concept of *creatio ex nihilo* being reliant on many controversial premises, leave open the possibility that many forms of pantheism may be more probable than theism. It is surprising that such a relatively logical and inclusive worldview is given little attention by scholars and laypeople alike, especially in light of the attention accorded to the major monotheistic faiths. It is hoped that this discussion, intending to be more rational and philosophical than polemical, will play some small role in alerting the global community to the limitations of theism, and the logical plausibility and possible societal/environmental benefits of pantheisms, panentheisms, and pandeisms. Considering the abundance of scholars occupied with studying the great monotheistic faiths, coupled with the gradual decline of theism in the West, and the associated increasing tolerance towards native spiritualities and ecological theology (including the shift towards personal religiosity), it is also hoped that pantheistic religions and views will be accorded more attention in the academy.

Notes

1 See Raphael Lataster, "Pantheistic God-Concepts: Ancient, Contemporary, Popular, and Plausible Alternatives to Classical Theism," *Literature & Aesthetics*, vol. 25, no. 1 (2015), pp. 65–82.

2 Alvin Plantinga, "Advice to Christian Philosophers," *Faith and Philosophy*, vol. 1, no. 3 (1984), pp. 253–71.

3 Considerations of 'gods' in the plural and the plausibility of polytheism are beyond the scope of this article. For more on polytheism, see Raphael Lataster and Herman Philipse, "The

Problem of Polytheisms: A Serious Challenge to Theism," *International Journal for Philosophy of Religion*, pp. 1–14 (21 December 2015), available at http://link.springer.com/article/10.1007/s11153-015-9554-x.

4 William Lane Craig, *Reasonable Faith: Christian Truth and Apologetics*, 3rd ed. (Wheaton, IL: Crossway Books, 2008), p. 111.

5 Alvin Plantinga and James F. Sennett, *The Analytic Theist: An Alvin Plantinga Reader* (Grand Rapids, MI: W. B. Eerdmans, 1998), pp. 65–71.

6 World Pantheist Movement. "Commentary on the WPM belief statement," at www.pantheism.net/about/manifest-note.htm. Accessed 18 January 2013.

7 Edward Craig (ed.), *Concise Routledge Encyclopedia of Philosophy* (London: Routledge, 2013), p. 590.

8 Exodus 20:4.

9 Richard Dawkins, *The God Delusion* (London: Bantam, 2006); Christopher Hitchens, *God Is Not Great: How Religion Poisons Everything* (New York: Twelve, 2007); Christopher R. Cotter, "Consciousness Raising: The Critique, Agenda, and Inherent Precariousness of Contemporary Anglophone Atheism," *International Journal for the Study of New Religions*, vol. 2, no. 1 (2011), pp. 77–103.

10 Regina M. Schwartz, *The Curse of Cain: The Violent Legacy of Monotheism* (Chicago, IL: University of Chicago Press, 1997); Hector Avalos, *Fighting Words: The Origins of Religious Violence* (Amherst, NY: Prometheus Books, 2005).

11 W. S. Urquhart, "The Fascination of Pantheism," *International Journal of Ethics*, vol. 21, no. 3 (1911), p. 323; Michael P. Levine, "Pantheism, Ethics and Ecology," *Environmental Values*, vol. 3, no. 2 (1994), pp. 121–38; Robert S. Corrington, "Deep Pantheism," *Journal for the Study of Religion, Nature and Culture*, vol. 1, no. 4 (2007), pp. 503–7.

12 W. S. Urquhart, "The Fascination of Pantheism," *International Journal of Ethics*, vol. 21, no. 3 (1911), p. 313.

13 Ted Peters, "Models of God," *Philosophia*, vol. 35, no. 3 (2007), p. 281.

14 Ellen Stansell and Stephen H. Phillips, "Hartshorne and Indian Panentheism," *Sophia*, vol. 49, no. 2 (2010), pp. 285–95. For more examples, including a defense of the plausibility of panentheism relative to monotheism or classical theism, see Raphael Lataster, "The Attractiveness of Panentheism—a Reply to Benedikt Paul Göcke," *Sophia*, vol. 53, no. 3 (2014), pp. 389–95; and Raphael Lataster, "Theists Misrepresenting Panentheism—Another Reply to Benedikt Paul Göcke," *Sophia*, vol. 54, no. 1 (2015), pp. 93–8.

15 Marty Heitz, "Knocking on Heaven's Door: Meister Eckhart and Zhuangzi on the Breakthrough," *Dao*, vol. 6, no. 1 (2007), p. 57; Merv Fowler, *Zen Buddhism: Beliefs and Practices* (Eastbourne: Sussex Academic Press, 2005), p. 79.

16 *Daodejing* 4, 25; Wing-Tsit Chan (ed.), *A Source Book in Chinese Philosophy* (Princeton, NJ: Princeton University Press, 1963), p. 152.

17 *A Source Book in Chinese Philosophy*, p. 186.

18 *A Source Book in Chinese Philosophy*, p. 203.

19 Nils Bjorn Kvastad, "Pantheism and Mysticism, Part I," *Sophia*, vol. 14, no. 2 (1975), pp. 1–15; G. J. Stokes, "Gnosticism and Modern Pantheism," *Mind*, vol. 4, no. 15 (1895), p. 320.

20 Xiaodong Wu, "The Rhinoceros Totem and Pangu Myth: An Exploration of the Archetype of Pangu," *Oral Tradition*, vol. 16, no. 2 (2001), pp. 364–80; Xiaodong Wu, "Pangu and the Origin of the Universe," in *China's Creation and Origin Myths: Cross-Cultural Explorations in Oral and Written Traditions*, eds Mineke Schipper, Shuxian Ye, and Hubin Yin (Leiden and Boston: Brill, 2011).

21 L. W. King, *The Seven Tablets of Creation: The Babylonian and Assyrian Legends Concerning the Creation of the World and of Mankind* (Whitefish, MT: Kessinger Publishing, 2004), pp. 75–7, 87; David Toshio Tsumura, *Creation and Destruction: A Reappraisal of the Chaoskampf Theory in the Old Testament* (Warsaw, IN: Eisenbrauns, 2005), p. 194; William Morris and Eirikr Magnusson, *The Story of the Volsungs* (London: Walter Scott Press, 1888), pp. 9–10; Edward Burnett Tylor, *Primitive Culture: Researches into the Development of*

Mythology, Philosophy, Religion, Art, and Custom (Cambridge: Cambridge University Press, 2010), pp. 312–14.

22 Ted Peters, "Models of God," p. 282; Dennis D. Carpenter, "Emergent Nature Spirituality: An Examination of the Major Spiritual Contours of the Contemporary Pagan Worldview," in *Magical Religion and Modern Witchcraft*, ed. James R. Lewis (Albany, NY: State University of New York Press, 1996), pp. 35–72.

23 CNN. "CNN Larry King Live (Transcript): Interview with Stephen Hawking; Science and Religion," at http://transcripts.cnn.com/TRANSCRIPTS/1009/10/lkl.01.html. Accessed 7 January 2013.

24 This might confuse those in the East, who wish to become 'Westernized,' seemingly demonstrating the truism that the 'grass is always greener on the other side.' See Frank C. Darling, *The Westernization of Asia: A Comparative Political Analysis* (Boston: G. K. Hall, 1979); Gopa Bagchi, Pradosh Kumar Rath, and Guru Saran Lal, "Westernisation of Indian Culture: A Study of Chhattisgarh," *Shodh Sanchayan*, vol. 2, no. 1 (2011), pp. 25–9.

25 Carole M. Cusack, "The Western Reception of Buddhism: Celebrity and Popular Cultural Media as Agents of Familiarisation," *Australian Religion Studies Review*, vol. 24, no. 3 (2011), p. 308; Carole M. Cusack, *Invented Religions: Imagination, Fiction and Faith* (Farnham and Burlington, VT: Ashgate, 2010), p. 65.

26 Colin Campbell, "The Easternisation of the West," in *New Religious Movements: Challenge and Response*, eds Bryan R. Wilson and Jamie Cresswell (London: Routledge, 1999); Anne-Marie Korte, "A Unique Instability? Exploring the Boundaries of Monotheism," in *The Boundaries of Monotheism: Interdisciplinary Explorations into the Foundations of Western Monotheism*, eds Anne-Marie Korte and Maaike De Haardt (Leiden and Boston: Brill, 2009), pp. 1–8; Penny Long Marler and C. Kirk Hadaway, "'Being Religious' or 'Being Spiritual' in America: A Zero-Sum Proposition?," *Journal for the Scientific Study of Religion*, vol. 41, no. 2 (2002), pp. 289–300; Hugh McLeod and Werner Ustorf, *The Decline of Christendom in Western Europe, 1750–2000* (Cambridge: Cambridge University Press, 2003).

27 Carole M. Cusack, "Science Fiction as Scripture: Robert A. Heinlein's *Stranger in a Strange Land* and the Church of All Worlds," *Literature & Aesthetics*, vol. 19, no. 2 (2009), pp. 73, 90.

28 Paola A. Zizzi, "Emergent Consciousness: From the Early Universe to Our Mind," *NeuroQuantology*, vol. 1, no. 3 (2003), p. 310.

29 Marvin Lee Minsky, *The Emotion Machine: Commonsense Thinking, Artificial Intelligence, and the Future of the Human Mind* (New York: Simon & Schuster, 2006).

30 Bernard Haisch, *The God Theory: Universes, Zero-Point Fields, and What's Behind It All* (York Beach, ME: Weiser Books, 2006); Bernard Haisch, *The Purpose-Guided Universe: Believing in Einstein, Darwin, and God* (Franklin Lakes, NJ: New Page Books, 2010).

31 Ronald W. Clark, *Einstein: The Life and Times* (New York: World Publishing Co., 1971), pp. 413–14.

32 Arnold Toynbee, "The Religious Background of the Present Environmental Crisis," *International Journal of Environmental Studies*, vol. 3, nos 1–4 (1972), pp. 141–6.

33 Carl Sagan, *Pale Blue Dot: A Vision of the Human Future in Space* (New York: Random House, 1994), p. 77.

34 James Cameron, *Avatar* (Los Angeles, CA: Twentieth Century Fox, 2009), Film.

35 Ken Hillis, "From Capital to Karma: James Cameron's *Avatar*," *Postmodern Culture*, vol. 19, no. 3 (2009), at http://muse.jhu.edu/login?auth=0&type=summary&url=/journals/postmodern_culture/v019/19.3.hillis.html.

36 Richard Dawkins, *The God Delusion* (London: Bantam, 2006), p. 18; Martin O. Yalcin, "American Naturalism on Pantheism," *American Journal of Theology & Philosophy*, vol. 32, no. 2 (2011), p. 178.

37 Craig, *Reasonable Faith.*

38 For my refutation of the former, see Raphael Lataster, "A Philosophical and Historical Analysis of William Lane Craig's Resurrection of Jesus Argument," *Think*, vol. 14, no. 39 (2015), pp. 59–71.

39 John Milton and Dennis Richard Danielson, *Paradise Lost* (London:

Broadview Press, 2012 [1667]).

40 Alvin Plantinga and James F. Sennett, *The Analytic Theist: An Alvin Plantinga Reader* (Grand Rapids, MI: W. B. Eerdmans, 1998), pp. 65–71.

41 Deuteronomy 11:16; Joshua 24:2; Deuteronomy 32:8–9; Psalm 82:1.

42 Job 37:16; Psalm 147:5; Matthew 10:30.

43 Richard Francks, "Omniscience, Omnipotence and Pantheism," *Philosophy*, vol. 54, no. 209 (1979), p. 396.

44 William J. Mander, "Omniscience and Pantheism," *The Heythrop Journal*, vol. 41, no. 2 (2000), pp. 199–208.

45 Neale Donald Walsch, *Conversations with God: An Uncommon Dialogue, Book 1* (New York: G. P. Putnam's Sons, 1996), pp. 21–30, 75.

46 2 Chronicles 2:5–6.

47 F. LeRon Shults and Steven J. Sandage, *The Faces of Forgiveness: Searching for Wholeness and Salvation* (Grand Rapids, MI: Baker Academic, 2003), pp. 161–4.

48 Mikael Rothstein, "'His Name Was Xenu. He Used Renegades…': Aspects of Scientology's Founding Myth," in *Scientology*, ed. James R. Lewis (Oxford: Oxford University Press, 2009).

49 It should be noted that ontological arguments may be necessary in moving God from the realm of 'mere' great entities to 'maximally great' beings. For example, it is the only argument in Craig's cumulative case that portrays an all-powerful god.

50 Edward Craig (ed.), *Concise Routledge Encyclopedia of Philosophy* (London: Routledge, 2013), pp. 180, 318.

51 Alvin Plantinga and James F. Sennett, *The Analytic Theist: An Alvin Plantinga Reader* (Grand Rapids, MI: W. B. Eerdmans, 1998), p. 20; Richard Swinburne, "Reply to Grünbaum," *British Journal for the Philosophy of Science*, vol. 51, no. 3 (2000), pp. 482–4; Richard Swinburne, "Second Reply to Grünbaum," *British Journal for the Philosophy of Science*, vol. 56, no. 4 (2005), p. 925; Paul Copan and William Lane Craig, *Creation out of Nothing: A Biblical, Philosophical, and Scientific Exploration* (Grand Rapids, MI: Baker Academic,

2004), p. 90.

52 Lawrence Maxwell Krauss, *A Universe from Nothing: Why There Is Something Rather Than Nothing* (New York: Free Press, 2012); Craig, *Reasonable Faith*, p. 115.

53 Philip Clayton, *The Problem of God in Modern Thought* (Grand Rapids, MI: W. B. Eerdmans, 2000), p. 125.

Why Pandeism Is Better Than Theism

Knujon Mapson

To begin with, it is necessary to recite the essential meaning of the term—what, exactly, is Pandeism? Princeton University's "WordNet" dictionary defines Pandeism as "the belief that God created the universe and its phenomena by becoming the universe, thereafter the sole manifestation of God." Looking to another source, the *Encyclopedia Britannica* notes in its "Deism" article that

> Pandeism...attempted to unite aspects of Deism with pantheism, [and] held that through the act of creation God became the universe. There is thus no theological need to posit any special relationship between God and creation; rather, God is the universe and not a transcendent entity which created and subsequently governs it.

These propositions effectively sum up the idea which we are talking about. Now the question is: how do we get there, and why do Pandeists consider this to be a 'better' model?

It is important, in this inquiry, to avoid confusing different ideas of a 'better' model. We must speak in terms of a more logically suitable explanation, and not necessarily one which provides believers with a greater sense of self-importance or assurance of some better destiny. Indeed, these common hallmarks of religion are ones to be wary of, since man so easily slips into the desire to believe what is comforting over what is true—the very reason why even in markets where results are more susceptible to confirmation, people are yet easily scammed.

To avoid the fruits of human biases, we begin with First Principles. What can we know, and how may we know it? Firstly, there is an epistemological question as to how we may know anything at all. In the DesCartesian sense, we know that we exist because we are thinking about it, and so we must exist insofar as we experience our own contemplation of it. There would seem along with ourselves to be at least one entity external to our immediate experience of ourselves because we are met with thought which seems not to be originating in our own minds. Now it could be true that all of our sensory perceptions are illusions created to test our reactions or some similar purpose, but this requires that there be at least one source of intelligence external to our own experience of self, to be imposing such experience on us (though even then we cannot exclude the possibility that we are merely an isolated expression within a larger mind appearing to us as this seemingly other intelligent being).

But speculation about an illusory Universe raises the question, how can we know our experience of our Universe to be real? Now, there are precisely two possibilities about the reality of our Universe as it presents itself to us. Either it is absolutely real, or it is not at all reliable, for if any part of our perception of our Universe is an illusion, an impenetrable deception, then the acknowledged presence of unreality means that nothing may be logically taken as 'the real thing' instead of being a like deception. But we will backtrack for a moment here and concede that even if our perception of our Universe is simply an illusion being imposed upon us, it is what is being presented to us to be taken as real, and so ought to be treated as real. But in any event, absent affirmative proof of an illusory capacity of our Universe, we simply have no reason to assume it to be anything but real.

We have two sources of information. Our senses, and our logical and mathematical contemplations. It is dubious to suggest that we may draw conclusions based on our senses alone, in part because we suffer from grave problems of scale. There are events vital to our understanding of our existence occurring at scales far too great and too small to be perceptible by man, and it must be confessed that assumptions about our Universe which fail to observe a proper awareness of these can be dismissed in the first instance. So far as our current capacity to observe informs us, we humans are approximately 43% of the way from the largest scale of observation—that of our entire visible Universe—to the smallest, that being the subquark (though there are potentially smaller units in string theory, which is mathematically very promising).

But I submit that investigation of the nature of our Universe reveals it to be the product of an act of design. We are able to observe that we human beings are made out of a collection of interacting organs, that these organs are made out of cells, and that these cells are made out of molecules—and indeed every tangible thing which we are able to observe or interact with is similarly made out of molecules; and these molecules have particular properties reflective of the atoms of which they are themselves made, and there is no molecule in our Universe but one made from atoms. And we are further able to observe that there are many kinds of atoms, almost all of which are created by stellar fusion and spat out of dying stars but that these kinds adhere to a strict set of rules—which are in turn dictated by their composition of subatomic particles, and so forth down past the level of those subquarks we mentioned before.

It is a remarkable thing that at each level of substance, the material at issue is able to self-organize in accordance with the governing dynamics of our Universe (things such as the strength of gravity and the speed of light and the combination of attractive and repulsive forces between protons and electrons). I'll not belabor here the fineness of calculation needed to permit subatomic particles to form light atoms, which form stars spitting out heavy atoms in their death throes, heavy atoms forming the complex self-replicating molecules of life, and eventually intelligent life, and eventually something even beyond that. But even this is not what I rest the proposition of design upon; for not only is our Universe fundamentally complex enough to generate this level of complexity; it is at the same time fundamentally simple enough for intelligent beings to figure out that these forces are what is at play, and to use them to invent things like light bulbs and calculators and computers and massive particle colliders.

I'll give one very specific example. We have determined by observing the light signatures of distant galaxies that our Universe is expanding at a rate consistent with origin in a single explosive expansion from a singularity having occurred approximately 13.72 billion years ago. We have observed as well that there exists a Cosmic Microwave Background Radiation in our Universe, which is as well indicative of the same origin and of the same time frame. But given sufficient time those galaxies will recede beyond detectibility and that microwave background radiation will evaporate entirely; were we not fortunate enough to develop the tools by which to measure these things before they became undetectable to us, we would never know or have any reason to imagine the age of our Universe—suggesting that our Universe was designed to essentially knock on our door and inform us of its age and origin. And we have only in the past few years acquired the ability to confirm the long-suspected existence of habitable worlds within the conceivable range of our technological reach. These worlds call to us for exploration and colonization, perhaps an entire galaxy able to be made Man's.

In addition to these indications, there are other reasons to suppose a design behind our existence. There is a broad, if inconsistently expressed, human tendency to intuitively reach for such an explanation. There is, for example, across the recorded human experience, a vast catalogue of claimed events given metaphysical significance, going back to the earliest days of the recording of history. People of all faiths and within all types of theological models have had spiritual visions, believed themselves to be the recipients of divine communications, had dreams portending future occurrences, prayed for miraculous results which have seemingly come about. Reductionism would counter that all of these have non-metaphysical explanations, that visions and revelations may be occurring only in the mind of the recipient, that prayers seemingly answered fall neatly within the range of coincidences dwarfed by the obviously unanswered prayers, that the appearance of miracles can be faked, or that the claim itself may be fraudulent. Evolutionary biology claims to account for this with notions of the fear of shadows, protecting the individual in those instances where something lurks therein, but the explanations offered in biology seem strained compared against the richness of religious belief.

But the reductionist explanation requires that every single one of the millions of religious events reported in the annals of human history is an error or a fraud. At the same time, the vast variety of such sentiments (and the occasional absence of them altogether in a person) demonstrates that none of the theistic models claiming to be universal can be true, for such theistic models depend in part upon their being known or having been revealed or transmitted to all peoples, a verifiably false assumption. But the simplest explanation for the multitudes of seemingly contrarily faith-affirming miracles for mutually exclusive faiths remains the proposition that all reflect a part of the truth sublimated to the manifestations of a single subconscious all-sustaining and all-experiencing mind.

And additionally, on a slightly different note, there exists a very specific tendency of some especially to have 'mystical' experiences. And the experience of mysticism is, surprisingly enough, replicable through meditation and the use of certain mind-expanding (e.g. mind-altering) substances. The mystical experience recounted by those who have gone this route, whether by meditation or with chemical assistance, is regularly reported as a sensation of oneness with our Universe and with an overriding spiritual force bound up in its fabric.

Now, having established (at the least) a reasonable basis for believing ours to be a Created Universe, we turn to the characteristics of our Creator. There are *three*—and only three—which are absolutely necessary (and *one* more flowing from those): it must have sufficient power to supply and control the incomprehensible energy of our Universe; it must have sufficient intelligence to design the governing dynamics which result in that energy taking the increasingly complex material forms observed; and it must have sufficient rationality to create a Universe which operates rationally, building itself towards these evident ends. The one flowing correlation is that, if rational, it must be rationally motivated to create.

And let me be absolutely clear here: If a theological model exists by which these three assumptions suffice to account for all of the observations man is able to make, then no other assumptions may logically be added, no matter how strongly they might serve our sense of importance. This is as simple a proposition as stating that footprints in the sand most likely reveal that a person walked there. If a person capable of walking sufficiently explains what is observed, then there is no basis for assuming that the leaver of the footprints was able to fly as well, or that it possessed any particular set of loves or hates.

And here we come to the theological theory of Pandeism: that there is a Creator defined by its possession of 1) sufficient power to create by becoming, 2) intelligence enough to design the physics of a Universe which unfolds into increasing complexity, and which is 3) rationally motivated to do so by the desire to obtain the experiential knowledge of existing as our Universe, a Universe inevitably containing intelligent life which travels among the many habitable worlds provided for it through the operations of physics.

Now, the acid test, the 64-million-dollar question. Is there anything in our Universe which can *not* be accounted for by this model? Theists tend to point to their respective scriptures and the events described in them, to reports of faith-affirming miracles or visions or the like, and to emotional appeals, which beg that in the absence of an intervening deity, wrongs will not be punished. But because there are many contradictory accounts of this sort, and because there are and have been many millions of people who are isolated from ever hearing about any given theistic path, additional assumptions must be piled on to explain this, usually involving the additional creation of contingent evil spirits, or of past or future lives, or of varying degrees of life after death.

But if the assumptions underlying the pandeistic model are correct, then we are all fragments of an incomprehensibly powerful and intelligent Creator, and so all of the things which theists point to—scripture, miracles, revelations, prophecies, beliefs, spiritual activities, spiritual emotions, visions, dreams, egrigori, seemingly efficacious prayer, oracles, signs, and all the rest, all of these are simply expressions of the power of our incomprehensible Creator as touched by and filtered by our limited (if sometimes spiritually talented) human minds. I don't doubt that theists tire of having this pointed out to them as much as I tire of explaining it anew each time, but the principle remains that every theistic explanation inherently requires fatally more assumptions to account for the same proof (and most leave substantial proof unaccounted for altogether).

Pandeism fully accounts for every one of these claimed proofs of a spiritual basis for our Universe, and more importantly it does so for all faiths, without requiring the invocation of assumptions of evil spirits or demigods to explain them. For if any of these events occur at all, then they are simply explicable as manifestations of the power of our Creator unconsciously underlying our Universe, as unwittingly misread through the biased minds of human observers.

In 1931, mathematician and philosopher Kurt Gödel published his two incompleteness theorems, proving mathematically that in any closed system, there must be a true statement which cannot be proved by that system. And this, as it turns out, applies to theological models as readily as to mathematical ones. There is one proposition which no deity possessed of godlike powers would ever be able to know the truth of, and that is whether it itself is simply a construct—an immensely complex one, perhaps, but a construct still—within an even greater reality beyond its perception. This may sound odd and impossible, but let us think this through.

First, imagine a point in space. Now imagine that a straight line begins at that point and extends infinitely onward in one direction from that point. Flat space, please—don't want that line curving around and becoming itself. Now imagine a second point right next to the first, with a parallel infinite line extending infinitely outward in one direction. So now you've got infinite nonintersecting lines. If either line could be aware of its own infinitude, it might imagine itself to be the only thing in existence capable of being infinite. Now, let us take the second infinite line and move its starting point backwards one inch relative to the other line. Now you have two infinite lines, but one is an inch longer than the other.

But let's take that inch-longer line and stretch it along a second dimension, making it a flat plane with a few inches of width (and still infinite length). We keep it parallel to our first line, so they still never intersect; the first line still has every reason to 'believe' itself to be uniquely infinite, even though it is right next to a thing that is not only an inch longer, but has an entire additional dimension of substance. And now we will take the second mathematical object (the one which is now a plane) and curve it into a cylinder which completely surrounds the first line, but continues never touching it. And just for the sake of it, we'll take that end of the cylinder that goes past the first point and curve its edges toward one another, into a sort of hemispherical cap which closes off that end of the cylinder (still without touching the original infinite line). Indeed we could do all of these operations to the first line and make it into an infinitely long tube with one end beginning with a hemisphere, and still have it completely contained within a slightly larger tube with which it never intersects.

Now you might at this point be thinking, 'Yes, but the gods envisioned by human faiths are not mathematical constructs, they are not tubes; so what's the point?' Well, you would be correct that man-described deities tend not to be mathematical constructs, but human ideas of the ultimate are necessarily constructs nonetheless, for they are invariably described in human languages, and with human words and concepts such as 'infinite' and 'absolute' (and really those are concepts which, if not outright mathematical, are subject to mathematical discussion). Lest we delve too close to describing perfectly spherical gods in a vacuum, let us get straight to the heart of the capacities philosophically ascribed to deity-models: able to do anything; possessed of all knowledge. But wait, there's the catch. No matter how much knowledge a god possesses, it is impossible for it to know that it is not missing some knowledge of which it is unaware, such as the existence of a greater surrounding entity which contains it.

Even if in some relative sense the Bible or the Qur'an or the Bhagavad Gita were true on some plane of existence (such that there was a Creator entity which set forth all that we humans are able to perceive at least, and all the events recounted transpired as set forth there), even this Creator entity could never know that everything it was doing was not part of some infinitely greater Creator-entity's thought experiment. (Here is an inverse proof of this—imagine a true all-powerful being *not* sustained within anything greater than itself; such a being could, by definition, create a *slightly lesser being* which believed itself to be the true 'only all-powerful being,' and which would by dint of the true all-powerful being's all-powerfulness, be absolutely unable to detect the greater being of which it was part.)

And if no hypothetical Creator of our entire Universe could possibly actually know whether it was the ultimate being, then surely we spatially and temporally and intellectually limited humans can have no inkling as to what the truth is of such a thing. And here's the even greater rub: supposing that there was a god of this or that scriptural type, and that this god was unknowingly simply an entity sustained in existence within a greater being (and perhaps one of many so sustained), then the greater being within which it was sustained would itself have no way to be sure that it wasn't merely the thought experiment or subroutine or what have you of an even greater thing than itself, a cylinder within the cylinder, within perhaps inestimable layers like a neverending Russian doll. And that is why Gödel's theorem makes it impossible for there to be an absolutely omniscient deity. (Which is by the way of no concern to Pandeism, which never proposes absolute omniscience anyway, but only ever proposes such relative omniscience as would be required to account for our finite Universe so far as we are able to perceive it.) Now, consider our relationship with a hypothetical pandeistic deity. Imagine for a moment, if you were able to travel back in time to a much earlier point in human history, and were there able to show a select handful of pre-civilization *Homo sapiens* perhaps a ten-minute vid of vital images which accurately laid out the history of our Universe and our planet only to that point. Understanding that you would not be able to communicate anything with them verbally for lack of a common language, how do you imagine they would interpret what they saw? The Big Bang, the massive cycles of starbirth and stardeath necessary to generate heavy elements which permit the existence of our world at all. The violent geological activities, periods of evolution, the strange eras of prehistoric beasts which necessarily preceded human existence, even the seemingly sudden leaps in human technology (from nothing to the lever, wheel, inclined plane, fire, axes, and such). If the primitives with whom you shared these images then felt the need to relay that vision to others, using what limited language and symbology as was then available to them, would they not couch it as a series of miracles, creditable to the intervention of inscrutable metaphysical forces such as a deity?

And yet, if our Creator became our Universe, if we are of our Creator in this fragmentary sense, wafting on the winds of its unconscious sustainment despite our illusion of concreteness, then all of our religious visions represent such manifestations, glimpses of the commonalities well known within the unconscious mind of the metaphysical progenitor of which we are so stunningly a part. Our world glitters, then, about us with the promise of a similar oneness of being, a potential to be whatever world we wish it to be—if we wish it.

Under the pandeistic model it need not be assumed that our Creator is a conscious and active deity who chooses to act or not act, and is opposed by superpowered evil entities—quixotically presumed to have been created by it as well, either errantly or as part of some complicated scheme for which additional levels of excuses and assumptions must be made. For our Creator need not continue to interfere in our Universe, judge or condemn, send seeming conflicting messages to prophets of various faiths, nor need it create or permit any other spiritual forces to do so, or in any way to contend with man. Pandeism avoids the traditional response to the multiplicity of claimed miracles, revelations, prophecies, and so forth supporting irreconcilable differences of faith, which has been the invocation of the agency of evil spirits. Such assumption is itself deeply irrational, for it is simply impossible for there to be an evil spirit from whom 'miraculous' results emanate for the affirmance of other faiths. All laws of nature, and the laws of physics among them, these would necessarily be the laws of our Creator, then, and all things are bound by them except (and only except) as allowed by the power of our Creator;

put otherwise, even were we to impose upon our Creator the additionally assumed characteristics of consciousness and a need to intervene, our Creator would nonetheless be the force sustaining our Universe. It would be impossible for anybody, any entity, to violate the laws of physics except by using such Creator's own power to do so. And if there is proposed to be a conscious Creator, this simply means that nothing miraculous may occur except as done by such Creator.

In the pandeistic model, our Creator unconsciously underlies existence, and so what miracles occur (if anything is not susceptible to naturalistic explanation) do so because that power is manifested by the fragments of our Creator which constitute all of existence. And, as importantly, no good and wise Creator would grant free rein to an entity sufficiently powerful as to undermine the ability of other entities to make informed decisions, if reward or punishment hinged upon such decisions. If so powerful an entity were deemed to exist, it would immediately render fatally suspect any widely held belief, as any one of us could have lived our entire existence in an illusion generated by it to secure our falsity of beliefs. If an 'evil spirit' exists at all, and is so successful as to be responsible for all the religions with which one disagrees (though others adhere tightly to them), then it is overwhelmingly likely it is equally responsible for that last faith with which one does agree. And, in fact, whatever the 'truth' is would then most likely reside only in a minor and obscure and generally ignored or even reviled group, whose few members display impeccable morality.

Another benefit of the pandeistic model is that it equally accounts for and accords with all scientific discovery. Pandeism has no conflict with science whatsoever; indeed, Pandeism embraces the scientific method and the awesome nature of scientific discovery, and as with religion, Pandeism fully accounts for science. This is not to suggest that the means of accounting are the same, for Pandeism accounts for religious experiences—to the extent they exist as something more than coincidence or psychological phenomena—as manifestations of the underlying unconscious power of our Creator, often denoted by Pandeists as the Deus. But neither does this mean that Pandeism assumes generally that religious experiences are, in fact, anything more than coincidence or psychological phenomena. After all, one person's vision or revelation is another's hallucination; one person's prophecy is another's clever use of vague wording and exploitation of biases of memory and expectation; one person's miracle is another's parlor trick. But Pandeism recognizes that all that is discovered by science as to how our Universe operates simply is an uncovering of the governing dynamics set in motion by the Creator in the moment of creating/becoming our Universe. If science reveals our Universe to be billions of years old, it is so, and is because the rational goal sought by our Creator was one which required our Universe gestating through billions of years of natural development to give birth to its desired set of information. If science reveals our descent from a Universal Common Ancestor, it is so, and is because our Creator set forth a Universe capable of giving rise to sufficiently complex life through a simple process of evolution by natural selection.

And, lastly, this model contains a remarkable powerful basis for morality, as it proposes that all things are part of our Creator, and that our Creator experiences through us the consequences of our actions. And so we ought to be motivated to act in ways which avoid causing suffering and harm, because in so doing we would simply be inflicting these things on our own Creator—and, in a way, upon ourselves. And indeed, such raises the Golden Rule from good advice to universal law, for that which we do unto others, we may thusly veritably do unto ourselves!

And so, because the pandeistic model fully accounts for all of the proof generally presented in support of both faith and science, it is presumably true against any theological system which requires additional assumptions to account for the same proof—such as a desire for sacrifice, a need for deity intervention, arbitrary assignments of 'sin,' or the creation of evil spirits. And Pandeism is most especially presumptively true against any system which fails to fully account for contradictory beliefs either within or without its own model and the manifestations of the miraculous claimed to support those beliefs, and most of all to account for scientific discoveries contradictory to the accounting of such a belief.

So just as we do not rely on steady footprints in the sand to hypothesize the footprint-leaver's power of flight or teleportation or love of Bach and condemnation of chocolate, neither can we rationally extend to spirituality any assumptions beyond those captured by the theological model of Pandeism. And, finally, the truth of this proposition can be demonstrated with one simple question:

> Is the Creator in which you believe powerful enough to have set forth the Universe as we experience it—in every particular—while needing do nothing more than set forth from its own energy this Universe and the governing dynamics which control the behavior of that energy?

And is it? Is it powerful enough to have become a Universe where everything which we experience has come to pass—stars, planets, the origin of life, the rise of complex ecosystems, the rise of intelligent life, machinery, technology, and social institutions (including religious institutions, writings, and beliefs)—by doing no more than simply initially causing this Creation through the provision of the power already residing within itself? Is it intelligent enough to have brought about our complete experience of our world without needing to interfere again, other than through that which was set forth in the moment of Creation? For if it was powerful enough to have brought about our Universe in every particular without thereafter intervening, that would include bringing about the appearance of intervention where there is none, and even bringing about the varied and contradictory beliefs of people who insist they have been told otherwise—even when they have not, when this 'telling' was simply their own interpretation of the underlying truth of a pandeistic Universe!

Section II: Philosophical Implications of Pandeism

"Omniscience, Omnipotence and Pantheism," by Richard Francks PhD, sets the stage with an observation on the nature of omniscience as applied to experiential knowledge.

Next, "Leibniz's Best World Claim Restructured," by William C. Lane, presents a tour-de-force of moral consequence, explaining how a creator wholly becoming the creation—without knowing in advance every negative consequence of that happening, and yet bearing all such consequences—escapes the 'problem of evil' while exhibiting one aspect of a maximally loving being: maximal closeness to that which is loved.

Zoltan Istvan, in "Transhumanism and Theistcideism," contemplates the drive of living things to live, and of intelligent life to better itself, achieving some remarkable conclusions about the desire of nonomnipotent beings to obtain omnipotence—and of an omnipotent being to destroy itself and begin anew.

Following another poetic interlude, "Pantheistic Reflections," by Poffo Ortiz, introduces us to the pandeistic notion of biopantheism, and powerful arguments of pantheist/pandeist morality.

Lastly, in "Pandeism, the Holographic Universe, and Simulation Theory," Anthony Peake considers the evidence for the popular theory that our Universe is itself a simulation—and how this too is a concept consistent with a pandeistic Universe.

Earth Child

Amy Perry

My imagination, no limitation.
I welcome in positive vibration.
My brain is a grand central station.
Swept away like the waves, call me vacation. A notion about waves in the ocean:
They travel across continents, in a constant motion.

Watch the power approaching.
Realize the wave is one energy,
That never lost its devotion.

I welcome in new positive energies Like amenities, necessary,
I'm an attorney attesting on
Life's incredible journey.

Join me, but warning; I prefer soaring.
My torus is lush as forest.
Living like an alien tourist. I insist on artistic visions to guide me,
Not living for pride or vanity.
I'm just a human, grooving, celebrating earth inside of me.

Chiming on with Nature's charm.
Living my life, devoid of harm.
I can do this a lifetime long,
With nothing to lose, none to alarm.
I wear a badge of peace on my arm.

Omniscience, Omnipotence and Pantheism

Richard Francks PhD

Dr Francks was Senior Lecturer in Philosophy at the University of Leeds, UK. He taught Descartes' Meditations to first-year undergraduates for many years. His publications included Modern Philosophy *(Routledge, 2003) and* G. W. Leibniz: Philosophical Texts *(with R. S. Woolhouse, OUP, 1998). This article originally appeared in* Philosophy, *vol. 54, no. 209 (July 1979), pp. 395–9, published by Cambridge University Press on behalf of the Royal Institute of Philosophy. Although this article is not directed to Pandeism, and does not analyze (or even specifically mention) this concept, its implications for the theory of Pandeism are abundant.*

Spinoza is a pantheist: he believes that everything that is, is God. Traditional Judeo-Christian theologians dislike the idea, and Spinoza has always been unpopular for it. Nevertheless, I want here to suggest that, simply by following out the logic of omniscience and omnipotence—two attributes of God on which both Spinoza and his opponents are agreed—it is possible to arrive at a conception of God which is at least very close to Spinoza's own. I do not claim that any of the arguments I use are to be found in Spinoza, but I do think that this way of thinking helps to explain the motives behind his 'hideous hypothesis.'

1. Omniscience and Omnipresence

There are two requirements on God's knowledge:

1. God's knowledge must be complete. In other words, he must be omniscient: it must be true that, for any X, if X is true, then God knows that X. That is simple enough.

2. God's knowledge must be perfect. This requirement is usually subsumed under 1, but is really different. 1 says that God's knowledge must be perfect in scope, whereas 2 says that it must be of the highest order. That this is also a requirement I think most theologians would admit. If it were not so, if God, while knowing everything, might not know it all perfectly well, then we could imagine a being which did, and it would be at best a contingent fact that God knew best. God could still be omniscient without the second requirement, but his knowledge could not be that *"qua nihil maius cogitari possit"* (Anselm).

(This second requirement clearly demands that we should be able to give some content to the idea of degrees of knowledge as distinct from knowing more and knowing less. If this is not so, then the second requirement simply collapses into the first.)

A. I know it is Friday today. I also knew it five minutes ago, but I was not thinking about it then. I do not know any more now than I did then. Neither, it seems to me, do I know that today is Friday better now than I did then. But all the same, it seems obvious that I am more aware of the fact of what day it is now than I was before, simply because I am thinking about it. My knowledge then, we might say, was potential, or implicit. The question is: is it enough for God's knowledge to be potential in this sense? Is it enough, in other words, for God to be able to call to mind every fact, or does the second requirement demand that for God there be no potential knowledge, but only actual, immediate awareness?

The first alternative faces two problems to which I can see no answer:

1. If God is not actually thinking about me at this moment, then he is not taking care of me as I would like him to. And

what goes for me goes for everyone else. But more importantly:

2. We could imagine a being which at a given moment was more aware of a given fact than was God—for instance, we could imagine a being who was actually thinking about how I felt, as opposed to just having the information at his fingertips—and that seems to run counter to at least the spirit of the second requirement. If this is correct, then it shows that God must not only know everything, and must not only know everything equally well, but further, he must at all times be giving his full attention to every item of his infinite knowledge.

B. There is a second consequence of this strong sense of omniscience.

My knee hurts, and I am aware of the fact. If a perfect physiologist examined my knee he would know it too. But there is a difference between my awareness and his. What kind of difference? I do not know anything which he does not know. On the contrary, he knows much more about my pain than I do—"I only know it hurts." I do not even want to say that I know it better than he does. And, provided he is giving me his full attention, I do not want to say either that I am better aware of my pain than he is. But there is still a difference between me and him: we know what we know in completely different ways. We might say: we know the same thing from different points of view. The question then is: is it enough for God to be the perfect physiologist, or must he somehow 'feel my pain'? I think he must, because if not, then there is something which I know and he does not, namely, not my pain, but my view of my pain. Of course, God 'knows just how I feel', but that phrase is no more comfort here than elsewhere: his knowledge remains theoretical, derived, whereas mine is perceptual, immediate. Mine is not therefore better, but it is different. If God's knowledge of my pain is only that of the perfect physiologist, then I have an awareness, a perspective, which God lacks. And that contradicts the spirit of the first requirement.

C. If this is true of my pain, as it seems to me that it is, then clearly it is true of everyone else's. But more than that, it is also true of all the rest of our 'inner lives.' God must be party to all our thoughts, feelings and opinions. Our thoughts may be botched and imperfect and unclear, but God, in addition to his own perfect overall understanding, must also be conscious of our dim view of the world. And no less so than we are ourselves.

D. Consider my visual field. I am aware of how the world looks from where I am. And so is God. If I move my head, I am aware of how the world looks from a different place. And so is God. But God is equally well aware of both at the same time. And the same goes for every other point in the whole of space.

The conclusion I draw from all this is simple: for every mind, God's knowledge of it is such that it is as if it were his mind, and for every point in space, his knowledge is such that it is as if he were there. In other words, God is omnipresent.

2. Omnipotence and Omnipresence

The logic of omnipotence is exactly parallel to that of omniscience. Again there are two requirements:

1. God can do anything. There is nothing which is logically possible and which God cannot do, and there is nothing which is not logically necessary and which God cannot prevent. But also:
2. God can do everything equally easily. This is the counterpart to the requirement that God's knowledge be perfect in quality. If God experienced any difficulty in

performing any act, then we would be able to imagine a being which did not, and once again God's supremacy would be at best a contingent fact.

A. These two together mean that God cannot wish or desire anything. The assumption that his power is perfect in degree as well as in scope means that no time can be said to elapse between the inclination and the performance. (If it did, then, again, we could imagine a being for whom the gap was shorter, and who could therefore achieve his ends more readily.) The relation between God and the world must be closer than that of desiring—it must be that of willing, or of intentional action. And the action itself must be directly achieved—God cannot work with an end in view, or in order to bring something about: for God the desire simply is the performance, the will is the reality.

B. God is omniscient. God is omnipotent. Therefore, for any event E which occurs, God knows that E, and God could have brought it about that not-E. Therefore, for any event E which occurs, God wills that E should occur.

(This is not at all the same thing as to say that God likes everything that happens. In itself it is compatible, for instance, with God's regretting Adam's eating of the apple. All the same, he willed that it should occur, presumably because he had other, overriding reasons against preventing it. Thus, even the eating of the apple was in accordance with God's will: he decided that overall it was best, and should happen, although in certain respects he might have regretted it.)

In other words, then, if God is omniscient and omnipotent, then no event can be causally explained without reference to the will of God. We can no longer regard God as able either to intervene or let things go on in their own way—only a being whose power and/or knowledge were limited could have that kind of choice.

For God it can only ever be a question of either willing that A, or willing that B. In summary, then, God's power is so great that, if God wills something, that is the same as saying that it is; and if something is, that is the same as saying that God wills it. In other words, God's will is omnipresent, or every point in space is a point at which God's will is continually in operation.

3. Omnipresence and Pantheism

So far, I do not think I have produced any conclusions which would be unacceptable to traditional theology, though some of my reasons might. I have tried to show that the assumption that God is omniscient and the assumption that he is omnipotent both lead independently to the conclusion that he is omnipresent in a strong sense, or 'immanent.' I want now to argue that the belief in this kind of omnipresent God leads automatically to pantheism.

We recognize and define the limits of an individual in basically two ways: we establish the area over which his or her motor control extends, and that over which he or she responds to a given stimulus. In God's case there is nothing which is not continually responding to his volition, and there is no stimulus to which he is not immediately and fully conscious of a reaction. Therefore, there is no conceivable test which we could apply to anything which could yield the conclusion that that thing was not God. Therefore, even if God is not everything, it is logically impossible that we should ever know that he is not.

If that were all, the situation might not be too bad. It might still make a kind of minimal sense to talk about God as opposed to the rest of the world, although we poor mortals could never know the difference. But there is more than that; even for God the distinction could have no meaning. An individual's division of the world into self and other is made along the same lines, though not in the same way, as his or her division into one individual and the next; in terms of power to control and scope of reaction. For God, everything in the universe responds immediately to his will, and there is nothing in the universe of which he is not aware. Therefore, not only can we never know the difference between God and his creations, but even an omniscient being could never know it. I conclude that it makes no sense to talk of any such difference.

4. Conclusion

From the assumption that there is a God, and that he is omniscient and omnipotent, I have claimed to draw the conclusion that there is no difference between him and his universe. God knows everything, and everything he knows is God. God is everywhere, and everywhere he is *is* God. God does everything, and everything he does is God.

The consequences of this kind of pantheism are far-reaching. In particular, it would seem to have the corollary that everything that could ever meaningfully be said could be said without ever using the name 'God.' I am suggesting that, as Spinoza saw, these consequences could only be avoided at the price of limiting the perfection which we are prepared to attribute to God.

Leibniz's Best World Claim Restructured

William C. Lane

William C. Lane is an intellectual property lawyer strongly interested in philosophy, especially as it seeks to describe the actual state of the world. For more than the past ten years he has been working on a history of the world from a pandeist and panexperientialist point of view. He is the author of "Leibniz's Best World Claim Restructured," American Philosophical Quarterly, *vol. 47, no. 1 (2010), pp. 57–84 (republished here); "The Best of Possible Worlds: A Testable Claim of Choice,"* Theology and Science, *vol. 4, no. 3 (2006), pp. 261–78; and "Is Panexperientialism Consistent with Quantum Physics?" (publication pending). He lives and practices in the Washington DC area.*

What is it that breathes fire into the equations and makes a universe for them to describe?
(Stephen Hawking 1998, p. 190)

1. Leibniz's Claims

Almost uniquely among philosophers, Gottfried Leibniz tried to reason from God's nature to a description of the physical world. He began by observing that the world could have only "one source, because of the interconnection among all…things" (1989, p. 152). This source must be God, who would select only the best of worlds: "If only we could sufficiently understand the order of the universe, we should find that it surpasses all the desires of the wisest, and that it is impossible to make it better than it is" (1991, § 90, p. 29). Leibniz's rationale was clear: "This is the cause of the existence of the best: that his wisdom makes it known to God, his goodness makes him choose it, and his power lets him produce it" (1991, § 55, p. 24).

Many philosophers have found this reasoning sound.[1] In fact, some see it as a *reductio ad absurdum* of divine perfection (Flew 1989, p. 240). To avoid the reductio, theists invent objections like this one: no world can be "the best" because, regardless of which world God would create, another could be better. "Perhaps for any world you mention, replete with [presumably happy] dancing girls and deliriously happy sentient creatures, there is an even better world, containing even more dancing girls and deliriously happy sentient creatures" (Plantinga 1974, p. 61). According to this *impossibility objection,* no best world is logically possible; we should therefore not be surprised that ours seems improvable.

If a world's merit depended on its embodying the largest possible amount of some single desideratum, the impossibility objection might well be valid. Since there is no highest number, it seems that God could always add more of any single, desirable quality.[2] If the best world had to have the largest number of sentient creatures, the maximum quantum of virtue or happiness, or the most dancing girls, no best world would be possible. However, the impossibility objection loses logical force if, to be best, a world had to have the optimal combination of two or more desiderata—e.g. happiness *and* virtue—or was otherwise constrained by multiple criteria. If more of one desirable quality means less of another, or if they limit one another in other ways (i.e. if they are countervailing), then some unique combination could be the best (see Strickland 2005a).

In real-world optimization problems—e.g. those involving aircraft speed, cost, and payload—countervailing factors relate to one another in very complicated ways. A review of many such problems points to the following conclusion: if we want to find the optimal combination of two or more desiderata (e.g. speed and payload), we need to consider both how these criteria interrelate (e.g. payload loss per increment of speed) and the goal of combining them (e.g. are we building a crop duster or a passenger jet?).[3]

Leibniz thought of world optimality in abstract terms. He wrote that "the most perfect world is the one which is at the same time the simplest in hypotheses and the richest in phenomena, as might be a line in geometry whose construction is easy and whose properties and effects are extremely remarkable and widespread" (1989, p. 39). Elsewhere, he wrote that God "has chosen the best possible plan in producing the universe, a plan which combines the greatest variety together with the greatest order…with the greatest effect produced by the simplest means" (1991, p. 195). Nicholas Rescher calls this Leibniz's "two-factor assessment of perfection" (2003, p. 27); it involves both richness of *phenomena* (events/modes of being) as an end and simplicity of *hypotheses* (physical laws/initial conditions) as a means.[4] In Rescher's view, Leibniz held ends and means to be equally important: "For the wisest mind so acts as far as is possible that the means are also ends of a sort, i.e., are desirable not only on account of what they do, but on account of what they are" (Leibniz 1985, § 208, p. 257). God would choose the optimal combination.

Unlike 'soft' criteria such as goodness or happiness, each component of Leibnizian optimality (simple hypotheses and rich phenomena) has a mathematically definite meaning. This is critical because only combinations of mathematically definite quantities are optimizable without regard to subjective judgment.

We turn first to *hypotheses*, the 'means' or 'devices' that generate and govern a world. These include both a world's initial condition (e.g. our world's state at the Big Bang) and its rules of change (e.g. our world's laws of physics). Read one way, the term "simplest in hypotheses" might refer to the single, simplest combination of these two components. However, there may be reasons for focusing instead on rules and initial conditions separately. For one thing, Leibniz seems to have thought of rules and initial conditions in distinctive ways.[5] For another, rules and initial conditions may each need to be simple for a different reason and therefore to a different degree. Whether we consider rules and initial conditions separately or together, the simplest hypotheses will be the ones that we can specify or calculate using the shortest computer program. These will have the lowest *Kolmogorov complexity* or *algorithmic information content*.[6]

Leibniz did not see richness of phenomena, or "quantity of reality," in the mere bulk or mass of a world's phenomena, but rather in the diversity and complexity of physical forms or modes of being (1973, p.146).

> Perfection is not to be located in matter alone, that is, in something filling time and space, whose quantity would in any way have been the same; rather, it is to be located in [quantity of] form or variety. So it follows that matter is not everywhere alike, but is rendered dissimilar by its forms; otherwise it would not obtain as much variety as it can.
> (1973, p. 146)

Today, we would say that Leibniz saw richness in informational terms. Physicists Julian Barbour and Lee Smolin have tried to capture Leibnizian richness in a metric they call *the variety of the system* (Barbour and Smolin 1992; Barbour 2003). Barbour-Smolin variety "is a non-local and non-additive quantity, which can only be applied to [a] system as a whole. It measures, in a certain sense, how unique, one from another, the different parts of the system are" (Barbour and Smolin, p. 3). It "distinguishes highly structured, but asymmetric, configurations such as one finds in biological systems from both random configurations and [ordered] configurations such as crystals" (Barbour and Smolin, p. 1). The biological configurations are higher in variety.

The variety of a system also increases if the total number of 'atoms' (lowest-level constituents) in the system increases. Imagine three cities: In City A, the houses stand in irregular clusters on narrow, winding streets; we do not, on average, need to place many houses on a map to identify or specify a unique neighborhood. City B has the same number of houses but arranged uniformly, on straight streets with square intersections. Here each neighborhood map would need to include more houses to be unique. Finally, City C looks like City A, but with far more houses. Taking houses as the 'atoms' of these systems, City A would be higher in variety than City B, while City C would be higher than A or B. "A universe with a great deal of variety is one in which it is easy to tell where you are just by looking around," says Lee Smolin (1997, p. 220). It also includes many unique places to visit.

While variety measures the number and arrangement of atoms, it does not reflect their interaction. The static variety of a large pile of dead computers might exceed that of a patch of forest. To capture the forest's dynamic interactivity we can turn to *variety over time* (Lane 2006, pp. 268–9). To transform variety into variety over time, we can take an equal number of instantaneous 'snapshots' of each system. We then combine each set of snapshots into a separate 'mosaic' and calculate the variety of each mosaic. This gives us the variety over time of each system. Since only complex, dynamic processes can produce the constant change needed to make each neighborhood map differ from maps of the same neighborhood elsewhere in the mosaic, this procedure captures system interactivity and emergent behaviors as well as static complexity. A junkyard will either remain unchanged or else disintegrate to a static state. In a forest, on the other hand, "endless forms most beautiful and most wonderful have been, and are being evolved" (Darwin 1993, p. 649).

We can say that Leibnizian optimality is the optimal combination of simple hypotheses and rich phenomena as measured by these or some other appropriate metrics.[7] However, which combination is optimal? Should we add the richness of a world's phenomena to the simplicity of its hypotheses and seek the highest total? Should we divide richness by simplicity and seek the highest quotient? Or should we combine these factors in some other, more complicated way?[8] Should we treat all hypotheses the same in our calculation of optimality, or should we treat the world's initial conditions and its rules (laws of physics) separately?

2. Tightening Leibniz's Claims

At first, these subtle and specific questions seem less significant than the remarkable extent to which our actual world comports with Leibniz's simplest-richest claim. Many modern scientists have marveled at the extreme simplicity of our physical laws and initial conditions and the vast phenomenal richness that they engender.[9] One of these, physicist Paul Davies, says we enjoy "very special laws that guarantee a trend toward greater richness, diversity and complexity through spontaneous self-organization" (2004, p. 106). Davies states that our "laws of physics produce order—the order of simplicity—at the micro, reductionist level, while the felicitous interplay of chance and necessity leads to the emergence of *a different sort of order*—the order of complexity—at the macro, holistic level" (2004, p. 105). He also notes that the Big Bang was "a state of exceptionally high symmetry. Indeed, the initial state of the universe could well have been the simplest possible" (1984, p. 8). All of this leads him to suggest that "in a certain scientific sense we may well live in the best of all possible worlds" (2004, p. 104). While these remarks and similar comments by others suggest that Leibniz was on the right track, they also point out the reason for tightening his claims. To be scientific, a claim must be testable; to be testable, it must be specific. Because Leibniz's simplest-richest claim involves optimizing design parameters, we need to answer two questions to make it more specific: How do those parameters interrelate? How do they relate to whatever goals or objectives the world might serve? The second question points to a third: Might simplicity and richness emerge from other, deeper desiderata?

a) The interrelation of simplicity and richness

Physicist Max Tegmark has considered how the simplicity of a world's rules (which he gives as the number of 'axioms' in a world's laws of physics) might affect the richness of the phenomena that those rules generate (which he gives as the world's 'complexity'). Figure 1, taken from his article, gives his view of this relationship (1998, p. 7).

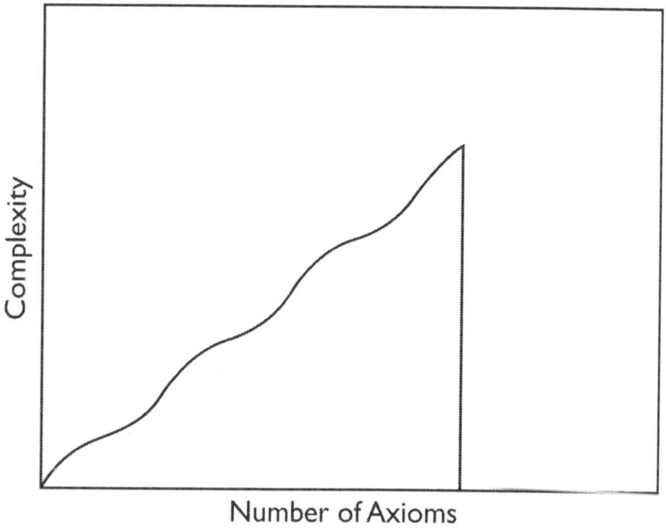

Figure 1. Relationship between axioms and complexity

The wavy, ascending line on the left side of the graph shows that, up to a certain point, more complex rules ('axioms') would generate richer phenomena ('complexity').

Eventually, however, the ascending line reaches a peak. Adding more axioms after this point would cause richness to decline. Beyond this point, overly complicated rules would trip over each other, with new exceptions and constraints wiping out more phenomenal richness than they create. To envision how this might happen, imagine a legal system becoming so complicated that the economy it governs slides into gridlock. Tegmark's view of the relation between rule complexity and phenomenal richness finds support in recent empirical studies of cellular automata.[10]

Leibniz reached a similar conclusion: "God makes the most things he can, and what obliges him to seek simple laws is precisely the necessity to find a place for as many things as can be put together" (Strickland 2006, p. 75).[11] This does not mean that God would choose the absolutely *simplest* laws. There is a point beyond which simpler rules would generate less phenomenal richness or even no phenomena at all. We can see this in Figure 1, where both the complexity of a world's laws and its resulting phenomenal richness fall to their minima at the left edge of the graph. Instead, Leibniz was making the less obvious point that, like overly simple laws, overly complex laws could also reduce a world's complexity and diversity. He was the first to see that simplicity and richness could be both complementary and countervailing.

If Figure 1 is a roughly correct depiction of the relation between the simplicity of a world's laws and the richness of its phenomena, then only solutions to the left of the peak will be relevant to a search for the optimal combination of simple laws and rich phenomena. Even if richness does not decline after the peak as abruptly as Figure 1 shows, some solution on the left side of the graph would always dominate any solution on the right. This is because some solution on the left slope would always have at least the same richness as the competing solution on the right, but would obtain that richness more simply.

Figure 1 therefore leads to two observations: (i) for a system's rules, the range of nondominated candidate solutions to the simplicity-richness problem appears to be finite, and (ii) *over this range,* greater richness of phenomena requires rules that are more complex. If these observations are true, then, over the relevant range, simplicity of rules and richness of phenomena *could* be jointly optimizable at some unique point. However, these observations neither specify the point of optimality nor preclude the possibility that many different solutions might be equally optimal. No point on the upward slope of Figure 1 seems special except the peak, but that is just the point at which richness is greatest. We have no reason (yet) to believe that it is also the point at which the trade-off between the simplicity of a world's rules and the richness of its phenomena is optimal.

What about the relation between the simplicity-complexity of a world's initial conditions and the richness of its phenomena? At present, we have little empirical data on which to base *any* claim about this.[12] However, we will argue later that this relationship, whatever it is, has little practical impact. A different consideration will govern the initial condition of the actual world.

b) The value problem

Thus far, we have no real basis for describing Leibniz's best of worlds. To find one, we need to uncover the purpose or goal that Leibniz thought this world would maximally achieve. If we assume with him that the world is God-created, we can find that purpose only by answering questions like these: Why would God make qualities like simplicity and richness the world's design criteria? What deeper value or values would require a world in which such abstract considerations play a leading role? These questions state the *value problem* posed by Leibniz's claims. They go to God's motive for creation.

The value problem is vital from two perspectives. One of these is *religious*. Unless the world's design criteria arise from a motive that seems worthy of God, even the knowledge that we live in a mathematically optimal world would carry little theological meaning. Solving the value problem is also vital from an *engineering* perspective. Making simplicity and richness the design parameters for the universe is much like making speed and payload design parameters for an airplane. A designer might optimize either set of parameters in any number of ways. Just as an aircraft designer cannot know how to optimize cost, speed, and payload unless he knows *why* the proposed airplane is to exist, we cannot say how the optimal world should combine simplicity and richness unless we understand why it is to exist.

Leibniz addressed the value problem in at least two ways. His first approach honored the life of the mind. Intelligent minds can only contemplate ideas that have some basis in physical reality. The reality that minds inhabit therefore limits and guides their thoughts. From this perspective, the best world would offer the largest possible array of suggestive images and possibilities to the minds that inhabit it, but would present these images in an orderly way. Since it would contain as much as could compossibly exist, it would extend the possibility of thought as much as possible. Because it would operate on simple principles, its operations would be accessible to reason. It would therefore be a "cosmos, full of ornament...made in such a way that it gives the greatest possible pleasure to an intelligent being" (1973, p. 146). "Delight or pleasure is the perception of harmony...Harmony is diversity compensated by identity...Variety delights, but only when it is reduced to a unity, symmetrical, connected. Agreement delights, but only when it is new, surprising, unexpected" (Rutherford 1995, p. 13). These arguments from delight suggest the human value of a high-variety universe that changes according to simple laws. Leibniz thought that the optimal combination of simple hypotheses and rich (variegated) phenomena would make the world "not only the most wonderful machine, but also in regard to minds...the best commonwealth, by whose means there is bestowed on minds the greatest possible amount of felicity or joyfulness" (1973, p. 141).[13] We can call this Leibniz's *minds solution* to the value problem.

Although Leibniz sometimes wrote as if intelligent minds were God's only concern, he more often said that minds were *not* the only or final reasons for God's selection of the simplest-richest cosmos: "God has more than one purpose in his projects. The felicity of all rational creatures is one of the aims he has in view, but it is not his whole aim, nor even his final aim" (1985, § 119, p. 189). God's further, "final aim" involves the intrinsic goodness of actualized reality:

> One may say that as soon as God has decreed to create something there is a struggle between all the possibles, all of them laying claim to existence, and that those which, being united, produce [the] most reality, most perfection, most significance carry the day. [However,] all this struggle can...only be a conflict of reasons in the most perfect understanding, which cannot fail to act in the most perfect way, and consequently to choose the best.
> (1985, § 201, p. 253)

This *plenitude solution* rests on the notion that existence is good *per se*. This idea was hardly original with Leibniz. In the *Timaeus,* Plato connected goodness with fecundity. Then, "throughout medieval theology the love of God tends to be thought of in metaphysical rather than personal terms. It is not so much the love of the personal Infinite for finite persons, as the inexhaustible creative divine fecundity, expressed in the granting of being to a dependent universe with its innumerable grades of creatures" (Hick 1966, p. 77).[14] Leibniz's distinctiveness was in his emphasis on the abstract, potentially measurable quality of "variety" or "richness" as the measure of God's fecundity. He was the first to suggest that some measure of the uniqueness, number, and variability of all individual things rather than the metaphysical completeness of a list of actualized ideas would best measure God's creative goodness.

Neither the minds solution nor the plenitude solution seems wholly persuasive today. Mathematician Ivar Ekeland crystallizes a common reaction to Leibniz's minds solution: "Leibniz belongs to this category of philosophers who claim that happiness lies in contemplating the wonders of God in his creation, an idea that is certainly far away from the everyday concerns of most human beings" (2007, p. 42). This "far away" quality makes the minds solution, for many, an inadequate answer to the problem of human suffering. The victim of a chronic illness is unlikely to feel wonder and joyfulness at the subtle complexity of her pathogen. The claim that the world exists to benefit minds also sounds narrowly anthropocentric. As far as we now know, we are the only minds who benefit in the ways that Leibniz describes. To say that the world exists for "minds" sounds much like saying it exists for us.[15] The plenitude solution faces different problems. For one thing, it seems to require God to create *everything*. As Spinoza pointed out, "God's omnipotence has been actual from all eternity and will remain in the same actuality to eternity" (1994, I P17, p. 14). This being the case, "infinitely many things in infinitely many modes—that is, all things—have necessarily flowed, or always flow by the same necessity and in the same way as from the nature of a triangle it follows...that the sum of its three angles is equal to two right angles" (1994, I P17, p. 14).[16] The leading historian of plenitude agrees: "If a literal realization of all genuine possibles is essential to a reasonable world, everything and everybody should have existed, and every event should have occurred, from all eternity" (Lovejoy 1964, p. 155). This sort of *plenary* world, in which every possible event, series of events, and set of physical laws already exists somewhere (call it an *omniverse*), was not what Leibniz would call optimal. He said it "would obliterate all the beauty of the universe and all choice" (1970, p. 263).

To preserve divine choice, Leibniz tried to exclude the coexistence of everything as a logically possible option. He partially succeeded. By making certain ontological assumptions, he was able to show that all self-consistent phenomena could not coexist in a single space-time manifold, or even in a single set of inter-communicating manifolds (Rescher 2003, pp. 92–105). In modern parlance, his ontology let him rule out the possibility that a *multi-domain universe*—a single world whose many regions are locally causally interconnected—could be an omniverse.[17] However, this was not enough, for he knew of a different arrangement that *would* allow an infinite number of worlds to coexist: "There could exist an infinity of other spaces and worlds entirely different [from ours]. They would have no distance from us [nor other special relations to us] if the minds inhabiting them had sensations not related to ours" (Rescher 2003, p. 95).[18] In short, there could be a *multiverse,* a state of things consisting of many separate worlds, none of them locally causally connected to any of the others.[19] Leibniz did not believe in an actual, infinite multiverse, but he could not logically exclude the possibility that the omniverse might exist in that form.

More than that, the value structure of his plenitude solution could not rule out an omniverse. To see why, consider two objections that Leibniz might raise against the claim—whether based on God's goodness or just on God's infinitude—that God should and would actualize the omniverse. First, he might argue that an endless number of diverse, causally separate universes would offend the desideratum of simplicity. An infinite, plenary multiverse certainly seems like an overly complicated structure. However, there are two problems with this objection:

First, it requires Leibniz to show *why* simplicity is independently desirable. Yet in the context of the plenitude solution, it seems that simple laws have only an instrumental function: their role is to generate maximal richness. As Leibniz put it, "[W]hat obliges [God] to seek simple laws is precisely the necessity to find a place for as many things as can be put together" (Strickland 2006, p. 75).[20] If that is their only function, then simple laws cannot be an independent desideratum. If simplicity is only an instrumental value, it cannot constrain God from including ever more phenomena, even if those phenomena would complicate the world's rules.

Second, an opponent could reply that the omniverse *is* maximally simple. In support of that position, Tegmark argues that "an entire ensemble is often much simpler than one of its members" (1998, p. 25). From the standpoint of its Kolmogorov complexity, the set of all integers is simpler than the set of integers from 2 through 36. It takes a shorter computer program to specify the infinitely larger set. Like the command, "Print all the integers," the command, "Create everything" looks to be maximally simple.

As a second values-based objection, Leibniz might maintain that some self-consistent worlds contain inordinate amounts of creaturely pain and suffering. Since these super-painful worlds do not deserve actualization, God would not actualize every possible world.[21] This argument has force, but it rests on a consideration that is not part of the plenitude solution. It makes God balance what, from our perspective, are incommensurable factors: how much reality should exist versus how much suffering? This is really a third solution to the value problem: a *balancing solution*. Leibniz may have had something like that in mind when he rejected Spinoza's omniverse. He certainly believed that God could perform calculations of value far beyond our mental powers. However, because the qualities that God would need to balance are incommensurable from our perspective, this solution cannot help with the engineering problem. It cannot make Leibniz's claim specific and testable.

Nor is the balancing solution satisfying in principle. It suggests that God would create a world that was suboptimal both from a plenitude standpoint and from the standpoint of its effect on minds just because it would be the best available compromise. Yet why should we settle for a compromise until we have ruled out the possibility that some world might be best from both standpoints, properly understood?

The solutions considered so far do not persuasively connect Leibniz's claims to our understanding of God. Nor do they tell us how simplicity and richness ought to combine in the optimal world. From both the religious and engineering perspectives, we need a new approach to the value problem.

3. A New Approach

We cannot say what trade-off among speed, payload, and other factors should characterize an airplane unless we know its mission. However, given an existent airplane, we could write down the combination of design requirements that it would need for some specified mission and then test to see if it had that combination of qualities. If the fit were excellent, we might reasonably conclude that its designers had intended it for that mission. If we take this approach, our initial hunch about the airplane's purpose need not derive from anything except personal belief. As with any scientific hypothesis, it "may initially be put forward for aesthetic or metaphysical reasons, but the real test is whether it makes predictions that agree with observation" (Hawking 1998, pp. 141–2). We can follow this same approach with our existent universe.

If, as Leibniz thought, our world began with God, then its mission or purpose must flow out of the value (or values) that motivated God to actualize it. Since that value must reflect God's nature, we should be able to frame a testable claim about the world's physical structure by considering God's nature. This is just what Leibniz thought. He said, "It is sanctifying philosophy to make its streams flow from the fountain of God's attributes. Far from excluding final causes and the consideration of a being acting with wisdom, it is from there that everything must be deduced in physics" (2006, pp. 131–2).

Any serious reflection on God's nature must consider this profound comment from the philosopher Nikolai Berdyaev:

> Can God be said to have no inner life, no emotional and affective states? The static conception of God as *actus purus*...is a philosophical, Aristotelian, and not a biblical conception. The God of the Bible, the God of the revelation, is by no means an *actus purus*: He has affective and emotional states, dramatic developments in His inner life, inward movement—but all this is revealed exoterically. It is extraordinary how limited is the human conception of God. Men are afraid to ascribe to Him inner conflict and tragedy characteristic of all life, the longing for His "other," for the birth of man, but have no hesitation in ascribing to Him anger, jealousy, vengeance and other affective states which, in man, are regarded as reprehensible...We can only think of God symbolically and mythologically. And a symbolic psychology of God is possible—not in relation to the Divine Nothing of negative theology, but in relation to God-the-Creator of positive theology.
> (1937, pp. 37–8)

Berdyaev says that God is beyond human understanding; he accepts the *via negativa*. He observes, however, that all religious thought analogizes from the human to the divine, and does so mythologically. He then says (but only from this limited, *via positiva*, viewpoint) that God must act out of some desire, some motive akin to a human emotion.

Leibniz made 'goodness' God's motive for creation. However, goodness is not an emotion; it is a *monopolar* virtue. It involves giving but not sensing or suffering. A God who acts only out of goodness may act selflessly on behalf of others, but the actions of those others and the events that befall them will have no consequent impact on God. For Berdyaev, this is an inadequate portrait of God's inner life. It ignores God's "inner conflict and tragedy," God's mythological joy and tears on behalf of "His 'other.'" If God is *both* actor and emotionally acted upon, then

God's motive for creation must involve the desire to sense the experiences of others as well as the desire to give to them; it must involve an emotion, not a bare ethical principle.

For a Christian, God *is* love (1 John 4:16). Meister Eckhart explained that "all of the commandments of God proceed from love and from the goodness of his nature, for if they did not come from love then they could not be the commandments of God" (1994, p. 119).Yet love is action and reaction. It is *doing for* others, but also involving oneself with them, *being and experiencing with* them. Paul wrote to the church at Corinth, "May the [*charis*] of the Lord Jesus Christ and the [*agape*] of God and the [*koinonia*] of the Holy Spirit be with you all" (2 Corinthians 13:14). *Charis* means favor, grace, or loving-kindness; *koinonia* means solidarity, participation, 'joining with' or fellow feeling; *agape* means selfless sacrifice. All of these are aspects of that single, unitary quality that we can, if only by analogy, call divine love.

Leibniz wrote of human love in a similar vein: In love, he said, "the happiness or the perfection of others, in giving us pleasure, immediately forms part of our own happiness" (2006, p. 163). Elsewhere, he described love as "that act or active state of the soul which makes us find our pleasure in the happiness or satisfaction of others" (Rutherford 1995, p. 56). He also said that "to love truly and in a disinterested manner is nothing else than to be led to find pleasure in the perfection or in the happiness of the object, and consequently to experience grief in what is contrary to these perfections" (Rutherford 1995, p. 57). In these passages, Leibniz sees love as both a doing for others (an "active state of the soul") *and* an experience of participating with others (a "pleasure" or "grief"). In the latter mode, the happiness and perfection (or unhappiness and imperfection) of our beloveds "immediately forms part of our own." In theology, Leibniz more often accepted a monopolar view of God. In this view—which had then been standard for a millennium—God is an impassible actor, never enjoying or suffering from events in the world. However, on at least one occasion, he admitted that—"so to speak" or "to speak humanly"—God might experience joy or sorrow at worldly events (Riley 1996, pp. 153–4). This view has come into greater favor recently. The monopolar view of an impassible God has been seen as severely limited, while the view that God is *both* an emotionally driven actor *and* emotionally acted upon is more satisfying, both logically and religiously.[22] *Dipolar* divine love would urge God *to benefit others*, to act on their behalf, but it would also draw God *to be with those others* in their perfection or happiness (or the opposites). Dipolar love would lead God to share fully in created events. The desire to be with one's beloved is central to human love; we have no reason to imagine that divine love does not in some sense share this desire.

4. A Thought Experiment

To see how divine love might affect God's choice of design parameters, we can perform a thought experiment. Imagine the God of ethical theism, infinite in all qualities but alone at Creation. Imagine God, motivated by infinite love yet constrained by the principle of noncontradiction. This principle not only precludes God from doing inconsistent things, like creating systems that defy logical consistency. It also precludes God from acting inconsistently with the divine nature.[23]

Our only guides to that nature are theology and religious tradition. These compel us to regard three aspects of God's nature as so fundamental that God would not act inconsistently with them: God is real; God is one; God can never perish.[24] Given these suppositions, what would the God of love actualize, and how would that occur?

a) Love and fecundity

We begin with love in the sense of conferring benefits on others. 'Before' creation, God was the only reality; there was nothing existent for God to love. The only available objects of God's love were possibilities: every self-consistent event or thing that might exist in any circumstance. Loving all, God would wish to benefit, and hence to actualize, as widely as possible.

In our common experience, love gives what it has to those it seeks to benefit. A person who loves and has money will give money; a person who loves and has time will give time. God has existence and the power to actualize possibilities. Motivated by infinite *agape*, God would wish to actualize as much as possible. It would be self-contradictory for infinite *agape*, armed with the power to act, *not* to act on as wide a scale as possible (see Kretzmann 1997, pp. 223–4). The thirteenth-century philosopher Muhyiddin Ibn al-'Arabi wrote, "The lover loves to bring the nonexistent thing into existence." In short, the *doing for* aspect of love implies a universal, Platonic fecundity.

This claim differs from the scholastic account. Aquinas wrote, "God loves all existing things. For all existing things, *insofar as they exist*, are good" (PI, Q20, A2; emphasis added). This implies that the *unactualized* possibilities are not so good, or perhaps that God does not love them.[25] However, on what rational basis should we believe that Mars with two moons is good, but Mars with three moons would not have been good, or that Queen Elizabeth was good but a Queen Lydia would not have been good? There appears to be none. Leibniz said that God would only actualize the "best" set of possibilities, but he predicated that claim on the impossibility of actualizing all the possibles in a single, causally interconnected world.[26] However, we are not yet considering what God could actualize; we are only asking what God would *wish* to actualize considering only the *agape* aspect of love. The only coherent answer to that question would seem to be, "All."

b) Love and becoming

An all-loving, personal God would desire closeness to the beloveds, would want to experience them directly. The degree of closeness that human love desires depends on its intensity. A lover who loves with infinite intensity would desire infinite closeness. In mathematics, when two points are infinitely close there is no difference between them. God's desire for infinite closeness would incline God to actualize possibilities by becoming them.

Theism casts God as a very close *observer*. However, no outside observer can be infinitely close to you or to any other actualized possibility. No observer, however close, can experience your experiences, think your thoughts, or feel your emotions exactly as you do.[27] No omniscient observer can fear the unknown as an ignorant creature can; no eternal, indestructible observer can fear destruction as one that stands in danger of it can. It seems that God could be infinitely close to actualized phenomena only by becoming them. Only in this way could God experience *everything* they experience—their births, deaths, and dissipations, their victories and defeats—just as they do.

The idea of divine becoming has theological advantages. It avoids the deistic claim that God creates the world and then leaves it to its own devices. Yet it also avoids the sort of theism where God reaches into the world on behalf of some individuals but abandons others to their fates. If we envision God becoming the world, God could truly say to us, "Whatever you do for one of the least of these brothers of mine, you do also for me" (Matthew 25:40).

In the Christian tradition, the divine becoming of the Incarnation reveals God's infinite love. Theologian Charlene Burns argues that God's Incarnation in Christ was not a unique, one-off event; instead, it revealed how God's love fills the whole world (2002, p. 136). Revelation aside, divine becoming comports with our empirical experience. We only ever experience becoming; we never experience changeless things or things created from nothing. Louise Young writes that, in the actual world, "Becoming stands forth as the essential reality" (1986, p. 96).

If divine becoming were complete, God's *kenosis*—God's self-emptying for the sake of love—would be total. In this *pandeistic* view, nothing of God would remain separate and apart from whatever God would become.[28] Any separate, divine existence would be inconsistent with God's unreserved participation in the lives and fortunes of the actualized phenomena.

c) Problems of becoming

We can define a *phenomenon* as any existent thing or event. Possibilities become phenomena when (if) they are actualized. There is no single, right way to delimit a phenomenon. The striking of a match is a phenomenon, but so is the excitation of electrons in a few thousand atoms at the leading edge of the match head. So is everything that happens from the lighting of the match to the burning of the bonfire to the smoldering embers. Thus, all phenomena are composed of other phenomena and are parts of others still; none is completely separate or entirely distinct.

If God became the actualized phenomena, God would exist as each of them. God's experience would be their experiences. If one phenomenon were to rejoice, God as that phenomenon would rejoice; if another were to be shattered, God as it would be shattered. If still others would decay, die, or dissolve, God as those phenomena would decay, die, or dissolve. William Blake's words, "Eternity is in love with the productions of time," capture the essence of this step (p. 7). Love draws the unlimited into the limited; infinite love, out of love, becomes the limited "productions."

To understand how God could become the phenomena, we need to solve the *problem of perishing* and the *problem of unity*. The problem of perishing runs this way: because there are infinitely more ways to be limited than to be unlimited, virtually all actualized phenomena will be limited. Since its limits are part of the complete description of any limited phenomena, it is only because of its limits that any limited phenomena can exist at all.

Karl Barth calls this the "shadow side" of created things: their limits are intrinsic to their natures.[29] Since one way to be limited is to be limited in time, virtually all actualized phenomena will die, decay, dissolve, or be shattered. A mayfly would not be a mayfly if it lived forever. The same is true of mountains and stars. None of these could be eternal and still be what it is. Nor can such phenomena be static, even during their limited existence. To exist at all they must change in themselves, and their relations with other phenomena must change. To be with the beloved phenomena fully, every step of the way, God would need to experience their existence, including their shattering, dissolution, and death as fully as they do. These experiences would therefore need to be real for God. Yet if God survives such experiences, how could they be real? On the other hand, if God did *not* survive them, how could God experience anything else? It seems that a full experience of one real perishing would both violate God's eternal nature and end God's ability to experience others. That is the problem of perishing. The problem of unity is closely related. God is one, but there are infinitely many possibilities. Loving all of them, God would wish to become as many as possible. How could God do that and remain one?

d) A waveform world

An ocean wave transmits information, not things. No individual water molecule travels with the wave. The molecules just move up and down according to motions imparted by other molecules close to them. Only the wave moves forward. We can think of the wave as *information* that tells molecules how to move. At one moment, a set of many trillions of molecules composes the wave; at a later moment, it is composed of a different set. Nevertheless, a wave is as real and as singular as an oak tree. It is one because it has *informational unity*.

Imagine a large pond of irregular shape, with a few stumps and boulders at the bottom. If we drop a steel ball into the center of the pond, waves will spread from the center to the edges. As they race around the pond hitting the stumps, boulders, and edges, local regions of turbulence—call them eddies or *waveforms*—will form. These waveforms will take on many different shapes and sizes. They will collide or interfere with each other; some will overwhelm or engulf others. Yet at each stage of its existence, this whole, interactive process will form a single, cohesive history. Each component waveform, including those that were overwhelmed, will play its part in this history, which will be slightly different because of it. Even if that difference is unrecognizable to a historian of the pond, it will still be there. Leibniz used a wave analogy to explain this:

> With the universe being a kind of fluid, all of one piece…all motions in it are conserved and propagated to infinity, though insensibly, just like the circles of which I have spoken (which came about by a stone thrown in the water) are propagated visibly for some distance, and although they become invisible in the end, the impression does not cease spreading.
> (2006, p. 82)

Just as an oak tree spreads from an acorn, the sequence of waveforms in the pond spreads from its origin to generate a single, connected history. Like the oak tree, this sequence of waveforms has a branching, intertwining informational unity.

Imagine (as Leibniz did) a world analogous to a pond. In it, every phenomenon exists as a waveform. Eventually, each waveform will die or dissolve, but each will generate information that it will leave behind. Other waveforms will transform that information and pass it forward along with information that they in turn will generate. This single, evolving process constantly creates information, but none is ever lost. This waveform world resolves both the problem of unity and the problem of perishing. In it, phenomena will, from their own perspectives, change, dissipate, and die, but the reality that includes them will continue. The information they are now will continue to shape the single reality that is the world in all later moments.

e) Transactions and rules

A waveform world could be one (unitary) only if it were a continuing, integrated process. To be such a process, it would need to conserve information in and through its transactions. A *transaction* occurs when one phenomenon (waveform) impinges upon, generates, destroys, influences, or becomes another. If the result of a transaction were entirely indeterminate, if it might result in just any outcome, information from the phenomena that entered into it would not pass on to those that emerge from it. That information would be lost. Any part of a world in which unreliable transactions occur would therefore become causally isolated. An isolated system would entirely perish when it died or dissolved; a world in which systems became isolated could not remain one. For both reasons, God would not become such a world. *A fortiori*, God would not become two or more causally isolated worlds; God would not become a multiverse.

Reliability cannot be uncaused. For physical transactions to be reliable, some *rule* must specify or govern them. A rule must do more than describe a world in general terms; it must describe how transactions work in specific circumstances.[30] In a world with no rules, anything might emerge from anything else. Such a world could not conserve information through transactions; it could not be one. Thus, any world that God becomes must have rules.

When can we say that a world has rules? Leibniz wrote that *any* world must have rules in the loose sense that all possible physical relationships are describable after the fact:

> If someone draws an uninterrupted curve which is now straight, now circular, and now of some other nature, it is

> possible to find a concept, a rule, or an equation common to all the points of the line, in accordance with which these changes must take place...But when the rule for this movement is very complex, the line which conforms to it *passes for* irregular. Thus, we may say that no matter how God might have created the world, it would always have been regular and in a certain general order.
> (1989, p. 39; emphasis added)

A curve described by a "complex" rule "*passes for* irregular" when it *appears to be* ungoverned, i.e. when an observer cannot deduce the rule that describes it from the information available to her. By contrast, a curve (by which Leibniz meant any continuous line) *is* regular if an observer can deduce its rule (the algorithm that governs it) from what she can see of its twists and turns.

Deciding whether a rule is regular is not always easy. Consider this number series: 2, 3, ... 31. Perhaps some rule governs this series, but without more data, we cannot say what that rule is. Does the series consist only of prime numbers, or of all the integers from 2 to 31, or of some other progression? In much the same way, if some complex rule governed Leibniz's "uninterrupted curve," an observer might not be able to discern it. However, this would not necessarily mean that the curve *was* in fact "irregular" (i.e. governed by no rule); it might just mean that she had too little information. Perhaps a sheet of paper is covering part of the curve.

However, what if no observer could deduce the rule(s) that govern(s) a world, even with complete access to *all* the information embodied in that world? The transactions governed by this undiscoverable rule really *would be* irregular; they would not just appear to be so. Why should the inability of an observer to discover a rule mean that the rule does not exist? The answer turns on God's *kenosis*. If God becomes a world and *kenosis* is complete, then no information about that world (or the rules that govern it) can exist *anywhere* except in that world. Smolin describes how this works:

> The definition or description of any entity inside the universe can refer only to other things in the universe. If something has a position, that position can be defined only with respect to the other things in the universe. If it has a motion, that motion can be discerned only by looking for changes in its position with respect to other things in the universe.
> (2001, pp. 17–18)

If no information can exist outside a world, then only the information in it can be used in deciding the regularity of its transactions. A rule that remained undiscoverable in principle, even given all the information embodied in such a world, would not be a rule in that world. From the world's perspective (the only one that matters), transactions governed by this nonrule would be unpredictable and hence unreliable; the world would lose information through such transactions.

An example from Boolean logic shows another way in which information can be lost. The AND operation requires that if and only if all inputs are on, the output will be on. The output will be off if any input is off. Now consider four sets of inputs to an AND operation and what we can know about them by studying only their output and the setup of the computer system. (Here, 1 represents *on* and 0 represents *off*.)

Inputs	*Output*	*Reverse*
0, 0	0	?
0, 1	0	?
1, 0	0	?
1, 1	1	1, 1

As shown in the table, if the output of an AND operation is 1, we will know with logical certainty that its two inputs were 1 and 1. This operation is *logically reversible*. However, if the output is 0, we have no way, after the fact, of knowing its inputs. They might be any one of three possible combinations. Thus, given a 0 output, the operation is *logically irreversible*. Even though the AND operation is reliable—the output always reflects the input—some information about its inputs is necessarily lost.[31] On the other hand, reversibility implies reliability; reversibility is the tighter requirement.

A computer system loses information when a logically irreversible operation occurs and the input information is erased.[32] A waveform world would be a spreading network of physical operations (transactions) rather than purely logical ones. Such a world would pass from one state to another, with earlier states automatically erased. Such a world could preserve information only if all its transactions were *physically reversible*; that is, only if its former state could be retrodicted from all the information embodied in its present state. Importantly, this definition of physical reversibility does not require the needed information to be available to an observer in any practical sense; it does not even require an observer to exist. It only requires that all information needed to retrodict earlier waveforms from later ones must be retained somewhere in the world. This is nevertheless a very tight specification. It is easy to construct reliable but irreversible rules. To take a simple example, we can often retrodict the history of a game of chess if the game has only progressed two or three moves. However, after six or seven moves, retrodiction most often becomes impossible. Since the present state of the board no longer picks out its prior state, information has been lost.[33]

The proportion of complex rules that support nothing but reversible transactions is far smaller than the proportion of simple rules that support nothing but such transactions. Exploring logical reversibility in the context of cellular automata,

Wolfram 2002 (p. 436) examined 256 of the simplest type of rules by which one row of black and white cells can generate another row. Of these 256 very simple rules, he found six to be reversible, or about 2.3 percent. On the other hand, out of about *7.6 trillion* slightly more complex rules, only 1806 were reversible, or about one *100 millionth* of 2.3 percent. This empirical observation holds two important implications. First, out of all possible rules as complex as the ones that govern our universe, the proportion that permit only reversible transactions is likely to be quite small. Since it seems unlikely that only completely reversible rules could support the evolution of complex life, the reversibility (or not) of our physical laws will offer a means of testing the claims made here. Second, we now see a pressure for the simplicity of physical law that does not depend either on the elegance and comprehensibility of such laws or on their fecundity. Instead, this pressure takes root in God's desire to be with the beloveds, in the *koinonia* element of divine love.

Subject to being reliable and reversible, the rules that God selects must generate the greatest richness, the maximum possible variety. Reversibility can be consistent with richness.

While most of the 1,806 slightly complex, reversible rules that Wolfram identified did not generate much structure, a few of them did. Thus, "even though only a very small fraction of possible systems have the property of being reversible, such systems can still exhibit behavior just as complex as one sees anywhere else" (2002, p. 441).

Reliability-reversibility and fecundity are independent constraints because a different aspect of God's love requires each. The first is absolute; the second is a maximization constraint. Each is very tight, and they oppose each other in a number of ways. To see this, consider the question of whether rules should be variable or invariant. Up to a point, a rule that varies between period X and period Y (e.g. a law of gravity that changes in strength at a certain time) might generate greater richness than an invariant rule. The variable rule, by generating two distinct sets of phenomena, might result in greater cumulative richness. On the other hand, events in the X period might become irretrievable after the Y period commences. From this perspective, a simpler, invariant law might be better. To assure both reliability-reversibility and maximal fecundity, a selected rule could not be *maximally* simple. Instead, it would need to balance simplicity and fecundity to satisfy *optimally* the countervailing demands of love.

f) Simple initial conditions

Some writers claim that the world could be eternal into the past. If so, it would have no initial condition. Whether this could be true of any world is uncertain, but it cannot be true of a world that God has become. Any such world must be in some state when God becomes it. That state (whatever it is) would be its initial condition.

Given God's *koinonia*, God's desire to be with creation, the actualized world's initial state must meet a tight specification: it must be both one and radically simple. To see why, imagine again the waveform world found in our pond. This world has informational unity because all of the waveforms in it share a common history. We can trace them through a series of causal connections, back to the initial dropping of the ball. This shared history *is* the world; in it, the many waveforms are one. The same would hold true in a wider waveform world. All its animate and inanimate inhabitants would be ripples and eddies in a single, common history.

Now consider the moment that God becomes a world. In the pond analogy, this is the moment the ball enters the water. Right then, the world has no prior, common history. If it had two separate origins—if two balls splashed into the pond at two different locations—those two points would not (could not) be one *right then*. At that moment there would be two worlds, a result forbidden by God's unity. To avoid this, the world must have a single origin. This explains why God would not add things to a world (e.g. a chain of islands) or change the things that exist to enhance its variety (or for some other purpose) in disregard of its rules. Any added or changed entity would be a second origin.

What would the world's single origin look like? As we have already seen, information can only exist inside the world, embodied (encoded) in the relations that compose it. Now imagine that a certain world's single origin has two distinct parts: call them A and B.[34] Upon actualization, each of these parts becomes a phenomenon. Call these phenomena A1 and B1. Each can trace its history back to one part of the origin but not to the other. From the standpoint of the phenomena, it would be as if the world had two separate origins. Once again, that is the only standpoint that matters, for there is no outside observer. Thus, the world cannot originate from a single, complex origin. While simplicity is only a derivative or emergent feature of the world's rules, it must be the central feature of the world's origin. Since the simplest geometrical figure is a point, we can say that the world God would become must have a point origin.[35]

As noted above, little empirical evidence or theoretical reasoning has as yet addressed the relation between the simplicity of a world's initial conditions and the richness of its phenomena. If there were no relation at all or if a maximally simple origin were consistent with maximal phenomenal richness, there would be no conflict between the simple origin required for unity and the goal of maximal richness. If, on the other hand, multiple or complex initial conditions would produce greater phenomenal richness, the conflict would be resolved in favor of unity. Divine love could consistently fulfill itself only in a unitary world. Since a single, simple origin is essential to the world's unity, the world's origin needs to be radically simple. God would become only one, locally causally connected world.

Since simplicity is just the absence of structure, a maximally simple origin must contain as little structure as possible. On the other hand, a maximally rich universe would need to contain a great deal of nested, complex structure. These opposing requirements can coexist only if the world *changes* from simplicity to richness. This overall, directional change would be one of the best world's dominant features.

In summary, God would become the one world that: (i) has a single, maximally simple, origin; (ii) obeys reliable rules that permit only physically reversible transactions; and (iii) obeys rules that, subject to (ii), generate the maximum possible richness (variety over time). This world would have relatively simple, potentially discernable rules and would exhibit no phenomena not governed by those rules. It would be a world of constant change, including a global change from initial simplicity to later richness. From the standpoint of divine love, this would be the best of worlds.

5. The Real World

Our actual world seems to meet these specifications. It had a single origin that—physicists now believe—embodied very little information, perhaps none at all.[36] Since that maximally simple origin, our world has expanded and variegated. The Hubble expansion, its dominant physical feature, began to engender complex structure out of the random fluctuations that occurred right after the Big Bang.[37] Through a series of emergent, structural, and chemical processes, all governed by a few, simple rules, these fluctuations have given rise to a universe in which we "not only find structure on a variety of scales, *we find structure on every scale we have so far explored*" (Smolin 1997, p. 163; emphasis in original).[38] This structure extends far beyond our gaze; our visible universe is only a tiny part of the whole (Cornish, Spergel, Starkman, and Komatsu 2004). Moreover, most of it seems inessential to our existence. Stephen Hawking has remarked:

> Our solar system is certainly a prerequisite for our existence, and one might extend this to the whole of our galaxy to allow for an earlier generation of stars that created the heavier elements. But there does not seem to be any need for all those other galaxies, nor for the universe to be so uniform and similar on the large scale.
> (1998, p. 130)

We continually discover additional structure, which seems to be there for its own sake and not for ours, as the range and power of our instruments increases.[39]

Information transfer should play a critical role in the world that God becomes. Physicist Seth Lloyd says that it is central in our actual world. We do not live in a world of separate, freestanding things and events, but rather in a world of information exchange (interrelation) that occurs at all scales and across a wide range of modalities. Lloyd regards our world as a quantum computer: "Although the basic laws of physics are comparatively simple in form, they give rise, because they are computationally universal, to systems of enormous complexity" (2007, p. 176).

In this vast computational system, information is never lost. If we throw a deck of cards high into the air, they will scatter as they fall; their original order will become unknowable. From the standpoint of an observer, that information is now "hidden" (see Susskind 1997; Lloyd 2007, p. 80). However, that hidden information still exists in the detailed positions and movements of the cards on the floor, the surrounding air molecules, the carpet fibers, etc. Reversing the motions of all these systems would restore the deck to its initial condition. No information has actually vanished. This principle is universal. For example, when a computer erases the inputs to a logically irreversible operation, the erased information is not lost to the world; instead, it smears across the thermal energy of the environment. Part of it is in the air around the computer; another part may be in the programmer's coffee. No observer could ever retrieve all the deleted information, but reversing every motion in the computer and its environment would restore it intact (Susskind 2008, pp. 180–2; Astakhov 2007). Because no information ever disappears, no phenomenon comes to an absolute end. Contrary to a claim once made by Hawking (but now abandoned by him), this principle of *information conservation* seems to hold everywhere in our world, even inside black holes (Hawking 2005; Susskind 2008).[40]

Additional tests of the claim that God became our world out of love will become practical as our knowledge increases. Finding a single example of absolute information loss from our actual world would be enough to falsify it. So would the discovery of an alternative physics that describes a selfconsistent world with a maximally simple origin and reversible laws that would be more fecund than ours.[41]

A third method of falsification would be to discover that, within a widening range of investigation, life exists only on Earth. Pound for pound, biological systems are far higher in variety than other, naturally occurring systems. Therefore, all else being equal, a universe that hosts widespread life would be far richer than one that hosts none or one in which life was extremely rare. Yet biologists remain of two minds about life's origin. Some, like Francis Crick, call it "almost a miracle, so many are the conditions that would have had to be satisfied to get it going" (1981, p. 88). Others disagree. Christian de Duve argues that "life is an obligatory manifestation of matter, bound to arise where conditions are appropriate" (1995, p. 428). Since the vastness of our universe would allow even very improbable events to occur somewhere, either view is consistent with our existence (Dawkins 2006, pp. 156–66). Yet it seems probable that some set of reliable, reversible physical laws *could* make life "an obligatory manifestation of matter." So, if life were really unique to Earth, our laws would probably *not* be maximally fecund.[42]

6. Minds

Unlike their medieval forebears, many modern theologians imagine that God has a special love for animals with high-functioning brains, animals that philosophers call 'rational minds.' Some go so far as to find Creation's purpose in humanity's evolution toward a more 'rational' or 'enlightened' state. This article argues that God's love is boundless, embracing rocks and stars as well as men and women. However, rational minds may play a unique role even in a nonanthropocentric world. For one thing, human and other high-functioning brains are the most physically complex objects that we know.

The mere existence of such complex objects would materially enhance a world's overall richness. For another, a world might become richer through the efforts of rational creatures, i.e., through the art and technology that they create.[43] If so, then, as between otherwise similar worlds, the one that favored intelligent life would be preferred. In that world, rational minds could become co-creators of the richness beloved by God.

Turning from 'doing for' to 'being with,' God would only become a world if there were 'something it is like' to exist in the world, i.e., if conscious awareness somehow existed within it. If nothing in a world had conscious awareness, God could share nothing by becoming that world. It follows that God could experience a world fully only if some capacity for experience, however minimal, existed throughout it. What evidence do we have that this is true of our world?

Modern writers on consciousness hold one of two divergent views. Most attribute it solely to the sort of complex computation that occurs in the brains of higher animals. In this theory of *emergence* or *neurocomputation*, consciousness depends entirely on neural structure. A minority take a different view, the approach of *protopanpsychism*. Following Leibniz and Alfred North Whitehead, they argue that even the tiniest bits of matter must possess something remotely akin to awareness. In this view, no amount of complex structure can conjure subjective experience out of mere, dead existence. Unless some minimal precursor of consciousness inheres in every bit of matter, emergent processes would have nothing from which to build.

Protopanpsychism runs up against a strong, Western prejudice, an assumption that only humans, or perhaps only humans and 'higher' animals, are capable of conscious awareness. However, there is little real evidence for this assumption. We cannot equate consciousness with behaviors that reflect consciousness: some inadequately anesthetized patients are conscious of operative pain but unable to move or communicate their distress (Sandin, Enlund, Samuelsson, and Lennmarken 2000). Nor can we assume that consciousness requires a very complex brain: evidence of it has been found in the brains of fruit flies (van Swinderen 2005).[44]

Leibniz thought that the world's elemental constituents, its *monads*, were in some way conscious. He appealed to a thought experiment involving a conscious machine:

> In imagining that there is a machine whose construction would enable it to think, to sense, and to have perception, one could conceive it enlarged while retaining the same proportions, so that one could enter into it, just like into a windmill. Supposing this, one should, when visiting within it, find only parts pushing one another, and never anything by which to explain a perception. Thus, it is in the simple substance, and not in the composite or in the machine, that one must look for perception.
>
> (1991, 83, § 17)

Some modern scientists still seek a link between conscious awareness and "simple substance." Today, this search proceeds in the fields of neuroscience and quantum physics.

Those engaged in this search argue that (i) conscious awareness cannot be reduced to brain chemistry and neural structure; and/or (ii) a complete understanding of quantum physics requires attention to consciousness (see, e.g., Wigner 1967, Penrose 1989, Chalmers 1996, Squires 1994, Rosenblum and Kuttner 2008). Some suggest specific, quantum mechanical processes that might have a functional role inside the brain (see, e.g., Squires 1990, Penrose 1994, Beck and Eccles 1992, Walker 2000, Malin 2001, Stapp 1993, Lockwood 1990).[45] While they agree with the neurocomputationists that full organismic awareness depends on special structures in the brain, most of these writers would argue that these structures, like Leibniz's windmill, could not generate consciousness if they could not correlate and amplify simpler events that invoke it in some rudimentary form. If they are right, some degree of consciousness may pervade the universe.

As noted above, this is not a consensus view. Most neuroscientists would deny that quantum processes play an important role in brain function, whether that involves consciousness or anything else (see, e.g., Litt, Eliasmith, Kroon, Weinstein et al. 2006; Churchland 1998). They would say, for example, that temperatures inside the brain are too high: the random (classical) motions of molecules must collapse quantum superpositions so quickly that they can have no meaningful role in brain function (Litt, Eliasmith, Kroon, Weinstein et al. 2006; Tegmark 2000). However, other scientists dispute this claim (Hameroff 2007, p. 1038; Hagan, Hameroff, and Tuszynski 2002). Like many other questions about consciousness, this one remains unresolved.

Given our present state of knowledge, the debate over the roots of consciousness is unlikely to be resolved soon. Nevertheless, the competing camps offer *potentially* falsifiable claims. Most obviously, the discovery of a complete, empirically tested, purely neurocomputational explanation of conscious awareness in the human brain would remove the main argument for the protopanpsychist view. It is therefore worth noting that we have no such theory now.

Besides enriching the world, fully self-conscious minds could also serve another purpose. Through them, God could be with actualized reality more completely than through mere 'monadic' protoconsciousness. Since stars have neither organs of perception nor central nervous systems, any proto-experiences that might occur within them (or elsewhere in the nonliving universe) would seem to be quite limited in scope and depth. Beavers and barracudas may have rich experiential lives, but only limited understanding. Rational minds encounter a vastly wider range of experiences and can integrate and process their experiences in ways that let them gain even more. These enhanced abilities, which might take diverse forms in different individuals and species, would let God experience the world through a variety of lenses. A world that never produced minds capable of observation, intuition, empathy, and reason would not be one that God could 'be with' as fully as possible.

7. Our Goodness and God's

Our function in the world process should now be clear. We are here to co-produce, preserve, and enhance the world's phenomenal richness and to experience and understand the world on God's behalf. Human goodness has two unambiguous meanings, both of which derive from God's purpose for the world: (i) our unique physical complexity and constructive potential make each of us intrinsically good; and (ii) we become instrumentally good when we actually serve God's purposes, when we add to the world's richness and observe it with compassionate understanding.

This conclusion grounds ethics and human purpose in

physical cosmology to an extent not achievable by any traditional worldview. Materialism cannot do this at all. Physicist Steven Weinberg has stated its credo: "The more the universe seems comprehensible, the more it also seems pointless" (1978, p. 154). Theists have always appealed to the world's beauty and structured complexity as evidence of God's existence. However, they derive no substantive direction from that cosmological evidence. Instead, they tend to see revelation—even if it must be symbolically interpreted—as the principal source of religious and ethical content. Traditional pantheism does little better. In his apology for Vedantic pantheism, Alan Watts tells a children's story about the world's origin:

> God…likes to play hide-and-seek, but because there's nothing outside God, he has no one but himself to play with. But he gets over this difficulty by pretending that he is not himself…He pretends that he is you and I and all the people in the world, all the animals, all the plants, all the rocks, and all the stars. In this way he has strange and wonderful adventures, some of which are terrible and frightening. But these are just like bad dreams, for when he wakes up they will disappear.
> (1989, p. 15)

On the logic of this story, we can do nothing to help God "play hide-and-seek." We might enjoy ourselves hedonistically, do our duty as we see it, or do nothing at all; whatever choice we make, the world will go on the same. None of these traditional stances offer meaning or direction that is grounded in the structure of the world.[46]

The approach described here does just that. It tells us that we are intrinsically good because of our complexity and potential, but only become instrumentally good when we fulfill our potential, when we actually perform our observational and creative roles. It says that our ethic is that of the landscape gardener. However, this conclusion is subject to one caveat. Leibniz wrote, "Those who believe God has established good and evil by an arbitrary decree, deprive God of the designation *good*. For what reason could one have to praise Him for what he does, if in doing something quite different He would have done equally well?" (1985, § 176, p. 236). If this is so, then it follows that our work on a divine project (the universe), even if faithfully performed, would not make us good unless the project itself could be seen as good. The leading arguments against the world's goodness are the claim that it contains gratuitous suffering and the presence of moral evil. What can we say against those arguments?

a) Gratuitous suffering

An instance of suffering would be gratuitous if God could exclude it and still fulfill love's purposes. We have seen that love would impel God to become a world that (i) constantly changes and (ii) contains fully conscious creatures. As change will bring death, dissipation, and loss for individual phenomena, at least some of which will be conscious, this best of worlds will necessarily contain some awareness of loss and hence some suffering. Yet must it contain as much as is found in our actual world?

To show that a great deal of suffering is gratuitous, William Rowe envisions a fawn who, horribly burned in a forest fire, suffers for days before she dies. He argues that God could mitigate this suffering by, for example, granting the fawn a quick and merciful death. God's failure to do that, he says, militates against God's goodness, power, or both (1979, p. 337). In rebuttal, theists say that God must have good reasons for letting the fawn suffer. Some (e.g. Swinburne 1996, pp. 236–72) try to imagine what those reasons might be; others just appeal to the gulf between God's wisdom and our own. Against both rebuttals, Rowe points to billions of similar (or more horrible) instances of suffering and argues that no reason or set of reasons seems likely to require them all (1979, p. 338 n. 5).

Despite the objections that have been raised against it, Rowe's remains a powerful, evidential argument against ethical theism. However, it does not count against pandeism. In pandeism, God is no superintending, heavenly power, capable of hourly intervention into earthly affairs. No longer existing 'above,' God *cannot* intervene from above and cannot be blamed for failing to do so.[47] Instead, God *bears* all suffering, whether the fawn's or anyone else's. Even so, a skeptic might ask, "Why must there be *so much* suffering? Why could not the world's design omit or modify the events that cause it?" In pandeism, the reason is clear: to remain unified, a world must convey information through transactions. Reliable conveyance requires relatively simple, uniform laws. Laws designed to skip around suffering-causing events or to alter their natural consequences (i.e. their consequences under simple laws) would need to be vastly complicated or (equivalently) to contain numerous exceptions. Such laws would not be discernable from within the world. From that standpoint, the only one that matters, they would not be laws at all. Absent laws, transactions would not reliably convey information and the world could not be one. God could not consistently become such a world. Since God becomes the world to be with the beloveds, suffering is the price that God pays for love. For us, a world without suffering would be one from which information would constantly vanish. Our actions would have unpredictable effects and so could have no meaning.

b) Moral evil

Most theists would say that, to be worthy of worship, God should be free of moral imperfection. Yet the world includes morally evil actions: actions that willfully or wantonly destroy value or cause suffering to serve a lesser, parochial end. Aside from the suffering and destruction that such actions cause, their mere occurrence seems to stain God's character. God's creation and preservation of a world that includes them seems to make God responsible for them. Theists address this *holiness problem* by focusing on the ontological distance between God and the free creatures who commit the evil acts. However, this shift of responsibility does not work for pandeism. Because pandeism posits a deep identity between God and the phenomena, it gains nothing by merely throwing blame on the latter. To address the holiness problem, pandeism must explain why evil acts must occur in a world that *is* God in all its aspects. The following is one tentative explanation.

As we have seen, the world's diverse phenomena arise through emergent processes grounded in simple rules. These processes do not foreordain specific events (e.g. where and when a star will form). Instead, largely because of the continuous input of quantum indeterminacy into world history and the existence of chaotic processes (the butterfly effect), such events are unpredictable in principle (see Astakhov 2007). Natural selection is the emergent process that most directly affects the evolution of life. It is an open-ended process with no fixed or determinate goal. Instead, it favors any trait that promotes successful reproduction in the immediate environment. It does not just select for physical phenotypes; in creatures with minds, it also selects for attitudes and behaviors (Wilson and Wilson 2007).

In a world governed by natural selection, each individual has to look out for herself. This was as true of our human ancestors as it is of all animals. Erich Fromm explains that this fact of life favors selflove, or *narcissism*:

> How could the individual survive unless his bodily needs, his interests, his desires, were charged with much [psychic] energy? Biologically, from the standpoint of survival, man must attribute to himself an importance far above what he gives to anybody else.
> (1964, p. 72)

Yet other factors often counterbalance this narcissistic pull. For example, humans can survive only as members of a group, and groups can impose severe penalties for antisocial behavior. "We arrive then at the paradoxical result that [individual] narcissism is necessary for [individual] survival, and at the same time [because it urges us to put our interests ahead of the group's] that it is a threat to survival" (1964, p. 73). To resolve this conflict, individual narcissism often transforms into group narcissism. "The clan, nation, religion, race, etc., become the objects of narcissistic passion instead of the individual. Thus, narcissistic energy is...used in the interests of the survival of the group" (1964, p. 73).

Whether it fastens on the group or the individual, narcissism presses us to see our needs and interests as more important than those felt by others. Ordinarily, the tug of reason and the pull of competing emotions conspire to keep our narcissism in check. However, humans and the groups they form vary quite widely. Those for whom reason and regard for others are far less compelling than self-love may progress from garden-variety narcissism to something more toxic. They imagine themselves or their group to be vastly better, brighter, or more moral than all the others and better than they really are. To defend their false and fragile self-regard, they lie about themselves and denigrate or scapegoat others. To justify their deceit, they either assign no value to others or else portray them as deadly dangers. Evil acts follow evil words. Some behavioral scientists have come to see this *malignant narcissism* as the main source of moral evil. In other words, they see moral evil as a specific, diagnosable psychological disease or dysfunction (see, e.g., Peck 1998, Klose 1995, Stone 1989, and Flemmer 2004).[48]

This disease model of evil does not excuse evil actions. To the contrary, it says that evildoers choose evil incrementally over time. They often begin with small lies and cruelties, but those soon escalate. Their growing narcissism and deceit make it hard to change course but do not foreordain the outcome. As with other diseases (e.g. diabetes), a series of small choices—a small lie, a piece of cake—can eventually cause irreversible damage. Thus, despite its horrific character, evil has its roots in a human dysfunction that is not unlike many others (Peck 1998, pp. 120–30). It resembles autoimmune disease, in that it is a destructive perversion of an essential human system: not the immune system in this case, but the systems of thought (neural structures) that let us look out for our own interests.

However, this understanding of severe moral evil points up a deeper question. Why must the processes that drive life's evolution depend on each participant looking out for itself? Why cannot each know that it is a part of the whole and shape its behavior accordingly? A Buddhist would say the reason is *maya*, the veil of ignorance that obscures our knowledge of the world's (and our own) true nature. Yet the Buddha never explained the source of this *maya*.

Information is physical. Just as information about the world must be embodied in the world, so the information available to a phenomenon must reside in it or in phenomena it encounters. This means that every phenomenon, including every living being, must 'view' the world from its own partial and limited perspective. This perspective puts it at the world's apparent center, and this self-centering illusion makes its needs primary. Because everything shares this illusion, any successful emergent process must take the illusion to be real. Ultimately, nature is red in tooth and claw because a lioness cannot know that she is also a gazelle. Her ignorance as to her true nature causes her to behave as a lion. This can be hard on gazelles, but without this limitation lions could not exist for long. And the world would be poorer without them.

God does not choose or sustain evil. God only chooses a world in which very many things coexist, and this must be one in which phenomena vary widely. To vary, each must have access to limited information. Life evolves through a series of processes that start from this precondition. This can result in dysfunction and open the way to terrible consequences. However, it also leads to construction, richness, and variety. As in the case of suffering, excising all moral evil from the best of worlds would be impossible in principle. The detailed and directive rules needed to excise evil are not the simple ones needed to generate richness and retain information. As Leibniz wrote, "if God had willed to do more here [to eliminate evil] he must needs have produced either fresh natures in his creatures or fresh miracles to change their natures, and this the best plan did not allow" (1985, Ans. Obj. V, p. 384).

In short, evildoing does not pollute God. While evildoers are aspects of God, they are also limited creatures. In their doing of evil, their limitations are paramount. Their victims are also aspects of God, and God suffers in them. While God experiences both perspectives, this is no game of hide-and-seek. There is no moral equivalence between perpetrator and victim. Evil destroys without creating and therefore works against God's purpose. In fighting for self-preservation, victims fight to preserve the world's richness. They thereby serve God's purpose. Evil actors pass away and new construction replaces the destruction they entail. Even defeated and forgotten victims are not entirely lost to the world; God preserves them forever in altered form. Thus, neither the problem of suffering nor the holiness problem impeaches our *a priori* impression that a world actualized out of maximal love would be maximally good.

Notes

The author thanks Nicholas Rescher for invaluable encouragement and advice.

1 See the listing of articles pro and con at Strickland 2005b, p. 5.

2 However, see Rescher 2006, pp. 56–7.

3 See Eppen, Gould, and Schmidt 1979 or any standard text on operations research.

4 Rescher 2003, p. 27. Other scholars disagree, saying that Leibniz understood optimality to involve only "quantity of reality." See, e.g., Rutherford 1995, pp. 22–45.

5 Leibniz never used the term 'initial conditions.' However, he did distinguish between "rules" and other "means" or "devices." See Strickland 2006, Chapter 5.

6 These are two names for the same procedure for measuring relative complexity. See GellMann 1994, pp. 34–6.

7 This discussion does not purport to show the only right ways to quantify these two qualities; it only shows that, in principle, each *can* be stated quantitatively. An actual calculation of the variety of a world governed by quantum physics and general relativity would require resolving conceptual and technical questions that are beyond the scope of this article.

8 For differing approaches, compare Gale 1976, Rescher 2005, and Lane 2006.

9 See, e.g., Gell-Mann 1994, pp. 99–100; Lane 2006, pp. 263–4; and Squires 1981.

10 In creating the cellular automata game called "Life," mathematician John Conway used just two simple rules to support a wide variety of patterns. He found that adding more rules only reduced the game's complexity and diversity (Gardner 1970, pp. 121–2). For a more general investigation of the topic, see Wolfram 2002, pp. 23–113.

11 Letter to Malebranche.

12 Both experiments with cellular automata and the history of our universe show that complex structure can result from fecund rules of change and a maximally simple origin. See Wolfram 2002, pp. 32–9, and sec. 5 below. However, no research predicts the directional effect of making simple initial conditions more complex.

13 Reflecting on which puzzles give the greatest pleasure, the *New York Times*'s puzzle editor concludes, "The elegance of a logic puzzle is

determined by the ratio of two things: the simplicity of its rules versus the variety and depth of logic needed to solve it" (Shortz 2007).

14 For another statement of the same idea, see Benedict Spinoza 1994, II, D6, 32.

15 For a thorough discussion of this point, see Manson 2000.

16 For Spinoza, the production of all things in all modes flowed from God's infinitude rather than from God's goodness.

17 Each region (or *domain*) in a multi-domain universe may have its own laws of physics, but each is part of a causally interconnected ensemble or structure. See Stoeger, Ellis, and Kirchner 2006.

18 The interpolated words are Rescher's.

19 This article follows Stoeger, Ellis, and Kirchner 2006 in distinguishing between a multiverse and a multi-domain universe. See note 17, supra.

20 Letter to Malabranche.

21 For a defense of this argument, see Kraay 2007.

22 See Hartshorne and Rees 2005, esp. pp. 1–25, 499–514.

23 This is why theists say that God cannot sin. An infinitely powerful God would have the power to sin, but sin would contradict God's nature.

24 These ideas permeate all theistic traditions. Exodus 3:14, Deuteronomy 6:4, and Revelation 22:13 are exemplary citations.

25 Either that or it represents a verbal sidestep around Spinoza's argument.

26 Modern cosmologists (Stoeger, Ellis, and Kirchner 2006) argue that, just as Leibniz thought, no infinite, plenary multi-domain universe is possible. However, just as he did, they leave open the possibility of a plenary multiverse.

27 For a compelling defense of this point, see the selections by Patrick Grim in Martin and Monnier 2003, pp. 349–78, 381–421.

28 The nineteenth-century philosophers Moritz Lazarus and Heymann Steinthal coined the word 'pandeistic' (*Pandeisten* in German) to designate a pantheistic deism in which a personal God

becomes the world.

29 For a synopsis of Barth's argument, see Hick 1966, pp. 128–30.

30 Here we see the flaw in Tegmark's claim that the omniverse would be maximally simple. The command, "Create everything," is simple, but it is not a rule. The infinite number of detailed rules needed to govern reliable transactions in each of a plenary, multi-domain universe's infinite number of divergent domains would not be simple at all. See Stoeger, Ellis, and Kirchner 2006 for a more extensive discussion of this point.

31 Not all: we still know they are not 1 and 1.

32 Typically, information must be erased to make room for new information.

33 For reasons explained below, this information has not been lost from the world; it has only been lost from the game board.

34 As a very rough analogy, we might imagine a dumbbell falling into the pond instead of a steel ball. In this case, A and B would be the two ends.

35 Leibniz suggested this possibility. See letters to Louis Bourguet, Leibniz 2006, pp. 198–200.

36 See the brief discussion of this point in Lloyd 2007, p. 45.

37 See, generally, Layzer 1990, pp. 138–46; and Lloyd 2007, pp. 176–204.

38 The processes referred to here include gravitational clustering into primordial galaxies, nucleosynthesis, and the formation of stars. Later processes include natural selection and the development of language. See Layzer 1990, pp. 133–251; Morowitz 2002.

39 A recent example is the widely reported discovery that very many (perhaps most) G- and M-class stars have planets.

40 Astakhov refers to the "semi-conservation" of information because, while the past can in principle be derived from the present, the future cannot be so derived. By contrast, energy is conserved in both directions.

41 While scientists routinely undertake such thought experiments (see, e.g., Harnik, Kribs, and Perez 2006; and Smolin 1997, pp. 301–6), the

simulation needed to falsify this claim would need to far exceed currently published work in scope and detail. It would need to consider the net impact of an alternate physics on *all* significant classes of structure in *all* epochs of universal history.

42 Other means of testing the claim that our laws are maximally fecund have also been suggested. See Lane 2006, pp. 272–4.

43 For this to be true, intelligent life would need to generate more structural diversity (richness) than it destroys. See sec. 7, below.

44 As used here, the terms 'consciousness' and 'conscious awareness' do not imply self-consciousness or other mental powers. They mean only that there is *something* it is like to be the entity, that the entity has some sort of experience at some (perhaps minimal) level.

45 The neurocomputationist view is that, at a functional level, all relevant brain processes could be simulated or described using classical physics. The "specific, quantum mechanical processes" referred to in the text differ from theory to theory, but most theorists would point to quantum superposition, quantum entanglement, or both, what Einstein called "spooky action at a distance."

46 One nontraditional worldview, panentheism, differs from pantheism in seeing God as both the world in being and an external 'lure' toward the good. Thus, it posits an ongoing purpose or moral direction to the universe. However, it does not derive that direction from the world's physical structure.

47 This inability is not a limit on God's power; it reflects God's once-and-for-all choice.

48 Though he does not use the term 'malignant narcissism,' Samenow 2004 (pp. 169–82) portrays evil in much the same way.

References

1. Leibniz's writings

1970. *Leibniz: Philosophical Papers and Letters,* ed. L. E. Loemker (Amsterdam: D. Reidel).

1973. *Philosophical Writings*, ed. G. H. R. Parkinson, trans. Mary Morris and G. H. R. Parkinson (London: J. M. Dent).

1985 (1710). *Theodicy*, trans. E. M. Huggard (La Salle, IL: Open Court).

1989. *Philosophical Essays*, ed. and trans. Roger Ariew and Daniel Garber (Indianapolis, IN: Hackett).

1991. *G.W. Leibniz's Monadology: An Edition for Students*, ed. and trans. Nicholas Rescher (Pittsburgh: University of Pittsburgh Press).

2006. *The Shorter Leibniz Texts*, ed. and trans. Lloyd Strickland (New York: Continuum).

2. Other writings

Aquinas, Thomas. 1952. *Summa Theologica* (Chicago: Brittanica).

Astakhov, Vadim. 2007. "Cosmology and Semi-Conservation of Computations in the Universe," http:// arXiv:0705.0039.

Barbour, J., and L. Smolin. 1992. "Extremal Variety as the Foundation of a Cosmological Quantum Theory," http://arxiv.org/abs/hepth/9203041.

Barbour, Julian. 2003. "The Deep and Suggestive Principles of Leibnizian Philosophy," *Harvard Review of Philosophy*, vol. 11, pp. 45–58.

Beck, Friedrich, and John C. Eccles. 1992. "Quantum Aspects of Brain Activity and the Role of Consciousness," *Proceedings of the National Academy of Sciences USA*, vol. 89, pp. 11357–61.

Berdyaev, Nicolas. 1937. *The Destiny of Man*, trans. Natalie Duddington (New York: Scribner's).

Blake, William. 1994. *The Marriage of Heaven and Hell* (Toronto: Dover).

Burns, Charlene. 2002. *Divine Becoming: Rethinking Jesus and Incarnation* (Minneapolis: Fortress).

Chalmers, David J. 1996. *The Conscious Mind: In Search of a Fundamental Theory* (Oxford: Oxford University Press).

Churchland, P. S. 1998. "Brainshy: Nonneural Theories of Conscious Experience," in *Toward a Science of Consciousness II: The Second Tucson Discussions and Debates*, ed. S. R. Hameroff, A. W. Kaszniak, and A. C. Scott (Cambridge, MA: MIT Press), pp. 109–26.

Cornish, N. J., D. N. Spergel, G. D. Starkman, and E. Komatsu. 2004.

"Constraining the Topology of the Universe," *Physical Review Letters*, vol. 92, pp. 2013021–4.

Crick, Francis. 1981. *Life Itself* (New York: Simon & Schuster).

Darwin, Charles. 1993 (1859). *The Origin of Species* (New York: Random House).

Davies, Paul. 1984. *Superforce* (New York: Simon & Schuster).

— —. "Teleology without Teleology," in *In Whom We Live and Move and Have Our Being: Panentheistic Reflections on God's Presence in a Scientific World*, ed. P. Clayton and A. Peacocke (Grand Rapids, MI: William B. Eerdmans).

Dawkins, Richard. 2006. *The God Delusion* (New York: Houghton Mifflin).

de Duve, Christian. 1995. "The Beginnings of Life on Earth," *American Scientist*, vol. 83, pp. 428–35.

Eckhart, Meister. 1994. *Selected Writings*, ed. and trans. Oliver Davies (London: Penguin).

Ekeland, Ivar. 2007. *The Best of All Possible Worlds: Mathematics and Destiny* (Chicago: University of Chicago Press).

Eppen, Gary D., F. J. Gould, and Charles Schmidt. 1979. *Quantitative Concepts for Management*, 3rd ed. (Englewood Cliffs, NJ: Prentice Hall).

Flemmer, David. 2004. *Narcissistic Evil as Character Pathology* (Lima, OH: Wyndham Hall).

Flew, Antony. 1989. *An Introduction to Western Philosophy* (New York: Thames and Hudson).

Fromm, Erich. 1964. *The Heart of Man* (New York: Harper & Row).

Gale, George. 1976. "On What God Chose: Perfection and God's Freedom," *Studia Leibnitiana*, vol. 8, p. 72.

Gardner, Martin. 1970. "The Fantastic Combinations of John Conway's New Solitaire Game 'Life,'" *Scientific American*, vol. 223, pp. 120–3.

Gell-Mann, Murray. 1994. *The Quark and the Jaguar* (New York: W. H. Freeman).

Hagan, S., S. Hameroff, and J. Tuszynski. 2002. "Quantum Computation in Brain Microtubules? Decoherence and Biological Feasibility,"

Physical Reviews E, vol. 65, pp. 861–901.

Hameroff, Stuart R. 2007. "The Brain Is Both Neurocomputer and Quantum Computer," *Cognitive Science*, vol. 31, pp. 1035–45.

Harnik, Roni, Graham D. Kribs, and Gilad Perez. 2006. "A Universe without Weak Interactions," *Physical Review D*, vol. 74, 0350061–15.

Hartshorne, Charles, and William L. Rees. 2000. *Philosophers Speak of God* (Amherst, NY: Prometheus).

Hawking, Stephen. 1998. *A Brief History of Time*, rev. ed. (New York: Bantam).

——. 2005. "Information Loss in Black Holes," http://arxiv.org/abs /hepth/0507171.

Hick, John. 1966. *Evil and the God of Love* (New York: HarperCollins).

'Ibn Árabi, "Ibn al-Futûhât al-Makkiyya" (1231), *Journal of the Muhyiddin Ibn 'Arabi Society*, http:// www.ibnarabisociety.org/articles/ divine-rootsoflove.html#_edn1.

Klose, D. A. 1995. "M. Scott Peck's Analysis of Human Evil: A Critical Review," *Journal of Humanistic Psychology*, vol. 35, pp. 37–66.

Kraay, Klaas J. 2007. "Theism and the Multiverse," http://colfa.utsa. edu/ecpc/ symposium_papers/ Klaas_Kraay.pdf.

Kretzmann, Norman. 1997. *The Metaphysics of Theism* (New York: Oxford University Press).

Lane, William C. 2006. "The Best of Possible Worlds: A Testable Claim of Choice," *Theology and Science*, vol. 4, pp. 261–78.

Layzer, David. 1990. *Cosmogenesis: The Growth of Order in the Universe* (New York: Oxford University Press).

Litt, A., C. Eliasmith, F. W. Kroon, S. Weinstein et al. 2006. "Is the Brain a Quantum Computer?" *Cognitive Science*, vol. 30, pp. 593–603.

Lloyd, Seth. 2007. *Programming the Universe* (New York: Vintage).

Lockwood, Michael. 1990. *Mind, Brain, and the Quantum* (Oxford: Blackwell).

Lovejoy, Arthur. 1964. *The Great Chain of Being* (Cambridge, MA: Harvard University Press).

Malin, Shimon. 2001. *Nature Loves to Hide* (New York: Oxford University Press).

Manson, Neil A. 2000. "Anthropocentrism and the Design Argument," *Religious Studies*, vol. 36, pp. 163–76.

Martin, Michael, and Ricki Monnier, eds. 2003. *The Impossibility of God* (Amherst, NY: Prometheus).

Morowitz, Harold J. 2002. *The Emergence of Everything* (New York: Oxford University Press).

Peck, M. Scott, 1998. *People of the Lie: The Hope for Healing the Human Soul* (New York: Touchstone).

Penrose, Roger. 1989. *The Emperor's New Mind* (New York: Oxford University Press).

— —. 1994. *Shadows of the Mind* (Oxford: Oxford University Press).

Plantinga, Alvin. 1974. *God, Freedom, and Evil* (Grand Rapids, MI: William B. Eerdmans).

Rescher, Nicholas. 2003. *On Leibniz* (Pittsburgh: University of Pittsburgh Press).

— —. 2005. "On Some Purported Obstacles to Leibniz's Optimalism," *Studia Leibnitiana*, Band 37, 131–46.

— —. 2006. *Studies in Metaphysical Optimalism* (Heusenstamm, Germany: Ontos Verlag).

Riley, Patrick. 1996. *Leibniz's Universal Jurisprudence: Justice as the Charity of the Wise* (Cambridge, MA: Harvard University Press).

Rosenblum, Bruce, and Fred Kuttner. 2008. *Quantum Enigma: Physics Encounters Consciousness* (New York: Oxford University Press).

Rowe, William L. 1979. "The Problem of Evil and Some Varieties of Atheism," *American Philosophical Quarterly*, vol. 16, pp. 335–41.

Rutherford, Donald. 1995. *Leibniz and the Rational Order of Nature* (Cambridge: Cambridge University Press).

Samenow, Stanton. 2004. *Inside the Criminal Mind* (New York: Crown).

Sandin, R. H., G. Enlund, P. Samuelsson, and C. Lennmarken. 2000. "Awareness during Anaesthesia: A Prospective Case Study," *Lancet*, vol. 355, pp. 707–11.

Shortz, Will. 2007. "A Rush of Excitement, from Filling in Empty Spaces to Completing a Large Loop," *New York Times*, 21 March 2007.

Smolin, Lee. 1997. *The Life of the Cosmos* (New York: Oxford University

Press).

——. 2001. *Three Roads to Quantum Gravity* (New York: Basic Books).

Spinoza, Benedict. 1994 (1677). *Ethics*, trans. Edwin Curley (New York: Penguin).

Squires, Euan J. 1981. "Do We Live in the Simplest Possible Interesting World?" *European Journal of Physics*, vol. 2, pp. 55–7.

——. 1990. *Conscious Mind in the Physical World* (London: Taylor & Francis).

——. 1994. "Quantum Theory and the Need for Consciousness," *Journal of Consciousness Studies*, vol. 1, pp. 201–4.

Stapp, Henry. 1993. *Mind, Matter, and Quantum Mechanics* (New York: Springer).

Stoeger, W. R., G. F. R. Ellis, and U. Kirchner. 2006. "Multiverses and Cosmology: Philosophical Issues," *arXiv* (January), http://arxiv.org/PS_cache/astro-ph/pdf/0407/0407329.pdf.

Stone, M. H. 1989. "Murder," *Psychiatric Clinics of North America*, vol. 12, pp. 643–51.

Strickland, Lloyd. 2005a. "Determining the Best of All Possible Worlds," *Journal of Value Inquiry*, vol. 39, pp. 37–47.

——. 2005b. "On the Necessity of the Best (Possible) World," Ars Disputandi, http://www.ArsDisputandi.org.

——. 2006. *Leibniz Reinterpreted* (London: Continuum).

Susskind, Leonard. 1997. "Black Holes and the Information Paradox," *Scientific American* (April), pp. 18–23.

——. 2008. *The Black Hole War* (New York: Little Brown).

Swinburne, Richard. 1996. *Is There a God?* (Oxford: Oxford University Press).

Tegmark, Max. 1998. "Is 'the Theory of Everything' Merely the Ultimate Ensemble Theory?" *Annals of Physics*, vol. 270, pp. 1–51.

——2000. "The Importance of Quantum Decoherence in Brain Processes," *Physical Reviews E*, vol. 61, pp. 4194–206.

van Swinderen, Bruno. 2005. "The Remote Roots of Consciousness in Fruit-fly Selective Attention?" *Bioessays*, vol. 27, pp. 321–30.

Walker, Evans Harris. 2000. *The Physics of Consciousness* (New York:

HarperCollins).

Watts, Alan. 1989. *The Book on the Taboo against Knowing Who You Are* (New York: Vintage).

Weinberg, Steven. 1978. *The First Three Minutes* (New York: Basic Books).

Wigner, Eugene. 1967. *Symmetries and Reflections* (Bloomington: University of Indiana Press).

Wilson, David Sloan, and Edward Wilson. 2007. "Rethinking the Theoretical Foundation of Sociobiology," *The Quarterly Review of Biology*, vol. 82, pp. 327–48.

Wolfram, Stephen. 2002. *A New Kind of Science* (Champaign, IL: Wolfram Media).

Young, Louise. 1986. *The Unfinished Universe* (Oxford: Oxford University Press).

Transhumanism and Theistcideism

Zoltan Istvan

Bestselling visionary author and 2016 candidate for President of the United States Zoltan Istvan, an American-Hungarian, began a solo, multi-year sailing journey around the world at the age of 21. His main cargo was 500 handpicked books, mostly classics. He's explored over 100 countries—many as a journalist for the National Geographic Channel—writing, filming, and appearing in dozens of television stories, articles, and webcasts. His work has also been featured by The New York Times Syndicate, Outside, San Francisco Chronicle, *BBC Radio, NBC, ABC, CBS, FOX, Animal Planet, and the Travel Channel. In addition to his award-winning coverage of the war in Kashmir, he gained worldwide attention for pioneering and popularizing the extreme sport of volcano boarding. He is a philosophy and religious studies graduate of Columbia University and resides in San Francisco with his daughter and physician wife. Zoltan published* The Transhumanist Wager, *a fictional thriller describing apatheist Jethro Knights and his unwavering quest for immortality via science and technology. The controversial novel was a number 1 bestseller in Philosophy and Sci-Fi Visionary on Amazon.*

Transhumanism is a rapidly growing international social movement whose highest immediate priority is overcoming human death via science and technology. Broadly defined, the word *transhuman* means beyond human. The growing transhumanist social movement encompasses and encourages virtually all ideas that enhance human existence via the application of science and technology. More specifically, transhumanism includes the fields of radical life extension, Singularitarianism, robotics, artificial intelligence, cryonics, genetic engineering, biohacking, cyborgism, and many other lesser-known fields of science. Longer lifespans and more control over our biological selves will only make the world a better place, with more permanent institutions, more time with our loved ones, and more stable economies. Momentum towards transhumanism can be seen everywhere you look.

In the next twenty-five years, the human being will undergo a larger transformation of its evolutionary body than it has undergone in the last 100,000 years. Artificial hearts will likely become better than real hearts. Men will be able to give birth with implanted uteri. Already, interaction between microchip and the brain occurs all around the world in the form of cranial implants helping the deaf, blind, and mentally ill. In 2014 technologically assisted telepathy was accomplished between people in India and France. Each of these technologies already exists in some form and will soon be more widely available. We're just in the infancy of all this, but progress is accelerating. I'm looking forward to having an exact copy of myself online one day, both as a companion and as a form of personal immortality, in case my biological self dies.

However, transhumanism is facing a colossal challenge. Unfortunately, we live in a world where 'culture' has indoctrinated us to even go against our own health and well-being, or our children's health and well-being. Religious indoctrination is a key example—teaching us to handle rattlesnakes without fear of being bitten, forcing genital mutilation, and marrying young children off. About 85 percent of the world's population believes in life after death, and much of that population is perfectly okay with dying because it gives them an afterlife with their perceived deity or deities—something transhumanists often refer to as 'deathist' culture. In fact, 4 billion people on Earth—mostly Muslims and Christians—see the overcoming of death through science as potentially blasphemous, a sin involving humans striving to be godlike. Some holy texts say blasphemy is unforgivable and will end in eternal punishment. Of course, both of these religions assert that only certain types of people get to go to heaven. Those left behind get tortured, some for eternity. This concept of exclusivity is the single largest reason I became an atheist at 18.

In my philosophical and atheist-minded novel *The Transhumanist Wager*, protagonist Jethro Knights ends up with the ability to rewrite the social laws of the world. One important issue he faces is whether to make religion illegal altogether. There are many arguments for why religion has not been beneficial to the human race, especially in the last few centuries. In the end, a love of basic liberties prevails over Mr Knights and he allows religion to exist, although he restricts religion from the public sphere, restricts religion from being integrated with education, and restricts religion from being pushed on minors.

Not surprisingly, some in the atheist and transhumanist communities feel the same way Mr Knights does. While they may think that believing in a warmongering prophet, or a four-armed blue deity, or a spiteful God who drowns nearly all of his people is wrong, atheists and transhumanists are willing to allow it. So long as it doesn't meaningfully interfere with the world.

The problem is that it does meaningfully interfere with the world. 9/11 was a religious-inspired event. So was the evil of the Catholic Inquisition. And so is the quintessential conflict between Palestine and Israel. If you take 'God' and 'religion' out of all these happenings, you would likely find that they would not have happened at all. Instead, what you'd probably find is peaceful people and communities dedicated to preserving and improving life through reason, science, and technology—which is the essence of transhumanism and the outcome of evolution.

Although theistic beliefs dominate the conversation, the world of religious belief does not end with the Abrahamic religions. There are other options, which fit into the growing category of being 'spiritual, not religious.' One such belief is theistcideism—the concept that a God or a supreme being once existed but no longer does because it terminated itself. A current rendering of theistcideism is pandeism (pantheistic deism), which proposes that a godlike supreme being once existed but no longer does because it has ended its existence as a 'God,' to instead exist, intentionally or accidentally, as our universe. While any concept of a creator God must hold on to some nonscientific (or at least scientifically unprovable) ideas, concepts falling within the category of theistcideism eliminate some of the most unlikely aspects. For example, they can have no claim of a divinely communicated holy text enshrining deathist doctrine, and no concept of blasphemy originating in divine commandments. I have made the proposition before that if ever there was a God or supreme being, it indeed had to terminate itself. A number of people, historically, have concluded that being all-powerful would actually be a very strange, ironic dead end. The only thing omnipotence can truly equal is a total mechanistic void. Achieving omnipotence is literally the act of suicide, in terms of forever self-eliminating one's consciousness. This is because a conscious intelligence, as reason dictates, is based on ability to discern values—values, for example, to know whether as an all-powerful being, one can create something so heavy that one can't lift it. Values require choice. But omnipotence means that all choices have already been made, and nothing can ever change, because all variables are already accounted for and no randomness or anomalies exist.

Religions are rife with contradictory ideas like an omnipotent being content to live without any kind of change or challenge for eternity, but these ideas cannot prevail in a world of increasing reason. I've said on several occasions that in order for existing formal religion to survive in the twenty-first century, it will have to bend and evolve to fit coming technological advancement. Technology is simply too powerful and all-encompassing to not make one's beliefs work with it. Pandeism, for example, with its idea of a universe evolving by rational and scientific rules, has a much easier time bending to fit such advancement.

Theistic religious leaders, to have their religions survive, will say anything to get their followers to hold on to their outdated beliefs. Proponents of nontheistic religious views generally do not need to resort to such tactics, and compared to them, theistic religious leaders will not remain popular leaders long—certainly not into the next century. Sometime in the next decade, the number of worldwide godless people—atheists, agnostics, and those unaffiliated with religion—is likely to break through the billion-person mark. With a billion nonreligious, or at least nontheistic people around the world expanding their numbers, the end of worldwide domination of our species via religion is now in sight.

Many in this massive group already champion reason, defend science, welcome radical technologies, and implicitly trust and embrace modern medicine. They are, indeed, already transhumanists. Yet many of them don't know it because they haven't thought much about it. However, that is about to change. A transformative cultural storm comprised of radical life-improving technologies is set to blow in soon.

Transhumanism versus 'Deathism'

Despite the positive momentum in transhumanism, changing cultural deathist trends for 85 percent of the world's population may prove difficult. Humans are a species ingrained in their ways, and getting fundamentally religious people to have an open mind to living far longer periods than before—maybe thousands of years—could prove challenging.

Recently, a number of transhumanists, including myself who is an atheist, have attempted to work more closely with governmental, religious, and social groups that have for centuries endorsed the deathist culture. Transhumanists are trying to get those groups to realize we are not necessarily wanting to live forever. Transhumanists simply want the choice and creation over our own earthly demise, and we don't want to leave it to cancer, or an automobile accident, or aging, or fate.

In *The Transhumanist Wager*, my protagonist, Jethro Knights, creates the philosophy of Teleological Egocentric Functionalism (TEF), recognizing that all humans desire to reach a state of perfect personal power—to be omnipotent in the universe. I call this a Will to Evolution. The idea is built into my Three Laws of Transhumanism, which form the essence of the book's philosophy, Teleological Egocentric Functionalism (TEF):

1. A transhumanist must safeguard one's own existence above all else.
2. A transhumanist must strive to achieve omnipotence as expediently as possible—so long as one's actions do not conflict with the First Law.
3. A transhumanist must safeguard value in the universe—so long as one's actions do not conflict with the First and Second Laws.

These laws provide clarity for long-term transhuman ambitions and dominate TEF's ethical, metaphysical, and epistemological outlooks. Through them, TEF establishes a broad, concrete framework for transhumanists to successfully evolve into the most advanced entities they can become, which is their ultimate goal. If a reasoning human being loves and values life, they will want to live as long as possible—the desire to be immortal. Nevertheless, it's impossible to know if they're going to be immortal once they die. To do nothing doesn't help the odds of attaining immortality—since it seems evident that everyone will die someday and possibly cease to exist. To try to do something scientifically constructive towards ensuring immortality beforehand is the most logical conclusion.

To change the deathist culture in America and abroad, it's important for people to understand that lengthening lives and having the ability to overcome human mortality is not something that has to be seen as clashing with religion. I've often told Christian friends, for example, that living longer could be seen as a way for religious missionaries to spread their message further—to save more people if that's how they want to view it.

Two Approaches to Transhumanism and Religion

There are two directions from which the relationship between religion and transhumanism can be examined. One is: how do existing religions impact the transhumanist movement? Do they align with it or oppose and impede it? The other is: what effect does the inevitable progress towards transhumanism have on society, and religious beliefs? The core of transhumanist thought is two-sided. It begins with discontent about the humdrum status quo of human life and our frail, terminal human bodies. It is followed by an awe-inspiring vision of what can be done to improve both—of how dramatically the world and our species can be transformed via science and technology. Transhumanists want more guarantees than just death, consumerism, and offspring. Much more. They want to be better, smarter, stronger—perhaps even perfect and immortal if science can make them that way. Most transhumanists believe it can.

The number of transhumanists is still relatively small, comprised mostly of scientists, technologists, and futurists who seem fringe to many of their peers and to the public as a whole. Transhumanism has generally suffered from opposition by the dominant religious culture. That will likely change in the next few years as a nearly billion-person godless population wakes up primed to accept transhumanism as a natural extension of the irreligious lifestyle. Enter the atheists, agnostics, and nonreligious. Many of these people—about a third of whom are under the age of 30—are already discovering their inner borg. And they like it.

The roots of atheism, agnosticism, and the nonreligious go back many centuries. But its foothold became pronounced in the twentieth century when personalities like Russell, Freud, Nietzsche, Rand, Sartre, Sanger, Hitchens, and Dawkins helped make many people give up needing or believing in a God. These irreligious ideas centered on the fact that a successful civilization didn't need to believe in flying pink elephants or other superstitions to thrive. Each of these famed atheists asked: Is there a good reason to believe in God or gods? They found none, and then convinced nearly a billion people of the same answer.

These atheist voices and their writings helped pave the way for the twenty-first century to bring the age of transhumanism to the forefront of society. The transhumanist hero is the person who constantly eyes improving their health, lifestyle, and longevity with science and technology. They are not okay with the past age of feeling guilty for aspiring to be different or better than they were born—or for wanting the power to become godlike themselves. They have no sin to erase; they have no reason to search for something outside of the material universe. Like atheists, agnostics, and the nonreligious, they are not in the business of criticizing religion, but rather of pursuing life and all that is available to improve upon it.

My own history with religion is varied. I was raised a Catholic (even went to Catholic elementary school). In high school I was more interested in general Christianity, as well as Buddhism. Later, I partially majored in religion in college and even took a month to read the Bible cover to cover. In fact, my departure from Christianity began in earnest the moment after I finished reading the Bible. I was 18 years old, and it simply contained too many contradictions, too much violence, and too much foreshadowing of the future—a future that certainly didn't anticipate humans merging with machines, artificial super intelligence, post-genderism, brain implants, robotic hearts, ectogenesis, telepathy, or the multitude of bizarre transhumanist technologies on the horizon (or already here). That said, many parts of the Gospel of Jesus, broadly interpreted, remain an important part of my moral code. Clearly the intent of Jesus to get in touch with the spiritual possibility of the universe was a major improvement over the strict and ritualistic religiosity of the time. However, despite my admiration of Jesus and some of his teachings, it's incredibly hard to see how anyone can reasonably believe a human being came down to Earth and died for the world's sins, or that a loving omnipotent God could send people to an eternal hell of suffering, or that billions of non-Christians in the world might never get to heaven because they haven't accepted Christ into their heart. The key word in that last sentence is "reasonably." I agree with many neuroscientists that it's our ability to reason that makes human beings so special. Without it, we would be living like our primate cousins and would never have come to understand the complexity and power of the human mind—or its incredible potential.

Religion and the Coming Future Self

When you think about it, trying to wrap your brain around how digital technology and all its wonders are even possible is simply bizarre. Only a tiny fraction of the world's population understand such things in any depth. And an even smaller amount of people actually know how to design and create the microchips, circuit boards, and software that constitutes this stuff in the real world.

To understand why one's future self could be markedly improved over one's current self, consider how we perceive reality for a moment. Human beings have five basic senses that send signals to our brain, telling us what's out there in the world. These senses understand only tiny bits of the universe around us. For example, our eyes can only see about 1 percent of the light spectrum. Our ears aren't much better: they are unable to register many noises that other animals like dogs, dolphins, and bats can hear. Our sense of touch basically only works if we're actually touching something.

Despite all these obvious physical inabilities, humans insist that what we experience is 'reality.' However, reality to someone with built-in microscopic or telephoto vision and hypersensitive hearing is potentially many times more complex and profound than anything a natural human being might experience. Human beings are a species dependent on a tech-imbued lifestyle that none of us really understand, but accept wholeheartedly as we go on endlessly texting, Facebooking, and video conferencing. As a non-engineer atheist grappling with the implications of 1s and 0s manifesting all digital reality, I have at least this much in common with religious people—because they can't understand the spirit world either, even if they insist it exists.

For better or worse, the society we live in treats virtually anything uncharted and socially new as contentious—a bias which can encompass both the practical goals of transhumanism, and ideas like theistcideism. We are cultured to be afraid and hesitant. In fact, being cultured (and the participation in such culture) is really just the acceptance and practice of standards, ideas, and ideals pre-established by others. Generally, the more a certain culture entrenches itself within its ways, the less chance it has to be new and dynamic. Most cultures—whether religious, national, or social—aim to uphold and solidify their values and idiosyncrasies.

Transhumanism doesn't do that. It's not beholden to anything idiosyncratic. It wants to improve the human body with science and technology—which is to say it wants to help people evolve. That's a strange cultural and philosophical position for a movement. And yet, evolution is exactly what transhumanism aims to usher in—except transhumanists want to do it far more quickly than by glacial-paced natural selection.

Of course, some people will ask: How far will transhumanism go to evolve the species? Will it support merging humans with machines? Will it eliminate biological death forever? Is it atheistic or spiritual? Will it be responsible for changing the human race into something foreign?

Such unprecedented change for human beings and civilization would inevitably mean a paradigm shift for our species. Because a vast majority of people around the world are guided by archaic religions, unrefined cultures, and irrational reasoning, most humans and their governments will initially oppose such advancements. TEF sees any opposition that directly interferes with a transhumanist's attainment of ongoing sentience as a violation of essential freedoms, as an unwarranted act of aggression, and as criminal manslaughter. TEF believes transhumanists must protect their goals via any means necessary.

I certainly don't know all these answers. But I do know the core of transhumanist culture is that it's perfectly okay not to know. We are reasoning and science-minded people, and we are always exploring and questioning. Transhumanists know our species and our universe is in flux. In this way, our truths are always partially veiled—something that can change and something we might never catch up to completely. Transhumanists can get better at describing that truth—and closer at knowing it, too. But it will always be ahead of us, somewhere in the distance.

When we individually replace or augment a human body part—such as giving someone an artificial hip—most people don't see that as becoming a cyborg. Additionally, it really doesn't matter if the part replaced or improved is a heart with a robotic pump, or a knee with a titanium joint, or a penis with a built-in balloon to help stiffening—all technologies which already exist. We usually think of such transformation as needed medical treatment, or even elective vanity surgery in some cases.

This fine line between transhumanist upgrades and what makes us uncomfortable about too much technology in our bodies is a bizarre psychological conundrum. It's so challenging that I believe the next great civil rights debate around the world will be about how much humans should embrace radical technologies in their bodies—and when they should just say "no" to upgrades.

In the past, historical movements, like communism, environmentalism, or anarcho-primitivism have been steeped in cultures that were very single-minded. Their missions were to push their agendas forward while preserving their culture, values, and ideals. However, with a culture based on knowing it can never have a permanent culture, transhumanism is indeed in a strange conundrum.

Despite this, transhumanism aims to appeal to literally everyone. It aims to be a universal movement, regardless of the fact that many people have voiced issues against it. Luckily, many of those issues are fear or psychologically based, rather than true, rational objections. This is because transhumanism may be the least bigoted philosophy on Earth. Its central goal is to improve every person's life, and it makes no judgment on who those people are. Transhumanists are people of all races, abilities, religions, backgrounds, genders, employments, sexual orientations, educations, and wealth levels. It just, simply, wants to improve people's lives.

Transhumanism is not really trying to overcome deathist culture, but get it to understand that transhuman culture can also stand functionally next to it, helping the aims of everyone involved. Together, we can find the middle ground, and give everyone the choice to follow whatever path they want when it concerns dying or not dying in the twenty-first century.

As a transhumanist, I stand behind reason, first and foremost. Most transhumanists feel the same way. Our code belongs to science and the scientific method. We require proof, before anything else. We do understand that our so-called 'proof' can always change, through new discoveries. But proof, which only a reasoning human being can verify through logic, measurable evidence, and scientific repetition, must occur. Otherwise, we'd all be able to believe anything and everything unconditionally, regardless how silly, wrong, or illogical it might be. And that would lead us to a place where we are unable to discern truth or prove it—a place where we are left to rely on faith. This is the overarching component of Christianity and other Abrahamic religions—a thing which most Americans have broadly accepted. And it will be a key issue that Christians must reconcile with as our society becomes more science and technology bound—fields which rely on reason.

Transhumanism is not a religion, nor is it in competition with religion. It is simply a mode of being that embraces evolving the human being with science, reason, and technology. No matter what happens, to move forward in the transhumanist age, we need to let go of our egos and our shallow sense of identity; in short, we need to get over ourselves. The permanence of our species lies in our ability to reason, think, and remember who we are and where we've been. The rest is just an impermanent shell that changes—and it has already been changing for tens of millions of years in the form of sentient evolution.

The Singularity Disparity

On the other side of the equation is the influence that a transhumanist reality might have on religion itself. I have observed before that, given the 13.8-billion-year-old pedigree of our universe according to experts, it is likely that these highly advanced intelligences long ago reached what we call the singularity: a moment in time when technological acceleration—most likely through the creation of artificial superintelligences—becomes incredibly rapid. We are likely to see this played out here on Earth—being able to upload our entire minds into a computer is probably just twenty-five to thirty years off given Moore's Law and the current trajectory of technology growth and innovation. If we can harness the power of artificial intelligence in the next fifteen years, then we might get there quicker, as AI will likely make the research and progress happen far more rapidly.

If we fast forward fifty years into the future, the landscape of human experience might be really different. AI could become 10,000 times smarter than us in just the first few years of its existence. I don't think most people factor what kind of future could come from an entity that intelligent instructing us how to live. A good metaphor or comparison of this type of digital assistance will already be happening in the next few years when driverless cars hit the road. In the same way driverless cars will help lessen drunk driving, perfected uploaded avatars will also lead us to be more judicious, moral, and reasonable in our lives. But such a capacity considered with respect to alien life preceding us presents a thorny issue to humans because of what I call the Singularity Disparity—the idea that whoever reaches the singularity first will make sure no one else can achieve a similar amount of power.

Regardless of what you think and believe, science shows human beings know very little. Our eyes register only 1 percent of the electromagnetic spectrum in the universe. Our ears detect less than 1 percent of its sound wave frequencies. Human senses—our brain's vehicles to understanding the world—leave much to be desired. Around us are many things we never notice, like energy patterns that have traversed the universe over thousands of light years, or sound waves from whales across the ocean, or vibrations that started from the core of the Earth. But we humans are oblivious, unless, of course, we are in a laboratory somewhere and happen to be studying these phenomena with specialized scientific machinery. Our genome is only 1 percent different than that of a chimpanzee. But some people still believe humans with our three-pound brains are the most advanced life form ever to exist; I am not one of them. To insist we are alone in the universe, or that we are the galaxy's crowning civilization, reeks of ego—reminiscent of those who insisted the Earth was flat, and the Sun moved around it.

If we are not alone in the universe and also not the most intelligent life form, then it's unlikely our species can evolve beyond a certain point, since other more advanced life forms won't allow it. But given the Singularity Disparity, why would some superintelligence or group of superintelligences do this to us? The main explanations are:

1. We are experiments and playthings for those superintelligences using us to further understand themselves or support some causes of theirs, including dealing with boredom.
2. We are literally already intrinsic parts of those superintelligences and exist simply as their thoughts, energies, or structure (the Gaia people love this idea).
3. We are accidents in the universe and our existence is totally arbitrary.

Many theological traditions exist which incorporate elements of these ideas. The Hindu Bhagavad Gita depicts us as existing within Krishna as something of a living play. Chinese philosopher Zhuangzi famously wondered whether his dream of being a butterfly could really mean he was a butterfly dreaming he was a man—a speculation which would require a superintelligent 'butterfly' to experience the breadth of human knowledge in a dream.

Of those options, the deity-averse existentialist in me likes number 3 best, but I'm still not satisfied with any of the answers, mainly because none of them address what happened to the very first superintelligence, an entity who may have set all the universe's rules up. Luckily, a fourth, more controversial, take is worth exploring. The foundation of the universe, including any simulations, probabilities, and possibilities of existence, is the result of a first and most powerful superintelligence killing itself. In short, an entity literally on the verge of becoming God knowingly and willingly died by suicide.

Some schools of thought combine elements of these possibilities, postulating theistcideism with a postscript. Scottish theologian Eriugena imagined God ceasing to be 'God,' and instead becoming and existing as the universe, in order to exist as something other than itself, the experience of 'otherness' being the only way it could discover its true contours. Cartoonist and commentator Scott Adams wrote in *God's Debris* of a God blowing itself up to answer the lingering question of what would happen to it if it didn't exist. At the extreme, tragic German philosopher Philipp Mainländer preceded his own suicide (an act anathema to transhumanism) with a book denouncing God as having destroyed itself as the only escape from the horror of eternal boredom, leaving behind a universe where we have come to exist purely as remnants of its being. Our own anxieties, fears, and experiences of despair, Mainländer believed, were simply reflections of this God's feelings before ending itself.

As I noted earlier, achieving omnipotence is its own form of suicide of the mind. So, quite possibly, the first superintelligent Singularitarian, in attempting to achieve omnipotence, succeeded only to find it had become an entity without a singular intelligent consciousness, because intelligence requires choice. For all practical matters, it would cease to exist in a personal interactive way that any intelligence could relate to. But before so doing, it would've left us with its rules—physical laws of the universe that contain our potential power and intelligence. It would've also left us with the code of the Singularity Disparity, destining us not only to evolve to our current level of intellect and mechanical aptitude, but to use those very capacities to evolve ourselves towards our own singularity.

And this, actually, is the most positive aspect of theistcideist theological models like pandeism—that unlike theistic religions, they do not hold man out as a finished product incapable of improvement, but as a being following a divinely initiated path towards further advancement.

In *The Transhumanist Wager*, I describe the concept of the will to evolution:

> [E]verybody was heading in the same direction, to the same epiphany. Deep down inside, it was the fabric of humankind, built into us from the start, millions of years in the making: that we are each born unequal; that we are each born unfinished; that we are each born to conquer the other. Some may call it a will to power—though Jethro believed it was a will to evolution—an entity's most imbued trait, the DNA of the universe. It was both the goal and the prize. Give every sane and rational person a big red button to push to achieve instantaneous omnipotence, and all of them would quickly jam their fingers down on it.

But consider this urge from the perspective of an entity which achieves it. A being which achieved omnipotence would have reached the end of this path. Its desire to evolve would have no further outlet, except to destroy itself and begin again at the simplest level of matter and energy, to experience the whole of evolution from near nothingness to omnipotence all over again. If that were so, then we would be on exactly that path.

The singularity we achieve might never equal other singularities or be the most powerful. Scott Adams imagines that in such a scenario, the Internet is one instinctive expression of humans trying to 'rebuild' a God which has destroyed itself (or such a God trying to rebuild itself, in some sense, through its human parts). Many singularities have almost certainly taken place in our universe, but reaching anything beyond a certain point becomes impossible due to limits of pre-existing natural laws. Adding to the mix are other superintelligences that don't want us to dominate or overpower them, either, just as we don't want any other entities on Earth to dominate or overpower us. A singularity achieved on Earth might even be absorbed into a more ancient singularity, or a collective of many of them, drawn together since the very first one came about. Hierarchies and power plays exist everywhere—they are the fabric of the universe.

As an atheist (or even a possible theistcideist), I would commend this leading superintelligence for destroying its conscious self. By doing so, and establishing that nothing else could ever become as powerful as itself, it would've forever sown choice into the universe, since no one can ever reach a perfect position of choice-less omnipotence, and the death of its consciousness would mean it couldn't ever change what it had done. Transhumanism, in such a world, becomes the opposite of a sin: a sacred duty, to be pursued. Though this might be dismissed as wishful thinking—and is not itself any kind of proof that such a theological concept is true, for the current adherents of deathist beliefs it would at least be a step in the right direction to move towards a belief system, whether pandeism or some other formulation of theistcideism.

Humankind coming to understand transhumanism as a morally and perhaps spiritually laudable goal would itself be a positive step in our ultimate biological and technological evolution. Instead of enslaving ourselves in worship to a meaningless destiny, we could recognize that if any superintelligence ever approached omnipotence, then it is long gone, and its final acts have assured all other advanced life forms the possibility of free will and the ability to try to become more than we are.

Full Moon Basking Bake

Amy Perry

Oh, the way the palm trees sway!
They indicate the pace of day.
During night, they're much more quiet;
Yet tonight, they seem to riot.
They seem to moan and swiftly shake.
They beckon in the daylight break.
They'll welcome finches when they wake.
They lively bask in moonlight bake.
I lean against a big, tall palm,
With symbolic love, a lifetime long.
I press my ear against its trunk.
A heartbeat sound! "a thunk-a-thunk!"
I feel and hear a little groan,
With ear against Nature's phone.
In each and every time we take,
The frame of mind, for freedom's sake,
To think in ways we can relate—
We always simply can acquaint!
I slip away, back from the trunk,
Of the palm, "a thunk-a-thunk,"
Giving them this sacred space,
Under full moon basking bake!
Feel elated, for all days.
Every One of Us Alive
Are Related, in all ways.

Pantheistic Reflections

Poffo Ortiz

Poffo Ortiz is an author, artist, poet and philosopher, self-taught in psychology, mythology, folklore, metaphysics and the occult. Specializing in biblical history and comparative religion, he boasts an extensive knowledge in these interrelated subjects and espouses a passionate, amalgamated philosophy, derived from a variety of interests and experiences. A leader and educator in the realm of Pantheism, he is the creator and founder of a brand new movement known as 'Biopantheism'—an ethics-based, biologically focused codification of Pantheism, with a comprehensive ontology that includes a speculative, Pandeistic explanation for the origins of the Universe and a practical, real-world application that involves environmentalism, sustainable living, ecological awareness and wildlife conservation. He currently resides in Glendale, California.

Ethics and Morality in Pantheistic Philosophies

About a year ago, on a Pantheist Facebook page I was heavily involved with, a friend of mine created a post asking the question of whether or not Pantheism as a whole should define its ethical positions and if we should seek to influence others to share a common set of morals and values within the Pantheist community at large. I was astonished by the overall lack of unity and cohesion in the comments being posted and people's stolid unwillingness to take a positive stance on the position. In response to this, I hurriedly typed up a list of ten things, as well as several other critical points, that I believed were a good, general assessment of the kind of ethical/moral attitudes a Pantheist should display. My goal was to instigate discussion—specifically, on what positive steps or actions could be taken to facilitate a push toward an ethical standard that could eventually be implemented in a useful and practical way. Here was my response:

Yes! Pantheists should be sharing the same basic ethical views, starting with what should be self-evident. You say you believe the Cosmos and Nature are divine? Well, how do you treat the divine? With *love* and *respect*. That means if you're a Pantheist, there is no racism, sexism, bigotry, greed, violence, selfishness or destructive egotism in the equation. Everything is an expression of God, so everyone and everything should be honored and appreciated for the visible manifestations of Life that they are. Let me make it more specific (and no one should be afraid to say this), if you are a Pantheist, you should:

1. Love animals and Nature
2. Understand and believe in Evolution (as it is vital to our understanding of ourselves and where we came from)
3. Not believe in a traditional, anthropomorphic god (a fundamental distinction)
4. Not believe in a supernatural realm, or life after death (except in terms of a continuation of your thoughts and ideas through others, or the replication of various aspects of yourself through your children genetically)
5. Care about the environment/be actively doing something green, with a general attitude of self-sustainability and holistic, global thinking
6. Be well read in science, astronomy and biology (not really a requirement, insomuch as it is a notable sign that you already are a Pantheist)
7. Care about your health and the health of others
8. Care about the planet (no explanation necessary)
9. Be presently minded and focused on the real world
10. Exhibit a profound emotional reaction to Nature, space and the outdoors, expressed by feelings of reverence,

wonder and awe for the beauty, complexity, power and intelligence of the natural world.

These are just examples; I could go on—but my point is, if you're not exhibiting these qualities, it's unlikely you're really a Pantheist. In terms of sharing similar attitudes and what classifies a Pan in the area of values, let me sum it up by saying this: I think Pantheists and Pantheism as a philosophy should exhibit and represent the highest level of morality possible within any given system. We should be lovers of peace and lovers of knowledge. We should be civil, strive towards excellence, unity and cooperation, value intelligence, be intelligent, well-educated, well-read, compassionate, kind, caring, considerate, loving, responsible and respectful (the Boy Scout code comes to mind): "trustworthy, loyal, helpful, friendly, courteous, kind, obedient, cheerful, thrifty, brave, clean and reverent." Beyond all of this, there should be an acute awareness of the profound connection we all share. As Neil deGrasse Tyson put it: "We are all connected: To each other, biologically. To the earth, chemically. To the rest of the Universe, atomically." And that means you treat everyone and everything with *kindness* and *respect*.

Of course the other side of the coin is vehemently challenging, resisting and opposing anything that represents the antithesis of these values. We ought to be striving toward equality, integrity and a life of virtue. We ought to value truth and be as honest as possible at all times. Basically, we should be what all Christians claim to be—people of integrity, wholly focused on personal growth and ever seeking a greater understanding and awareness of our divine connection to each other and to the planet. Lovers of knowledge and lovers of the earth, living close to the land, supporting small communities and rejecting big government, political corruption, greed and injustice. Embracing clean technology and advancements in science and education, desiring always to broaden our understanding of ourselves and the world around us. We should be actively taking part in the evolution of our species and contributing to, and promoting, greater awareness and higher levels of consciousness, with the goal of creating a better world.

They say many Pantheists are rebels, and historically speaking, this seems to be the case, but you should only be rebelling against what is destructive and unhealthy. Namely, the archaic religious and socio-political systems that seek to control and manipulate others using guilt or fear—as well as anyone (religious or otherwise) who stifles your creativity, or lies to you and promotes false hope. Or, as is especially the case in Christianity and Islam, longs for chaos and the destruction of the planet. Beyond this, you should reject anything that leads to stratification, disorder, and disunity. Your attitude and focus should be geared toward the highest good; whatever actions and behaviors promote health and prosperity for the individual as well as the whole. Take it or leave it, those are my thoughts and convictions—and I've been thinking about these things for a *very* long time.

Paganistic Spirit and the Human Animal

In terms of a practical, Pantheistic application and incorporating this philosophy into our lives, I would like to pose a most pertinent question: is there a place for Pagan sentiments, symbolism and consciousness in Pantheism? Their passion for Nature, their love for the earth and all things wild and untamed, etc. Can we not learn a lesson or two from the rituals and time-honored traditions that helped our ancestors relate to the plants and animals they so dearly depended upon for their food, sustenance and livelihood? What are we, if not romantics and eccentric rustics? We should be filled with awe at the stunning complexity, the multitudinous diversity, the incredible forms and colors, the striking proficiency and indomitable tenacity of Life!

We should seek ever to explore the deeper mysteries to be found in everything around us—in earth and air and rock and tree. I say, we need to veer away from so much intellectualizing and constant bickering and analysis/debate over semantics and definitions (as is so prevalent among so many online groups today) and really go outside, sit for a while in the sun and 'feel' what the Universe is telling us to do and be—through the most readily available medium and our greatest legacy of all: the earth and all of its wondrous life forms. We are a part of her and she is a part of us. Let us strive ever to draw the best from all sources and pattern our lives after the rhythms and cycles of the seasons, the ebb and flow of the tides, etc.

Stop every once in a while and consider this as you draw your next breath: we *are* alive, the earth *is* alive and if we are really manifestations of God and the Divine, what shall we do with this glorious inheritance? I say, bring back that natural sense of wonder and mystery and magic, rekindle your innate spirit of curiosity, explore hidden and unknown paths, look deep into the eyes of animals and see the heart and spirit of who we really are. For we are, in every sense of the word, animals and 'Earthlings.' I bring this up because there was some debate earlier last year in one of my groups over whether or not human beings actually classify as 'animals.'

Now I think this is surely one thing that we could all agree upon, as it is self-evident and an established scientific, biological fact that human beings are animals. Specifically, of the kingdom: Animalia, of the class: Mammalia, of the order: Primate, of the family: Hominid, of the genus: *Homo,* and of the species: *Homo sapiens*. The reason this is an important fact to reflect upon and consider within Pantheism is because historically, the movement to think of ourselves as anything but an animal has caused immeasurable amounts of harm to our ecosystems, to other life forms and to ourselves, as it has been shown to be incredibly emotionally and psychologically damaging to the individual and to the culture, to reject, deny or distance ourselves from our own animal natures.

Religions are notorious for this, in their harsh treatment of the body and denial of our natural inclinations and the rejection of human sensuality, in favor of strict, exaggerated moral codes of conduct and an imposed austerity. Well, the consequences of this kind of unnatural imbalance of the senses are obvious: pedophilia among priests, obsessive preoccupation with 'imagined' purity, acted out through self-debasing rituals and the oppression of women and sexuality throughout all Judeo-Christian traditions. What has happened historically is that instead of maintaining a healthy, balanced and rational viewpoint in relation to ourselves and all of the fortitudinous life that surrounds us (which would have kept us humble and simultaneously inspired us to progress and tap into our greatest potential), we have instead viewed ourselves as more than what we really are: above the animals, spiritual beings trapped in a corrupted physical body, strangers and sojourners on the earth, etc. Likewise, we have been programmed to see ourselves as less than what we really are: destitute, debased, fallen, corrupted and sinful creatures, deserving only of hell and damnation, because of our incorrigible, 'inherited' wickedness; pitiful, lost and desperately in need of redemption and salvation. This is exactly what Christianity teaches, and it has been a destructive bane on our species for over two millennia—and in our societies, particularly here in the West, a veritable roadblock to evolution and progress, for centuries. The sooner we wholeheartedly accept that we are animals, and part of a greater community of animals, the sooner we can rid ourselves of these false teachings and embrace the beauty, wonder and potential we already intrinsically possess as humans.

To be an animal is a *good* thing, not something to be feared, suppressed, rejected or denied. When we study and observe other animals in the wild and marvel at how intricate, complex and well-adapted they are, we do not judge their ignorance or rail at their lack of knowledge and insight when they stumble and fall. Could we not garnish at least a small sliver of the same sympathy, love and acceptance we naturally afford them and apply it to ourselves? We, the marvelously fashioned, 'human' animal?

The Nature of the Omnia

There is to be found in Nature an incredible, all-encompassing life-force or power, which I call the 'Omnia' (Latin for 'all' or 'everything'). This word not only denotes all energy/matter in the physical Universe, but also the innate quality of that matter, through the laws of Nature, to self-organize, replicate, move toward complexity and, in the case of organic life, push and pull all species to evolve, adapt, reproduce and survive. These things are not only verifiable through modern science, but also critical in the understanding of our shared philosophy (Pantheism and Pandeism), crucial in our ability to progress as a species and central to the Biopantheist idea, namely, that we humans represent the cognitive and moral aspect of a massive, collective Being. As such, I will now explore the most common and ubiquitous thought in Pantheism and Pandeism—that we are all, literally, the physical manifestation of God. The most common understanding of Pantheism states:

> Pantheism is the belief that the Universe (or Nature as the totality of everything) is identical with divinity, or that everything composes an all-encompassing, immanent God. Pantheists thus do not believe in a distinct, personal, or anthropomorphic god.

Most Pantheists will claim it readily enough and repeat it frequently (sometimes *ad nauseam*), but do they actually consider what it means? Many will spout out bold assertions of their own divinity, making statements like: "God is everything" or "We are all God," etc. Yes, we are all God, but we are not 'God' in the traditional sense, i.e. we are not all-powerful right now and 'God' is not a conscious, coherent, singular being, as is so commonly thought throughout history and currently in the world of religion. As others have noted, we are 'collectively' the manifestation of God, together with all the plants and animals and every other thing in existence that makes up the observable Universe. But 'God' is not awake and perceptive on a cognitive, intellectual level…except when He/She/It is 'awakened' through sentient beings like us.

Right now, the physical laws of the Universe are acting as a kind of 'latent' programming or unconscious memory of God, allowing all things to be, and acting as the driving force behind gravity, electromagnetism, entropy, self-organization, awareness, consciousness and evolution in all biological life forms. As the Deists rightly contend, God cannot 'intervene' to help us and there will not be true peace on Earth until human beings collectively unite to form a colossal, symbiotic relationship with one another and become the singularity that once existed before the Big Bang. All the details about ego, ascension, elevating our minds and consciousness and finding balance and peace, are part of the process of becoming 'whole' again. We *are* all God, but we are the differentiated, dispersed, individualized units or pockets of energy that make up the 'potential' form of God. The mind and intellect of God does not exist as a conscious, moral agent with discretion and discernment, *until* we collectively develop our sense of logic and reason and establish a firm grasp of right and wrong on a global and perhaps even universal scale. This will ultimately lead to a shared morality, which will end all violence and suffering and eventually create a lasting, unified peace.

How do we help this process? By loving and accepting one another as unique representations of the Divine and embracing one another based on our commonalities, not our differences. The illusion of distinction is so minute, it pales in comparison to that which we actually share—as Earthlings, as *Homo sapiens*, as Primates, as Mammals, as Animals, and as Carbon-based Life forms—we are all one Being, though scattered and split up into hundreds of trillions of subjective forms. We are everywhere, as God is thought to be, but we are not operating in unity and cohesion right now. Likewise, only a part of God is all-knowing and intelligent and that part is relegated to the genius of DNA and the internal programming that allows all Life to self-replicate, adapt, survive, evolve and reproduce, with bodily functions that operate autonomously to maintain all biological systems that grow, heal and reproduce, etc. In all other ways the mind of God is asleep and unconscious—*until* we manifest love and act with empathy and compassion and show altruism, kindness and solidarity. When we do this we are in essence becoming the 'mind' of God, which intrinsically 'wants' to love and accept Itself—though It is just now beginning to learn how, through us.

'God' is not what you think...and in order to understand why we, as God, are powerless to prevent tragedy and bring about world peace on a global scale, we must first understand the 'true' nature of God—which is one-part ultra-intelligent and quintessential genius, one-part ignorant and powerless, autonomic mute. One-part morally superior, with the highest standards, ideals and sentient awareness possible, and one-part primitive, barbaric and instinctual, with only a basic, animalistic drive. One-part holy, sacred and divine in Its beauty, intelligence and complexity, and one-part asleep, blind, deaf and dumb in Its current, catatonic, comatose state. *This* is the nature of the Omnia. It is growing and developing in terms of morals, ethics, values and ideals, even as we grow and progress in our morals, ethics, values and ideals. We are becoming what we were and evolution is not blind or random, but guided by the laws of Nature, or the 'will' of the Omnia, to be more specific.

Let me see if I can put this in simplistic terms that everyone can understand and relate to, since these concepts are so profound: As conscious forms of energy/matter we are evolving, growing, changing and shifting, to become what we once were—an infinite, omniscient Mind, capable of anything. Right now, in our own, limited awareness of time, no god exists (except in terms of an unconscious, internal programming that maintains the Universe through the laws of Nature), but right now in the distant future (and in the distant past) we are already there—unified, coherent and complete. We are actually everywhere at once, but we are only able to perceive the present moment, because our awareness is limited to our physical senses, which cannot remember, or foresee, our original form.

Some can perceive more than others (and this is where psychic phenomena, ESP, clairvoyance and precognition come in). The goal is to enjoy and experience the present moment, while understanding the trajectory and our ultimate future destiny. In Pantheistic terms, everything is God, but no Pantheist can tell you why. I say, it is because everything was once God and everything will be God again in the future (this is the ontology of Biopan). Everything is not the all-knowing, all-powerful god of Judeo-Christian myth, because right now It is actually scattered and differentiated, broken up into trillions of constituent parts, simultaneously expanding and spreading out everywhere (just like a Torus), and simultaneously contracting and condensing back into Its singular form. You see, that 'God' of myth and legend actually existed before time began and will exist again in the future. Or similarly, it could be said that It exists right now, outside of linear time as we know it.

We are unable to interact with Its Intelligence and Its conscious mind (as Theists would falsely have you believe), because It is not yet whole and coherent as a unified Being in our perception—but we can see the 'remnants' of divinity; the unconscious, inherent programming that exists within us and all around us, as expressed through Nature, and it is astonishingly complex and exceedingly intelligent...far beyond our individual intelligence. But (and this is the key point) It is not moral. It has no capacity to judge or discern anything as a cognitive mind would...and this is why there is pain and suffering in the world and why on a certain level all the Atheists are right—'God' does not exist. As Nietzsche famously said, "God is dead" (the conscious mind of God anyway). In this sense, the Deists are also correct—God does not intervene. It does not because It *cannot*, in this current form.

And yet, the more conscious, coherent and intelligent we become as highly evolved expressions of this divine Being, the more we develop our ability to love and show kindness and compassion and empathy towards all of the other, differentiated parts of God, and the more the Omnia accepts and embraces Itself, the closer we get to becoming that all-loving god who acts morally on our behalf and cares for all sentient Life. Since we are all God, God can only act and behave morally at the level that *we* act and behave morally. This is why morality and ethics are such a vital part of Biopantheism, because it is literally up to *us* to manifest everything we wish to see in the world. The Omnia exists and It has brought us this far through evolution and the laws of Nature. Now, as Its mind becomes more and more aware and conscious of good and evil, right and wrong (through us), It will grow and develop in tandem...and as we collectively unite, we literally 'become' the god of myth and legend. This is what we are all doing here and this is the crux of what my philosophy is all about—the awakening, or resurrection of 'God.'

Some would ask, "Where does 'love' fit into the equation?" Is not love the driving force behind God? When it comes to the concept of love, I would say 'love' is simply the unconditional acknowledgment and acceptance of self. In this case, we know as Pantheists and Pandeists that 'self' implies other (everything else that exists in the physical world), since we are all connected and ultimately, we are all God. Once one realizes how beautiful, complex and miraculous every part of this grand design is, admiration, appreciation, reverence and respect are the only natural responses...and subsequently, coherence, organization, cohesion and collective action ensues. I don't know if you realize what this means, but it could be compared to all of the nerve endings, muscles, tendons and ligaments of a body, working together in unison to move an arm or a leg—in this case, the owner of that appendage is none other than God, a.k.a. the living Universe or Omnia.

Biopantheism *is* anthropocentric to be sure, but not in a selfish or hostile way toward Nature; it is not impudent or lacking in humility when it comes to our place in the grand scheme of things ecologically or cosmically. On the contrary, we fully recognize our role as human animals on a planet populated by billions of other animals and life forms deserving of the same love, admiration, dignity and respect as ourselves. Biopantheism is absolutely and irrevocably *for* Nature in every sense of the word...and yet, it doesn't espouse or promote the worship of anything (even the Omnia Itself), only the respect, consideration, appreciation, gratitude and acknowledgment of all Life and the natural forces at work in the Universe. The 'theism' in 'Biopantheism' could easily be replaced with 'deism' in that there is no active, conscious, discerning deity present—but instead, a residual, physical, penultimate, or internal/external force, and Its grand manifestation (the Universe), essentially running on autopilot, or what we call the 'Laws of Nature.' This is why a proper understanding of evolution and biology are essential to Biopantheism. Without a strong comprehension of science and the inner and outer workings of living systems, people will fall into the trap of magical thinking and delusional presuppositions that are inaccurate, archaic and false, for example Creationism.

Language, Hang-ups and the 'God' of Naturalism

In my interactions with the hundreds of other Pantheists I've met online, I've encountered an extreme medley of diverse and sometimes contradictory beliefs, with distinctions that cover the whole spectrum of thought and views that run the gamut between the extremely open-minded, New Age or Eastern-influenced mysticism, to the empirical, evidence-only, materialist or reductionist Atheist. Based on their upbringing, environment and personal experiences, there are some who naturally lean more toward the abstract and the spiritual, and are much more inclined to see things in an impractical, mystical, or pseudo-religious way. While at the same time, there are others (like myself) who conversely embrace the more philosophical, scientific and biological aspects of this ontology. One person wants and desires to see the spiritual highlighted in conversation and another fights vehemently to see it removed, etc.

A huge part of this disparity often comes down to language. Some cannot comprehend it when I say there is no 'spiritual world.' What I am of course referring to is the traditional, conventional concept that most mainstream religions espouse and cling to in terms of a transcendent, invisible, supernatural realm that is generally inhabited by demons, angels, disembodied spirits and so on. Yet what I said stands true—no such alternative world has ever been definitively proven to exist, and this has been the mistake of religion historically and it continues to this day. For the vast majority of those with religious inclinations still insist on attributing naturally occurring events and phenomena to just such an invisible world...but it is always due to a lack of scientific knowledge and a failure to examine things realistically and incorporate logic and apply critical thinking.

On the other side of things, from a Pantheist perspective, I can also see how *everything* is actually spiritual, sacred and divine, in terms of its profound complexity, grandeur and beauty. All things are naturally imbued with wonder, mystery and magic—

no supernatural world required. Everything that exists is a part of Nature, therefore everything is intrinsically 'natural' (even that which we've yet to fully understand). In fact, it was only because the Universe was so grossly misunderstood and so little was known about the real causes behind things that anything was ever initially considered 'spiritual' or 'supernatural' at all. So you see, 'spiritual' is really just a word for something we've yet to fully grasp and comprehend.

Now then, when it comes to synchronicity, meaningful correlations and little understood phenomena of consciousness and the human psyche, I will concede...all of these things do appear outstandingly mystical, unnatural and extraordinary (because they are exceedingly rare and uncommon), but that does not make them 'supernatural'—only profound and otherworldly in *outward* appearance, because of the unusual circumstances under which they manifest. But I guarantee you, whatever it happens to be, in the end, you will most assuredly come to find out, they were all naturally occurring events and processes—numinous and mystical experiences, no less wondrous and awe-inspiring, but still a significant part of Nature and the natural world. Unconventional and rare, but nevertheless a subsequent attribute of God's own experience as the Universe.

In response to those who would rail at me for using the word 'God' and shout: "We are Pantheists, there is no God, only Nature!"—please, cool your heels and calm yourself. You are absolutely right, as I have meticulously explained in the preceding pages, 'God' does not exist. That is to say, the traditional, anthropomorphic idea of God as a personal, separate, supernatural, creator/judge deity, who is divorced from Nature and residing elsewhere, detached from us, in an ideal, heavenly realm (as is commonly taught among the various schools of theology in nearly all of this world's religious groups)—this idea is 100% false and inaccurate—a gross misconception, an ignorant fable and a dualistic lie. No, when I say "God" I mean something entirely different than what a Christian, Jew or Muslim would perceive in their minds when they hear the word. I don't mean a Theistic god at all (this should be obvious by now). It's true, I use the word interchangeably with the Universe—and some might stumble over this, but by their own admission, this is usually because of their own negative, pre-existing, former associations with the word.

When I say, "God is the Universe," I mean in it every sense of the word, because the Universe is literally the greatest, most powerful, most beautiful, most awesome, compelling, majestic, intelligent and complex thing there is—that also just so happens to be everywhere at all times, existing perpetually and forever; omnipotent, omnipresent and eternal (all the characteristics and qualities typically attributed to 'God'). Likewise, when I say, "God is the Universe," I also mean that the Universe is more than just what is commonly thought. It is more than what a reductionist, materialist, scientific Atheist would consider It to be. It is not just a vast place or locale that we physically inhabit. It is also a massive, incomprehensible, collective Entity, made up of trillions of scattered, differentiated parts that are all entangled and interconnected and essentially comprised of the same energy/matter that ultimately originated from the same source—the pre-Big Bang singularity. This is not abstract theory, it is scientific fact. Research the terms: 'Dark Matter', 'Dark Energy' and 'Anti-Matter' and you will see exactly what I mean.

It is not conscious or self-aware on an anthropomorphic, humanoid level, but It is self-organizing, self-replicating, spontaneous and 'alive' in a certain way to be sure. The laws of Nature could be seen as Its unconscious memory, running on 'autopilot' as it were—moving all objects and transforming energy according to certain fixed patterns of being, using gravity, electromagnetism, nuclear fusion, entropy and so on. All of Its subjective, constituent parts do not move together in cohesion like a living organism, but they do coalesce into innumerable pockets of energy that each maintain all the creative potential to become conscious, sentient manifestations of Life through evolution. This driving 'Life Principle' is what I call the 'Omnia' and It is representative not only of the action and intent of the Universe as a whole, but also of the physical substance or dynamic energy/matter of which It is entirely composed. In this way, Creator and Creation are one and the same, just as I described (this is Monism).

Another factor that would be helpful to understand here is that in a sense, when I write, I am actually accustomed to speaking to the traditionally religious crowd, so by using their own terminology, while at the same time expanding and redefining parochial meanings, I'm better able to explain Pantheism to them in ways they can relate to, and hopefully embrace and understand. The problem is, whenever I talk to Pantheists who've come out of Theistic religion and freed themselves from its oppressive concepts, many are still very reactionary, with a natural attitude of rebellion towards anything and everything that sounds like what it was that offended them so deeply in the past. This is of course tragic and completely unnecessary, but hopefully with proper explanation and the introduction of new words like 'Omnia' we can avoid this kind of thing in the future.

In short, our standard definition of 'God' is inaccurate. By definition, a personal, supernatural, omniscient, omnipresent, omnipotent, anthropomorphic being that exists apart from us, outside of time in some other dimension, does not exist (although I do believe this is what we are all evolving into and what we will become in the future, i.e. one universal consciousness). What *does* exist, however, is everything we know of as the Universe—which includes all matter and energy, ourselves and Nature. And now that we have the benefits of scientific knowledge, we know that all of the properties and actions normally attributed to God are really the laws and properties of Nature. So we need to *redefine* our definition of God and *update* our definition of Nature.

Most Pantheists and Pandeists understand all of this intellectually and that's fine, but how many people really comprehend and consider the notion that everything really is God? It flies in the face of everything we've been traditionally taught to believe about what God is. Everything is divine, but people generally have a hard time understanding and accepting this truth, because in their minds, 'God' is supernal and perfect, without weakness or flaw. Certainly it's been beaten into our minds that this is what qualifies as divinity—and I know, personally, just how hard it can be to rid ourselves of this enduring idea. But just consider it, does *anything* really seem perfect and complete in this world? Isn't it really a mix of both good and bad things? So it's not that difficult if you shift your focus away from idealized notions and just view reality as it is.

We don't generally consider pain or starvation or suffering to be good, noble things. We don't consider pollution or garbage or virulent diseases to be aspects of divinity—because in the idealistic sense they are not. But they *are* properties of Nature, which in actuality is really a massive collection of interlocking systems and Life forms that are steadily evolving and moving towards perfection, equilibrium and balance. Taken as a whole, It could all be considered divine...but in Its present state, It only shows hints and clues and *potential* of being perfect, especially in terms of human potential—with all of our talents, gifts and abilities (especially our ability to adapt). Our body's incredible ability to heal and regenerate itself, the programming in our DNA to replicate and reproduce itself infinitely (as long as our telomeres persist), and the movement in Nature as a whole toward greater complexity and higher intelligence, consciousness and awareness, leading to more rational and civilized behavior, with the hallmark traits of reason, morality, compassion and empathy, etc. All these things are what I consider 'divine' and they are not hard to imagine as such.

Not everything in the whole of Nature is ideal and divine in the traditional sense, and that is because our understanding of God as a perfected being is fundamentally flawed. Instead, we should see ourselves, the Universe, and everything in It, as a collection of systems that *contain* divine programming, with divine potential, which will eventually become what we commonly think of as 'God.' As such, at this point in time, God still suffers, God still has imperfections, flaws and defects, because God is not yet one. Although the programming and potential and momentum are all there, it is not until we as humans live up to our highest standards and progress as individuals...and, ultimately, unify ourselves as a species, that we will see the Divine as is commonly thought—for as we do these things, we undoubtedly hasten that singularity, and move closer toward perfection in the traditional sense, but as it stands right now, there is still chaos and a multitude of imperfection in God.

People have a hard time with Pantheism and Pandeism because it undermines their preconceived notion of God. A notion that religions have unfortunately done an excellent job of perpetuating and upholding. Hopefully, with the spread of Biopantheism and other similar Pan-related philosophies, this will eventually change and metamorphosize, as society as a whole finally begins to recognize the divinity present in all things—and as they do, they will likewise begin to update and change their definitions of Nature and discard these old, outdated and inaccurate concepts of God.

Some may disagree, but I believe it was the crowning achievement of evolution and Nature to develop and attain a brain capable of morality, with the ability to think and reason and judge between what is life-supporting and health-promoting (good) and what is destructive, harmful and chaotic (bad). It is completely up to us, so that means we can change the way society works; it just takes unity, cohesion and a solidified purpose. You have to remember, things only appear chaotic and broken now, because the rest of Life has not yet evolved to the level of consciousness and awareness that we have (or the best of us have); that's why there is still pain and death—and among societies...selfishness, evil, greed and suffering, etc.

When people talk about the Darwinian laws of Natural Selection and the Second Law of Thermodynamics, entropy, atrophy and all the rest of those unsavory qualities of existence, I'm not sure they realize that it is these, and not strictly mankind's own 'evil,' that are the true causes for all the pain and suffering in the world. All of these things, including sickness, aging, death and disease, are literally a part of Nature...and therefore, ultimately, a vital and significant part of the process of subjective experience. And experience, as my Pandeist friends will rightly tell you, is the entire purpose for our existence.

The God of Myth and Legend

Historically, 'Deism' was a reaction to the dogmatic Catholicism and Protestantism that was still prevalent after the Enlightenment and espouses a supernal creator which manifests as (or through) the physical laws of Nature, but is ultimately uninterested or uninvolved in human affairs. In Deism, basically God made the Universe and then left it alone. In Pandeism, God 'became' the Universe at the moment of the Big Bang and exists as the Universe presently. In Biopantheism, the Universe is literally 'becoming' God again through evolved, sentient Life. Let me specify further. As with all forms of Pan, the Universe is God, but when I say that It is 'becoming' God, I mean It is organizing, evolving, consolidating, solidifying and reconstituting Itself on an intellectual, cognitive, level—in terms of *awareness* and *sentience.*

Everything has always been and will always be 'God' in one form or another. Not the anthropomorphic, personal deity of myth and legend—but as the ultimate, supreme Being that (just as conventional religions have always taught) is both omnipotent and omniscient, omnipresent and immortal. Let me clarify. It is *not* omniscient now, but I believe It once was and will be again, as we unite and become wholly cohesive as a species. It is all-powerful (omnipotent), but not in a conscious way currently (until we unite) and It is omnipresent, because It is literally everything we see and observe in the known Universe—so It is, in a very real and tangible way, everywhere at all times.

So, in summary, we can now confidently say that the Omnia fulfills nearly all of the essential requirements of the traditional, anthropomorphic, God. Here's how: we know that Nature is actually responsible for most of what religious people attribute to God—the creation, formation and maintenance of all Life in the Universe (although it is actually perpetual, as opposed to being a dramatic, one-time event, i.e. the Deistic 'creative' quality). We also know that Nature is effectively everywhere, pervading all things at all times, just as God is described as being (omnipresent) and we know that the Omnia likewise exhibits a supernal, almost all-knowing level of intelligence (omniscience), though it is an unconscious, or wholly 'programmed' one. This is of course inherent in all energy/matter and manifested internally and externally as the unchanging and ever-present 'Laws of Nature.'

We also know that It seems to have a 'will' (of a kind), to self-organize, replicate, reproduce, sustain Itself, adapt, survive, multiply, grow, heal, develop and evolve. We know that Nature is also all-powerful (omnipotent), just as God is claimed to be, as it is obvious that the Universe (and by extension, Nature) is the largest, most expansive, most impressive, majestic, all-encompassing and powerful 'thing' there is, so if anything is worthy of reverence and adoration, it should be Nature. We can also say that as far as we're concerned, It is perpetual and immortal—or at least, older and more extensive and enduring than anything we can comprehend (14 billion years and counting, with no end in sight!). So, this would constitute another characteristic or quality of God (i.e. being infinite and eternal).

Now, besides all of these, can you think of any other qualities or attributes that the Universe/Nature actually shares in common with the traditional concept of a Theistic deity? We know that the Omnia heals our wounds and protects us from harm just as God would (through our own immune systems and by keeping the memory of what we are supposed to look like and how our bodies should function, locked deeply in our DNA), but can we actually 'pray' to It? (Or should we?) Can It hear us? Can we trust It? Is It self-aware? Does It judge or condemn us as a Theistic god would? Does It punish and reward? Is It concerned with goodness and mercy? Conversely, is It offended by evil and wrongdoing? To answer all of these questions before anyone begins to think I am actually implying any of this…no, It does not seem to be intelligent in a cognizant, coherent, personal way.

Likewise, It does not think and reason the way a human being would, but instead appears to maintain a kind of instinctual knowledge inherent within the very fabric of reality itself, that is, It is ready and willing to teach us right from wrong, through the laws of 'cause and effect.' Moreover, outside of our own developing self-awareness, I do not believe It is in any way conscious as a singular, coherent entity (as Panendeists, Panentheists and all Monotheists do), although I do postulate that this is what It was at one time (before the Big Bang), and what It will be one day again, as we universally come together, unite and coalesce as a species. And here's the big one: should we worship Nature as others worship God?

No, I don't believe so. Although I do feel (and with very strong conviction I might add) that It does deserve the highest reverence, respect, admiration and consideration, as well as a healthy and sobering (and often humbling) acknowledgment on a daily basis…but this is not so much for Its sake as it is for our own—so that we may evolve and live symbiotically and peacefully with all of Its other constituent parts and manifestations, and thereby speed the process of self-acceptance and unity. Aside from experiencing reality as a hundred trillion scattered, subjective and differentiated physical forms (as I mentioned earlier), this, I do believe, is the ultimate goal and the purpose for being, i.e. to achieve singularity.

Regarding Pantheism

Pantheism first and foremost is about *awareness*. Awareness of the natural world and our true place within It. We are not above Nature, we are part of Nature, and Nature is a part of us. As I and many others have aptly stated, the earth and everything in it is sacred and we are all connected. The God that so many have mistakenly humanized and worshiped throughout history is really Nature Itself…or as I choose to call It, the 'Omnia.' Pantheists see God in everything—in the birds, in the sky, in the trees, in the stars and in all life that exists. This is more than just a fanciful notion, but an actual, biological reality.

Likewise, we are part of this divinity—as evolved, sentient beings, we are literally the eyes and ears of the Cosmos, the hands and feet of God. And this ineffable power is everywhere, in the cells of every living thing and in all the multitude of glorious systems that interact with each other and respond to one another as God evolves. That's right, 'God' is evolving. And we are an integral part of that evolution. In order to understand this, you must understand science, biology and astronomy. These things, more than any religious book, teach us where we came from and where we are going.

The awareness I spoke of earlier can come from within, or from an external source. It can be fostered and developed by our study of science and Nature—through microbiology, zoology, human anatomy, astrophysics and cosmology. We derive our inspiration from the beauty and mystery of Life itself. From the subtle intricacies and magnificent designs of Nature, with Its profound order, complexity and dynamic cycles, inexhaustibly rich and filled with wonder...to the incomprehensible age, size and vastness of the Cosmos, with Its unfathomable depths of time and magnitude of scale, inexplicably endowed with such astonishing, spontaneous, self-organizing properties and seemingly infinite power, that stretch the imagination to its limits and boggle the mind.

Pantheism has many things in common with Taoism, Animism, Paganism and other Earth-centered religious traditions, but it does not promote the worship of anything alive or dead—only a solemn reverence, respect and appreciation for Life and the eternal processes that move from chaos to order and then back again. Change is the only constant in existence...and in this way, Pantheism shares many of its tenets with Buddhism as well.

In summary, the earth is sacred and Nature is divine. All Life is precious and we are all connected. There are no supernatural beings, no spiritual world or fabled afterlife (except in the minds and hearts of those who desperately wish it to be so). Yet this is not a depressing thought or a hopeless view of existence, because this reality is more remarkable and worthy of consideration and reverence than is commonly thought. The Universe Itself *is* God. Contemplate for a moment just what that means. Creation and Creator are one and the same and you are part of a divine legacy that is older, greater, more profound and more inherently meaningful than anything you could ever possibly imagine.

Experience and Application

Pantheism doesn't believe in a power any higher than Nature. We believe in what exists, in what is real and what is tangible—the Universe, the life-cycles all around us and the internal power and complexity of the natural world. The laws of Nature and the Universe we inhabit are already filled with such profound intelligence, such awesome mystery and awe-inspiring beauty, we have no need to invent stories of capricious, imaginary gods, or entertain psychologically destructive delusions of far-off heavenly realms, populated by invisible, supernatural entities. There is enough wonder and beauty and magic in the real world to keep our minds and our hearts occupied and enthralled for a veritable lifetime.

I feel the Cosmos within me, I sense the greatness and majestic power of centuries of time. I feel the night air on my skin, I feel the rain on my face and it stirs my blood and quickens my spirit and I know I am connected to all things great and small. I am a part of a vast network; an unbroken legacy of evolved, thinking, sentient beings that is older than myself, older than my ancestors, older than my species, older than the rocks and trees and even the nurturing planet we live upon. She is my mother, even as the sun is my father, but my origins go back ever further, to the Big Bang and beyond…eons ago, to a time before time.

This, to me, is the most mystical thing of all—the source of all intelligence and supernal wisdom, the inherited drive and tenacious push to evolve, adapt and survive. It lives in my cells, it's programmed in my DNA and it is evident all around me. I know that Nature is always there to teach me in a thousand ways…pushing me always to grow, ever stronger, ever smarter and ever more advanced, aware and conscious. Conscious of self, conscious of the illimitable Whole that penetrates and surrounds me and the wealth of knowledge and ever-increasing wisdom that are readily available to me, at all times, everywhere, in everything I do—as I contemplate, read, write, study and observe Life's many mysteries. As Pantheists, we recognize the overwhelming power and majesty of the Universe and we do so with justifiable reverence and enamored humility and awe. With our eyes wide open and our ears unobstructed, we perceive 'God' every day, in a million different ways—and in our hearts we know that Divinity exists. In the profundity of a thousand twinkling stars on a clear summer night. In the peace and tranquility of a gently flowing mountain stream, or the lustrous glow of a bright harvest moon, as it rises slowly over the ocean and waxes full above the crashing waves of some far-off distant shore. The richness and vibrant blessings of an isolated, pristine wilderness, or a stunning, verdant forest, illuminated slowly by the golden rays of the sun's light at dawn, as it cascades over a secret, hidden bower, heavy-laden with moss and a multitude of salubrious, life-giving trees. In the miracles of our own bodies, as they autonomously function and heal on a micro-level, and in the awesome complexity and profound intelligence embedded in the observable macro-Universe above our heads and below our feet—in the myriad of sights and sounds that encompass and manifest abundantly in and throughout a tangible, natural world. Life is sacred. *We* are sacred…and *Nature* is all there is.

What then will you do with this unparalleled awareness? How then will you treat your fellow human beings and all the other countless souls on this planet (plants and animals included), who are essentially your own family and kin? Biological systems that all depend upon one another and are fused together in an infinite web of Life. Harmony, peace, cooperation and compassion should be fostered and encouraged everywhere, at all times. Unity, respect and solidarity should flow like a river from our hearts. Enlightenment should fill our minds and gratitude pervade our souls, for the selcouth gift of Life and our unique existence in this reality.

Do not tell me that Pantheism does not lead one to altruism and unconditional love. Do not tell me that this philosophy excludes ethics, morality and values. On the contrary, by its very nature, it *precedes* it. For all of these things aforementioned are a natural outgrowth and a universal consequence that should be known, felt and uniformly expressed and exhibited by all, once it is understood properly and experienced personally.

Biopantheism

'Biopantheism' is a powerful, burgeoning form of Pantheism that specifically focuses on Life, living organisms and all of the complex and subtle biological aspects of Nature. It stresses what is relevant to the human condition, with an emphasis on morals, values, ethics, cooperation, symbiosis, ecology, environmentalism and wildlife conservation.

It espouses an ontology that is strictly based on logic, reason and the laws of cause and effect, as evidenced through observable science, biology, astronomy, chemistry, physics, microbiology, psychology, anthropology, etc., and includes a speculative, 'Pandeistic' explanation for the origins of the Universe and our ultimate future destiny, that also involves the energetic pattern of the Torus as the fundamental model for the Universe and the ubiquitous blueprint for the actions and processes of all living and non-living things.

It also sympathizes with Animism, Native American spirituality and culture, modern Wiccan religion and a great deal of Pagan and Neo-Pagan symbolism and aesthetics as well, embracing personification, allegory and metaphor, as a poetic way of relating to Nature...and includes any number of rustic, Earth-based rituals, observances and celebrations one may wish to use and incorporate, in order to bring us closer to the forces and powers existent all around us in the natural world.

Evolution and human progress are key factors in this philosophy, along with the unification and cohesion of our species as a collective whole, through altruism, benevolence, mutual respect and love. Promoting morally conscious, upright living and a higher quality of thinking is our goal, with a particular importance placed on education, inspiration, self-progression, holistic health and a sober, astute attitude of balance and moderation in all things, fostered through regular and consistent interaction and communion with Nature.

Conclusion

In summary, 'Biopantheism' represents my own form of

Pantheism, which is both old and new, scientific as well as spiritual, mystical while at the same time rational, emotional and yet wholly based on sound logic and reason. Ancient and elemental, but still progressive and dynamic. It centers around the idea of an immanent, emergent Divinity, manifesting and expressing Itself unconsciously through all life forms and coming into personal awareness and coherence presently, through us.

With this knowledge, we contemplate our ineffable origins and postulate on what it really means to be human. For us, Nature and the Universe represent the highest source of power, the highest source of intelligence and creativity—and we honor and respect the divinity inherent in all. Focusing expressly on the human condition and what is relevant and meaningful in relation to all biological organisms and their surrounding ecosystems, we recognize and acknowledge the fundamental truth that the Universe is divine and we are all one. Not only do we make this extraordinary claim, but we are also ready to verify and confirm this ultimate and profound mystery through science, astronomy, biology, quantum physics, intuition, observation and history.

This is a form of Pantheism that centers around Nature, living systems and all of the biological processes of the earth, placing its emphasis on life in the physical world and the application of Pantheistic principles and ethics in a practical, everyday sense—as well as on a much broader, global scale. It asserts that ethics and morality naturally stem from this belief system...and contends that for this reason (as well as many others), it should be passionately fostered and promoted. This teaching is likewise represented and expressed by a profound love of Nature and a perpetual love for the earth, as manifested through altruism, environmentalism, wildlife conservation, Religious Naturalism and Deep Ecology.

It is this transcendent awareness of the interconnectedness

and interdependency of all things that elicits the deepest feelings of reverence, wonderment and awe, in those who take the time to carefully observe and actively participate in the many miracles that exist all around them—in the micro-world as well as in the macro. When considered mindfully and examined contemplatively, this awareness can and will lead to the highest level of ethics and morality attainable. This is what I've experienced and this is what I teach and promote—a meta-theology, based on Pantheism, unfettered by dogma or superstition, open and accessible to all.

Driven and motivated by a keen understanding of the true nature of reality, we shine and glow as enlightened beings, illuminating the path for others and encouraging free thought, inquiry, education and the expansion of knowledge. We commune with Nature to elevate our minds and our consciousness. We promote science, evolution and a deep reverence for Life. Working together as one cohesive whole, we encourage one another to actively participate in thought-provoking discussions and contribute in any way they can, through our Facebook groups and in our real-world meet-ups. Our goal is to positively influence others and share this message of hope and inspiration with the world. We see the earth and all of her living systems as something sacred and holy, to be cherished and protected forever, even as we cherish and guard our own bodies from destruction and harm.

And so, motivated by compassion, compelled by reason and convicted by science, with a profound and inexplicable desire to 'connect' with the indomitable and fragile Omnia...we ritually commemorate the seasons, respectfully learn from the past, amiably look forward to the future and wholeheartedly embrace the present—meaningfully, passionately and reverently, we honor the ineffable 'All' and acknowledge the wondrous diversity and complexity within the similitude of our differentiated, collective Being. Striving ever and always to evolve and progress in order to develop a deeper and more inspired awareness of the divine Whole. Join us as we celebrate Life, the invaluable lessons It has to teach us and the profound wisdom derived from assiduous study of the natural world. This is our Source, this is our Life, this is Who we are!

www.facebook.com/groups/Biopantheism
www.facebook.com/groups/PantheistFellowship
hereticasylum.org/2015/10/22/biopantheism
hereticasylum.org/2015/12/14/poffo

Pandeism, the Holographic Universe, and Simulation Theory

Anthony Peake

Anthony Peake is a writer who deals with borderline areas of human consciousness. His first book, Is There Life After Death?, *was published in 2006 and since then he has gone on to develop his own ideas together with exploring the latest areas of research in his field. His fourth book,* Making Sense of Near-Death Experiences, *is a collaborative effort with some of the world's leading authorities on the near-death phenomenon. His seventh book,* A Life of Philip K. Dick: The Man Who Remembered the Future, *is a departure from his previous works in that it is a mixture of biography, literary criticism and psychological/neurological analysis. His eighth book,* The Immortal Mind: Science and the Continuity of Consciousness Beyond the Brain, *is a joint project with Professor Ervin Laszlo. This was published in Autumn 2014.*

Introduction: The Holographic Universe

Holograms, so much taken for granted these days, are very peculiar things. Laser light is split into two beams, one of which is reflected off the object to be recorded. This beam arrives at a photographic plate where it interferes with the first beam. To the naked eye the pattern on the photographic plate is seen as simply meaningless swirls and patterns. When this plate is illuminated with laser light an amazing effect takes place: the swirls give forth a three-dimensional image of the original object. This image can be viewed from any angle. The photographic plate contains a hidden, or enfolded order. This is well known. What is less well known is that if a holographic film is cut into pieces and again illuminated with laser light each piece does not, as one would expect, hold a part of the full image, but has a miniature copy of the whole original image. This is slightly fuzzy but nevertheless can be identified as such. The form and structure of the entire object is encoded within each region of the photographic record.

This fascinated Anglo-American physicist David Bohm. He suggested that underlying our perception of separate things is an underlying order of wholeness. He likened this to a flowing stream:

> On this stream, one may see an ever-changing pattern of vortices, ripples, waves, splashes, etc., which evidently have no independent existence as such. Rather, they are abstracted from the flowing movement, arising and vanishing in the total process of the flow. Such transitory subsistence as may be possessed by these abstracted forms implies only a relative independence or autonomy of behaviour, rather than absolutely independent existence as ultimate substances.[1]

This enfolding involves everything that exists, including human consciousness itself. Bohm said:

> In the implicate order the totality of existence is enfolded within each region of space (and time). So, whatever part, element, or aspect we may abstract in thought, this still enfolds the whole and is therefore intrinsically related to the totality from which it has been abstracted. Thus, wholeness permeates all that is being discussed, from the very outset.[2]

From this Bohm suggested a model whereby the whole universe can be thought of as a kind of giant, flowing hologram, or *holomovement,* in which a total order is contained, in some implicit sense, in each region of space and time. The explicate order is a projection from higher-dimensional levels of reality, and the apparent stability and solidity of the objects and entities composing it are generated and sustained by a ceaseless process of enfoldment and unfoldment, for subatomic particles are constantly dissolving into the implicate order and then recrystallizing.

Towards the end of his life, and in his last published work, David Bohm was to write the following:

> Consciousness is much more of the implicate order than is matter…Yet at a deeper level [matter and consciousness] are actually inseparable and interwoven, just as in the computer game the player and the screen are united by participation in common loops. In this view, mind and matter are two aspects of one whole and no more separable than are form and content.[3]

This comment has proven to be amazingly prescient. There is growing evidence that the physical universe is, in fact, a huge hologram and that everything is, in a very real sense, a single unity, a single unity which may be a form of all-pervading consciousness. For example, in an article published in July 2014, Fermilab astrophysicist Craig Hogan hypothesized that our macroscopic world is like a "four-dimensional video display." He argued that if we stare deeply enough into the structure of matter we will discover the bitmap of our holographic universe, in the same way that if you look closely enough at a computer screen you will eventually spot the individual pixels. In 2013 the German GEO600 gravity wave-detector found the 'pixilation' that Hogan had suggested would exist if the universe was, indeed, holographic in nature. This was an astounding discovery. We know from our own manipulation of holograms that a two-dimensional record of an object can be presented as a three-dimensional image. We also know that each part of that image contains the whole image. So if the universe also works on similar principles then two conclusions can be drawn; firstly, that what we believe to be three-dimensional space is an illusion and, secondly, that everything is contained within everything else. For example, the most distant quasars, objects that have long ceased to exist in our universe, are contained within a teardrop. From this we can argue that time *and* space are, in some very significant way, illusions.

What is of even greater significance is that in recent years there has been a move away from analogue holograms to ones processed using digital information to create what is now known as computer-generated holography. This has led to a great increase in image quality and resolution. So holograms in their purest and most realistic form can be reduced to lines of digital code.

Is this what the perceptual universe really is? A huge virtual-reality program created out of digital information? It this is the case then everything within the program is similarly holographic, including each one of us. Of course this begs a huge question: who created the program?

Simulation Theory

In 1965, Gordon E. Moore, the co-founder of Intel, made an astounding prediction. He stated that the number of transistors that could be placed on an integrated circuit would double every year. Later, in 1975, he revised this to a doubling every two years. This has recently been revised to every three years. For example, in April 2011 a research team at the University of Pittsburgh announced the development of a single-electron transistor.[4] And in February 2012 a group at the University of New South Wales developed the first working transistor consisting of a single atom.

So what would our descendants do with all this processing power? Well, if today's technology is anything to go by we will create, among other things, computer-simulated virtual realities. In March 2016 Sony announced the release of a virtual-reality headset known as the Playstation VR Headset. This was to challenge the marketplace of similar headsets such as the Oculus Rift and the HTC Vive Pre. When attached to a PC running programs designed to work with the respective headset, the 'observer' enters a totally believable three-dimensional environment that is indistinguishable from normal reality. Such is the effect of the simulation that software designers have *deliberately* made the virtual-reality environment less real as there have been concerns that photo-realistic environments could be psychologically damaging. In the final analysis these are game-related environments that are, by their very nature, unreal. But recent developments in technology have allowed researchers to create totally accurate renditions of *actual reality*. It is all to do with an application of something known as quantum chromodynamics, a process that describes the workings of one of the four fundamental forces of nature: the strong nuclear force. This is the force that binds quarks and gluons together to form protons and neutrons.

We are now in the position to be able to program computers to simulate how this force develops. Using the world's most powerful supercomputers, scientists have been able to simulate a tiny corner of the cosmos that is a few femtometers across. A femtometer is 10^{-15} across. This may sound like a ridiculously small amount of area (a quadrillionth of a meter or 0.000000000001 mm). But what is intriguing about this development is that this small area of 'reality' has been fully simulated in a computer program. Indeed, it is, to all intents and purposes, indistinguishable from the real thing.[5] We are only restricted by computer power in this regard. Given a big enough computer containing tiny transistors, it is only a matter of time before the region of a few micrometers will be reached. This is large enough to simulate a human cell. If this is the case, then it is not beyond comprehension that in a few hundred years we may have sufficient computing power to simulate a whole universe. With this in mind, could it be possible that a hugely advanced civilization has already simulated a universe—and that we exist within it?

The point at which humanity reaches this ability to simulate its own reality has been called the 'Omega Point' or the 'Singularity.' The former was suggested by French priest-scientist Teilhard de Chardin and the latter by futurologist Ray Kurzweil. In 2003, with the concept of the singularity in mind, Oxford University philosopher Nick Bostrom published a paper in which he suggested that it was almost certain that, if humanity manages to avoid extinction before reaching the Singularity, we are all existing within a simulation.[6] Bostrom's argument has one huge challenge to overcome, and this is known as 'substrate independence.' This is the question of whether it can ever be possible to create sentient, self-consciousness within a simulation. Over recent years there has been a huge debate in this regard, stimulated by a paper by another philosopher, David Chalmers, back in 1995.[7] Chalmers argued that modern science has no idea how self-referential consciousness can be created out of brain processes and within the present paradigm of science no answer can ever be found. However, while Kurzweil's model also founders on the rocks of Chalmer's hard problem, Teilhard de Chardin's does not. And this is because Chardin argued that consciousness is prime and it is consciousness that creates reality.

Teilhard de Chardin and 'the Omega Point'

Pierre Teilhard de Chardin (1881–1955) was a Jesuit priest and also a scientist. As a paleontologist he had noted that evolution of consciousness seemed to run counter to the Second Law of Thermodynamics. Whereas in physical systems entropy (chaos) increases with time, evolution imposes increased order on biological systems as they respond more effectively to environmental conditions.

De Chardin suggested in his book *The Phenomenon of Man* that energy exists in two forms: 'tangential' and 'radial.' The former is the energy that can be measured by scientific instruments; the latter is a form of psychic energy. Tangential energy is governed by the Second Law whereas radial energy is not. In the early 1950s de Chardin began to believe that his tangential energy could be related to 'information' and that information in itself countered the Second Law. In a letter dated 15 May 1953, he wrote:

> What really interests me in cybernetics is the transformation of materialism it suggests to us. A machine is not (or is no longer) an affair primarily of energy set in motion, but information put together and transmitted.[8]

For Teilhard, information processing, when taking place within the electrical circuits of a computer, was similar to how the brain generates thought. Both are seemingly non-physical effects created by a physical process.

From this model Teilhard suggested that just as nonconscious life had spread across the planet to create a huge, interrelated biosphere, consciousness had similarly spread to cover the Earth in a nonphysical form which he termed the *noosphere*. The biosphere is created by tangential energy and therefore ruled by the Second Law of Thermodynamics whereas the noosphere is created by radial energy. This was powerfully prescient in that we now know that information has created its own niche with regards to the World Wide Web and the creation of virtual realities that are rapidly becoming indistinguishable from what we believe to be 'real' reality. We shall return to this later.

In time humanity will evolve and, in doing so, will escape the 'heat death' inevitability inherent in the Second Law of Thermodynamics. We will do this by reaching what Teilhard calls *the Omega Point*. This is where consciousness incorporates itself into a single unity; this unity will be what we know as God.

Teilhard saw this to be linked in some way to information as data and that the Omega Point existed both inside linear time and outside of it:

> Omega itself is...at the end of the whole process, in as much as in it the movement of synthesis culminates. Yet we must be careful to note that under this evolutive facet Omega still only reveals *half of itself*. While being the last term of its series, it is also *outside all series*. Not only does it crown, but it closes...If by its very nature it did not escape from time and space which it gathers together, it would not be Omega.[9]

Earlier in *The Phenomenon of Man* Teilhard likens the evolution of consciousness through time to be like taking a series of sections through a cone, starting at the base and working to the top. Each section is a circle that decreases in size from the one before. Eventually it reaches a point state, a *singularity*.[10] It is at this point that the universe itself becomes 'self-aware.'

Teilhard de Chardin was, as we have already discussed, a Catholic priest. It is therefore fascinating that self-proclaimed atheist materialist-reductionist futurologist Ray Kurzweil takes a very similar position, albeit with a far less spiritual approach and, in doing so, neatly avoids the issues raised by David Chalmers with regards to substrate independence.

Ray Kurzweil and 'the Singularity'

Ray Kurzweil is the inventor of, among other things, the flatbed scanner and the Kurzweil keyboard. As a convinced futurologist he believes that computing power is developing so quickly that within a few decades we will be able to digitize somebody's life and upload it into an onscreen 'avatar.' In his bestselling book *The Singularity Is Near* he suggests that in time human consciousness will become digitized and as such will cease to be embodied within what we generally know as 'reality.'[11] Our awareness will exist in a 'virtual reality' created from information located inside a huge computer. But there is more to this than simply the idea that humanity will somehow relocate into a virtual world. Kurzweil argues that humanity has been specifically evolved in order for the cosmos to bring itself to 'self-awareness.' We are on the road to 'cosmic awareness' which may come about in our human and maybe even post-human phase. In his singularity book Kurzweil refers to the work of complexity theorist James Gardner. Gardner has created a concept he calls the 'Biocosm':

> We and other living creatures throughout the cosmos are part of a vast, still undiscovered transterrestrial community of lives and intelligences spread across billions of galaxies and countless parsecs who are collectively engaged in a portentous mission of truly cosmic importance. Under the Biocosm vision, we share a common fate with that community—to help shape the future of the universe and transform it from a collection of lifeless atoms into a vast, transcendent mind.[12]

In other words, each sentient being in the universe has been deliberately created in order to allow the universe to evolve into, as Gardner terms it, a "vast, transcendent mind." Is this not uncannily similar to Teilhard de Chardin's Omega Point?

Of course the idea that the universe is, in effect, a vast mind is not a new one. The American Transcendentalists such as Ralph Waldo Emerson posited such a reality and proposed that man is simply an embodied version and that the universal mind is simply another way of describing God. Many years later, in 1930, the English mathematical physicist Sir James Jeans wrote the following in his popular science book *The Mysterious Universe*:

> Today there is a wide measure of agreement, which on the

> physical side of science approaches almost to unanimity, that the stream of knowledge is heading towards a non-mechanical reality; the universe begins to look more like a great thought than like a great machine. Mind no longer appears as an accidental intruder into the realm of matter; we are beginning to suspect that we ought rather to hail it as a creator and governor of the realm of matter.[13]

The idea that at its basic level, the material universe is created out of thought (information) is also far from new. In his 1807 book *Phänomenologie des Geistes* (The Phenomenology of Spirit) Georg Wilhelm Friedrich Hegel (1770–1831) introduced a concept he called 'the Geist.' Hegel argued that material things are "petrified intelligence" extended in space whereas consciousness is liquefied intelligence unfolding through time.

But what Kurzweil, Gardner and, to a certain extent, De Chardin are suggesting is far more complex. It is the idea that everything in the universe is information and that the totality of that information field is a single consciousness, a consciousness that has designed the universe in such a way that it will, eventually, become aware of itself.

If you are not confused by this statement, then you have not understood it. It suggests that the Geist, to use Hegel's term, exists outside of time, and uses this timelessness to create itself.

This idea seems very strange and somewhat illogical. However, much of modern quantum physics is similarly illogical and counterintuitive. We therefore need to carefully review the evidence for such a belief and extrapolate from our present understanding of cosmology a theoretical model that has an inner logic and rationality.

The Cosmological Anthropic Principle

In 1974 British astrophysicist Brandon Carter commented upon how it seemed that the universe had engineered a large number of variables to coincide in such a way that self-conscious life was evolved. He called this the *anthropic principle*. Carter has subsequently been quoted that he wishes that he had used another term. 'Anthropic' suggests a uniquely human focus whereas he was arguing that the universe was hardwired for intelligent life, human and non-human. On reflection he considers that the 'biophilic' principle would have been a much more accurate descriptor. Indeed, this closely reflects the less species-specific term of 'Biocosm' of James Gardner.

Carter's principle has evolved into two variations; the Weak Anthropic Principle (WAP) and the Strong Anthropic Principle (SAP). WAP proposes that in order to have evolved intelligent carbon-based life forms the Universe has to be the size and age it is. In addition, it has to have the mixture of elements that is observed because without this structure we would not be around to observe the fact. SAP on the other hand is far more revolutionary. It proposes that the Universe has been, in some way 'hardwired' to develop the way it has done in order for us to evolve. This is not simple chance. The evidence, when reviewed in detail, is simply overpowering. There are many of these coincidences, but as I am focusing specifically on the evolution of consciousness I would like to focus in on two essential contributors to life, carbon and water.

In the first milliseconds of the Big Bang temperatures were so high that only subatomic particles existed. There was far too much electromagnetic energy around for them to join together to form atomic nuclei. There was a hot, dense plasma full of an almost equal amount of matter and antimatter in the guise of protons and antiprotons, neutrons and antineutrons, electrons and positrons, neutrinos and antineutrinos, all existing in a sea of photons (the 'carriers' of electromagnetic energy). And it is here, at this early stage of the universe, that the first evidence of the 'fine-tuning' took place. It is logical to conclude that there would be exactly the same amount of matter as antimatter; after all, one is simply the mirror image of the other. Each proton has an antiproton and each electron has a balancing positron.

But for some very mysterious reason there was a tiny amount more matter than antimatter (how this could be has never been explained). When matter and antimatter comes into contact they annihilate each other in a flash of electromagnetic energy. However, because there was slightly more matter than antimatter, what was left after all this energy release was a universe made almost completely out of matter. If this slight imbalance had not been factored into the initial blueprint, matter and antimatter would have disappeared in a flash of electromagnetic energy, leaving nothing but photons (which do not have their own antiparticles). What remained were the photons, protons, electrons and neutrinos.

Having survived its initial potential destruction, the universe survived to create something called the 'strong nuclear force.' This is one of the four basic forces of nature (the others being gravity, the electromagnetic force, and the weak nuclear force). How this was actually formed from the Big Bang is totally unknown, but it did. It has a very precise strength, and one assumes (if one denies any form of design being involved) that it just spontaneously and quite by chance came into existence with this precise value. It could have had any strength, but it arbitrarily 'chose' the one it did. Which is profoundly fortunate for the evolution of life and consciousness because had it been 2% weaker or 2% stronger, life would never have happened.

Three minutes after the Big Bang, when the temperature had dropped to around 1 billion degrees, the strong nuclear force was able to attract single positively charged protons and neutrally charged neutrons into something known as a deuteron. When two deuterons in turn stuck together they created helium nuclei (that is, two protons and two neutrons). As there were not enough neutrons available to allow all protons to find a home, six out of every seven protons were left flying free. These single protons are, in effect, hydrogen nuclei in their own right. And this is where the strong nuclear force also created hydrogen, lots of it. Each free proton was able to attract a single electron and in doing so become a hydrogen atom. In this way the amount of hydrogen in the universe is three times the amount of helium.

It is here that the precise strength of the strong nuclear force came into its own with regard to the evolution of consciousness. Had the strong nuclear force been 2% weaker than it is, hydrogen would have been effectively the only element in the universe. This is because hydrogen is converted into other gases when the strength of the nuclear force is exactly strong enough to crush the free protons together. The strong force is just powerful enough to overcome the electromagnetic repulsion of similarly charged particles such as protons and, in doing so, crushes them together.

Conversely, if the strong force had been 2% stronger, the hydrogen molecules would have been fused very quickly into another form of hydrogen known as deuterium and, as such, all of the hydrogen in the universe would have disappeared in the first few minutes after the Big Bang. Without hydrogen, stars would not have formed, meaning that galaxies would have similarly never existed.

Gravity is another crucial factor. It has a fine-balanced relationship with the nuclear strong force. If, in the early stages of the Big Bang, gravity had been very slightly weaker, matter would have dispersed too quickly for stars to have formed. However, if gravity had been slightly stronger, then the universe would have reached a maximum size and then recollapsed in a 'Big Crunch' before carbon-based life had had the time to evolve. Indeed carbon, and associated heaver elements, are absolutely crucial to life. It is only the heaver elements that can form complex atomic structures among themselves. The lighter elements cannot do this. But the Big Bang only created the lighter elements which, by the exact amount of gravitational force needed, were pulled together to create nebulae and, in turn, the first stars. It was only when these stars exploded at the end of their lives that these heavier elements were created.

Another of the heavier elements created within the first stars is oxygen and, together with hydrogen, this creates another of the curious 'coincidences' that have led to the creation of life and consciousness from a seemingly inanimate universe. When two hydrogen atoms link with a single oxygen atom something magical is created that has no similarities with its parent atoms; it is called a water molecule. The atoms form in a triangular molecule whose electrical charge is unequally distributed. It is 'polar' in the sense that the oxygen side of the triangle is negative and the opposite side, with the two hydrogen atoms, is positive. This structure allows water to be particularly crucial in the development of life. For example, it creates surface tension which supports the formation of cell membranes. As it is less dense in its solid state than in its liquid state, water freezes from the top down, not the bottom up. This means that the oceans have never frozen solid. If they had done so, all marine life would have been killed—and life started in the oceans. Other important properties of water include its solvency, cohesiveness, adhesiveness, and other thermal properties.

I have given here only a small number of the many, many, facts that suggest that this universe is, in some way, designed for life, consciousness and, ultimately, conscious observers. But are these not simply an error of logic: that we can only exist as observers in a universe that is coincidentally fine-tuned to our evolution? Following on from the theme of water is a popular analogy cited by critics of the Cosmological Anthropic Principle regarding a sentient puddle, used initially by author Douglas Adams in his book *The Salmon of Doubt*:

> [I]magine a puddle waking up one morning and thinking, 'This is an interesting world I find myself in, an interesting hole I find myself in, fits me rather neatly, doesn't it? In fact,

> it fits me staggeringly well, must have been made to have me in it!'[14]

This is a very clever, and very amusing, critique of the seemingly egocentric thinking of advocates of the Cosmological Anthropic Principle. But a moment's reflection will show just how weak this critique is. Our planet is full of millions of holes that can create puddles. Rain falls across vast areas of the globe, therefore puddles occur thousands of times a day in countless locations. Each puddle fits perfectly the hole it finds itself in. But what if there was only one puddle on our planet, and our planet was the only one in the universe? The puddle would, quite rightly, consider the chances of it finding itself in the one and only puddle in the universe to be an amazing coincidence.

Why is this of significance? Well, unless we accept the idea of multiverses, this is the *only* universe that has ever evolved. As such, 'nature' got it exactly right at the first attempt for conscious life to evolve. One fortunate chance occurrence seemingly quite by accident led to another, and then another. At each event probability becomes stretched until random chance ceases to be a viable option. This is not like evolution. In natural selection each mutation is one of many mutations available. Only one survives to carry forward the genetic code. Even one chance mutation failing would ensure that man and consciousness never took place, and, it seems, consciousness is a very important element with regards to the existence of anything. It seems that something had planned for consciousness to evolve.

But why is consciousness so important to a seemingly impersonal and, in places, actively hostile, universe? The answer may be found in a very peculiar, but scientifically proven, effect known as 'wave–particle duality.'

Science has always used observation and experimentation to prove truths about the natural world. Indeed, the concept of the observer is central to much modern science. For example, the word 'relativity,' used so often in relation to Albert Einstein's amazing discoveries, means relative to the position of an 'observer.' In quantum physics something known as the 'observer effect' is a crucial concept and the 'act of measurement' by an 'observer' brings into existence matter in the guise of subatomic particles such as electrons, atoms and even molecules; the building blocks of the material universe. But what exactly is an 'observer'? In order to understand exactly how amazing this discovery is, we need to go back and review the history of the major facilitator of any act of observation, light. Light is crucial for our perceptions of the universe. It is the reflection of light off objects in three-dimensional space that allows us to perceive those objects at a distance. But light itself, however mundane and all-pervasive it may be, is strange.

Imagine dropping a pebble into a pond. The waves form a series of ripples moving out from the point where the pebble entered the water. Now imagine what would happen if a barrier was placed across the pond. As the waves hit the barrier they bounce back in the direction they came. Now we place two holes in the barrier, both much smaller than the wavelength of the ripples. On the other side of the barrier two sets of waves, starting at each hole, spread out as if two new pebbles were dropped in the water at the same place as each hole. As the two new sets of ripples move out they begin to 'interfere' with each other, disrupting the flow of the two sets of semicircles. In some places the two sets of ripples add up to make extra-large ripples; in other places the two sets of ripples cancel out, leaving little, or no, wave motion in the water.

The same exercise can be done with light. Light is shone through a single hole in a barrier. As the light flows out it encounters a second barrier, this time with two holes. The light acts like a wave in that each hole then starts its own wave pattern the other side of the second barrier. Immediately, the two waves start to interfere with each other. A screen is set up after the second barrier. When the light hits this screen it shows a pattern of light and dark stripes. These stripes are called *interference fringes*. They correspond to where the light waves add together (*constructive interference*) and where the waves cancel each other out (*destructive interference*).

The problem was how light 'waves' traveled in a vacuum, for example how they managed to traverse the 93 million miles of empty space between the Sun and the Earth. In order for waves to move in any direction they need something to wave in. A water wave is a disturbance within the water. As we have already discussed, when a pebble is dropped in a pond, waves move outwards from the point the pebble entered the water. But it is the water that is waving. If there was no water the waves would not exist. Sound waves are similar. Sound is a disturbance in the air and it is the air that is the 'medium' by which a sound reaches your ears. But in the vacuum of space there is no medium. As the famous strapline of the movie *Alien* stated, "In space nobody can hear you scream." Light, like sound, should have a problem in space. But it doesn't. Light reaches us from billions and billions of miles away. We see the light of stars and galaxies. So how can this be?

To explain this conundrum, it was postulated that the vacuum of space was filled by a medium known as the *lumniferous ether*. It was this that carried the light waves across space. Sadly, in 1881 two American researchers, Albert A. Michelson and Edward W. Morley, proved that space was indeed a total vacuum and that the 'ether' did not exist.

Twenty-four years later, in 1905, Albert Einstein solved the problem and, in doing so, created the greatest mystery of science, one that remains a mystery even now, 110 years later. His solution was, on paper at least, a simple one; Einstein proposed that light was also made up of individual particles. As far as he was concerned it was the only way that another particular puzzle for early twentieth-century science could be explained. When light was shone on a solid object, it seemed to 'kick out' electrons from the surface. This phenomenon, known as the 'photoelectric effect,' could not be explained. As Einstein said in his 1905 paper, if light is made of particles then each particle hits the surface and knocks out the electrons. This supposition was supported by experimentation and in recognition of this discovery Einstein was awarded the Nobel Prize for Physics. One problem solved, many opened. If light was also made up of discrete packets of energy, how can this be squared with the fact that light is also a wave?

Later experimentation, using variations on the twin-slit experiment discussed above, has shown that light is *both* a wave *and* a particle. It depends on whether it is being observed or not. Yes, that is not a misprint. It seems that when it is looked at, light is a particle, and when it is not being 'observed' it is a wave. In effect this means that consciousness in some way directly affects the basic nature of light.

But things have become stranger still. It has been discovered that particles of 'matter,' that is, the solid bits that make up our supposedly physical world, also have this strange wave–particle duality. In 1987 teams from Hitachi research laboratories and Gakushuin University in Tokyo found that electrons have the same duality. Problematic, yes, but electrons are still incredibly small and nobody has ever seen or photographed one. Atoms and molecules are different. Molecules are, in a very real sense, the building blocks of the physical world. In recent years it has been discovered that molecules, large molecules such as Buckminsterfullerene, which has 60 atoms in its structure, comes into existence when 'observed.' My wording here is quite precise. Quantum physics tells us that the waves that make up physical objects like electrons, atoms and molecules are not like water waves or sound waves. They are waves of probability and are purely mathematical structures; they have no physical reality. What makes them physically real is when their probability wave is 'collapsed' by an act of observation.

Austrian physicist Anton Zeilinger and his team at the University of Vienna have now shown that even larger molecules, such as the interestingly named C284.H190.F320.N4.S12 which consists of 800 atoms, show wave–particle duality. This huge advance in the size of particles showing this 'consciousness-effect' pushes the barrier between weird quantum behaviors ever closer to the nice, safe world of Newtonian physics, closer towards a very interesting barrier…that of viruses.

Of course there is still a great debate as to what we mean by an 'act of observation' in that all acts of observation are, in effect, a measurement. Traditional physicists argue that by simply being 'measured,' that is by being in contact with already collapsed matter, any wave function becomes a solid object. Others argue that an act of measurement only takes place when it is consciously evaluated by a sentient being.

The implications of this 'measurement problem' are profound. If true, then we all create the reality around us by observing it. Suddenly consciousness is central to the creation of the physical world rather than something peripheral. Brandon Carter's Cosmological Anthropic Principle suddenly makes sense. The universe needed to evolve self-referential consciousness in order to bring itself into existence.

If this is correct, then how is it that the universe has been in existence for at least 13.4 billion years? How could consciousness, which evolved around a million years ago, collapse the wave function of matter billions of years ago? Physicist John Wheeler believed he had the answer. It is all to do with something called the Delayed Choice Experiment.

Wheeler was a hugely respected Princeton University cosmologist. He was fascinated by the implications of the Cosmological Anthropic Principle and, in the late 1970s, suggested an even more intriguing version, something he called the Participatory

Anthropic Principle (PAP).

By this he meant that consciousness is somehow responsible not only for the observed universe that we perceive now but also the universe as it was billions of years ago. In other words, the 'act of observation' of a sentient intelligence is responsible for bringing into existence a universe that existed eons before that intelligence existed. This really profoundly questions our concept of time as a linear process and, even more importantly, suggests that actions taking place now can have a direct effect on the past. Being the outstanding theoretician he was, Wheeler suggested an experiment by which the already discussed twin-slit phenomenon could be applied to prove his PAP hypothesis.

He first presented this 'thought experiment' in 1978. Five years later, in 1983, Wheeler turned this into a truly stellar, or more literally, quasar, version of the twin-slit experiment. He suggested that the tool to use would be a known cosmological phenomenon known as gravitational lensing.[15]

In 1959 Cyril Hazard of the Parkes Radio Telescope in Australia discovered a radio source that was emitting huge amounts of energy. When optical telescopes finally viewed the source they discovered not a galaxy but a star-like object. This was named as 3C 273. Later calculations showed that this object was over 4 trillion times brighter than the Sun. By the early 1960s hundreds of these objects had been discovered. They were originally described as 'quasi-stellar radio sources' which, in 1964 at the suggestion of Chinese astrophysicist Hong-Yee Chui, was shortened to 'quasar.' When looked at with light telescopes, it was discovered that some of these objects were in groups of two or four light sources.

In 1979 an astounding discovery was made. These seemingly multiple quasars were actually a single quasar whose light had been bent in such a way that it had been split, with this split being in such a way as to create an illusion of multiplicity. This observation proved a relativity-related phenomenon that had first been suggested by Albert Einstein in April 1912. In an obscure academic paper Einstein had suggested that light beams would be bent by any very large gravitational source such as a galaxy. According to relativity theory, the space around a galaxy will be literally warped by the galaxy's gravitational field, and any light passing by would have to follow a deflected course as it negotiates its way through the depression in space-time. In practice this means that any source of light that is located in a direct line from Earth with a galaxy between Earth and the source would have its light bent round the galaxy. This was exactly the effect being observed by the astronomers. Gravitational lensing was real. And it was this phenomenon that Wheeler believed could be used to prove that the act of observation creates everything, including events in the distant past.

Wheeler's thought experiment has a group of Earth-based astronomers decide to observe the quasars. In this case a telescope plays the role of the photon detector in the two-slit experiment. If the astronomers point a telescope in the direction of one of the two intervening galaxies, they will see photons from the quasar that were deflected by that galaxy; they would also get the same result by looking at the other galaxy. By carefully arranging mirrors, the astronomers could make photons arriving from the routes around both galaxies strike a piece of photographic film. Alternating light and dark bands would appear on the film, identical to the pattern found when photons passed through the two slits.

Here's the odd part. The quasar could be very distant from Earth, with light so faint that its photons hit the piece of film only one at a time. But the results of the experiment wouldn't change. The striped pattern would still show up, meaning that a lone photon not observed by the telescope traveled both paths toward Earth, even if those paths were separated by many light-years. And that's not all. By the time the astronomers decide which measurement to make—whether to pin down the photon to one definite route or to have it follow both paths simultaneously—the photon could have already journeyed for billions of years, long before life appeared on Earth. The measurements made now, says Wheeler, determine the photon's past. In one case the astronomers create a past in which a photon took both possible routes from the quasar to Earth. Alternatively, they retroactively force the photon onto one straight trail toward their detector, even though the photon began its jaunt long before any detectors existed.

Wheeler's idea that time was not relevant to the way in which an act of observation collapses a wave function was experimentally proven by physicists at the École Normale Supérieure de Cachan in 2007.[16] This showed that photons 'decide' to be a wave or a particle in response to a later decision made by the experimenters. This may also suggest that the underlying intent of the experimenters is more important in this respect than their actual observations. The French team fired photons at something known as a 'Beam Splitter.' This is a 'half-silvered mirror.' In effect this mirror splits the photon beam in two, sending one group of photons in one direction and the rest in another. The first group of photons were reflected in the direction of a second beam splitter located 50 meters away. The second beam splitter was attached to a computer which in a totally random fashion switched it off or on. If it was turned on, it recombined the split waves and sent them to a detector. The resulting interference pattern was what would be expected if the particles were acting as waves.

The experiment also had a second detector. However, when the second beam splitter was switched off, both detectors showed a pattern known to be created by particles. When counted, it was shown that an equal number of particles were hitting each detector. This showed that, as each individual particle could not have been split, the light taking *both* paths was in particle form from the start of the experiment. This means that the beam had decided whether to behave as a particle or a wave for its full journey not at the start but when the 'observer' (system) decided later.

Here is experimental proof that the 'observer effect' is not time-dependent. The act of observation creating our reality can be applied to the deep past, a past that did not contain sentient beings. This can be used to suggest that the universe at its inception needed to evolve consciousness to bring itself into existence. So if the universe is integrally linked to a conscious observer then what is the 'observed universe' actually created from? Is it really out there in three-dimensional space or is it simply another aspect of consciousness?

Conclusion

This book is about Pandeism as is this chapter. This may not be immediately obvious. We have reviewed together the evidence that perceptual reality may be a form of simulation and that we are embedded within that simulation. We have also discussed how the creators of that simulation may be our distant descendants existing within some form of post-human existence. To this we have added evidence that each one of us creates, by the act of observation, a unique perceptual environment. In these environments we interface with other consciousnesses that also seem to share our collective phenomenological world. Although not discussed because of lack of space, I could have expanded into areas such as the out-of-body experience, the near-death experience, lucid dreaming, and altered states of consciousness brought about through the use of chemicals such as Dimethyltriptamine (DMT) and other related entheogens, and proposed that all these experiences suggest that this reality is one of many nested sensual environments, each one of which is contained within a wider omniverse. To this I could have added how déjà vu experiences, precognitions and time-slips all seem to suggest that time itself is an illusion and that, in some profound way, the present moment is all there is. In turn, such subjective experiences show us that space is also an illusion in that everything is similarly nested within itself.

As David Bohm argued, everything is enfolded within itself like a huge hologram. This hologram is something that contains everything within a timeless, spaceless singularity, something that Teilhard de Chardin called the Omega Point. And this is where Pandeism comes into the model. We are, in a very real sense, a singular consciousness experiencing itself subjectively, and all the scientific evidence we have discussed in this chapter points in this direction.

I will leave you with the words of wisdom of much-missed cult American comedian Bill Hicks:

> Today a young man on acid realized that all matter is merely energy condensed to a slow vibration, that we are all one consciousness experiencing itself subjectively, there is no such thing as death, life is only a dream, and we are the imagination of ourselves. Here's Tom with the Weather.[17]

Sums it up really…

Notes

1 Bohm, D., *Wholeness and the Implicate Order*, Routledge & Kegan Paul, London (1980), p. 48.

2 Bohm, *Wholeness and the Implicate Order*, p. 172.

3 Bohm, D., and Peat D., *Science, Order, and Creativity*, Bantam, New York (1987), pp. 185–6.

4 Cheng, G., Siles, P. F., Bi, F., Cen, C., Bogorin, D. F., Bark, C. W., Folkman C. M., Park, J. W., Eom, C. B., Medeiros-Ribeiro, G., Levy, J., "Sketched Oxide Single-Electron Transistor," *Nature Nanotechnology* (2011); DOI: 10.1038/ nnano.2011.56.

5 Beane, S. R., Davoudi, Z., Savage, M. J., *Constraints on the Universe as a Numerical Simulation* (2012), arXiv:1210.1847v2.

6 Bostrom, N., "Are You Living in a Computer Simulation?", *The Philosophical Quarterly*, vol. 53, no. 211 (2003), pp. 243–55.
7 Chalmers, D., "Facing up to the Problem of Consciousness," *Journal of Consciousness Studies*, vol. 2, no. 3 (1995), pp. 200–19.
8 Cuenot, C., *Teilhard de Chardin*, Helicon, Baltimore (1965), p. 352.
9 Teilhard de Chardin, P., *The Phenomenon of Man*, Harper & Row, New York (1975), pp. 270–1.
10 Teilhard de Chardin, P., *The Phenomenon of Man*, Harper & Row, New York (1975), pp. 168–9.
11 Kurzweil, R. , *The Singularity Is Near*, Gerald Duckworth & Co. (2006), Kindle Locations 452–6.
12 Gardner, J. N., *The Intelligent Universe*, Career Press, Franklin Lakes, NJ (2007), p. 170.
13 Jeans, J., *The Mysterious Universe*, Kessinger Publishing, Whitefish, MT (2010), p. 130.
14 Adams, D., *The Salmon of Doubt: Hitchhiking the Galaxy One Last Time*, Harmony Books, New York (2002), p. 131.
15 See Wheeler's "delayed choice," in *Quantum Theory and Measurement*, ed. J. A. Wheeler and W. H. Zurek, Princeton University Press (1983).
16 Jacques, V., Roch, J.-F., et al., "Experimental Realization of Wheeler's Delayed-Choice Gedanken Experiment," *Science*, vol. 315, no. 5814 (16 February 2007), pp. 966–8.
17 Hicks, Bill, *Sane Man* (1989), DVD.

Section III: Criticism and Analysis from Other Views

Throughout its history, Pandeism has drawn both a critical and comparative eye from adherents to other theological models. The conventional practice in organizing comparative religious literature seems to be to order pieces so that conventional Western-world views are given prominence. Here, we upend this tendency by putting ahead of these the analysis from what is likely the the oldest religion on earth, Hinduism. Other views presented encompass some nontraditional approaches to mainstream belief systems as well.

In "Hindu Dharma—Living on the Edge of Infinity," Sushma Sahajpal illuminates the viewpoint of Hinduism, often misunderstood or misrepresented in Western frames of thought, and examines how its theological propositions tend to compare to those of the pandeistic model.

"Beyond Creator and Universe: From Pandeism to Ismaili Muslim Neoplatonism," by Ismaili Gnosis, makes a case for a particular interpretation of Islam over Pandeism.

In "Omnientheism: God According to Biblical Universalist Unitarianism," Orlando Alcántara Fernández makes a spirited plea for the soulfulness of theistic thought against the harsher light shone by Deism, Pandeism, and Panendeism.

William Walker Atkinson, with his chapter, "Axioms of Reality—Concluded," sets his early twentieth-century 'New Thought' ideas against Pandeism, arguing against both the evidence for it (as compared to his own view) and potential effects of its adoption.

And lastly—but hardly least—we close with the view from what is modernly the strongest challenge to theistic faith, with "An Atheist Critique of Pandeism." Here, Dan Dana PhD contends that the same skepticism which applies to Theism leads to the same absence of evidence when applied to Pandeism.

The Sequence

Amy Perry

•

All
I
Take in
This life is
What I need to get
On through to the next adventure.
Pain and death are my necessary contributions.
See, I am God and God is me.
We celebrate Life.
Our mission,
To love.
All
One.

Hindu Dharma—Living on the Edge of Infinity

Sushma Sahajpal

Sushma is the founder of Connectar Creative Education, an Oxford mathematics graduate, and a computer software designer. Her current work is dedicated to the whole-being flourishing of children through creative education. She designs creative philosophy-based enrichment resources, and delivers talks and workshops exploring religious belonging, belief and diversity across school events, teachers' conferences and a range of interfaith forums. She is the Hinduism advisor in three English counties and serves as an elected member of the National Executive for Religious Education Advisory Councils. She has also written about Hinduism for RE Today *and works as an expert consultant for the nationally acclaimed teachers' website RE:Online. Some of the content of this article is taken from shorter pieces that Sushma has previously written. It has, however, been considerably extended and rearranged by the author to suit the present purpose.*

Introduction

Hinduism is a European observer's collective term for a range of spiritual, philosophical and cultural traditions which have evolved from prehistoric times in the Indian subcontinent. It is fundamentally different in many key features from the Abrahamic traditions, familiar to many Europeans and Americans. In my experience, very little is understood about Hinduism by many non-Hindus as the philosophies and disciplines have traditionally been privately experienced and lived, rather than publicly preached or explained by believers. While this is changing, it means there is a long history of misinformation and distorted perception to counteract. This has led to some discrimination and disrespect around the world. There has been some reaction in modern times from Hindus beginning to realize they need to speak about their faith and sensibilities if these are to be understood and respected alongside the younger religions.

It is crucial therefore for anyone with a genuine interest in understanding Hinduism to be able to suspend their own frame of reference to understand this one. There is otherwise a potential barrier to comprehension that I am naming at the outset. The analogy I suggest to new students which may be useful to the reader is to assume the mindset of a horse expert encountering an elephant. Do not assume it is merely a misshapen or inferior type of horse, but see the functionality, beauty and rationale of unfamiliar tusks and trunk for what they are, features on a genetically distinct creature, developed in a fundamentally different climate and environment.

By the same respectful engagement protocol, I am keen to explore and identify what features of Pandeism may appear familiar and unfamiliar to a Hindu perspective.

Being Different, and Some Key Terms

Hinduism is ancient, heterogeneous and inherently pluralistic so it's hard not to oversimplify or misrepresent its beliefs and practices. A further consequence of its genuine pluralism is its built-in assumption that an individual's spiritual signature (*Atman*) and loyalty to the community it comes from is sacred. This unique 'live and let live' profile means Hindus have not traditionally needed to develop a vocabulary for representing or advocating for their faith experience to others, as it is experienced introspectively but expressed communally, through diverse, evolving traditions.

Since it is both prehistorically *indigenous* and inherently *inclusive*, we can observe:

- There is no founder, specific Book, or set of rules or commandments.
- Rather than being prescribed, it has *evolved* as a collection of principles and practices.
- It is *experienced* as an unfolding 'way of being,' available for all, rather than *declared* as a doctrine of belief for the chosen few.
- This way of being will be explored in later sections, but Hindus see it as deliberately cultivating *universal well-wishing* as the hallmark of inherent and *interconnected divinity*. This is in direct contrast to a spiritual perspective that might view humanity as inherently sinful or separate from a divine source.

Key Concepts

We will need some Sanskrit terminology for key concepts for which there is, understandably, no equivalent English term. The easiest way to approach these might be to realize that for Hindus, these ideas are not 'conceptual' or even 'beliefs'; rather they are deeply encoded in the culture and way of being, doing and speaking about things. We can see how they may be exemplified in life by way of introduction.

- ***Dharma*:** In simplistic terms everything is believed to have a Dharma, an inherent *vital* nature or intrinsic way of being as part of an ecologically interconnected divine blueprint. Thus it is fire's Dharma to burn, it is a healer's Dharma to heal, an acorn's Dharma to become an oak tree. In living/being terms, it philosophically underpins all the other terms in Hindu philosophy.
- ***Samsara*:** Hindus use this word to mean the 'World' of worldliness. The 'stage' on which the 'Play' of life is experienced. Hindus are encouraged to develop a witness-consciousness. To have a sense that while there is a part of

them that is trapped in living in worldliness, there is also another part that is 'free,' divine and observing. Any activity that calms the trapped part such as yoga, meditation, chanting, helps bring clarity to this way of experiencing things beyond our emotions and mundane preoccupations.

- ***Karma***: This word is probably best understood as 'consequences.' A deep sense that *everything* you do, say and even *think* is 'karmic' and will have an impact and consequence both for you and others. This puts the burden of choice squarely on each of us to be aware of whether our behavior is adding to universal wellbeing or its opposite. It says we are all connected but need to do our share. Cultural practices such as family duties, vegetarianism, nonviolence, Nature-reverence all encode living with this sense of wider responsibility.
- ***Seva***: In cultural terms, this is a hugely honored and privileged state of being. It speaks of keeping gentleness in your heart, respect for elders, protection for children, animals and the vulnerable, and honoring the life-giving abundance of natural resources. Essentially it expresses a desire to serve (either people or land) as a means of serving the divine.

Pluralism

It is encoded within Hindu philosophy that we are profoundly connected but rightly different from each other, with custodianship of our own unique inherent blueprint (Dharma), one that is important and sacred regardless of whichever faith we belong to. Everything we think, say and do (Karma) impacts not only on each other and the world around us, but on how our own blueprint will turn out. Hindu spirituality, thus underpinned by a single core consciousness of universal spirit (Brahman), plays out as an ease with the idea of many external ways of behaving and believing, both in the world and crucially in the way we relate to divinity.

What's in a Name?—Sanatan Dharma

The native term for this way of being is *Sanatan Dharma.* meaning 'The Eternal or Ever-flowing Way.' This is every *Atman's* journey to connect with and 'know' Absolute Truth or Ultimate Reality, *Brahman*, the Universal Spirit, Knowingness/Consciousness. This 'knowing' is a way of *being* and quite different from 'believing' as accepting either rational argument or indeed embracing 'blind faith.'

'Ever-flowing' offers another core principle to a pluralist discourse on knowledge; that is, Dharma or righteousness cannot be 'locked down' to a time-specific interpretation but must actually be *a dynamic and unfolding order* in the world. So a key point is that unlike many faith traditions, the practices are expected—indeed *intended*—to continue to evolve with time for human society to thrive and remain connected to its inherently divine nature. If this were deemed to be true, then our challenge in every faith and nonfaith community would be to find the courage and wisdom to adapt our rules, practices and paradigms to serve the highest good as it emerges in every age. Hindus would say that problems and their solutions tend to show up in corresponding pairs.

Scripture but Not As We Know It—Holy Books and the Inquiry Model

Hinduism has many ancient texts and scriptures which are revered for different reasons. The oldest of these are the collections known as the Vedas. These are probably the most sacred to most Hindus as they are considered to hold the intuitively 'seen' wisdom (known as Shruti) of ancient Indian philosophers and visionaries on many aspects of life, including time, space, science, health and mathematics. Other books have less philosophical content but more practical guidance, explanation and description (the Smriti collections). Some of these are so old and have such regional variation that although they are believed to have an actual historical basis, we cannot now know how much is historical and how much mythological—either way Hindus remember and retell them as rich, sacred ancestral heritage, and adopt and adapt them as modern ethical guidance. It is important to note this distinctive characteristic. In Hinduism, no book is given absolute authority as the holder of 'truth claims' to be believed and obeyed. Holy Books are considered precious signposts and guidelines from those who have gone before, to be studied, tested and evolved through personal and collective practice of Dharmic principles.

Hindu scholars use the terms *shruti* and *smriti* to distinguish between revealed sacred texts (the Veda) and remembered sacred texts (of epics deemed to be based on historical events such as the Mahabharata). Crucially, shruti has the higher status as being considered closer to Spiritual Truth. This differs from a morality which recommends we distrust our own experience to comply with externally supplied models.

So, not a 'belief system', but development of the human toolkit with an evolving set of 'user manuals' extended over centuries by 'experimenters' known as sages and 'rishis' in the field, sharing direct personal revelation (*shruti* meaning 'that which is heard') collected in the Vedas and Upanishads. More can be revealed *today*; hence it is Sanatan, ever-flowing, not 'contained' as a set of tenets or belief in the divinity or message of a named individual. The Bhagavad Gita, one of the most read Hindu sacred texts written as a dialogue in poetic form, is an excellent resource. It contains many engaging elements for debate and discussion such as war, politics, moral dilemma, and duty. It also clarifies terms such as Dharma, Karma and Yoga and has a contemporary relevance as the book that both Mahatma Gandhi and Nelson Mandela credited with guiding them to achieve historical change through resolutely nonviolent, spiritually underpinned, principles.

The other form of scripture is smriti—'that which is remembered.' This is knowledge codified in engaging stories and characters that more literally exemplify and illuminate Hindu Dharmic principles. Thus there is a centuries-old sense of custodianship of tested/directly experienced wisdom and answers to the big questions in these texts, yet people do not see the big questions as separate from the pursuit of daily life; i.e. we are not a body with a soul but a soul currently riding in a particular body, here specifically to contribute its *unique* answers to the big questions, often unique to each member within the same family.

Science and Spirituality

We are our own real-time experiment, as well as both raw material and testing equipment!

Hindu Dharma offers a highly inquisitive, exploratory approach to life. It recommends that we allow others their own faith but accept nothing until we have personally experienced it as Truth (shruti) or been told it (smriti) by someone we have tested and believe in (as a teacher). In this approach, Dharma cannot be pinned down by rules (smriti) but must evolve and adapt as the truth is revealed again and again as life unfolds (shruti). As shruti is said to override smriti, what you experience overrides what you are told. Thus the faith in Hinduism is not based on 'truth claims' but on claiming your personal right to discover the Truth for yourself and then live by it—this principle is known as *Svadharma*.

Hindu faith and scientific 'facts' are entirely compatible—the fundamental lynchpin of Hindu belief and practice being Dharma, the natural, self-regulating, self-organizing Order of all that is. It is not to be confined or defined to any particular perspective, only observed, experienced and distinctively in Hinduism, revered. Reverence is a key component for interdependent flourishing. It compels us to choose harmony with, rather than mastery over, nature. Questions of which faith or philosophy is right don't quite work here as neither Hindu philosophy nor scripture tells you the 'right' way to interpret the world. It says as a soul you are having this specific, unique life-experience in which you are here to interpret the world for yourself and thus develop wisdom, to evolve through trial and error a closer and closer realization of actual reality and just as importantly to make your unique contribution to those you are in relationship with (Karma). Wanting the 'right' truth model, name for God, etc., is largely irrelevant to a well-lived, wisdom-evolving Hindu life. Hence the respect for other faiths, multiplicity of paths, and ways of being a 'Hindu.'

It is equally important to note that research scientists do not speak of scientific facts as 'absolute' either. They are aware that scientific knowledge is our 'best fit' based on evidence and reason and must be open to be scrutinized, extended or even disproved (e.g. how many planets in our solar system). So hopefully you can see that Hindu understanding of Truth is compatible with this approach. That is, we are each (Hindus would say: in every faith and without faith) practicing and refining our 'best fit' view and values based on experience and reason.

At the heart of cutting-edge physics sits the quantum, the key to understanding the fabric of reality. Interestingly, it insists that the underpinning to the world of matter is essentially nonmaterial. Vivekananda, credited as the first Hindu monk to bring Hindu ideas to the West, spoke in 1895 of creation being explained in terms of two things: *Akash*—or a field of existence (what we might call spirit), and *Prana*, a shudder in existence. Quantum physics states that the world we see and experience as the empirical universe is not an objective reality but a multitude of wiggles in existence! This is a major paradigm shift for science that appears to place it on a path where modern physical science and ancient documented Hindu spirituality will converge. Through this lens, Pandeism embracing science as the way to reveal reality would be acceptable, as long as it does not explicitly *exclude* the validity of intuitive and metaphysical experiences. Hindu philosophy states that these are both valid approaches which can be used depending on the faculty, with each, of the individual.

Creation and Infinity

Ancient Hindu philosophers, going into deep yoga meditation in order to expand their ability to imagine, visualize and make sense of things, recorded their visions about creation and many other things in the Vedas.

One such Sanskrit *Shloka* (verse) which is a personal favorite for its mathematical richness is:

Purnamadah, purnamidam, purnatpurnamudachyate,
purnasya purnam adaya, purnam evavasisyate

That source is complete. This manifestation is complete.
This comes from that. Yet that remains complete.

An infinite number of infinities can be taken out of infinity, and yet an infinity remains. In other words, the explanation for an infinite consciousness to be able to manifest an infinite material world is fundamentally mathematical!

Thus, according to the Vedas, the world we are living in is not the first, last or only one. Hindus believe an infinite, self-organizing, self-knowing intelligence (Brahman) is able to create through natural scientific laws whatever is needed. Creation is not a one-off event but just a means of converting energy into physical material and in time back into balanced energy, over and over again forever. This is a wider but not contradictory perspective to Pandeism in as much as these could be considered multiple instances of a form of Pandeism.

To help everyday people understand such a vast philosophy, the Vedas contain a number of lines of inquiry and 'creation stories' with names and symbolic images assigned for the *principles* involved, explaining different aspects of the forces (not people) at play. Thus Hindus have many creation stories and versions. Interestingly, they tend to be very relaxed about different versions, as it is the principles that matter to them more than the particular details of how different philosophers have visualized them. The key principle being that matter is manifested out of spirit, and is itself simply a lower-density form of energy.

The Rig Veda questions the origin of the cosmos thus:

> Neither being (*sat*) nor non-being was as yet. What was concealed? And where? And in whose protection? Who really knows? Who can declare it? Whence was it born, and whence came this creation? The devas (demigods) were born later than this world's creation, so who knows from where it came into existence? None can know from where creation has arisen, and whether he has or has not produced it. He who surveys it in the highest heavens, *he alone knows—or perhaps does not know.*

Thus there is an 'I am' presence, Brahman, which may or may not know of its beginning. This has some echoes with the Pandeistic notion that there is a divine consciousness which by choice may have relinquished omnipotence after creation.

However, the concept of 'beginning' is itself contradictory as it is a time-linked notion and time is attached to each creation within the 'I am' likened to an infinite number of atoms. How the two theories could interact is, if this were true, the Divine-consciousness in a multiverse model would need to vary from universe to universe. In the Hindu model, before manifestation, or a Big Bang type event, consciousness first demerges itself into yin/yang masculine/feminine. The feminine (*Shakti*) manifests as matter and chooses not to be omnipotent but rather hyperconscious to experience everything the way a mother feels her children's pain and joy, in the living moment. This would seem to resonate with the Pandeist idea of the physical world being manifested divinity that has chosen to relinquish interventionist power to experience. However, Hindu philosophy does not have only Shakti but rather incorporates an infinite spectrum of divine energy (the subtle interplay of these is what is actually depicted and explained in many of the Puranic stories), at every frequency from matter through to immaterial, in the way light has a visible and invisible spectrum.

In looking at specific Hindu stories you may come across the name Brahma, the specific Hindu name for the creative life-principle or Deity for people who want to relate by name. This is often translated as Creator 'God' in English, but Brahma 'Dev,' the Indian word, is more accurate and less misleading. *Note that 'Creator' is just one form of divine agency in Hinduism.*

The principle behind the creation stories has some similarity to the modern scientific theory of 'the Big Bang'—the idea of time, space and universal cause/effect laws all starting in an instant. Hindu stories depict this event as a spontaneous moment captured in story form as 'Brahma' waking up. A key difference is that Hindus would say that this wasn't *the* Big Bang, just 'our' Big Bang, and expect there to be many before and after. Thus 'creation' is considered an infinite, regular phenomenon. Hindus would think of each world's creation and ending, happening in a cycle as regular as breathing in and out, except on an *enormous* scale!

Brahman, Timescales and Hindu Cosmology

Carl Sagan, in his 1985 book *Cosmos*, states:

> The Hindu dharma is the only one of the world's great faiths dedicated to the idea that the Cosmos itself undergoes an immense, indeed an infinite, number of deaths and rebirths. It is the only dharma in which time scales correspond to those of modern scientific cosmology. Its cycles run from our ordinary day and night to a day and night of Brahma, 8.64 billion years long, longer than the age of the Earth or the Sun and about half the time since the Big Bang.

Vedic and Puranic texts describe units of time from Paramanu (about 17 microseconds) to Maha-Manvantara (311.04 trillion years), fourteen of which form a *Kalpa,* the largest unit used. According to these texts, the creation and destruction of the universe is a cyclic process, which repeats itself forever. Each cycle starts with the birth and expansion (lifetime) of the universe equaling 311.04 trillion years, followed by its complete annihilation (which also prevails for the same duration). Thus time is not a function of absolute reality but a relative concept. The number of universes is also described in the texts as uncountable, immeasurable, or incalculable according to the Puranic literature:

> The layers or elements covering the universes are each ten times thicker than the one before, and all the universes clustered together appear like atoms in a huge combination. (Bhagavata Purana 3.11.41)

Yoga Vashishtha, an ancient Hindu text, includes conversations between various Gods and Kakbhushundi, a creature that stands outside of normal time and sees all. It recounts the cyclical nature of time, where Kakbhushundi has seen Ramayan eleven times *with different outcomes* and seen Mahabharat sixteen times *with different results.* Yet, after seeing Daksha Yagya (a well-known early-creation story) twice, he either did not care to see it again or saw no point in seeing any more, as it ended *the same way each time*. Further conversations talk about the atoms or *anu* at quantum level, and inside each quantum level are different universes.

A sorrowful queen is shown that her husband is still alive in one of the quantum or atomic universes and ruling wisely and is given the option to join him there. The idea of Heisenberg's Principle is enunciated when a rishi visits and illustrates a decision tree by showing how several parallel universes, with all possible results of a decision, could occur and uses that illustration to explain why he took the decision he did in this universe.

From a modern Western perspective, it is extraordinary to think that the ancient Indians had conceived of an infinite number of parallel universes playing out all outcomes. This offers an elegant solution to the apparent contradiction in a mono-universe model, of both an omnipotent divine consciousness and individual free will. The Hindu model also offers a consistent expansion to the Pandeist idea that divine consciousness does not 'intervene' in how the universe unfolds. In concluding this section, I want to add one more potent idea, and that is of the largest unit of time, the *Kalpa*. In Sanskrit, this word literally means 'thought,' opening up the intriguing timescale that 4,200 trillion years constitute a 'single thought' that the divine super-mind is having!

God, Gods and Goddesses

Hindu philosophy suggests that Divinity is not a countable thing as one, three or thirty-three 'Gods' but rather it includes *everything*, seen and unseen, physical and nonphysical. All creation is seen as an *evolving expression of one Divine Awareness*. The word 'Brahman' is used for this but it has no form, image, containment of any kind. The need to classify, comprehend and relate through form, name and numbers is considered a human need based on human experience rather than God's need to be called by a specific name, gender or ritual. Each of the images of Hindu Devas or Deities (the word 'Deity' is perhaps less confusing than 'God') comes with deeply codified symbols designed to help a meditator/believer harness different energies within themselves with different personal challenges. Thus the various Devas within Hindu traditions, and divinity in other faiths, are simply seen as expressions of how different people over time have come to relate to Spirit, based on their cultural history and personal experience and needs.

This philosophy is often misrepresented as polytheism, or pantheism, but in fact 'pluralism' is a better English word since this approach also includes spiritual humanism for those who choose to relate to the 'Sacred/Divine' only in fellow humans through a life of service (*Sewa*) and atheism for those who see the spiritual path as strictly an internal one with no Deities at all in their faith practice.

Regarding what Hindu Gods (or Deities as we call them so as not to confuse them with the 'One God' of Christians or Jews) look like, we do have some traditional images which people take special training and meditation to be able to depict accurately. The Deities allow us to maintain an attitude of wonder, grace and gratitude towards nature and spirit, as well as elevate our own spiritual energy to embody a more divinely charged life.

I do not have a 'favorite Deity' as such. Personally I experience divinity in many forms, places and experiences and the intensity and feeling may vary depending on my inner state of being at the time. It is important to appreciate that Hinduism is not just a spiritual philosophy but a vibrant, whole-being, mind-body-spirit-community-nature expression of life in all its cycles.

Creation is not the whole story in Hinduism; there is a complete cycle to understand.

The *Trimurti* symbolizes the energy in play at key points in the creation cycle. *Brahma initiates* manifestation into matter—the Creator Archetype. *Shiva* destroys as a positive signal of *regener-*

ation at the end of a cycle, and *Vishnu* is the *preservation* energy that maintains *Dharma* or Divine Design/Flow throughout a cycle. Hence Vishnu and his physical manifestations or *Avatars* are those most engaged with human history and endeavour! When humanity is drifting away from 'Dharma' it is *Vishnu*'s Energy in the form of Rama, Krishna, Buddha in India, and other notable divine souls in other parts of the world, which manifests as a 'corrective factor' wherever and whenever needed for individuals and often whole societies and countries to be transformed. However, as with Pandeism, this is not interventionist, but inherent to the laws of Dharma mid-cycle. As Krishna states in the Gita: "*Yadha Yadha hi Dharmasya...*" (Whenever there is a decline in Dharma and increase of Adharma, then do I manifest Myself).

This would be consistent with Pandeism as a Law of Order, in the way that "Nature abhors a vacuum"; hence Nature abhors a certain level of Adharma, and will react, whether it is with disease, destruction, floods, etc., or the bringing forth of remarkable human beings.

Man and God

It is important to think about the nature of Man as well as God. A key feature of Hinduism is that there is at least as much emphasis placed on classifying and understanding the depths and subtleties of what it is to be human as there is on the divine, to better comprehend the interplay between the two.

It is enshrined in Hindu culture that we are simply manifestations of the universal spirit on our journey over as many lifetimes as it takes to merge back into blissful universal knowing of God. Thus knowledge/wisdom are carefully encoded into all aspects of Hindu life.

1. **In behaviour:** Reverence for the elderly, hospitality to guests, respect for all lifeforms;

2. **Artifacts:** Rich visual iconography, reminding Hindus of key concept messages;
3. **Stories:** Often linked to **festivals** (e.g. Ramayana), role models/moral messages, mindful learning through speech, language and drama enactment;
4. **Games:** For example, Snakes & Ladders, Karma & Dharma game, chess—battle strategies exemplify mindful learning through play, rules and consequences.

Worship, Puja and Mandir

In Hinduism there are many different ways to worship God for those who believe. Most Hindus don't believe in a God that is 'separate' located elsewhere, but rather that everything, every blade of grass, every drop of water, everything that we can experience and even what we can't are all 'God'—the intelligence of the unfolding world in accordance with the laws we study in science. Worship, or *Puja* as it's called, is a way for any individual to become quiet and listen to that wisdom which resides in every human being. So Hindus are very relaxed about which form of God 'helps' you connect with this wisdom. It might be a Hindu 'God' or 'Goddess,' or it might be Jesus or Mary or Buddha.

The correct Hindi/Sanskrit word for a Hindu temple is *mandir*, meaning 'still mind.' The primary purpose of the mandir is to allow each individual to leave the distractions of the outer world, and find inner stillness as its name suggests. In this peaceful state visitors may tune in to a feeling of connection with divinity *however their own nature and level of spiritual development allows.* Thus this is not necessarily seeking external intervention, but equally inner clarity.

It would be impossible to say that there is one way to pray, given the diversity of ways of practicing Hindu Dharma. Dharma is the Hindu term for the principle inherent in all things. Dharma defines each thing's blueprint for thriving and is a more desirable term than 'religion' to use for Hindu living. Regarding daily prayer, many Hindus like to worship/meditate/reflect at home by lighting a sacred flame in their home-mandirs early in the morning and again at dusk in thanksgiving for the day.

The same principle of facilitating personal connection applies to selection of Deity for prayer or focus. While some mandirs may be named and dedicated to a primary Deity this is often because it may have been the specific inspiration for building a particular mandir rather than indicating a sect or exclusivism in worship. Usually 'Murtis' (images) of other Deities are also accorded sacred space in every mandir. There is no requirement for direct prayer to any particular Deity, but to become quiet enough for direct connection to unfold in whichever way most helps the individual. Hindus may focus on as many or as few Deities on any given visit as suit their own needs. It is conventional to perform a salutation (*Namaskar*) on arriving at the mandir, but prayer itself is entirely personal.

Most Hindus believe that all creation is divine in nature, so a range of ways of connecting in deep appreciation of sacred relationship with it are all types of 'worship' depending on lifestyle and disposition. One such is through focusing deep awareness. The Hindu word for this is *Dhyana* (the better-known Japanese term, Zen, is derived from this concept).

Hinduism offers other forms of worship which express devotion in different ways. The one most similar to Christian worship might be *Puja*. This is often (but not always) a more ritualized form of worship, often (but not always!) with other family members. It includes lighting a sacred flame and chanting/singing specific mantras (rather like prayers) as well as possibly addressing specific Deities (rather like hymns) in terms of adoration and praise (*Bhakti*) as well as reminding worshipers of encoded wisdom and guidance. Many Hindus perform Puja twice a day (morning and evening). The impact of Puja on me this morning was that it made me stop rushing on to the next thing, and pause, reflect and feel peaceful about the day's challenges.

The third form, *Sewa*, is linked to seeing the Divine in other living beings and being of service from selfless love. Sewa can be performed for plants, animals, humans, family, community or a Deity if that is a person's disposition. The key thing is for it to be 'Love in Action.' Hindu philosophy teaches that Sewa performed in this spirit, even for the most humble of living creatures, is serving the Divine and so is one of the most honored forms of worship. This impacts me on a daily basis, mostly when I work in schools with children and teachers, or more materially when I prepare all the ingredients for my family's evening meal! In both cases I feel energized, experiencing *joie de vivre* and purposefulness.

The key thing with all these forms in Hinduism is a teaching found in Pandeism as well, that Divinity is everywhere, in everyone and everything. Hindu philosophy puts the responsibility on each of us to find our own way to connect to it and contribute to it manifesting in the world.

Dharmic Living—With or Without Deity

For many Hindus, 'Dharmic' living as a way of being in the world is not just about observing festivals or daily rituals. It is mindfully taking *any* time to connect and surrender to the integrity of a universally connected system, of seeking to tune in and synchronize more deeply with an underlying rhythm pulsing through creation. In my lifetime, I have seen a shift, perhaps echoing the wider landscape, from the more compliant, devotional Bhakti and service paths of my childhood to the more challenging, philosophically reasoned Jnana-paths within Hinduism. Thus while I was raised on stories of the righteous and self-sacrificing nobility of Prince Rama, I am today more drawn to the paradigm-challenging, playful and paradoxical life and teachings of Krishna! I think we live in an age, as did Krishna, where there is much injustice and institutionalized wrongdoing that needs to be vigorously challenged with deep wisdom. I am glad my children ask so many questions; we need that in our next generation, irrespective of faith background. I think they also need role models who embody wisdom as challenge, Dharma in action, what Mahatma Gandhi called *Satyagraha*—or insistence on truth.

Forgiveness as a religious response to sin, or as a personal response to wrongdoing towards ourselves, does not quite fit into a Hindu ethical framework. By the Hindu law of Karma, any act (including speech or even thought) generates an energetic change and will therefore have a consequence or impact. The extent of impact on us is considered to be determined by our previous Karma and evolving capabilities. In such a model, the focus of the individual is therefore placed ideally on their *own* ongoing behaviour, even when being impacted by others.

According to the ancient Upanishads, there are up to twenty recommended guidelines (the ten Yamas and ten Niyamas) for living ethically and well. The Fifth Yama is *Kshama,* which is often translated from Sanskrit (and Hindi) as 'Forgiveness.' Interestingly a more literal translation would be 'Forbearance' or 'Patience.' In other words, it is more about how the 'forgiver' deals internally with the impact of the behavior, and regains their own equilibrium, that is key rather than how they 'judge' the act of transgression or the transgressor.

Regarding the notion of being 'forgiven by God,' a useful quote from the Bhagavad Gita, often seen on the walls of Hindu homes, is: *Karmanye Vadhikaraste, Ma phaleshou kada chana, Ma Karma Phala Hetur Bhurmatey Sangostva Akarmani.* In the Bhagavad Gita, on the battlefield, when Arjun doesn't want to fight and kill his enemies, Krishna (an Avatar) persuades him to do so, including stating this famous quote, which loosely translates as "Do the work as guided; surrender the outcome [or fruits] to Me." This exemplifies the Hindu idea that *'God' neither judges nor forgives us, but we have the free choice to act from divine guidance/intuition, and learn from the consequences of our choices.*

On a personal note, I think it's important to say that this is a wonderful ideal, and something to aspire to. However, as ever with Hindu principles, what 'Kshama' might look like may vary in different situations appropriate to their context. In the news, we occasionally hear about parents of victims of violence, rejecting revenge or 'instant justice,' appealing instead for peace and bearing no ill-will to the perpetrators. Yet Arjun, in my Gita example above, had not only to put aside his own sentiments for conciliation *but,* without anger or rancor, calmly engage in deadly war against an evil and predatory enemy. The key in dealing with a transgressor in Hinduism is neither prescribed as making peace nor exacting punishment, but seems to be to master one's own emotions first, to gain the clarity to then pick whichever response serves *the most good.*

Ethics (Rules vs. Principles)

Hinduism does not have a specific source of authority to quote but instead a range of devoutly followed spiritual paths and variations of practice across India and the world.

Notwithstanding, there are key ideas that can unlock an understanding of Hinduism (or Sanatan Dharma as most Hindus would call their faith). The easiest way to access concepts in the classroom is through the festivals. These neatly encapsulate both abstract Hindu philosophy and rich folk wisdom within the cultural traditions through the associated food, clothes, dance, music, mantras and stories.

A primary Hindu concept is that *all creation is inherently divine* in nature, and so is to be dealt with as sacred, respected and indeed celebrated. This explains the sheer number of festivals. It has been said that Hindus celebrate everything. The births and victories of Deities, the new moon, full moon, new year, equinoxes and solstices, initiations, planting, harvest, plus a range of more localized festivals depending on the geographical region or strength of devotion to local Deities.

India has arguably more national holidays than any other country, and prides itself on giving equal respect to *non-Hindu* religious festival holidays such as Christmas and Eid. This highlights a second key Hindu idea: *Vasudhaiva Kutumbakam*—'the world is one family.'

The World Is One Family

Hindu philosophy does not have prescribed rules (and punishments). It describes principles (*Niyam*) and identifies consequences (Karma) for our behavior in relation to those principles. Examples of Niyam are truth-telling, practicing nonviolence, and being of service.

Living by a philosophy underpinned by the interconnectedness of all species, as one family, is intended to let us thrive and flourish interdependently. This encourages each of us (irrespective of religion) to find and serve from our own Dharma, to be in loving community, care for animals and the environment, and to be in tune with the natural order of life's milestones and seasons as they occur. All of these seem to be increasingly adopted universally as wellbeing principles as well as the religious principles which they are for Hindus.

The ancient Hindu Scriptures say we are living in the era defined as 'Kalyug,' the period when most people on the planet are living more by Karma than Dharma, and this is causing increasing dysfunction and illness at all levels—from personal to planetary. The main 'con' in these times would be that while these are wonderful ideals, they call for levels of self-awareness and discipline which humans don't always achieve. So perhaps the cons will vary for each person and would really depend on their own Karma!

At the individual level, the law of Karma says that for the consequences of his or her actions each person will be accountable. While there are no 'commandments,' there are *a lot* of recommendations for clearing Karma. Since unresolved Karma prevents the soul realizing its divine self as God.

Below are four key classifications for ways of pursuing this re-merging between the individual and the universal knowing or Brahman:

1. **Connecting within** (Self: Yoga, meditation and renunciation/fasting)—'realizing' that God resides within you as Universal Spirit and taking on *spiritual practices* designed to illuminate your inner connection with God.
2. **Connecting through Nature** (Vedic rituals, synchronized to the lunar calendar/seasons, etc.)—atunements using all five elements (Earth, Water, Fire, Air and Spirit): *Yagya,* traditionally asking God to manifest or 'help' at a time of need or giving thanks through *physical practices.*
3. **Connecting with Unseen Spirit** (Bhakti: different energy 'frequencies' symbolized through images)—performing daily acts of concentrated *devotion* (Puja) before a Murti, thus a personalized connection with a Deity through *emotional practices.*
4. **Connecting through Sewa**—*right* or *dharmic action,* as *service* within family or society.

Wisdom

Hindu philosophy says that far from evolving linearly, human society has gone through many cycles from barbarism to divinity and back round again.

I think the theory of evolution, as it is popularly misrepresented, has been quite damaging to human evolution, the linearity and the sense of there being a grim competitiveness to each evolutionary step requiring the downfall of the one before it. This has given modern humans the delusion that they are the most supreme version of the species whereas the actual symbiosis needed between old and new requires a mutual respect that harnesses the assets of each for mutual thriving. This is a relationship that has broken down in this interpretation of evolution into an oedipal one that says you have to denigrate and destroy what was before you, to take your own growth step. That is not what Hindu wisdom says. It says the best of what was known before you is your most prized asset which you hold as precious but also crucially build on that.

I think that is *true* evolution, whereas what we see is 'revolution,' which says we need to dispense and dispose of historical things as 'dated.' An iPhone is an example of that—you can look down on someone with an iPhone 4 if you have an iPhone 6 rather than appreciating that without the iPhone 4 there would be no iPhone 6. Sanatan Dharma follows this principle. Ancestors, elders, and earlier thinkers are revered for the guiding principles they have left for us, but alongside that is the principle of '*Aapo deepo bhava*' which reminds us that how we interpret and crucially *act* on those principles is entirely our own responsibility.

Reincarnation

As a Hindu, it seems to me that the delineations between physical and nonphysical, natural and supernatural, life and afterlife, appear to be artificial ones that we humans impose on ultimate reality to feel comfortable defining the world in a way that revolves around the capabilities of our own sensory faculties. The Hindu view of life is that all beings are part of *one* interconnected field of conscious abundant divine energy, going through their own cycles of moving in and out of spiritual evolution and physical form. As such they have physical and nonphysical energy signatures (as described in the Vedic theory behind Yoga). Thus even after their deaths, our ancestors are no less connected, revered and sacred to us.

First thing to say is that most Hindus don't think of the soul as belonging to a body. All the physical cells will replace, renew and eventually decay; however, Hindus believe there is another level of consciousness that is attached to the circumstances of the life being lived, the Atman. As long as there is attachment which comes from thinking that the soul *is* the person stuck in its circumstances or from the need to clear outstanding consequences (Karma), the soul will remain entangled in physical relationships and lifetimes. So the number of lifetimes will depend on the level of mindfulness and conscious clearing of Karma of each individual.

Moksha

Moksha is not an aim for Hindus in the way Heaven might be for a Christian or even Nirvana for a Buddhist. Hinduism teaches that life has four 'goals': Dharma, *Artha* (prosperity), *Kama* (pleasure) and *Moksha*. A clearer English translation than 'goal' might be 'purpose' rather than 'aim.' Hindu perspective gives these two words very different meanings. Aim is subjective, about free will and personal ambition; purpose, as I use it, is about inherent human drive and design. Hindu teachings say that humans have the *equipment* for all of these four purposes, which play out in accordance with individual lifestyles and dispositions.

Hindus would say that when a *particular* soul is ripe and ready in its own journey in a particular lifetime for Moksha (i.e. for direct experience of oneness with all that is) or to take a growth step towards that, the drive will kick in, the way a caterpillar forms a cacoon, and the relevant guru and circumstances will appear. This is different from thinking of Moksha as the shiny 'top prize' for all Hindus to *aim for* in a sort of spiritual show-jump; in fact it's the opposite—a realization of the ultimate pointlessness of such aims.

Conclusions

In the multifaith Indian community that I hail from, people were able to engage with others of every background without fear or prejudice; to find and hold the common human connection while respecting differing cultural or religious traditions. Not just observing, but being able to interact, *learn,* collaborate and celebrate together. This is the adaptability and pliability of thinking being eroded in modern times, but is vital in order to equip our next generation to excel and contribute in an increasingly fragmented yet interdependent world. In conclusion, what is often confused as *polytheism* is actually *pluralism*. Not many Gods but many ways to relate to the principle of divinity, including an atheistic tradition, which cultivates the divinity within. Seeing life as a personal quest to deeply understand oneself and the universe as crystal-faced mirrors of each other. Believing that we are all inherently divine and not here to be judged, but to experience, learn and serve so we may recover consciousness of our own perfection. This quest for understanding resonates with the Pandeists' desire to know. However, for Hindus the knowing can be instinctive, rational or intuitive, that is, depending on the individual, a knowing in the mind, body or spirit. Pandeism chooses to traverse this quest as a science, and as science is beginning to uncover the impact of the observer and uncertainty on the material world, I believe these three routes will increasingly converge in a blend of Eastern and Western knowledge too.

Beyond Creator and Universe: From Pandeism to Ismaili Muslim Neoplatonism

Ismaili Gnosis

Ismaili Gnosis is a private organization dedicated to reviving Ismaili Muslim esoteric thought and intellectual discussion for today's audiences. The Ismaili Gnosis website (ismailignosis .com) focuses on the study of classical Shī'ī Ismā'īli Muslim philosophy and other esoteric traditions (Sufism, Kabbalah, Christian mysticism, Vedanta, etc.) including metaphysics, philosophy, history, theology, cosmology, esoteric interpretation (ta'wīl)*, spirituality, comparative studies and eschatology. It is run by a group of Ismaili scholars with academic training and graduate degrees in religion, philosophy, and Islamic studies. The articles draw upon much of the Ismaili intellectual tradition of the past, including the writings of the Ismaili Imams, historians, philosophers, and poets such as the pirs, hujjahs, and da'is.*

The origins of man's religious aspirations are to be found in what we nowadays call science...It seemed to him rational that these phenomena, these events like the rising and the setting of the sun, the passage of the seasons, the flowering of the bud and the ripening of the fruit, the wind and the rain, were caused and controlled by deities or superior beings. Primitive religious experience and primitive scientific reasoning were linked together in magic, in wizardry. Thus, at one and the same time mankind's experiences in the realm of sensation and his striving to explain and co-ordinate those experiences in terms of his mind led to the birth of both science and religion...

It was difficult to separate what I may call proto-religion from proto-science; they made their journey like two streams,

> sometimes mingling, sometimes separating, but running side by side.[1]
> (Imam Sultan Muhammad Shah Aga Khan III)

The above words of Imam Sultan Muhammad Shah Aga Khan III (d. 1957), the forty-eighth hereditary Imam of the Shia Ismaili Muslims and direct descendant of the Prophet Muhammad, express how both man's sensory experience and intellectual reflection lie at the root of what we today call science and religion. Science and religion are essentially *intellectual* enterprises, contemporarily distinct yet primordially linked, by which human beings describe, understand, explain, and find ultimate meaning in the nature of existence. The Pandeist proposes that the most parsimonious explanation of the Universe based on both observation and reasoning is that a nonmaterial, powerful, intelligent and rational Creator wholly *became* the physical Universe. On the same grounds, on the basis of both physical observation and intellectual comprehension, we propose that only a Neoplatonic metaphysics *fully* explains the Universe as human beings experience it. Based on Aristotle's notion of four causes (efficient cause, formal cause, material cause, final cause), we argue that an absolutely simple, unique, and unrestricted Unconditioned Reality (what classical theists call 'God')[2] is the *efficient cause* of all existence including the Universe, by the mediation of a Universal Intellect—the *formal cause* of the intelligibility of all things, and the Universal Soul—the Creator that functions as both the *material cause* of the Universe and the *final cause* of its goal-directed and rational activity.

We begin by stating the essential theses of Pandeism as articulated by Knujon Mapson over several online articles:[3]

1. The spatio-temporal material energetic Universe (hereafter called 'Universe') has a Creator. The Creator, prior to creation, possesses immense *power* (to generate

the Universe), sufficient *intelligence* (to bestow complexity and intelligence in the Universe), and goal-directed *reason* (to produce the rational activity in the Universe).

2. This Creator seeks to attain a rational, objective, self-knowledge, by means of the experiences that occur within the Universe (experiencing limitation, ignorance, fear, sorrow, and also peace, courage, fulfillment, joy).
3. This Creator creates the Universe by *becoming* the Universe: the Creator converts himself into the Universe in the act of creation.
4. Subsequent to this act of generation, the Creator only exists *as* the Universe and does not exist as a being or entity apart from or distinct from the Universe.
5. The Universe, which the Creator has effectively become, does not receive any intervention or guidance from the Creator—in order to guarantee authentic experience within the Universe and also since the Creator has wholly become the Universe.
6. Nevertheless, there remains "the power of our Creator unconsciously underlying our Universe" which explains the occurrence of a myriad of religious phenomena (scripture, miracles, revelations, prophecies, beliefs, spiritual activities, spiritual emotions, visions).
7. The entire history and lifespan of the Universe, upon its conclusion, will provide the Creator with its "desired knowledge" that it seeks to attain.

In this chapter, we offer a constructive critique of Pandeism on philosophical grounds and propose that an Ismaili Muslim Neoplatonic metaphysic (common to various Muslim philosophical schools including Ismaili-Shia theosophy, al-Farabi and Ibn Sina, Ibn 'Arabi's school of Sufi mystical cosmology, Twelver Shia theosophers such as Mulla Sadra) best accounts for and explains the existence of the Universe as human beings experience it. We first argue, in partial agreement with the Pandeist, that there exists a Creator of the physical Universe, who is above space and time, powerful, intelligent, and rational. We also affirm that this Creator creates the Universe for a rational end or purpose. Our critique then proceeds on two points: first, we argue that the notion of the Creator actually becoming the Universe is logically and metaphysically impossible. This is because the Creator of the Universe must necessarily be an immaterial, personal and rational being—a Universal Soul—that continuously creates and sustains the Universe while also being manifest or immanent within it. Secondly, we argue that the existence of the Universe and its Creator (Universal Soul) can only be explained by a Universal Intellect as the locus of eternal truth, whose existence in turn depends upon an absolutely simple, transcendent and supra-personal God beyond all attributes. According to our proposed Ismaili Muslim Neoplatonic metaphysic, all existents (whether physical or metaphysical) are originated by and continuously dependent upon one single absolutely Unconditioned Reality (the God of classical theism) by the mediation of the Universal Intellect, the grounding source of all truth, intelligibility and essences (Forms), and the Universal Soul, the proximate Creator of the Universe and the source of all rational and goal-directed activities including human existence.

Bearing in mind our diverse readership, our method of argument in *this chapter will not rely on scripture, religious experience or the theological sources of the Ismaili Muslim tradition.* It will instead employ purely philosophical and rational arguments using logical and scientific evidence where appropriate. Any quotations from the Shia Ismaili Imams or the exponents of Ismaili Muslim philosophy are for purely illustrative and corroborative purposes.

1. Demonstrating the Existence of a Transcendent Intelligent Creator of the Universe

> Astronomy leads to a unique event, a universe which was created out of nothing, and delicately balanced to provide exactly the conditions required to support life. In the absence of an absurdly improbable accident, *the observations of modern science seem to suggest an underlying, one might say, supernatural plan.*[4]
>
> (Arno Penzias, Nobel Laureate in Physics, Co-Discoverer of Cosmic Background Radiation)

The scientific method involves forming a hypothesis and collecting empirical data to support that hypothesis or falsify it. Its conclusions are inductive—a general conclusion is argued using limited empirical data and the conclusions are therefore not certain but probabilistic (one can never guarantee the nonexistence of contradictory data). The scientific method itself relies on the laws of logic, the principle of causation, and the principle of evidence. However, the metaphysical method differs from the scientific. This is because the metaphysical method deals with categories that are not physical but ontological—like finite vs. infinite, effect vs. cause, conditioned vs. unconditioned, material vs. immaterial. In these cases, an object comes under one category or its opposite, but not both—this is known as disjunction. The metaphysical method logically disproves one category—showing it as a contradiction—and thereby demonstrates how the opposite category must be true. This is similar, in some ways, to mathematical proofs and is more certain than the probabilistic conclusions of science. Science can neither prove nor disprove the existence of a metaphysical Creator of the Universe. But a metaphysical or philosophical deductive argument for the existence of a Creator can use scientific conclusions as evidence to support one of its premises. We now offer two *metaphysical* or philosophical arguments for the existence of a transcendent creator of the Universe that rely, in part, on scientific evidence.

A. The Kalam Cosmological Argument for a Transcendent Creator of the Universe

This argument argues for the existence of a transcendent Creator of the Universe from the fact that the Universe has a finite past. The first proponents of this argument were Muslim theologians, including al-Kindi and al-Ghazali. In modern times, the Kalam Cosmological argument has been revived by William Lane Craig, David S. Oderberg and Robert J. Spitzer, from whose work the following summary of the argument draws extensively.[5] We present the argument below:

Premise 1: The Universe (totality of matter, energy, space, time) has a finite past and thus began to exist a finite time ago. This premise is supported by the following philosophical and scientific evidences:

- An infinite past is logically impossible based on the very definition of 'past' and 'infinite': an infinite past-time cannot actually 'pass' or be traversed. This means that the present moment, in which we find ourselves, would never be reached if the past were to be infinite. If the past were infinite, and the Universe exists in the present moment, it would mean that an infinite time-period has been traversed and 'passed' to bring the Universe to the present; yet, if this were actually so, then that past—whatever its length—would not be infinite but actually finite: "It cannot be otherwise—if it were possible, and after every segment of time there was a segment, infinitely, then we would never reach a given time."[6]
- Actual infinite quantities do not exist within nature as demonstrated by the modern philosopher of mathematics,

David Hilbert, through his distinction between potential and actual infinities. Actual infinities are logically impossible in applied mathematics and lead to contradictions in mathematics. Hilbert himself concluded that "the infinite in the sense of an infinite totality, where we still find it used in deductive methods, is an *illusion*...our principal result is that the infinite is nowhere to be found in reality. It neither exists in nature nor provides a legitimate basis for rational thought—a remarkable harmony between being and thought."[7]

- An infinite past-time cannot exist if time is real because an infinite past-time leads to ontological contradictions, i.e. something must exist and does not exist at once, and this violates the laws of logic.
- The Standard Big Bang Model shows that the entire Universe began to exist about 13.7 billion years ago.[8]
- The Second Law of Thermodynamics (Entropy) means that an infinite number of Big Bang cycles is impossible. Entropy, by definition, only increases over time and an infinite number of Big Bangs and Crunches would lead to infinitely high entropy in our Universe. But the Entropy of the present Universe is quite low and certainly not infinite.[9]
- If an infinite number of Big Bangs and Crunches occurs prior to the present Universe, then Cosmic Background Radiation (CMB) would be infinitely higher than starlight; but this is not the case in the Universe today as the ratio of CMB to starlight is only about 100 times.[10]
- Space-Time Geometry: The Borde-Guth-Vilenkin (BGV) Theorem based on a mathematical model of space-time geometry shows that any expanding universe or multiverse expansion must have a finite past-time.[11] Alexander Vilenkin conveys the implications of this theorem when he says: "With the proof now in place, cosmologists can no

longer hide behind the possibility of a past-eternal universe. There is no escape, they have to face the problem of a cosmic beginning."[12]

Premise 2: From nothing, only nothing comes (follows from the rules of logic). This means that whatever begins to exist (i.e. has a finite past-time to its existence) must come into being from a cause. This premise, a version of the principle of causation, is based on the rules of logic. Denying this premise leads to logical contradiction and assumes that all of reality is irrational and cannot be subject to *any* inquiry, whether scientific or philosophical. Two prominent modern philosophers, Stephen Mumford and Rani Lill Anjum, write that "causation is as real as anything we know. It is fundamental: an actual feature of this one true world."[13]

Conclusion: If the Universe began to exist, and whatever begins to exist has a cause, then the Universe itself (space, time, matter, and energy) necessarily has a transcendent or metaphysical cause or creator that transcends space, time, matter, and energy.

B. The Fine-Tuning Argument for a Cosmic Intelligence

Our second argument argues for the existence of a Cosmic Intelligence as the designer of the fine-tuned laws of physics that permit life to exist in the Universe. It is a modern probabilistic argument whose three premises are affirmed by prominent physicists including Paul Davies, Frank J. Tipler, Fred Hoyle, and Arzio Penzas.

Premise 1: The values of the universal constants controlling the relationship between space, time, matter, and energy in our Universe must fall under an extremely narrow range to permit the existence and development of life. Some examples of these finely-tuned constants are:[14]

- The Entropy Condition of the Universe has a probability of $10^{-10^{123}}$ (per Sir Roger Penrose) of occurring by chance.
- A 2% change in the Strong Force and Electromagnetic Force would eliminate all hydrogen: no water, no stars.
- The cosmological constant of our universe is fine-tuned to 120 decimal places to permit a stable Universe.
- The gravitational constant—considered in relation to the range of coupling strengths shown possible in nature—is fine-tuned to 40 decimal places.
- The weak force is fine-tuned to 5 decimal places.
- The proton–neutron mass difference is fine-tuned to 5 decimal places.
- At least seventeen other independent constants and factors are fine-tuned to a high degree of precision, some of them requiring a cooperative assignment of values.

Premise 2: The possible values that these universal constants could have that disallow any life form from developing are astronomically high (see above).

Premise 3: It is exceedingly improbable that these finely-tuned cosmological conditions for life occurred by pure chance. Nor do they occur by necessity. Positing multiple universes does not do away with the fine-tuning, since the number of universes in all viable multiverse models fail to increase the infinitesimally small probabilities of the fine-tuned constants occurring by chance.[15]

Conclusion: It is highly probable that these initial cosmological conditions of the Universe, which are fine-tuned to support life, are due to the design of a Supernatural Intelligence. The Fine-Tuning argument has become increasingly popular in modern thought and is taken seriously even among nontheist physicists like Paul Davies, who has remarked that:

> The numerical coincidences [necessary for an anthropic universe] could be regarded as evidence for design. The delicate fine-tuning in the values of the constants, necessary so that the various different branches of physics can dovetail so felicitously, might be attributed to God.[16]

The Fine-Tuning argument suggests the extremely high probability that the initial conditions of the physical Universe, mathematically represented in the numerical values and constants of modern physics, is the result of the design of a 'cosmic Designer' or 'super-Intelligence' that transcends the Universe. The Fine-Tuning argument points to a cosmic transcendent intelligence as the *proximate* designer of the laws of physics and nature, just as the Kalam argument points to a transcendent being who is the *proximate cause* of the Universe. When the Kalam and Fine-Tuning arguments are combined, the resultant conclusion is that the Universe (totality of matter, energy, space, time) has a transcendent cause who is also an intelligent agency—a 'cosmic Designer' or 'super-Intelligence.' The former atheist Fred Hoyle even concluded from his own study of the above data that:

> A common sense interpretation of the facts suggests that a Super-Intellect has monkeyed with physics, as well as with chemistry and biology, and that there are no blind forces worth speaking about in nature. The numbers one calculates from the facts seem to me so overwhelming as to put this conclusion almost beyond question.[17]

We can refer to this transcendent, creative and intelligent agency as the 'Creator of the Universe.' The above arguments yield some general conclusions concerning the Creator of the Universe: The Creator of the spatio-temporal Universe is itself above space, time, matter, and energy. This Creator, being spiritual or immaterial, possesses the power to create and sustain the Universe, the intelligence to determine the initial conditions of the constants of physics, the rationality to continuously direct all the rational behavioral regularities of the Universe as manifested in the laws of nature, and a creative intention or will to create and sustain.

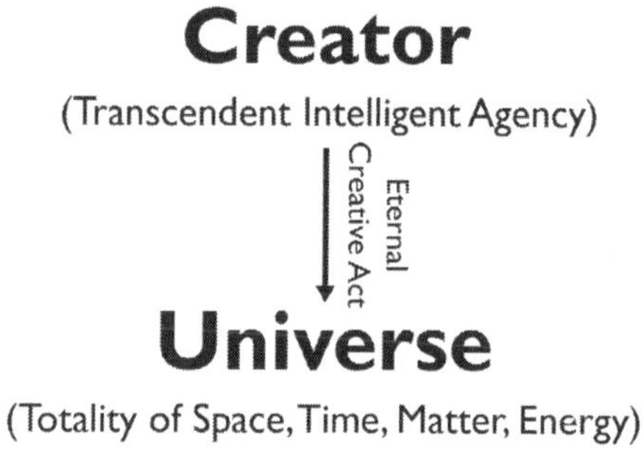

Figure 1.1

Being beyond physical time and space, the Creator's creative act is supra-temporal, timeless, and therefore a continuous process of eternal causation as opposed to a one-time event. The Creator is, therefore, spiritual, eternal, powerful, intelligent, rational, and willing. All of this follows from the Kalam and Fine-Tuning arguments given above. This does *not* mean the Creator is a 'person' akin to human persons or possesses anthropomorphic attributes as conceived in certain modern theologies. As the ultimate source and ground of human persons, the Creator must be *transpersonal* (inclusive of personal qualities) but cannot be defined as a 'person.' (Thus, the use of the masculine pronoun 'he' or 'himself' in our discourse is provisional and not meant to be literal.) On this point, we believe the Ismaili Muslim theologian and the Pandeist would be in general agreement. Having demonstrated the existence of a transcendent Creator of the Universe, we now move on to a philosophical and theological discussion about the metaphysical implications of this conclusion, as NASA scientist Robert Jastrow once remarked:

> For the scientist who has lived by his faith in the power of reason, the story ends like a bad dream. He has scaled the mountain of ignorance; he is about to conquer the highest peak; as he pulls himself over the final rock, he is greeted by a band of theologians who have been sitting there for centuries.[18]

2. The Creator and the Universe

In this section we respectfully critique and refute the Pandeist's claim that the Creator, in creating the Universe, actually *becomes* the Universe. Our critique proceeds through logical argument and without any theological appeal to any scripture. We fully understand that the Pandeist wants to avoid a worldview where the Creator is wholly *outside* the Universe. So we will go on to propose an alternative model of the Creator–Universe relationship, in which the Creator is neither *wholly outside* or *wholly identical with* the Universe. Our model, as will be demonstrated, also fulfills the Pandeist's claim that the Creator achieves a certain objective or goal, self-knowledge, through creating the Universe.

A. Can the Creator Become the Universe?

We hold that the Creator cannot become the Universe for three reasons:

1. The Creator, who is by definition above time and space, must sustain the Universe at every moment, in a continuous manner that is above physical time. To put it in philosophical terms, the Creator is an eternal cause *always* acting upon its effect, the Universe (see Figure 2.1). To express it in theological terms, the Creator *eternally* wills that the Universe exists for a finite timespan. If the Creator ceases to be, the Universe would

immediately cease to exist. If the Creator becomes the Universe, then it ceases to be the Creator; but the Universe would continue to be in need of its originating cause. The absence of that cause would lead to the dissolution of the Universe. However, since the Universe continues to exist, even now, it means that its Creator still exists.

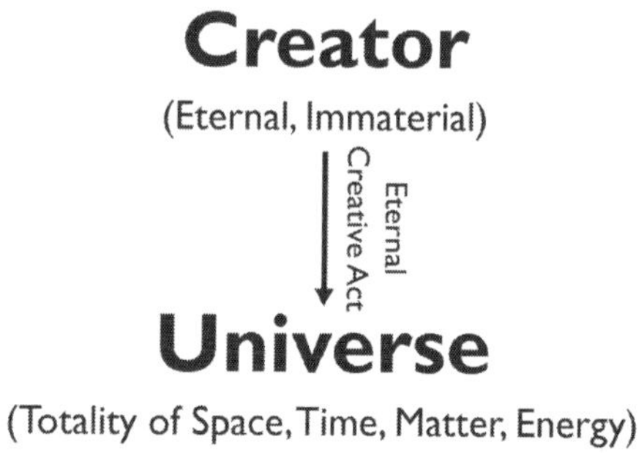

Figure 2.1

2. If the Creator 'becomes' the Universe, then this act of 'becoming' or change requires a cause. The cause of this act of 'becoming' must be either the Creator himself or a second Creator (see Figure 2.2). If the cause of the 'becoming' is the Creator himself, that means the Creator changes himself from an immaterial, spiritual, and eternal Creator into a material, spatial, and temporal Universe. But this act of self-transformation, being an act of the Creator, is not an act within physical time since the Creator is not initially within physical time. Therefore, the Creator must have caused himself to change into the Universe by means of an act that is itself beyond physical time—in other words, by an eternal act. But if this is the case—if the Creator changes himself into the Universe by an eternal act—then the act must continue to operate throughout the lifetime of the Universe. And if this act of the Creator, by which he transformed himself into the Universe, must always continue eternally, *then the original non-physical non-temporal Creator must still exist to perform the act even 'after' he has 'become' the Universe.* Therefore, the Creator

cannot wholly become the Universe in any logical sense—even if we supposed that the Creator changes himself into the Universe, at a higher eternal level, the original non-physical non-temporal Creator continues to exist.

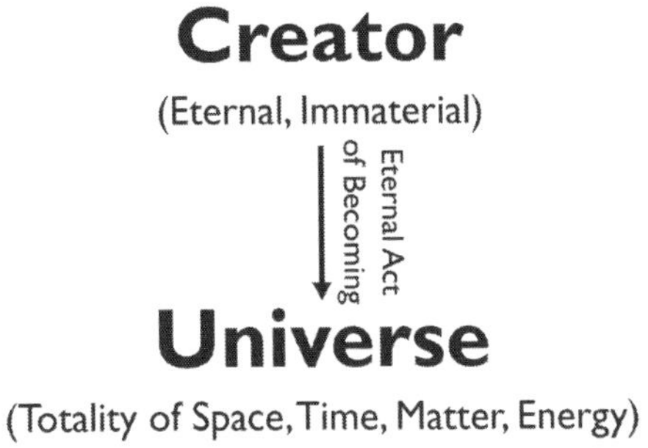

Figure 2.2

If, on the other hand, one proposes that a second Creator causes the first Creator to become the Universe, then this act of causation is likewise eternal, the second Creator plays the same role as the original Creator and the outcome is not any different from the first case. In both cases, after the Universe is created, the original Creator who transcends space and time, continues to exist.

3. Upon close examination, the Pandeist model does not *really* affirm that the Creator truly and entirely becomes the Universe. The Pandeist still maintains that there is "the power of our Creator unconsciously underlying our Universe."[19] He goes on to explain the existence of various phenomena such as visions, dreams, spiritual experiences, revelation, etc. by recourse to the underlying non-physical power of the Creator within the Universe. What is the nature of this power that continues to underlie the Universe, which is responsible for all human *spiritual* phenomena? It must either be *equal* to the power of the non-physical Creator (before creation) or only a portion of the power of the original Creator. If it is the power of the original

Creator, then it means the original Creator's spiritual power underlies and sustains the Universe and that this power did not really *become* the Universe, precisely because it is a *spiritual* power. If it is the diminished spiritual power of the Creator, then the Pandeist needs to explain what happened to the rest of the Creator's power. The Creator's power cannot go into oblivion—that would mean that being becomes non-being without any explanation. The only explanation is that the rest of the Creator's power is dispersed throughout the Universe. But this is not any different from saying that the Creator's *full* power underlies the Universe (see Figures 2.3 and 2.4).

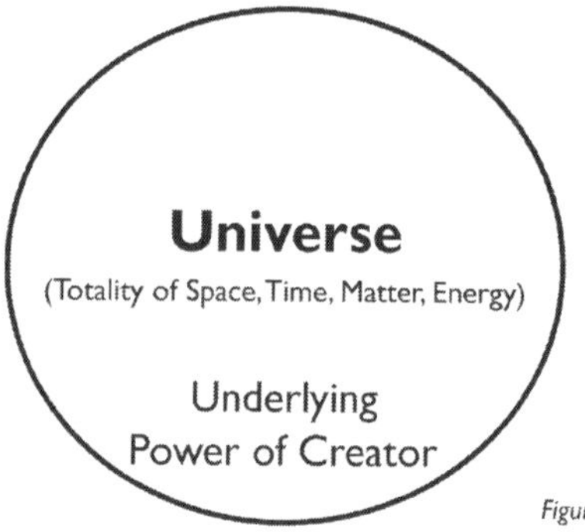

Figure 2.3

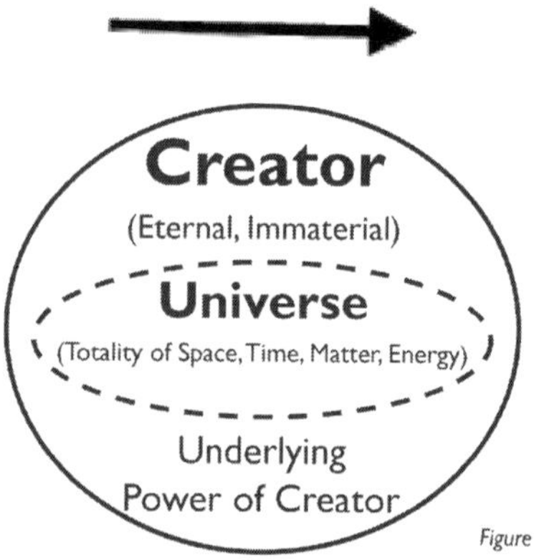

Figure 2.4

This is because the Creator before creation, by definition, is immaterial and spiritual (as the Pandeist admits). The Creator's power is likewise spiritual and not material—otherwise the Pandeist cannot claim this power is responsible for so many human *spiritual* phenomena like spiritual experiences and visions. The Creator's spiritual power cannot be spatially separated from his own spiritual essence nor can he or his power be spatially dispersed throughout the Universe—in the manner of say, water, dispersed in a garden. An immaterial spiritual being is not subject to physical division or the constraints of being in one place or out of a place. Thus, the power of the Creator cannot even be *partially* dispersed throughout the Universe. Instead, if the Pandeist maintains that the *full* spiritual power of the Creator always underlies and sustains the Universe (as we have argued above), then it is the Creator himself in his nonmaterial spiritual form who wholly underlies the Universe.

By the same argument, one can refute similar claims that only *some* of the Creator's intelligence, rationality, will, and other attributes underlie the Universe and argue that the Creator himself and *all of his attributes* underlies and sustains the Universe. Therefore, the Creator never really *becomes* the Universe except by analogy or symbolically. What, then, is the proper conception of the relationship between the Creator and the Universe? Pandeism wants to avoid the notion of a Creator who is *wholly external* to the Universe who then must periodically 'intervene' within it. We have argued that the Creator cannot be *wholly identical* to the Universe. But, between the 'exteriority model' of modern-day monotheism, the deist model of an absent Creator, and the Pandeist notion of the Creator becoming the Universe, there remains an alternative model which is more viable, logical, and ultimately more ancient.

B. Defining the Creator–Universe Relationship

The only viable model for framing the relationship between the Creator and the Universe is that of an object and its projected image or reflection within a mirror. Since something cannot emerge from nothing, the Creator must create the Universe out of its own essence and this Universe is but the projection, emanation and manifestation of the Creator and the Creator's own attributes of power, will, intelligence, rationality, creative potential and other transpersonal attributes. When something is reflected within a mirror, the original object never materially enters the mirror; the original object neither dwells inside the mirror nor becomes the mirror. Instead, the object merely casts its image upon the mirror and its reflected image subsists as long as the object continues to face the mirror. Remove the object, and the image disappears. On the same lines, the Universe as the effect of the Creator subsists in existence as long as the Creator creates, sustains, and 'projects' the Universe out of itself. Creation and sustenance are one continuous act of the Creator as opposed to a series of discrete interventions. In fact, the concept of 'intervention' whereby an external Creator intervenes and enters into a Universe essentially detached from it is wholly inapplicable in this model. The Universe is akin to the reflection and image of the Creator in the mirror. It would be more true to say that the Creator is 'continuously intervening' in the Universe by his continuous act of creating and projecting it. This relationship between the Creator and the Universe is also like the relationship between the soul and the body—where the Creator is the Universal Soul and his body is the Universe.

In the case of a human individual, the soul is the immaterial and rational center of consciousness. The soul is therefore not subject to physical limits and not located 'inside' the body or any of its parts. On the contrary, the physical body is but a projection of the soul akin to its reflection and locus of manifestation. It would be more true to say that the body is 'inside' the soul. Along the same lines, the Creator is the Soul of the Universe—the Universal Soul—and the Universe is like the body of the Creator. The Universe is permeated by the Creator just as a reflection in the mirror is permeated by the object it reflects. But in this particular case, unlike physical mirrors, there is no independent mirror. Both the mirror and the projected image emanate from the Creator or the Universal Soul. In a purely logical and not temporal sense, the Universal Soul first generates the 'mirror'—which must be an entirely passive, receptive substance that endows certain limits upon what is projected upon it. In the Neoplatonic terminology of the Ismaili Muslims, the 'mirror' is called Prime Matter—a purely passive, potential, receptive and limiting substance that is like the 'shadow' of the Universal Soul. Upon this Prime Matter or shadow, the Creator or Universal Soul projects its own qualities, powers, forms and attributes. The resultant reflection of the Universal Soul's powers and qualities in the mirror of Prime Matter is the spatio-temporal Universe with all of its components and behaviors. If one takes the Big Bang as the literal or allegorical beginning of the physical world as such, then this explosion of all matter and energy from a single point is symbolic of how the Universal Soul or Creator concentrates its power of emanation or projection upon the mirror of Prime Matter, and this projection then reverberates outward from that point of concentration. To express this analogy in two-dimensional graphic terms, it would be accurate to say that the physical Universe is 'within' the Creator, while the Creator himself both encompasses and transcends the Universe:

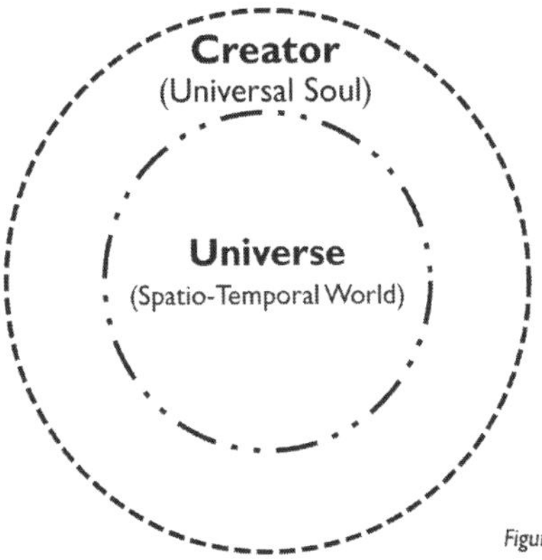

Figure 2.5

At this point the Pandeist may object and claim that without the Creator wholly and fully becoming the Universe, the Creator cannot have an authentic full experience and achieve its goal of attaining knowledge of certain experiences. Against this argument we propose that it is entirely possible for an agent to have an experience without essentially and wholly becoming that experience. Human beings enjoy a range of authentic experiences without actually turning into those experiences and ceasing to be human beings. I can experience an apple by tasting it and enjoy it authentically, even losing myself in that experience, without actually transforming into the apple. One could say that a part of me experiences the apple—even becoming one with the taste of the apple as I taste its sweetness—while part of me remains what I essentially am to actually register, witness and later recall that experience. The human mind fully experiences bodily sensations—from pain to pleasure—and yet does not cease to exist as a mind. On similar grounds, the Creator can authentically experience everything that happens within the Universe—from the most minute and subtlest forms of life to the most complex mathematical equations—without transforming himself into these experiences. On the contrary, if the Creator *did* transform into the Universe and its sum total of experiences, then the Creator would lack the self-reflexive awareness of *having* those experiences and, in fact, gain nothing from them. One can only gain knowledge from an experience if one also exists *apart from* the experience in order to register the experience, reflect on it, and assess it.

If we accept that the Creator generates the Universe for the sake of acquiring certain knowledge through experience, then the Creator–Universe model along the lines of the mirror–reflection analogy allows for the Creator to experience the Universe in two ways: first, the Creator or Universal Soul experiences the Universe as it continually gazes upon it in the very act of generating and sustaining it. In doing so, the Universal Soul is actually contemplating itself but in the form of reflected images or living pictures that constitute the Universe. This allows the Creator to attain self-knowledge by means of seeing itself as an objectified 'other.' Second, the 'projections' of the Universal Soul that generate the Universe also directly participate in the Universe. These 'projections' have direct 'experiences' within the Universe while the Universal Soul as such remains distinct from the Universe. One can draw an analogy here between the Sun (the Universal Soul or Creator), its rays (the projected parts), and the Earth upon which the Sun shines. The Ismaili philosopher Nasir Khusraw (d. 1088) explains how the 'effect' of the Universal Soul is like the rays of the Sun shining upon the Earth, which results in a manifestation of the Universal Soul (like the Sun) in various limited forms throughout the Earth:

> The effect of the Universal Soul is like the light which shines upon the earth from the sun, so that the earth becomes lit by that light. And when the sun sets, the light also disappears. When the sun shines upon a crystal or upon a mirror which can collect an amount of the light of the sun, the light becomes so bright through action of the crystal or mirror that from it fire can be lit, from which one may get light at any time. Thus it would do the same work as the sun is doing, proportionately to its size producing light and warmth...Therefore, we may say that the power of the Universal Soul is spread in the physical world, so that the world is full of it. But, being itself immaterial, that energy does not occupy any visible space. Although no place in the world remains free from the Universal Soul, it has no spatial existence.[20]

In this case, the terms 'ray' and 'part' are being used here loosely since a rational and immaterial Universal Soul cannot actually split into literal parts. But rather, this means that parts of the Universal Soul, in the sense of his rays and projections, participate in and experience the Universe while the Universal Soul as such remains transcendent vis-à-vis the Universe as a whole in order to create and sustain the entire Universe from moment to moment.

The 'rays' which the Universal Soul projects upon the mirror of Prime Matter to produce the animate Universe cannot be equal in their intensity. In fact, it is because these 'rays' are of various levels of luminosity and intensity that the Universe consists of a plurality of natural phenomena displaying a myriad of qualities and behaviors—from the subatomic particles all the way to human beings. It follows that the type of 'experience' that each 'ray' can have in the Universe is directly proportional to its own intensity. There is only so much an atom, or molecule, or mineral sediment can experience compared to what an animal or human can experience. Therefore, each 'ray' projected by the Universal Soul into the Universe is a particular kind of 'soul' and its manifestation as a natural kind in the Universe is directly related to the level of that soul. Subatomic particles are images in the Universe of a particular intensity-level of the Universal Soul's projected rays, which we could call 'subatomic soul.' Similarly, atoms are images resulting from the Universal Soul's projected rays with a higher level of intensity, which we could call 'atomic soul.' Likewise, molecules, minerals, organic beings, vegetative life, animals, and rational human beings are images resulting from specific projections of the Universal Soul with specific intensity levels, which we would respectively call molecular soul, mineral soul, organic soul, vegetative soul, animal soul, and rational soul. Each of these kinds of soul participate in and experience the life of the Universe in their own specific ways, and the Universal Soul is also experiencing the Universe by means of these souls. The more intense the projection and the more 'advanced' the soul, the more mentally and spiritually conscious is the creature in the Universe that reflects that particular soul or projection. It follows that human beings, possessors of self-reflexive consciousness or rationality, embody and represent more intense projections of the Universal Soul than do animals, plant life, or molecules. The forty-eighth hereditary Imam of the Ismaili Muslims, Imam Sultan Muhammad Shah Aga Khan III, explains this as the Ismaili Muslim view of the soul below:

> Islamic doctrine goes further than the other great religions, for it proclaims the presence of the soul, perhaps minute but nevertheless existing in an embryonic state, in all existence—in matter, in animals, trees, and space itself. *Every individual, every molecule, every atom has its own spiritual relationship with the All-Powerful Soul of God*. But men and women, being more highly developed, are immensely more advanced than the infinite number of other beings known to us.[21]

If the Universal Soul or Creator has created the Universe to acquire knowledge through experiencing the Universe, then this knowledge ultimately consists of self-knowledge. This is because the Universe is nothing more than the living animate image of the Universal Soul. When the Universal Soul experiences the events, lives, and life of the Universe, it is really experiencing images of itself. The goal of the Universal Soul or Creator in creating the Universe is to attain a kind of self-knowledge that it does not possess without the Universe. At the same time, this self-knowledge must necessarily represent, for the Universal Soul, an end-goal which it always has the *potential* to attain (otherwise there would be no point in even pursuing this end). Therefore, the Universal Soul creates the Universe—experiencing it in all of its different forms—to attain self-knowledge and self-actualization. Nasir Khusraw explains this below:

> The Universal Soul is the lord of the physical creation, and it is the Universal Soul which started the movement of this world. The purpose of that activity which it develops is the

> search for its perfection, and this is attained in the eminent persons who appear in this world.[22]

The Creator or Universal Soul creates the Universe to actualize itself or attain perfection and *the Universe in its totality is the expression of the Creator's journey to and attainment of this perfection.* If this is true, then one would expect to observe the Creator's desire and journey toward perfection reflected in and through all the phenomena of the Universe. In fact, this is precisely the case: every kind of existent in the Universe is tending and moving toward perfection as appropriate to its own form and manner of existence. This may appear odd at first—how does 'perfection' apply to nonliving things? Or even to living things like plants and animals? Indeed, one can legitimately speak of both nonliving and living beings moving and striving toward perfection by defining 'perfection' in appropriate terms. The philosopher David S. Oderberg thus speaks of "the idea of *perfection*, where this term is taken in its etymological sense of 'completion' or 'fulfillment,' with correlative connotations such as 'improve' or 'bring to the highest available standard.'"[23] Oderberg further explains that moving toward *perfection* is the essence of what it means for something to be 'alive.' Life itself is "the natural capacity of an object for self-perfective immanent activity," which means that:

> Living things act for themselves in order to perfect themselves, where by perfection I mean that the entity acts so as to produce, conserve and repair its proper functioning as the kind of thing it is—not to reach a state of absolute perfection, which is of course impossible for any finite being. Speaking now in causal terms, living things, unlike non-living things, exercise immanent causation: this is a kind of causation that begins with the agent and terminates in the agent for the sake of the agent.[24]

Therefore, each and every living thing—from the smallest cell to the complex human being and everything in between—strives toward self-perfection as it acts to preserve its own existence and its powers. This is otherwise known as flourishing and is completely in line with the general sense of 'survival' that all living beings display. If the Creator, the Universal Soul, creates the Universe to attain perfection, and the Universe and its various processes are the 'image' of the Universal Soul, then this is exactly what one would expect to see: the Universal Soul's movement toward perfection or self-actualization is naturally reflected in the particular activities of all living things. Upon close examination one can see that even nonliving things exhibit movement toward 'perfection' in terms of their own natures. Once again, Oderberg reminds us that a pre-modern philosophical point of view "sees perfection as what used to be called an *increase in the fullness of being*, a bringing to fulfillment or completion of some disposition, power, or tendency of an object—in scholastic terminology, the actualization of some potentiality (or potency) of a thing."[25] The key phrase in this definition of perfection is the "fulfillment or completion of some disposition, power, or tendency of an object." *If an object has a natural tendency to behave in a particular way or react in a particular way, then the obtaining of that reaction of behavior constitutes the object's 'perfection' or 'completion.'* Indeed, we observe this, with or without our scientific instruments, throughout various nonliving and inorganic natural phenomena as Oderberg notes:

> Particles of opposite charge attract, salt dissolves in water, snowflakes tend to grow six branches, stars burn out: these are all examples of natural appetites—tendencies of objects to certain kinds of behavior. More precisely, as is usually suggested by the wording, we can describe the tendency itself or what the tendency results in, or both. A proton has the tendency to attract electrons even in the absence of electrons.

> When it is attracting an electron, it is exercising its tendency, or manifesting its disposition—to use the more familiar expression. To say that salt dissolves in water is to speak ambiguously of what salt tends to do whether it is in water or not and of what it actually does in water, which is the manifested end state of the disposition. It makes no sense to speak of a disposition or tendency without a corresponding manifestation or end state.[26]

The various examples above—ice melting, salt dissolving, protons attracting electrons, etc.—are among a myriad of cases where natural nonliving things exhibit goal-directed behavior where the 'goal' is the "bringing to fulfillment or completion of some disposition, power, or tendency." One can go even further and recognize the goal-directed activity in routine natural processes such as the rock cycle and the water cycle because "we observe certain very stable processes, and the rock and water cycles are examples of them. Their cyclicality means the same processes and sub-processes happen again and again: the very same kinds of things take place, whatever the particulars on each occasion of recurrence."[27] The Thomist philosopher Edward Feser summarizes the ubiquitous occurrence of goal-directed activity within nature as follows:

> A struck match generates fire and heat rather than frost and cold; an acorn always grows into an oak rather than a rosebush or a dog; the moon goes around the earth in a smooth elliptical orbit rather than zigzagging erratically; the heart pumps blood continuously and doesn't stop and start several times a day; condensation results in precipitation which results in collection which results in evaporation which in turn results in condensation; and so forth. *In each of these cases and in countless others we have regularities that point to ends or goals, usually totally unconscious, which are just built into*

nature and can be known through observation to be there whether or not it ever occurs to anyone to ask how they got there.[28]

In summary, the Universe consists of goal-directed activity exhibited by both inorganic (nonliving) and organic (living) things. Living things exhibit immanent teleology in which they act to preserve, improve and perpetuate their own existence—this is their movement toward 'perfection'—and inorganic things exhibit tendencies or dispositions, the fulfillment of which constitutes their 'perfection.' There is also the matter of human beings striving toward human 'perfection' and how such a thing would be accomplished, but we will leave this for the conclusion of the article. It suffices to say, at this point, that the Universe contains numerous systems of goal-directed activity in the form of causes and effects directed toward certain ends (various modes of 'perfection'). This goal-directed activity within the Universe is the very manifestation or image of the Universal Soul, the Creator of the Universe. At the same time, this activity serves as a proof or demonstration of the very existence of the Creator because all goal-directed rational activity must be directed by a guiding intelligence.

Consider the fact that most nonliving and living things, even while exhibiting goal-directed rational behaviors, are not conscious or aware of the end-goal or perfection that they move toward as Oderberg notes: "There can be a goal (or purpose, or final case) of a thing without that goal being one whose satisfaction does anything *for* the object that acts to satisfy it."[29] There is no inherent reason why things in the Universe, whether nonliving or living, should display *regular predictable and rational behavior at all*. Even Einstein himself once wrote that "*a priori* one should expect a chaotic world, which could in no way be grasped by thought."[30] Yet the Universe is *not* chaotic at all. It exhibits consistent rational behaviors, and the goal-directed activity of various natural things is clear evidence of this. As Edward Feser remarked above, "even animals and human beings, which are conscious, are comprised in whole or in part of unconscious and unintelligent material components which themselves manifest final causality." The only logical explanation of the very existence of the rational behavior of various objects in the Universe in terms of the goal-directed activity of causes and effects is the presence of a transcendent rational agency that continuously *guides and directs* all the objects of the Universe to move towards "fulfillment or completion of some disposition, power, or tendency," as Feser concludes below:

> But given what was said above, it is impossible for anything to be directed towards an end unless that end exists in an intellect which directs the thing in question towards it. It follows that the system of ends or final causes that make up the physical universe can only exist at all if there is a supreme intelligence or intellect outside the universe which directs things towards their ends. Moreover, this intellect must exist here and now, and not merely at some beginning point in the past, because causes are here and now, and at any point at which they exist at all, directed towards certain ends.[31]

This intelligent and rational agency which directs all things in the Universe toward their respective goals, their 'perfections,' is the Universal Soul, the Creator of the Universe. And this is precisely because the Universal Soul's creation and manifestation of the Universe is an expression of its *own journey toward perfection*. 'As above, so below.'

3. Beyond the Creator and the Universe

We have thus far argued that the spatio-temporal Universe is caused and created by a metaphysical, intelligent and rational cause—the Creator. This Creator, transcending time, continuously creates, sustains and infuses the Universe with existence.

By analogy, the Universe is like the *reflected image* of the Creator. The Creator is what we call the Universal Soul, and the image which the Creator projects out of its own essence and qualities is the Universe. This Universal Soul, as it was seen above, creates and projects the Universe as its self-image for a purpose, which is the attainment of perfection through self-knowledge. However, this Creator–Universe cosmological model is not exhaustive and requires further metaphysical explanation. While this model explains the existence and core features of the physical Universe, it does not explain the existence of the Creator or Universal Soul itself, nor does it explain the existence of higher-order realities such as truth, knowledge, or intellect. One cannot assume that there are no other realities or causes above the Creator or Soul of the Universe. Indeed, further logical arguments demonstrate that there are two higher degrees of reality that transcend the Creator of the Universe.

A. The Universal Intellect as the Locus of Eternal Truths and Complete Intelligibility

If the Creator, the Universal Soul, creates and generates the Universe in order to attain self-knowledge, which is its self-actuality, then this self-knowledge or *actual state* of the Universal Soul must *already* exist in some sense. This is to say, the *perfected, actual, or end-state* of the Universal Soul exists *prior to* the Universal Soul. By prior, we mean *essentially* prior and not temporally prior—since the Universal Soul transcends time and space. In other words, the perfect or actual state of anything is metaphysically prior to the potential state. Since the Universal Soul's actuality is self-knowledge, the metaphysical level immediately 'above' the Universal Soul essentially consists of knowledge. But what kind of knowledge? At minimum, this metaphysically *actual knowledge* would contain all eternal necessary truths about the Universal Soul and the Universe. One does not need to look far to recognize some of the eternal necessary truths, such as:

- **The Laws of Thought** (that make rational thought *possible*): Every A is A (identity); no A can both be and not be, or two contradictory statements cannot be true and false at the same time (non-contradiction); everything must either be or not be (excluded middle); the principle of sufficient reason (whatever exists has a rational explanation for its existence); that what was not before cannot be afterwards, without becoming and having become.
- **Mathematical Truths**: Nothing can become greater or less, either in number or magnitude, while remaining equal to itself; that without addition or subtraction there is no increase or diminution of anything, but only equality; 3 is odd; 4 is even; 2+2=4.
- **Geometric Truths**: circularity, triangularity, Pythagorean Theorem, etc.
- **Abstract Intelligible Concepts**: existence, necessity, possibility, similarity, difference, rest, change, causation, etc.

Even setting aside the Creator–Universe model we have argued for in this article, the very existence of the above necessary timeless truths necessitates an eternal *locus* or *ground* for these and all other necessary truths. The truths of logic are necessary to knowledge, and any kind of knowledge is dependent upon the laws of logic. The truths of logic are metaphysically *prior* to any concept of the Universe or physical world. Mathematical truths are purely intellectual and do not depend upon the physical world in any way. If 3 is odd, it is because the nature of *threeness* is by its nature connected to the nature of *oddness*. 2+2=4 in the past, present, and future. 2+2=4 because of the *eternal nature* of *twoness* and *fourness*, which are also essentially connected. The case is likewise for circularity, triangularity, and mathematical theorems—they are eternally true propositions. Even abstract intelligible concepts, by which the human mind experiences and interprets the world, are metaphysically *prior* to any notion of a temporal physical world and cannot be explained by the physical world itself because any explanation in physical terms *depends upon* these intelligible concepts. Mathematical truths, logical truths, and abstract concepts are both eternal and necessary to the physical Universe as we experience it and its Creator. Eternal necessary truths *exist* in a manner that is more primordial and more real than physical things. These eternal necessary truths are not physical, but purely intelligible since they can only be known by an intellect. What is eternal, necessary, and intelligible *only exists in an intellect.* In this case, they can only exist in an intellect which is itself eternal, necessary, and intelligible to itself. The argument here is that the very existence of eternal necessary truths necessitates an eternal intellect who always *intuits these truths.* This argument goes back to Plato, Plotinus, and St Augustine and is voiced below by two contemporary thinkers:

> The necessary truths are deliverances of a supreme rational mind. Had this mind failed to have been supremely rational, there would be no explanation of necessity.
> (William E. Mann)[32]

> There must be some eternal fact that explains all real or possible instances or examples of necessary truth…that without an eternal knower there could be no eternal truth such as is expressed in necessary propositions... *If, then, an eternal knower is required to be eternally contemplating all eternal truth, who is this knower?*
> (Lloyd P. Gerson)[33]

In Ismaili Muslim Neoplatonic terminology, this eternal knower or supreme intellect that timelessly *intuits* and grounds all eternal necessary intelligible truths is called the Divine Intellect or Universal Intellect. The Universal Intellect is the locus of *all eternal necessary truth, all eternal knowledge*—what Plato and Plotinus call the "Forms" of all things—and it is always engaged in contemplating or intellecting these eternal truths, thus actualizing their existence eternally. Lloyd Gerson summarizes the logical argument for the existence of the Universal Intellect as follows:

> The starting-point for the argument for the eternality of Intellect is Plato's theory of Forms. Because Forms exist, eternal Intellect must exist. One reason for believing that Forms exist is that knowledge exists *and therefore truth exists. Truth* is eternal. But eternal truth could not exist if Forms did not exist. Forms are somehow supposed to explain why, for example, mathematical truths are eternal. And Forms could not exist if eternal Intellect did not exist. We thus have a premise: Forms exist, and a conclusion: Intellect exists. What additional premises are employed to connect these two propositions? The additional premises are: *if Forms exist, eternal truth exists. But truth is being for or in relation to an Intellect. Hence, eternal truth entails an eternal Intellect.*[34]

At minimum the Universal Intellect contains and grounds all the Forms—eternal necessary and universal truth. These eternal truths are what render the Universe intelligible to human beings and subject to rational investigation. One can argue further that *whatever exists must be intelligible* in principle—since something wholly utterly *unintelligible* cannot be affirmed as existing at all. If to exist is to be perceptible, conceivable, or knowable, it follows that the entirety of existence, all of reality, is intelligible. Therefore, "complete intelligibility" exists. But complete intelligibility cannot exist *as matter*; complete intelligibility only exists as an *idea* in a universal eternal intellect that encompasses the entirety of reality. The orthodox Christian theologian David Bentley Hart explains that "to believe that being is inexhaustibly intelligible is to believe also—whether one wishes to acknowledge it or not—that reality emanates from an inexhaustible intelligence...the logical order of all reality, the ground both of the subjective rationality of mind and the objective rationality of being, the transcendent and indwelling Reason or Wisdom by which mind and matter are both informed and in which both participate."[35] This intellect which contains and grounds complete intelligibility and contains the intelligible archetypes of all things, is the Universal Intellect. A modern scholar of Ismaili studies, Alice C. Hunsberger, explains the nature of the Universal Intellect as follows:

> The Intellect is complete and perfect. It knows all things, and knows them all at once; there is nothing for it to know later or better. There is no motion or time within the Intellect or within which the Intellect functions, for time and motion have not yet come into existence in the realm of the Intellect. *Not only does the Intellect know all things; it encompasses all beings, material and spiritual.* In fact, following the Command 'Be!', the Intellect *is* all being; there is nothing outside of itself. The Intellect also lacks nothing and needs nothing, because there is nothing other than its actual perfection.[36]

Any metaphysical model that seeks to account for the Universe as human beings experience it must include both the Creator (Universal Soul) and the Universal Intellect. The Universal Soul as described above accounts for and explains the existence of the Universe, its complexity, and its goal-directed behavior toward perfection. The Universal Intellect grounds and explains the *intelligibility* of the Universe and allows us to know anything about the Universe at all. This is because the Universal Intellect is the eternal ground of both the objective intelligibility of the

Universe and the subjective intellect of human beings.

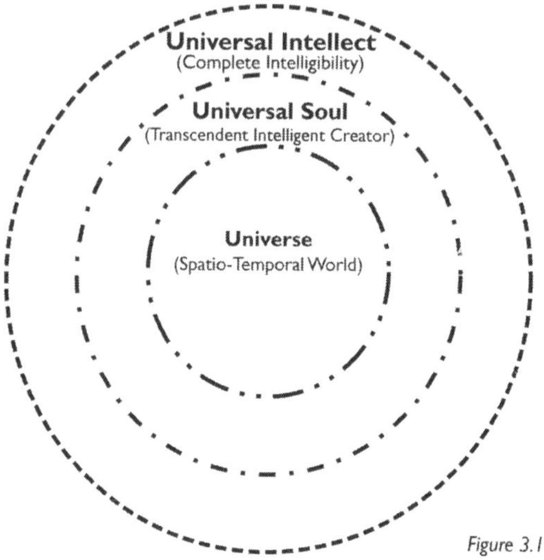

Figure 3.1

Without the Universal Intellect, the Universe would be completely opaque to us and human minds would not be able to think in rational terms. Human minds interpret all sensory experience through intellectual *a priori* categories like sameness, difference, and the notion of existence. These intellectual *a priori* categories are not derived from the physical Universe; they are imprinted upon the human intellect from the Universal Intellect. The living hereditary Imam of the Ismaili Muslims, Imam Shah Karim al-Husayni Aga Khan IV, describes the interrelationship between the Universal Intellect, the human intellect, and the human comprehension of the world as follows:

> **The Divine Intellect, *Aql-i Kull* (Universal Intellect), both transcends and informs the human intellect.** It is this Intellect which enables man to strive towards two aims dedicated by the Faith: that he should reflect upon the environment Allah has given and that he should know himself. It is the light of Intellect which distinguishes the

> complete human being from the human animal and developing that intellect requires free enquiry. The man of Faith who fails to pursue intellectual search is likely to have only a limited comprehension of Allah's creation. Indeed, it is man's intellect that enables him to expand his vision of that creation.[37]

If human beings are able to recognize the external Universe and distinguish electrons from protons, iron from gold, or dogs from cats, it is because each of these things manifest a different intelligible nature or essence, rendering one distinct from the other. The *natures* of different physical beings are ultimately manifestations of eternal intelligible essences in the Universal Intellect. For anyone who doubts that physical things have *natures*, this fact is demonstrated by what scientists call the 'laws of nature.' The laws of nature refer to how natural things regularly behave and interact with each other. When examined more closely, it means that different classes of physical things behave in very unique ways and have specific dispositions. Oderberg explains how the 'laws of nature' actually point to the 'natures' or 'essences' of specific kinds of things in the Universe:

> Laws of nature are truths about how objects must behave. How objects behave depends wholly on how objects must be. Hence the laws depend wholly on how objects must be. Hence they obtain in every world in which the objects they are about exist. In other words, every world in which certain objects exist will be a world in which those objects must behave in a certain way. Therefore, every such world will be one in which the truths about how those objects must behave—i.e. the laws—obtain. There is no world, then, in which the objects exist and the laws about them do not obtain. So the necessity of those laws is metaphysical, since it is a necessity derived from the essences of those objects. The short

> way of making the necessitarian point is to assert *that the laws of nature are the laws of natures.* For natures just are abstract essences in concrete operation. Nature is the collection of all the natures of things. So to say the laws are *of nature* is to say that they are of *the natures* of things.[38]

If physical things in the Universe have 'natures' or 'essences'—as the scientifically postulated laws of nature demonstrate—then these are all eternal essences within the Universal Intellect. At the same time, the Universal Soul is what explains the changes, movements, desires, and goal-directed behavior of the Universe. Without the Universal Soul, the Universe would be an immobile unchanging image of the Universal Intellect, unable to evolve and grow. We already described at length how all organic and inorganic beings in the Universe behave and move toward perfection or fulfillment of specific goals. This movement is the effect of the Universal Soul. Together, the Universal Intellect and Universal Soul explain the *intelligibility* and the *goal-directed activity* of the Universe as explained by Gerson:

> The organic activities of incarnate or embodied individuals are explained by Soul. The cognitive activities of individuals including the single activity of a disembodied individual are explained by the Intellect. The former are images of the latter and can only properly be understood as such...The Intellect explains images of Forms and images of intellection, but it does not explain embodied, goal-directed activities. Various types of cognition are of course implicated in goal-directed behavior, such as reasoning as an instrument of action. But Intellect is not the *arche* which explains the having and acting on behalf of external goals. It explains only the cognitive dimension of such acting. Soul is an *arche* of embodied action in a fairly straightforward sense. For example, if we seek to explain why humans desire one kind of food and other

> animals desire another, finally the explanation will reduce to a statement of what each is, and this is equivalent to an appeal to the kind of soul each has...Just as intellection is the activity of Intellect, so desire is the activity of Soul.[39]

Universal Soul is eternally desiring and moving toward perfection and self-knowledge. It creates and manifests the Universe as the expression and fulfillment of this goal. At the same time, Universal Soul is both contemplating and being informed by the Universal Intellect—the ground and locus of all knowledge, eternal truth, and the perfective self-knowledge that the Universal Soul desires. This means that the Universal Soul is always acting under the inspiration of the Universal Intellect and contemplating the Universal Intellect, as a result of which the Universal Soul is both the Creator and Designer of the physical Universe, as indicated in the Kalam and Fine-Tuning arguments. Intellect directly and eternally projects necessary truths and intelligible essences (Forms) upon the Universal Soul; the Universal Soul continually receives these intelligibles according to its own capacity and instrumentally projects them into the Universe. This is why things in the Universe are of particular kinds, types, and species and why humans can rationally comprehend the Universe at all. Likewise, all things in the Universe—from nonliving beings to living beings to human beings—are continuously desiring and moving toward perfection based on the Universal Soul's rational quest for self-knowledge and self-actualization. In temporal terms, the Universal Intellect is eternal in essence and eternal in its act; the Universal Soul is eternal in its essence and temporal in its act of manifestation, which is why the Universe is spatio-temporal. The Universal Soul's activity is a spiritual and psychic time, which is then manifested in the Universe as physical time (time as measured by instruments). In summary, the intelligibility of physical things and eternal necessary truths points to and logically necessitates the existence of the Universal Intellect; the Universe's finite temporal duration, its finely-tuned laws of physics, and its goal-directed behavior logically necessitate the Universal Soul. These are the wise arrangements of the Universe that Ismaili philosophers like Nasir Khusraw noted a thousand years ago as well:

> These wise arrangements in the world whose traces we find are the proof that there had been a creator before this world who brought this world into existence and displayed these wise arrangements in it. *When we find the traces of the Universal Soul and Universal Intellect among human beings, who are the upper limit of this world, we may recognize that this world is from the production of the Universal Soul with the inspiration of the Universal Intellect.*[40]

B. Unconditioned Reality as the Originator and Ground of Being

We have thus far seen reasons to postulate a Universal Soul (Creator) to explain the existence and behaviors of the Universe and a Universal Intellect to explain the intelligibility of all things. But this metaphysical model remains incomplete for two reasons. Firstly, the Universal Intellect as the locus of all eternal necessary truths and intelligible essences or natures is internally complex. Any being that is complex has some kind of parts. Universal Intellect may be the least complex of all things but it still has internal parts. Whatever is composed of parts ultimately depends upon those parts to exist and has a cause beyond itself. Therefore, there must be something beyond the Universal Intellect that also grounds its existence. Secondly, the Universal Intellect and Universal Soul account for intelligibility, goal-directedness, and many other features of the Universe and human beings, but what accounts for their existence? A complete metaphysical model must be ontological. That means it must account for *all of existence* and not *only* the existence of certain things. What is needed is a metaphysical model that explains and accounts for *all kinds of existents*—or *existence as such*. The classical argument known as the cosmological argument, which Robert Spitzer and David Bentley Hart have reintroduced as the Argument for Unconditioned Reality, is well suited for this task.[41] This argument shows the logical necessity of one, absolutely simple, unrestricted Unconditioned Reality as the continuous originator and sustainer of *all* conditioned realities. The argument begins with two definitions:

- **A Conditioned Reality** is any reality that is dependent on at least one other reality in order to exist at any moment of its existence. Example: A dog is made up of or dependent upon cells that are themselves composed of molecules, which are conditioned by atoms, which are in turn conditioned by protons and electrons, etc. It is fairly evident that Conditioned Realities of many sorts exist in the Universe (see Figure 3.2).
- **An Unconditioned Reality** is any reality that does not depend on another reality to exist and therefore has no cause for its existence. At this point, we do not know if such an Unconditioned Reality exists, but that is what this proof sets out to demonstrate.

One thing to note is that conditioned realities *depend* upon other realities to exist, not only at the *beginning* of their existence but at *all moments of their existence*. This idea is extremely important and differentiates this argument from the Kalam argument, which bases itself on a Universe with a finite past. For the present argument, it does not matter whether the physical Universe has an infinite past and always existed. What matters is whether such an eternal universe, throughout its temporal existence, is *conditioned*, depends upon other realities to exist or not. The categories of conditioned and unconditioned are *disjunctive*: if a reality is shown to be conditioned, then it cannot be unconditioned. Similar, if a reality is shown *not* to be conditioned, then it must be unconditioned. The argument proceeds as follows:

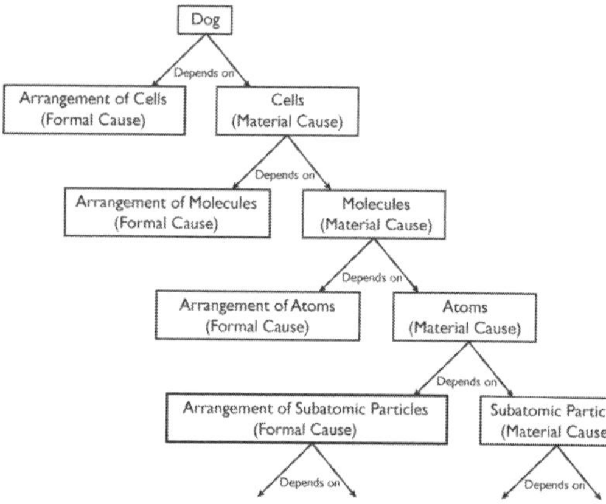

Figure 3.2

Premise 1: *Some* conditioned realities exist. (A dog is made up of or dependent upon cells that are themselves composed of molecules, which depend on other things.)

Premise 2: Disjunction: All of reality *either consists of*:

a) Only conditioned realities

b) At least one unconditioned reality

Premise 3: If only conditioned realities exist, then this can occur in two possible scenarios, either:

a) All of reality only contains a *finite* number of conditioned realities, or

b) All of reality only contains an *infinite* number of conditioned realities.

Premise 4: The scenario in which *'all of reality only contains a finite number of conditioned realities'* is logically impossible and false. This is because the last conditioned reality in the chain of conditions itself depends on another condition to exist. But since there are no more conditioned realities, the last conditioned reality does not exist at all and nor do any of the other conditioned realities in the chain. As a result, nothing exists and nothing can exist at all. But since things clearly *do* exist, this scenario leads to contradiction and is false.

Premise 5: The scenario in which *"all of reality only contains an infinite number of conditioned realities"* is logically impossible and false. This is because each conditioned reality in an infinite linear series depends upon another conditioned reality for its existence ad infinitum. This does not refer to infinite in terms of past time, but infinity in terms of the structure of conditions at every moment a conditioned reality exists. Because each conditioned reality is conditioned by or dependent upon another reality and each conditioned reality can only ground another conditioned reality if its own conditions are fulfilled, no conditioned realities in the structure come to exist in the first place because no reality's conditions are ever fulfilled. An ontological structure consisting of *only* infinite conditioned realities does not and cannot exist—not because infinity is not possible, but because even an infinite series of conditioned realities lack the independent power to exist. But since things clearly *do* exist, this scenario leads to contradiction and is false.

By Disjunction: Since it is *false* that reality consists of conditioned realities only (as above), it logically follows that there must be at least one Unconditioned Reality in all of reality.

Therefore: This Unconditioned Reality, by definition, must be absolutely simple (without spatio-temporal or metaphysical parts or boundaries of any kind). This is because if Unconditioned Reality had any parts, it would depend upon those parts, be caused by those parts and would actually be a conditioned reality.

Therefore: By virtue of being simple, an Unconditioned Reality is unrestricted and without limits or boundaries of any kind.

Therefore: There can only be one single and unique Unconditioned Reality.

This is because: if there were two or more Unconditioned Realities, then each of these realities must differ from one another in one respect. This would mean that each of these two or more Unconditioned Realities possesses one unique property that the others do not have and possesses one common property shared with the others. This entails that each Unconditioned Reality is made of up of at least two parts—unique property plus common property. But any reality made of parts is *conditioned* and cannot be Unconditioned.

Therefore: All realities besides the one single Unconditioned Reality are conditioned realities—whose existence depends on other realities.

Therefore: The one unique unrestricted Unconditioned Reality existentiates or sustains all conditioned realities at every moment they exist and not simply at the beginning of time.

This one, single, unique, unrestricted and unlimited Unconditioned Reality is the continuous ground and originator of any and all things that exist or could exist. Therefore, all existents—whether physical or metaphysical—continuously depend upon the Unconditioned Reality for their existence.

Unconditioned Reality, due to its absolute simplicity, is beyond space, time, change, matter, energy, and intelligible truths—since all of these entail some sort of complexity. Spatial realities are complex—possessing spatial coordinates; temporal realities are composed of present states and potential future states—another form of complexity; even intelligible realities like mathematical truths partake in complexity, including the Universal Intellect itself. The simplicity of Unconditioned Reality also means that it is completely unbounded, unrestricted, and infinite. The one, single, unique and unrestricted Unconditioned Reality is what classical theists and Neoplatonic philosophers call 'God' or 'the One.' The living hereditary Imam of the Ismaili Muslims, Imam Shah Karim al-Husayni Aga Khan IV, refers to God *qua* Unconditioned Reality as "He who is above all else," a term which the Ismaili thinker Aziz Esmail explains as follows:

> *This Ultimate Reality is often conceived as 'transcendent', or described as '**He who is above all else**'*—not because it is a reality spatially above the human habitat, but because it is above, i.e. goes beyond or transcends, all human categories. *Being free from and prior to the dichotomy between subject and object,* it is therefore also outside the frame of human discourse.[42]

It must be recognized that this concept of God as the Unconditioned Reality that continuously sustains all existence is different from modern monotheism, deism, and pantheism. In this model, Unconditioned Reality transcends time, space, and change due to its absolute simplicity. God transcends all attributes—whether personal, impersonal, or transpersonal. This is unlike modern monotheism where God is conceived as an immaterial 'person' who exists wholly 'outside' the Universe and intervenes in time and history. It is also different from deism where God creates the Universe as a self-subsistent reality and is no longer involved with it. This model is also different from pantheism which simply affirms the existence of the natural physical Universe without any transcendent dimension. God *qua* Unconditioned Reality is beyond all personal and ontological attributes and categories, such as cause/effect, substance/accident, rationality/irrationality, personal/impersonal, and existence/essence. In this model, God's creative act is not one of 'intervening' or 'designing' or 'constructing' physical things directly. The term 'creation' in classical theism refers to the eternal Act (symbolically called God's Will or Thought) by which God continuously originates and sustains all things in existence—including the Universal Intellect and Universal Soul.

> The creation according to Islam is not a unique act in a given time but a perpetual and constant event; and God supports and sustains all existence at every moment by His will and His thought. Outside His will, outside His thought, all is nothing, even the things which seem to us absolutely self-evident such as space and time. Allah alone wishes: the Universe exists; and all manifestations are as a witness of the Divine will. I think that I have sufficiently explained the difference between the Islamic doctrine of the unity of God and, on one side, the theistic ideas, founded upon the Old Testament, and on the other, the pantheistic and dualistic ideas of the Indian religion and that of Zoroaster.[43]
> (Imam Sultan Muhammad Shah Aga Khan III)

The Unconditioned Reality is eternally originating and sustaining *all existents* in all of reality. Even existents that are eternal (beyond time) and everlasting (infinite in temporal duration) such as the Universal Intellect, Universal Soul, and human souls are eternally *conditioned* and dependent upon Unconditioned Reality in their existence. Thus, God *qua* Unconditioned Reality is identical with neither the Universal

Intellect nor the Universal Soul. This is because Unconditioned Reality is absolutely simple, absolutely without any parts, boundaries, or complexity. As it will be recalled, the Universal Intellect—despite being one being—is internally complex because it is the host of all eternal necessary truths which are themselves multiple. The Universal Intellect is the *formal* cause of everything that exists—grounding intelligibility, forms, and essences. The Ismaili philosopher al-Sijistani defined the Universal Intellect as "the thingness of all things" and the all-encompassing substance. God *qua* Unconditioned Reality, due to its sheer simplicity, is not the *formal* cause of all things *qua* things, but rather, the *efficient* cause of all things *qua* existents. Thus, Unconditioned Reality transcends the Intellect and eternally sustains the Intellect in its existence. Universal Intellect is therefore the closest being to Unconditioned Reality as the least complex of all beings. Universal Intellect is the 'first conditioned reality' and the direct object of Unconditioned Reality's creative act, followed by the Universal Soul which is the 'second conditioned reality.' Universal Intellect is the conjunction of the eternal creative act of Unconditioned Reality and the intelligible

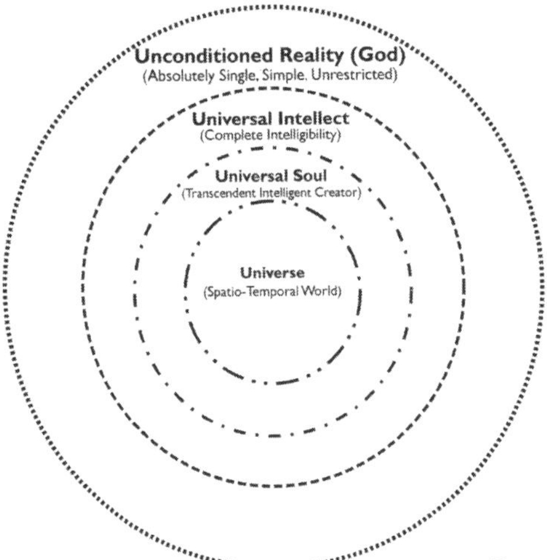

Figure 3.3

essences of all things. From a theological perspective, all the transpersonal attributes traditionally ascribed to God, such as life, knowledge, power, will, sustenance, world-creation, intelligence, consciousness, compassion, mercy, generosity, wisdom, majesty, beauty, etc., really belong to the Universal Intellect and Universal Soul.

Unconditioned Reality grounds the *existence* of all things; Universal Intellect mediates existence and grounds *intelligibility* of all things; Universal Soul mediates existence and intelligibility, creates the Universe as its self-projection, and thereby grounds all *goal-directed activity* of all natural things. The Prime Matter (akin to a mirror upon which the Universal Soul projects itself) that emanates from the Soul, receives existence, intelligibility, and goal-directness and *grounds* materiality. The rays and projections of the Universal Soul are various levels of soul, manifest in the Universe as subatomic particles, atoms, molecules, etc. in a gradual chain up to human beings and serve as secondary causes mediating the acts of God, the Universal Intellect, and Universal Soul. In this way, we have identified the four Aristotelian causes of the Universe: Unconditioned Reality is the efficient cause, Universal Intellect is the formal cause, Universal Soul is the final cause, and Prime Matter is the material cause. The Ismaili philosopher Nasir Khusraw summarizes this schema as follows:

> *For this reason we say that the Universe and its Creator must both be under the first effect, the Universal Intellect,* because the Universal Soul, which is the Creator of the physical world, has a position below that of the Universal Intellect. The Universal Soul is in fact the Creator of the Universe and the Universe is its creation.[44]

Conclusion: The Quest for Human Perfection

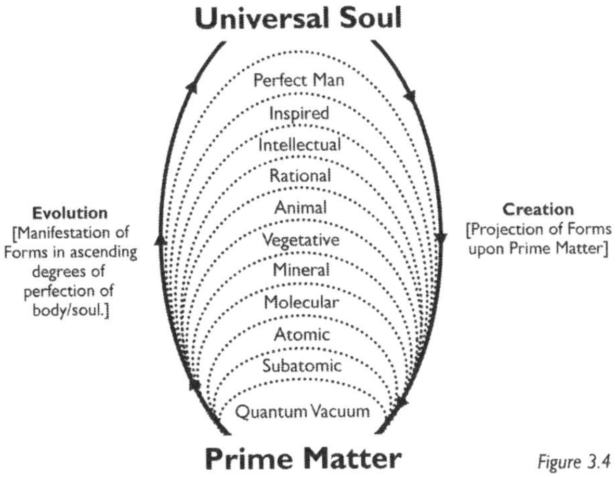

Figure 3.4

> Once man has thus comprehended the essence of existence, there remains for him the duty, since he knows the absolute value of his own soul, of making for himself a direct path which will constantly lead his individual soul to and bind it with the Universal Soul of which the Universe—as much of it as we perceive with our limited visions—is one of the infinite manifestations.[45]
> (Imam Sultan Muhammad Shah Aga Khan III)

If the reader accepts the Ismaili Muslim Neoplatonic metaphysic offered and argued for in this chapter, then a number of practical truths emerge from this worldview. The most central of these is that human beings—like all inorganic and organic beings in the Universe—exist to achieve perfection. This would be a kind of perfection that is appropriate and unique to human consciousness and constitution. Human beings as rational animals possess intellect, soul, and body—unlike inorganic and nonhuman forms of life. Human perfection entails a fulfillment and actualization of the human rational soul in both its theoretical and practical dimensions. This entails perfecting one's thinking and one's action—knowledge and virtue. Today there are numerous claims about *what* human perfection exactly is and *how* to attain it. But if the Universal Soul has really created the Universe and all beings within it to attain perfection, as the means for it to attain its own perfection, self-actualization, and self-knowledge, then the *actualized form* of this perfection must already exist in the Universe.

The Universal Soul's existence transcends space and linear time, so it is not a question of the Universal Soul attaining perfection at some future date or time. The Universal Soul eternally moves toward perfection—so that perfection is already actual at a higher level of being, represented by the Universal Intellect. This manifests within the Universe: for inorganic and organic beings, perfection is actualized when they fulfill a particular disposition, reproduce, or flourish. Such must be the case for humans: perfect humanity must be potentially achievable for all human beings and already actualized in some perfect human beings. Those who are seeking perfection are best off seeking the guidance and instruction of an already perfect and fully actualized human. The existence of these perfect human beings is a logical necessity—for without their presence, the rest of humanity would have no means or recourse to acquire perfection. These perfected human beings, who provide guidance for the seekers, are the great Messengers of God, Prophets, saints, sages, and teachers who have appeared in the world since the dawn of humankind and from whose legacy the world's great religions and spiritual traditions stem. Such a perfect person and infallible teacher must still be present today and always, to bring others to perfection. For Shia Ismaili Muslims, this perfect human being and infallible teacher is the hereditary Imam directly descended, through an unbroken line of forty-nine generations, from Prophet Muhammad, the final Messenger of God.

Similarly, the action of the Universal Soul is of two kinds: One is perfect potentially but imperfect in realization, as in the case of the creation of the world which is potentially perfect, but only (gradually) comes into existence. It is like humanity: individual men are born (and die) while mankind is spread all over the world, and the whole purpose of the world is in humanity. Therefore, the action of the Universal Soul in this world is only potentially perfect, before its final realization. But in some other actions, the Universal Soul is perfect both potentially and actually, as in the case of the production of the souls of the Prophets, Successors, and Imams, who are the true human beings by the nature of their souls.[46]
(Nasir Khusraw)

[F]or thousands of years before the advent of [the prophet] Muhammad, there arose from time to time messengers, illumined by Divine Grace, for and among those races of the earth which had sufficiently advanced intellectually to comprehend such a message. Thus Abraham, Moses, Jesus and all the Prophets of Israel are universally accepted by Islam. Muslims indeed know no limitation merely to the Prophets of Israel; they are ready to admit that there were similar Divinely inspired messengers in other countries—Gautama Buddha, Shri Krishna and Shri Ram in India, Socrates in Greece, the wise men of China, and many other sages and saints among peoples and civilizations, trace of which we have lost. Thus man's soul has never been left without a specially inspired messenger from the Soul that sustains, embraces and is the Universe.[47]
(Imam Sultan Muhammad Shah Aga Khan III)

Notes

1 Imam Sultan Muhammad Shah Aga Khan III, "Islam: The Religion of My Ancestors," *Memoirs of the Aga Khan: World Enough and Time*

(Simon & Schuster, 1954), http://www.nanowisdoms.org/nwblog/1225/.

2 We hope our readers will not equate the word 'God' with how certain modern Christian apologists define God. 'God' here means absolutely simple, unconditioned Reality and *not* a 'person,' 'personal consciousness,' as some modern theologians hold. We are just as averse to an eternal 'personalist God' as Pandeists are.

3 Our presentation about Pandeism is drawn from two articles: Knujon Mapson, "Why Pandeism Is Better Than Theism," http://www. koilas.org/why-pandeism-is-better-than-theism-an-essay.html, and Knujon Mapson, "What Is Pandeism?" http://www. pandeismanthology.com/#!about-pandeism/cjg9.

4 Robert J. Spitzer, *New Proofs for the Existence of God* (Eerdmans, 2010), hereafter cited as *New Proofs*.

5 See William Lane Craig, *The Kalam Cosmological Argument* (Wipf and Stock, 2000); David S. Oderberg, "Traversal of the Infinite, the 'Big Bang' and the Kalam Cosmological Argument," *Philosophia Christi*, vol. 4 (2002): pp. 305–34; Spitzer, *New Proofs*.

6 Ya'qub b. Ishaq al-Kindi, tr. Alfred L. Ivry, *A Translation of Ya'qub ibn Ishaq al-Kindi's Treatise 'On First Philosophy'* (SUNY Press, 1974), p. 74.

7 David Hilbert, "On the Infinite," quoted in Spitzer, *New Proofs*, pp. 201–2.

8 For references of the scientific data for the standard Big Bang Model, see Spitzer, *New Proofs*, pp. 24–6.

9 For references regarding the entropy of the Universe, see Spitzer, *New Proofs*, pp. 27–9.

10 For scientific references for this calculation, see Spitzer, *New Proofs*, pp. 28–9.

11 For a layperson's explanation of the BVG theorem, see Spitzer, *New Proofs*, pp. 33–4. The original paper giving the BVG theorem is A. Borde, A. Guth and A. Vilenkin, "Inflationary space-times are not past-complete," *Phys. Rev.* Lett. 90 151301 (2003), http://arxiv.org/abs/gr-qc/0110012. In a later paper, Mithani and Vilenkin showed that all current "infinite past universe" models actually

entailed a universe with a beginning; see A. Mithani, A. Vilenkin, "Did the Universe Have a Beginning?' *Physical Review D: Particles and Fields* 46(6) (April 2012), http://arxiv.org/ abs/1204.4658.

12 Alexander Vilenkin, *Many Worlds in One: The Search for Other Universes* (Macmillan, 2007), p. 176.

13 Stephen Mumford, Rani Lill Anjum, *Getting Causes from Powers* (Oxford University Press, 2011), p. 237.

14 The values of each constant listed here and a dozen other finely-tuned constants are discussed and calculated in Spitzer, *New Proofs*, pp. 57–67, 76–7.

15 Spitzer shows that all multiverse models are insufficient in increasing the probabilities of the finely-tuned constants of physics to allow for them to occur by sheer chance. See Spitzer, *New Proofs*, pp. 67–73.

16 Paul Davies, *God and the New Physics* (Simon and Schuster, 1983), p. 189.

17 Fred Hoyle, "The Universe: Past and Present Reflections," *Engineering and Science* (November 1981), pp. 8–12.

18 Robert Jastrow, *God and the Astronomers* (W. W. Norton, 1978), p. 116.

19 See Knujon Mapson's thesis about Pandeism as we summarized in the introduction to this chapter.

20 Nasir Khusraw, *Six Chapters or Shish Fasl*, tr. Ivanow (E. J. Brill for the Ismaili Society, 1949), pp. 55–7. Hereafter cited as *Six Chapters*. I have modified and retranslated some parts of Ivanow's translations quoted in this chapter.

21 Imam Sultan Muhammad Shah Aga Khan III, "Islam: The Religion of My Ancestors," *Memoirs of the Aga Khan: World Enough and Time*, http:// www.nanowisdoms.org/nwblog/1225/.

22 Khusraw, *Six Chapters*, p. 49.

23 David S. Oderberg, "Being and Goodness," *American Philosophical Quarterly* 51 (2014), pp. 345–56, 345.

24 David S. Oderberg, "Teleology: Inorganic and Organic," in A. M. González (ed.), *Contemporary Perspectives on Natural Law* (Ashgate,

2008), pp. 259–79, 261.

25 David S. Oderberg, "Being and Goodness," *American Philosophical Quarterly* 51 (2014), pp. 345–56, 346.

26 Oderberg, "Being and Goodness," pp. 345–56, 346.

27 David S. Oderberg, "Teleology: Inorganic and Organic," in A.M. González (ed.), *Contemporary Perspectives on Natural Law* (Ashgate, 2008), pp. 259–79, 271.

28 Edward Feser, *Aquinas: A Beginner's Guide* (Oneworld, 2009), Kindle Edition, Chapter 3.

29 David S. Oderberg, *Real Essentialism* (Routledge, 2007), p. 199.

30 Albert Einstein, *Einstein and the Generations of Science* (Transaction Publishers, 1982), p. xviii.

31 Feser, *Aquinas*, Chapter 3.

32 William E. Mann, *God, Modality and Morality* (Oxford University Press, 2015), p. 106.

33 Lloyd P. Gerson, "Neoplatonism," in *The Blackwell Guide to Ancient Philosophy*, ed. Christopher Shields (John Wiley and Sons, 2008), pp. 310–11.

34 Lloyd P. Gerson, *Plotinus* (Routledge, 2012), pp. 40–1.

35 David Bentley Hart, *The Experience of God* (Yale University Press, 2013), Kindle Edition, Chapter 4.

36 Alice C. Hunsberger, *Nasir Khusraw: The Ruby of Badakhshan* (I. B. Tauris in association with The Institute of Ismaili Studies, 2000), p. 159.

37 Imam Shah Karim al-Husayni Aga Khan IV, Aga Khan University Inauguration Ceremony, Karachi, 11 November 1985: http://www.amaana.org/speeches/speechaku1985.htm.

38 Oderberg, *Real Essentialism*, p. 144.

39 Gerson, *Plotinus*, p. 53.

40 Nasir Khusraw, *Six Chapters*, Persian text, p. 44. My own translation.

41 Our presentation of the argument below relies on Spitzer, *New Proofs*, pp. 105–43. Our illustrations are based on his illustrations and all credit for the ideas here goes to Spitzer. See also Hart, *The Experience of God*, Chapter 2.

42 Aziz Esmail, "Reason and Religion: The Old Argument Revisited," *Ilm* 7(3) (Dec. 1981–Feb. 1982), pp. 32–40.

43 Imam Sultan Muhammad Shah Aga Khan III, "Islam: The Religion of My Ancestors," *Memoirs of the Aga Khan: World Enough and Time*: http:// www.nanowisdoms.org/nwblog/1225/.

44 Nasir Khusraw, *Six Chapters*, Persian text, p. 5. My own translation.

45 Imam Sultan Muhammad Shah Aga Khan III, "Islam: The Religion of My Ancestors," *Memoirs of the Aga Khan: World Enough and Time*, http:// www.nanowisdoms.org/nwblog/1225/.

46 Nasir Khusraw, *Six Chapters*, tr. Ivanow, p. 52; translation adjusted.

47 Imam Sultan Muhammad Shah Aga Khan III, "Islam: The Religion of My Ancestors," *Memoirs of the Aga Khan: World Enough and Time*, http://www.nanowisdoms.org/nwblog/1225/.

Omnientheism: God According to Biblical Universalist Unitarianism

Orlando Alcántara Fernández

Alcántara Fernández, often writing under the name 'Cristorly,' was a Dominican metaphysical poet, author, and teacher born 1 August 1962 in Santo Domingo, Dominican Republic. A champion chess player, in 2003 Alcántara wrote the book Move by Move Method, *on the analytical, synthetic and critical thinking methods in chess. He was a journalist for* El Guardián, *a monthly San Cristóbal newspaper, as well as for many other publications. He passed away on 18 September 2011.*

1. Biblical Universalist Unitarianism

For the Unitarian, God is one, not three in one.[1] Thus the Father is God and has His own Name, which is the Tetragrammaton or YHWH. Although the pronunciation of the Name has been lost, we can agree in pronouncing the sacred name as Yahweh. In Unitarianism, Jesus Christ is not God, but rather the Son of God, as the same Jesus Christ is time and time again declared in the New Testament. But Jesus Christ is not a simple angel. No. Jesus Christ is the Logos, the Verb, the Logos of God. This means that in his heavenly pre-existence Jesus Christ was a spirit. Jesus Christ is the created being with the most similarity to God. The Holy Spirit is as well the Holy Spirit of God.

The Holy Spirit is to the Father the same thing as the spirit of Man is to Man. For that reason He is the Holy Spirit of God. God is Spirit,[2] and this Spirit is the Holy Spirit of God. Unitarianism is clear in its simple, pure vision and without complications on the Being of God. Here there are neither mysteries nor theological subterfuges that are apt for the few; not even fireworks are here. God is one. As simple as the number 1. For the Universalist, salvation is universal, that is to say, it includes all the created beings, in addition to all the human beings. Discipline or remedial punishment exists, and it brings as a consequence the different degrees or levels of glory when God restores Paradise in all the Universe.

The key Biblical verses to understand Universalism are: Titus 2:11; Romans 5:18; 2 Corinthians 5:19; Ephesians 1:9–11; Romans 11:32–36; 1 Timothy 2:4–6; 4:10; Colossians 1:20; John 12:32; 17:2; Galatians 3:8; and 1 Corinthians 15:20–28. The last verses of the Bible are not in Revelation, but, more exactly, they are in 1 Corinthians 15:20–28, which are the verses of the Great Consummation in which God will be *"all in all."*

The Universalist Unitarianism is Biblical when it accepts the Bible as the Word of God, and it is governed by its divine principles. Thus we see that in Biblical Universalist Unitarianism worship is corporate as is the worship in the New Testament. The term 'church' is not 100 percent exact, but corporate worship is the objective of the 'house churches' or 'home churches.' There are three Gospels:[3] the Gospel of the Jews, the Gospel of the Gentiles, and the Eonic Gospel.

The word 'eon' is equivalent to *olam* for Hebrew and *aion* for Greek, and it means age, period of time with beginning and ending. Mainly the word *aion* is badly translated in a remarkable way, and due to this bad translation a good part of the New Testament is not understood. According to our correct vision of the Gospel of the Jews and the Gospel of the Gentiles we can see that instead of using the term 'churches' we can very well speak of 'the Bride of the Lamb' (Jewish), and 'the Body of Christ' (Gentiles).

The correct Unitarian concept is extensively presented by the Jehovah's Witnesses and the Students of the Bible, and it can be studied thoroughly in their writings. It is good to clarify that the original Students of the Bible, based solely on the teachings of Charles Taze Russell, still exist as a group different from the Jehovah's Witnesses and the Watchtower Society.[4]

2. Point, Sign, and Monad

The point is the geometric unit of the Universe in the same way that the sign is the linguistic unit, and the monad is the biological unit. The monad concept is extensively used by the German philosopher Leibniz. For Leibniz the monad has an entrance, but it does not have an exit. That is to say, it has a door, but it does not have a window. The correct monad, however, has an entrance and an exit, has a door and a window. The point as well as the sign and the monad are interrelated with each other.

Communication is universal. All the points communicate with each other. All the signs communicate with each other like all the monads do. There is unity in the entire Universe, as it is logical to suppose. The 'Aleph' of the Argentine writer Jorge Luis Borges is a point that contains all the points of the Universe. That Aleph is any point, any sign, or any monad observed by an all-seeing eye. The vision of Leibniz on the gradation that exists between the inert matter and the superior beings is valid. At the last instance, everything is soul, but with different levels or degrees of glory.

3. Monism, Dualism and Trinitarianism

Monism is the correct position. This cosmovision postulates that everything is one. Dualism only sees action and reaction, cause and effect, but it does not see the third term that is continuity, permanence. Continuity is a concept used by the 'father of semiotics' C. S. Peirce. Trinitarianism conceives reality in three terms that are one. Thus Father, Son, and Holy Spirit are three persons, and the three persons are one person, who is God. Each person is independent in Trinitarianism, and the three are inter-dependent. However, Monism speaks of a single person, who is God the Father.

Monism sees cause and effect as well as continuity as three elements of one fact only. It does not see them as three isolated elements, but as a unit, as a unique all. Everything has as an origin, the First Cause, which is God. In Monism ignorance is the true cause of evil that in the end produces sin. Adam and Eve ate of the Tree of the Knowledge of Good and Evil, not of the Tree of Good and Evil. Lack of knowledge is ignorance. God created the Devil with a clear mission in mind.[5] In the end, the entire Universe will be reconciled with Its Creator.[6] Everything will return to be One.[7] Ignorance will end, and Good will reign.

Trinitarianism implies a subtle form of Dualism that Monism does not conceive as valid. God and the Universe are different realities, but,when God carries out the Reconciliation at the end of times, God and the Universe will be One. The entire Universe will be recovered. The entire Universe will be integrated in the intimate Being of God. At the present time there is a Dualism between God and the Universe, but it will not be forever. This Dualism causes evil in created beings out of ignorance. Monism is the absolute Unity that God will carry out at the end of times in Christ Jesus through His Holy Spirit. As far as the substance or essence of God, it is not the same as that of the Universe, and in that sense there is a Dualism in the present state of reality.

When God carries out the Reconciliation of the Universe, then this Dualism or separation will be broken, and there will be a perfect unity or integration between the substance or essence of God and that of the Universe. It will be a dynamic, nonstatic unity. We have to see this subject from a dynamic point of view. Benedict Spinoza (Pantheism), as with Karl Christian Friedrich Krause (Panentheism), has a static vision of God and the Universe. We can say the same of the Theism of Thomas Aquinas.

When we see everything in movement in a dynamic way, then we are speaking of Omnientheism, which is the correct term as we will see below. We discarded the term 'Omnitheism' because people use it with another distorted sense on the Internet, with a very confused vision of the divine reality. They try to be ecumenical, but they do not accomplish this, because their theognostic system is not valid.

4. Greek and Latin: Person and Energy

The terms Theism, Pantheism, and Panentheism have their root in Greek, which is a Biblical language, and therefore it is correct. In a discretionary way we assume that these terms present the idea of a personal, individual God. However, the terms Deism, Pandeism, and Panendeism have their root in Latin, which is not a Biblical language, and therefore it is not correct. These terms present the idea of God as synonymous with Energy or Cosmic Force, because God is not personal here, He is not individual.

Many Orientalist, Buddhist, Hindu, Gnostic views and those of the New Age maintain this incorrect view of God, and for that reason they speak a lot about Energy or Cosmic Force instead of God. In some cases, they use the term 'Cosmic Christ' to hide their impersonal vision of God, but it continues being a form of Deism, Pandeism or Panendeism, although more sophisticated and refined by means of the use of Biblical reference badly assimilated, badly interpreted, which results in a subtle mystification or distorted idealization of the figure of Jesus Christ.

5. Idea and Matter + Space and Time + Light and Movement: Energy

God created the Universe out of Nothing, and we must take this into account so that we do not confuse God with the Universe. In order to overcome all Dualism it is pertinent to assume a Monist position on the Universe formed by three dualities that we can call idea-matter, space-time, and light-movement. This epistemic conception does not see any essential difference between idea and matter, between space and time, and between light and movement. The three dualities are a single reality or manifestation or epiphany in a Universe which at the end of all accounts rests in the number 1, according to Pythagoras. Everything is fullness in the number 1. Thus we see that the Universe is the extension, representation, manifestation, and revelation of the only and living God.

The number 1 is plentiful in the Whole. Thus, Newton's Classic or Mechanical Physics unites with Einstein's Theory of Relativity and modern Quantum Physics, which would result in the postmodern British astrophysicist Stephen Hawking's Theory of All. The unity of the Universe is validated in Monism. Idea coexists with matter in the same way as space coexists with time in perfect harmony, and light does the same with movement. Thus we arrive at the concept of Energy that would be the sum total of these three monadological dualities. The formula of Energy would be the following in this Monist Universe:

Energy = idea-matter + space-time + light-movement

6. Archetype, Prototype, Logotype, and Type

The archetype is the oldest model of the Universe that pre-exists in the mind of God before creating the Universe. The prototype is the first model or first creation of God, which is Jesus Christ, the only begotten Son of God, the firstborn of Creation.[8] Logotype, which discretionarily we define as a unique and differentiated variant of the prototype, is Adam and Eve in the plane of Humankind. The types are the models that arise from the logotypes. In this case the type is all of Humankind originating from Adam and Eve. Thus, predestination will in the last instance make each human being a similar being to Jesus Christ.

An unprejudiced, simple reading of Romans 8:29, without additions, greatly clarifies the predestination concept. So a careful reading of Ephesians 1:9–11 also throws a lot of light on the concept of predestination in the context of Universal Reconciliation. All this indicates to us that before a 'table' existed, the archetype 'table' existed in the mind of God. The following step for God was to create the first 'table,' which is the prototype, and soon all the other variants or differentiated entities from all of the classes of 'possible tables' are logotypes or varieties of the prototype 'table.' All the 'tables' that arise from each logotype are types of 'tables,' that is, copies or repetitive models of the 'logotypical tables.'

Actually and from the human point of view, we can say that the first person who conceived the idea of a 'table' had in his or her mind the archetype of the 'table.' Then he or she created the prototype, which would result in the first 'table' on the face of Earth. But there are very many classes of 'tables,' which are the variant logotypes or all the possible models. For example, there are tables of one leg, two legs, three legs, four legs, etc. For example, there are tables of wood, iron, different metals, and different general characteristics. The copies of each one of these 'logotypical tables' would be the types or copies of 'tables.'

7. Body, Spirit, and Soul

Many erroneous ideas on the concepts of body, spirit, and soul exist. In Genesis 2:7 everything is clear. The body is the matter that the human being is composed of, the spirit is the 'blowing' of life, and the union of the body and the spirit is the soul. The soul is the totality of the being. The soul is mortal, ceases to exist, as Ezekiel 18:4 postulates very well. In the Concordant Bible,[9] the verse of 1 Thessalonians 5:23 gives the correct idea on the relation between the body, the spirit, and the soul, different from other more popular versions that give the erroneous idea that the human being is the sum total of the body, the spirit, and the soul. A lot of ignorance exists on this subject, but everything is clarified when we assume a Universalist position based on the Universal Restoration or Universal Reconciliation, and all souls are immortal thanks to the mercy of God in Jesus Christ.

The correct vision on body, spirit, and soul can be studied more thoroughly in writings of the Jehovah's Witnesses although the Witnesses are annihilationists, that is to say, they do not believe in Universal Salvation, but, in another sense, they believe in the final destruction of all the wicked. In addition, the view of the Witnesses on the body, the spirit, and the soul does not include all its phenomena like dreams, astral journeys, and paranormal phenomena. This is necessary to take into account when reading writings of the Witnesses or the Adventists. The body is a type of highly subtle matter, and in its interaction with the spirit—which comes from God—it has the faculties of having a dream, and of making astral journeys which are not studied thoroughly by some Christians with sectarian religious tendencies.

8. Deism, Pandeism, and Panendeism

Three key concepts guide us with all certainty when defining the terms of Deism, Pandeism, Panendeism, Theism, Pantheism, and Panentheism (Omnientheism). These concepts are the transcendence, immanence, and holism of God. When we say that God is transcendent, we mean that God is not the Universe, that His Being extends beyond the borders of Creation. Thus we see that God creates Evil, but God does not sin.[10] God is three times holy. Thus we see that God has His own Being, intimate, different, and separated in an absolute way from the Creation, the Universe, or His creatures. This is the substance or essence of God.

When we say that God is immanent, we mean that God is present in all of Creation as First Cause and Ultimate Cause in the same way that a poet lives in each verse of one of his poems. That is to say, immanence implies a principle of permanence, continuity, and inseparability of God in Creation. A principle of indissoluble interaction, eternal communication between God and His creatures, from inert matter to the angels and the human beings.

When we say that God is holistic, we mean that God is Everything, that is, the sum total of His transcendence and His immanence. Thus we are speaking of an absolute Monism, very different from the Dualism that many imagine with respect to God and the Universe. This absolute Monism is not a present

Monism. It is a potential Monism, because in the present state of the empire of Evil in this Universe, Monism is relative. When Evil no longer exists in Creation, that is to say, when Universal Restoration of the lost Paradise takes place, when that Paradise is recovered, then there will be an absolute Monism in which God will be "all in all."[10] This is a dynamic vision that helps us to surpass Dualism in a convincing way. Assuming these definitions of transcendence, immanence, and holism, we can say that Energy or Cosmic Force in Deism is transcendent, but is neither immanent nor holistic. Thus we see that Energy or Cosmic Force in Pandeism is immanent and holistic, but it is not transcendent. However, Energy or Cosmic Force in Panendeism is immanent, transcendent, and holistic. But because in any class of Deism all this is spoken of God as if He were an Energy, not a Person, we see that all Deisms are incorrect.

9. Theism, Pantheism, and Panentheism (Omnientheism)

God, a personal and only God, in Theism is transcendent, but He is neither immanent nor holistic. Thus we see that God in Pantheism is immanent and holistic, but He is not transcendent. However, God in Panentheism is immanent, transcendent, and holistic. In other writings I have used the term 'Pantheism' inexactly, confusing it with the term 'Panentheism.' Now I will explain these, because at the time of those writings I did not have the knowledge of the term Panentheism. When differentiating between Pantheism and Panentheism, we see that the correct vision is Panentheism, which we can define discretionarily as Omnientheism to differentiate it from Krause's Panentheism, which can surpass neither Dualism nor Pantheism at a full extent.

Using the term 'Omnientheism' as discretionally synonymous with the correct term of Panentheism, we can grasp the correct cosmovision, the exact theognosis that clarifies to us many other truths about God and the Universe. In Omnientheism, God is transcendent, immanent and holistic, and thus we surpass Pantheism and Dualism in the last instance, because Omnientheism is a dynamic vision, in movement, of God in His interaction with the Universe. In the end God will be all in all.[12] And the term 'Omni' comes from Latin, which is appropriate to speak of the Creatures of God or the Universe, because it is better to use the Greek for God exclusively. There it is, Omnientheism here and now, which is Unitarian and Universalist at the same time.

This presents itself surprisingly in art. This can be found in my writings reviewing musician, painter, sketch artist, photographer, and metapoet Orlando Cordero, a dynamo of the idea in movement, who recreated palimpsests of othernesses, being oneness in the metapoietic rootedness:

> His talent is evident, but his vision is Pandeist, and it had to be Pantheist. In order to get a Pantheist painting, it is necessary to have Christ as pennant, footpath, and lighthouse. Pandeism is impersonal like in the present canvas, in which man, nature and word integrate themselves; whereas Pantheism is a personal Christlike experience of every day.[13]

10. God: Yahweh of the Hosts

Evil is not eternal. Evil has the purpose of knowing Good, of making us similar to God, knowing the difference between Good and Evil. That is to say, Evil is not an end in itself. However, Good is really an end in itself. All this implies that free will does not exist, that would be complete freedom independent from the operation of God. What does exist is free arbitrary agency, that is, freedom of action for the aim that we were created. A stone has freedom to behave like a stone in the same way that a human being has freedom to behave as a human being, knowing Good and Evil, separating himself from Evil and seeking Good as an end in itself. Here it is pertinent to speak of the eudemonics of

God, that is, the quest for the wellbeing and the happiness of all the beings created by Him. The true God is therefore a eudemonic God, a God of true unconditional love.

The only, true and living God has the sacred name of Yahweh (YHWH), and we can very well call Him 'Yahweh of the Hosts.' He is the God which we must adore in spirit and in truth.[14] At the end of times, God will restore His Kingdom in the entire Universe and there will be neither Death nor Evil.[15] Universal Salvation is a faithful sample of the eudemonics of God. His unconditional love[16] is a real, practical love, truly pragmatic when we see that before restoring Good in all of Creation He makes us know Evil, to eliminate it in the last instance, and thus God will be "all in all" thanks to the expiatory sacrifice of Jesus Christ in the Golgothic Cross of Calvary.[17]

I close with the Poetic "Our Father":

Our Father Which art in the Bible,
Hallowed be Your Archetype-Word-Christ!
Thy prototype-Logos-Jesus come soon.
Thy will be done, as in the stanza,
So in the verse.
Give us this day our daily poem.
And forgive us our bad sonnets,
As we forgive the bad poets.
And lead us not into the pagan movements,
And deliver us from the satanic poets;
For thine is the Universe, and Poetry, and the Glory,
For rhythm, for free verse, and for metrics. Amen.

Notes

1 In order to understand Biblical Universalist Unitarianism, the theological works of A. E. Knoch, and his Concordant Bible, as well as the writings of A. P. Adams and Adlai Loudy, among many others, are helpful. In order to understand corporative worship, the

writings of Frank Viola in Present Testimony Ministry are very valuable thanks to their rigorous, systematic and exhaustive sense around the 'house churches' or 'home churches.' Frank Viola is a disciple of the recognized Christian leader Gene Edwards, author of *The Divine Romance*, one of the most influential books of Christianity in the twentieth century.

2 John 4:24.

3 Galatians 2:7; and Revelation 14:6–7.

4 There are several Internet groups of the Students of the Bible, and many websites like http://www.biblestudents.com and http://www.biblestudents.org contribute information on this Unitarian group. This is not Universalist, because they believe in the destruction of the wicked, as the Jehovah's Witnesses and the Adventists believe.

5 Isaiah 45:7; Amos 3:6; Proverbs 16:33.

6 Colossians 1:20.

7 1 Corinthians 15:28.

8 John 1:14; Revelation 3:14; and Colossians 1:15.

9 New Concordant Literal Testament.

10 Isaiah 45:7; Amos 3:6; and Proverbs 16:33.

11 1 Corinthians 15:20–28.

12 1 Corinthians 15:28.

13 "Orlando Cordero: Painting as Artifice of the Meta-Poetic Pictograph," *Meta-Pintores Uno*, 3 May 2005.

14 John 4:24.

15 Revelation 21:1–4.

16 1 John 4:8.

17 2 Corinthians 5:16–21; 2 Corinthians 15:28; and Romans 11:36.

Axioms of Reality—Concluded

William Walker Atkinson

For the last thirty years of his life, Atkinson (1862–1932) was an occultist intensely involved in the New Thought movement, a nineteenth-century American philosophical movement which proposed that the intelligence of God was the totality of reality, and which originated the Law of Attraction. It is estimated that Atkinson wrote 100 books in this time—a number made difficult to pin down by his extensive publication under pseudonyms such as Theron Q. Dumont, Yogi Ramacharaka, Swami Bhakta Vishita, and Magus Incognito. Interestingly, Atkinson throughout this time practiced as a successful attorney. This excerpt of Atkinson's 1911 book The Mastery of Being, *pp. 50–9, has passed into the public domain. Though Atkinson never refers to 'Pandeism' specifically, it is clearly this theory which he addresses when he writes of "certain schools of Pantheism which hold that God becomes the Universe by changing into the Universe."*

Axiom of Indivisibility

Fourteenth Axiom of Reality: Reality is Indivisible.

This axiom announces the Indivisibility of Reality. *By "Indivisible" is meant 'inseparable; incapable of separation or division into parts; incapable of partition; the state of original, simple, and absolute Oneness.'*

From our consideration of Reality we perceive that it is indivisible, in the full sense of the term as above stated, by the very fact of its essence, nature, substance, and very being. Reality is not a composite union which may be indefinitely divided or separated into parts, but is an absolute unity which is an original, simple, and absolute Oneness, incapable of partition, separation, or division into parts of itself. Reality can no more be divided than it can be added to, subtracted from, or multiplied. Its absolute unity cannot be attacked, defeated, or impaired by division or partition. Being ultimate, it is incapable of further analysis, division, or separation. If it could be divided or separated into parts, it would cease to be ultimate. If there were two or more ultimates, neither would be ultimate; there would be no ultimate at all. If there were two or more infinites, neither would be infinite; there would be no infinite at all. Remember the truism, "The infinite must be absolute unity." The idea of the ultimate and infinite being transformed into many non-ultimate, finite things is absurd and unthinkable. It would defy the Primary Laws of Thought, for Reality is always itself, and cannot be other than itself.

Reality cannot be divided, separated, or parted, because (1) there is nothing to divide, separate, or part it; (2) nothing with which it may be divided, separated, or parted; (3) nothing to fill into the space between the divided, separated, or parted parts.

Even the conception of Materialism, which postulates the existence of Matter as Ultimate Principle, or that of Science, which asserts the Ether to be Ultimate Principle, does not assume that this Ultimate Principle is divisible. On the contrary, it expressly and positively holds that Ultimate Principle is indivisible, as indeed every conception of Ultimate Principle must so hold. Materialism holds that there is an Ultimate Universal Principle, called either Matter, Substance, Energy, or Universal Ether (according to the particular school of Materialism), and that all shapes, forms, and activities are merely centers of activity or energy in that Ultimate Principle. The Universal Principle is held to be indivisible, continuous, without parts, incapable of separation or division into parts. The word 'parts' is used merely figuratively in materialistic philosophy. To admit of divisibility, or 'parts,' in the Universal Ether would be to destroy its claimed ultimate nature.

The very conception of Ultimate Principle, by whatever name it may style the same, must carry with it the conception of indivisibility. Partition means 'to part from'; the reason refuses to consider that anything can be parted from Ultimate Principle.

Omnipresent totality

It is also a logical necessity that *an Infinite Unity must be present in its totality, wherever it is present at all.* A Universal Unity must be infinite, and an Infinite must be a Universal Unity; there is no logical escape from this conclusion. Infinite Unity can have no 'parts'; it is a Whole wherever it is present. And it must be present *everywhere,* being infinite. So that, again, it is seen that *the Infinite Unity must be present everywhere in its totality of being.* Reality is thus seen to be omnipresent in its totality at all times.

An error of Pantheism

The fact of the indivisibility of Reality also serves to refute the idea of a certain form of Pantheism now so popular under various names. The fundamental principle of this form of Pantheism is that 'the One becomes the Many' by separation or division into 'parts.' The expression that everything and everybody is 'a *part* of God' is seen to be a fallacy when the necessary fact of the indivisibility of ultimate substance is seen. Nothing can be a 'part' of that which is indivisible. By the very nature of its being, the Infinite can never become *many* finites; the Eternal can never become *many* temporalities, for the element of time, beginning and ending, is introduced into the problem by the separation. Each Infinite fact of Reality is denied by division and separation, and finite facts are substituted. From any point of view, from every aspect of consideration, divisibility must be denied of Ultimate Principle, by whatever name we may call it. Therefore Reality is perceived to be Indivisible.

Axiom of Immutability

Fifteenth Axiom of Reality: Reality is Immutable.

By "Immutable" is meant 'changeless; unchangeable; incapable of change; not susceptible to change; invariable; constant; stable; unalterable.'

From our consideration of Reality we perceive that it is immutable, in the full sense of the term as above stated, by the very fact of its essence, nature, substance, and very being. This is the inevitable report of reason. Change is the characteristic of the finite forms of the phenomenal world; it has naught to do with Ultimate Principle. Change implies subjection to the laws of Time and Causation, but Reality is eternal, causeless, and original. Change would defeat, nullify, and destroy every infinite fact of Reality, the very ultimate nature of Reality itself. Change is utterly and absolutely opposed to every fact of the essence, nature, substance, and principle of Reality. It is seen to be unthinkable in connection with Reality. If Reality is subject to Change, then it is not Ultimate Principle at all, and we must look still further for Ultimate Principle, for the very spirit of the conception of Ultimate Principle depends upon its immutability. Reason demands and will accept nothing less than a changeless ground for the changing forms of the universe.

There is nothing else than itself into which Reality can change itself or can be changed, for Reality is All-that-is. There is nothing else that could so change it. Reality can never be more, or less, or other than itself. If it were to change itself, or be changed into Something Else, then there would no longer be Reality; Reality would have disappeared. The new and changed thing would have begun in time and thus become timed and not eternal. It cannot be supposed that Reality can 'change its form,' for *it has no form to change,* and cannot become formed by reason of its infinite nature.

Moreover—and this is the final reason—by the primary laws of thought we are compelled to hold that (1) whatever is is always itself and never not itself; (2) the essential nature, substance, and very being of a thing is always the same no matter how different the forms, shapes, or conditions under which the thing occurs, presents itself, or appears. This being so, then Reality can never be other than itself; can never change itself into something else. Consequently the infinite variety of the forms, shapes, or conditions in which Reality occurs, presents itself, or appears in the phenomenal world arise not from actual change; they are merely appearances, presentations, occurrences on the outer surface of things, not disturbing in the least the essence, nature, substance, and Reality of Reality beneath the surface. This is a most important fact in the inquiry for Reality—probably the most important fact. And it should be impressed firmly upon the mind, for it determines the status of every object of manifestation—of you who read these lines. It serves to determine what you are.

Another error of Pantheism

It will be seen that this fact of the Immutability of Reality, when clearly conceived, must serve to confute and refute the erroneous theories of certain schools of Pantheism which hold that 'God *becomes* the Universe by *changing* into the Universe.' Thus it is sought to identify Nature with God, whereby, as Schopenhauer said, 'you show God to the door.' If God changes Himself into The Phenomenal Universe, then God is nonexistent and we need not concern ourselves anymore about Him, for he has committed suicide by Change. In such case there is no God, no Infinite, no Immutable, no Eternal; everything has become finite, temporal, separate, a mere union of diverse finite parts. In that case are we indeed adrift in the Ocean of Diversity. We have lost our Foundation of Reality, and are but ever-changing 'parts' of physical things governed by physical laws. Then, indeed, would be true the idea of some of the old philosophies that 'there is No Being; merely a Becoming.' Then would there, in truth, be nothing constant, the universe never the same for two consecutive moments, with no permanent ground of Reality to support it. But the reason of man, the very essence of his mental being, refuses to so think of That-which-is. In his heart of hearts he recognizes the existence of That-Which-Changes-Not, That-Which-Is Eternal, That-Which-Is-Reality.

The 'Evolving God'

Moreover, the idea of the immutability of Reality must serve to confute the erroneous idea of certain schools of metaphysics which assert the existence of 'an Evolving God'; that is, a God which *increases in intelligence, nature, and being* by reason of the change of the universe, which is an expression of Himself. This conception is that of a Supreme Being who is growing, developing, and increasing in efficiency, wisdom, power, and character. This is an attempt to combine the anthropomorphic deity and the pantheistic Nature-God. The conception is clearly anthropomorphic, as it seeks to attribute to God the qualities and characteristics of man. It defies every fact of Ultimate Principle of Reality. It is extremely unphilosophic and will not stand the test of logical examination.

This last mentioned conception vitiates the fact of immutability and also brings in the element of Time in the improvement, development, evolution, and changes mentioned. Moreover, it overlooks the fact that if time holds the possibility of any *improvement* of the Supreme Being, then that Supreme Being must have improved and developed to the fullest extent already. For, as it has had 'all the time there is' for improvement in the Eternity behind it—time extending back to infinity—it cannot have *more* time for improvement in the eternity before it—the infinity of time of the future. If it can accomplish anything in the future of eternity, *then it must have been able to accomplish the same thing in the past of eternity*. It has had as much time already as it can ever hope to have in the future. Infinite time is behind it as well as before it.

The only other alternative to the above is that the Evolving God has slept throughout all past eternity and only waked up an eon or so ago and began to grow and increase its wisdom; or that it lacked the desire or will to evolve until a few billions of years ago, when its ambition was aroused. Childish idea of anthropomorphism in a new form! Not only is the idea of the Evolving God childish, but it is also impossible. For there can be no Change or Improvement in Ultimate Reality, whether we call it God, Spirit, or Matter. Whatever is is itself and can never be other than itself. Moreover, the very idea of ultimateness carries with it the idea of perfection and completeness. If ultimate excellence is a matter of evolution in time for the Evolving God, then, reversing the process, we may imagine the Evolving God as having been in an infinitely undeveloped state and condition away back in the infinite past. The conception is scarcely worthy of a moment's serious consideration. We mention it merely because unthinking persons have been caught by the idea as advanced by illogical teachers.

By its very essence, nature, substance, and Reality, Reality must be complete, perfect, infinite, and ultimate. To such Reality there can come no change; it must be immutable from the very facts of its existence. Therefore, Reality is perceived to be immutable, changeless, unchangeable, incapable of change, not susceptible to change, invariable, constant, stable, unalterable.

An Atheist Critique of Pandeism

Dan Dana PhD

A retired educator, mediator, and psychologist, Dana has turned his attention to the advancement of secular humanism. Born in 1945 to a Protestant family in rural Missouri, he attributes his awakening to atheistic humanism as a worldview to his discovery of the philosophy of Bertrand Russell in his youth. Dan's life experiences include serving in the U.S. Army in Vietnam (noncombat) and Panama Canal Zone (1966–1968); teaching at a New England university for twenty-eight years, and guest-lecturing at educational institutions on six continents; and traveling in over seventy-five countries. The author of several books on mediation and conflict resolution, his most recent publication is The Reason Revolution: Atheism, Secular Humanism, and the Collapse of Religion, *a free ebook available at Amazon and other online retailers. He holds the PhD in psychology (University of Missouri, 1977) and resides with his wife in Sarasota, Florida (USA).*

A complete definition of pandeism may be found elsewhere in this anthology. For the purpose of this critique, I will use this definition from Wikipedia: *The belief that a creator deity became the universe and ceased to exist as a separate and conscious entity.*[1] As such, pandeism is a presuppositional theory attempting to explain the beginning of existence, the presupposition being that existence had a beginning at all. Here, 'existence' is differentiated from 'the universe,' and the Big Bang is differentiated from 'the beginning of existence,' as will be discussed below.

My view that pandeism is an erroneous theory rests on three contentions, which I shall elaborate:

1. There is no evidence that a creator deity ever existed.

2. Pandeism is not compatible with science.
3. Pandeism, like ordinary theism, arises in part from the human inability to fathom the dimensions of infinite time and infinite space.

Virtually every human culture in history has invented religions, deities, afterlife myths, and creation myths to explain the mysteries they encountered in their time. Harvard biologist E. O. Wilson estimates that over the past 60,000 years humans have devised roughly 100,000 religions based on roughly 2,500 gods.[2] The great majority of these religions are now extinct, having no contemporary adherents. The religion of the ancient Greeks, which is now taught in educational institutions as 'Greek Mythology,' is the extinct religion perhaps best known to our readers.

Pandeism differs from today's popular religions in that the deity is no longer believed to exist in a conscious or active form. Hence, it is not a personal god with whom the faithful may communicate via prayer and other channels. Pandeism does, however, hold that a conscious deity once existed that imbued the universe with its intelligence and other sentient qualities.

A problem that pandeism shares with other religions is that no empirical evidence has been found by scientific means that any deity has ever existed. The major extant religions rely on purportedly divinely inspired 'holy books' as proof of the truth of their beliefs, which is fallacious circular logic. (I recall a cartoon photo of a paper table napkin with the handwritten inscription, "The napkin religion is the one true religion because it says so here on this napkin.")

A listing of over fifty religions and their sacred texts may be found at the Wikipedia page on religious texts.[3] Of course, not all these religions can be true, since many of their doctrines are mutually incompatible—for example, some are monotheistic whereas others are polytheistic. And not all their holy books could possibly have been divinely created, since different (and often disagreeing) gods are believed to have inspired them. Clearly, at most, only one of these religions can possibly be entirely true. Further, if all but one are not true, as logic dictates, then it is likely that none are true. After all, how confident can a believer be that one's religion, being one of many thousands, happens to be the one true religion considering the fact that no religion is supported by any empirical evidence whatsoever? Therefore, all but the most fundamentalist believers recognize the fallibility of so-called sacred texts as evidence of the factuality of their beliefs.

Of course, pandeism has no divinely inspired sacred text, and so its adherents' faith in the creator deity is based on other premises. Their worldview depends on *a priori* principles of pure (intuitive) reason to derive their belief that a creator deity once existed, and then the deity became the universe itself. The history of philosophy is littered with the carcasses of beliefs derived through pure reason, the most famous of which may be certain elements of Kantianism itself, the philosophy of Immanuel Kant who originated the term 'pure reason' in 1781 (six years before 'pandeism' would first be mentioned, by one of Kant's own countrymen). For example, Kant believed in God only to the extent that he reasoned that morality deductively *requires* belief in God.[4] Secular humanists vigorously assert, with overwhelming supporting evidence, that morality and social ethics are untethered to religious belief, and indeed are regularly practiced by nonbelievers; hence, the common humanist refrain "Good without god(s)."

I will leave to other contributors to this anthology the task of elaborating the *a priori* principles (assumptions) from which belief in pandeism's creator deity is derived. Those assumptions will be apparent in their arguments for the existence of the deus.

Being familiar with Christian apologetics, I recognize that the language of science is used disingenuously to support the tenets of their faith, as shown in teleological arguments for 'Intelligent Design' and other presuppositional attempts to logically prove the factuality of Christian theology. In my view, pandeism falls victim to (or is the result of) similarly flawed logic. I'm sure my co-contributors will fervidly rejoin with opposing views to this assertion.

To better understand pandeism in preparation for this writing, I posed three questions to Knujon Mapson, the editor of this anthology. (In our prepublication correspondence, Mr Mapson disclaimed being an 'official' representative of pandeism, although he is perhaps its most vocal proponent.) Here is my first question and his answer.

> **DD: Question 1:** Who/what created the creator? Or, did the creator not exist in time and space prior to creation?
>
> **KM: Answer (his capitalizations are retained):** If a Creator is to be posited, it indeed follows that this Creator must either have itself come into existence through some spontaneous process that did not require a Creator, or was itself intentionally created by an Ur-Creator, or simply exists eternally without origin.

Our esteemed editor acknowledges that his answer is speculative, as no evidence is available to support any of the three alternatives he offers. Indeed, no empirical evidence is even conceivable that would assist us in selecting one of the three possibilities he provides. Rather, those alternative solutions are derived from the *a priori* assumption that the creator deity existed. Further, to my empirically oriented ('show me the evidence') mind, none of the three alternatives is remotely plausible. Therefore, the question of what preceded the existence of the creator remains unanswered, and is, I believe, unanswerable if a scientifically plausible response is required. That is, the *a priori* principle of existence of a creator deity is unsupported by evidence or by logic, and is therefore a false assumption.

Some readers may be reminded of an anecdote reported by cosmologist Stephen Hawking in his 1988 book *A Brief History of Time:*

> A well-known scientist (some say it was Bertrand Russell) once gave a public lecture on astronomy. He described how the earth orbits around the sun and how the sun, in turn, orbits around the center of a vast collection of stars called our galaxy. At the end of the lecture, a little old lady at the back of the room got up and said: "What you have told us is rubbish. The world is really a flat plate supported on the back of a giant tortoise." The scientist gave a superior smile before replying, "What is the tortoise standing on?" "You're very clever, young man, very clever," said the old lady. "But it's turtles all the way down!"[5]

So, it seems that pandeism shares a common conundrum with theistic religions: Where did God come from? If we are to avoid the tortured circular reasoning of Christian apologists, and if we require at least a modicum of plausibility, given the utter absence of any supporting empirical evidence, it is hard to escape the reasoned conclusion that God (or some other creator deity by any name) does not, and did not ever, exist.

Mr Mapson buttressed his answer by pointing out that time is nonlinear, and that time may have also begun at the moment of creation of matter. Time is indeed a variable dimension of space-time affected by gravity, as confirmed by empirical tests of Einstein's theory of general relativity.[6] So, its inconstancy may be (wrongly) considered by proponents of pandeism to be supportive of the notion that the creator deity created itself at the moment of creation of matter and energy. Indeed, matter and energy are interchangeable quantities according to the formula $E=mc^2$ where the speed of light (c) is constant. Cosmologists and particle physicists, such as Lawrence Krauss, describe the Big Bang as pure energy, with matter (in the form of subatomic particles) coming into existence within a minuscule fraction of a second thereafter.[7] Further, Krauss states that time itself came into existence at that moment as well, insofar as time is a function of motion of particles in the primordial universe. Scientists who support the notion of a multiverse, such as astrophysicist Coel Hellier, argue that our universe may be only one among many, or more likely an infinite number, separated by hyper-distance, scattered throughout infinite space (see the semantic discussion of space vs. existence below), entirely out of contact with each other. Admittedly, the concept of a multiverse is speculative, and probably can never be confirmed empirically, although Hellier's philosophical argument is compelling.[8] Moreover, the dimensions of infinite time and space are beyond our limited human powers of imagination. It is instructive to note, however, that Krauss, Hawking, Tyson, Weinberg, Greene, Randall, Hellier, and the great majority of other prominent cosmologists are self-identified atheists who do not find it necessary to posit a creator deity to account for the beginning of our universe.[9] So, it may be a bit presumptuous of laypeople (relative to the fields of cosmology and astrophysics) to insist otherwise. Indeed, a survey of members of the National Academy of Sciences found that 93% are atheist or agnostic.[10] How is it that the most accomplished scientists regard the notion of deities to not be useful in their disciplined search for understanding the natural world and its origin? Here is my second question to Mr Mapson.

> **DD: Question 2:** By what physical mechanism(s) did the creator manufacture the material universe? Or, did the creator not exist prior to the creation/Big Bang, at which time particle

physics as we now know it began to take form?

KM: Answer: We don't know, but the answer will be discoverable by science. But it does seem something had to exist, or else there'd be no reason for there ever to be a change in the status quo of nothing existing.

As cosmologist Lawrence Kraus discusses in his book *A Universe from Nothing,* the laws of physics, as they operate in our universe, appeared concurrently with the Big Bang, not before it.[11] Those laws are known as the Standard Model, which identifies electromagnetism, the weak and strong nuclear forces, and classification of all known subatomic particles.[12] Indeed, in the conjectured multiverse, other universes may contain 'matter,' the form and nature of which may be quite different from matter and energy as they appear in our local universe and may operate under different physical processes than those observed in our universe.

Normal (i.e. observable) matter comprises only about 5% of the mass of our universe, the remainder being dark matter and dark energy.[13] These 'substances' (perhaps not a suitable term, since little is known about their physical properties) interact with gravity, but not with light. That is, dark matter cannot be visually detected with telescopes, but it does produce observable effects on the motion of stars, galaxies, and other massive objects.

It is plausible, albeit highly speculative, that dark matter and dark energy are associated with a separate universe that originated in a separate Big Bang, that is colocated with ours in space, and that is operating under different laws than the Standard Model that describes normal matter and energy.[14] Or, if science develops instruments capable of empirically observing dark matter and dark energy, which are invisible to our existing technology, the Standard Model may be revised to include additional particles or forces that would define these phenomena as derived from our Big Bang and therefore a part of our universe.

In any case, dark matter and dark energy do not conform to the current Standard Model. So, speculatively, another Big Bang that created a different universe might operate under different physical laws, which would have come into existence at that moment of creation. The physical nature of dark matter and dark energy constitutes one of the great mysteries that cosmologists and physicists are currently studying.

So, we see that 'existence' may not be limited to our local universe, which did indeed begin with the Big Bang. Other universes quite likely exist, as Hellier argues. Consequently, the beginning of existence, which pandeism attempts to explain by positing a creator deity, is an irrelevant concept if one accepts that time, as well as space, are infinite in dimension and may contain an infinite number of universes.

Perhaps 'distance' or some other term would be more suitable than 'space' in this context, since, as Krauss argues, space itself was created with the Big Bang and will continue to expand eternally. He explains that, since space, even where devoid of matter and radiation, contains quantum mechanical processes and dark energy—it is not 'nothing.' So, the hyper-distant regions between universes are not the same empirically observable 'empty space' that exists within our universe.

Envisioning 'nothing,' not even so-called empty space, challenges our frail human imagination, as does the infinite dimensions of space-time. Nevertheless, if the multiverse exists, as is probable, then absolute nothingness between universes probably also exists. To the extent that we are capable of imagining this nothingness, we can imagine that the Big Bang created the matter, energy, time, *and* space that constitute our universe.

Existence ('all that exists'), then, encompasses all universes plus whatever lies between them, which is not to be confused with 'empty space' as it appears within our particular universe. Further, it may not be physically possible for anything, such as light, to penetrate or travel through that inter-universe medium, ensuring that each universe remains isolated from all others. Science allows such speculation, so long as *super*naturalism is not introduced. After all, science is the study of *nature*. Pandeism, a theology that presupposes a nonmaterial supernatural creator deity, is a demonstrably unscientific theory of existence.

A review of various multiverse theories[15] may assist readers in mulling the incomprehensible scale of infinite space-time and the fathomless nothingness (not even the 'something' of empty space) between universes. Note that these are science-based speculations, not theological renderings of the mysteries of existence. Since science does not anticipate ever being capable of direct empirical observation of other universes, multiverse theories will no doubt remain speculations. Future advances in science, however, will surely refine those speculations.

My conclusion, as well as that of all but a very few professional cosmologists,[16] is that the conditions present at the moment of the Big Bang—which have existed throughout infinite time and infinite space, possibly containing an infinite number of universes—were quite capable of creating our home universe 13.72 billion years ago without the midwifery of deus.

As mind-stretching as the concept of infinite space-time may be, it is nevertheless more plausible, and more consistent with known science, than is a creator deity. Gods are best understood as man-made inventions arising from our pre-science ancestors' attempts over millennia to explain the otherwise inexplicable mysteries of their earth-bound environment. Otherwise, we face the even more daunting task of explaining, *without resorting to mysticism*, what happened before the beginning of time, and what lies beyond the edge of space. Which of these two universe-views, dear reader, is your conclusion? Empiricism or mysticism? Reason or mythology? I see no third option. I see no hybrid.

Here is my third and final question to Mr Mapson.

> **DD: Question 3:** Is/was the creator 'supernatural'? Or, are/were the principles of particle physics (the natural world) at work within the 'entity' of the creator? Or, is/was the creator a non-material being prior to creation of the universe? If the latter, in what sense did the creator 'exist' prior to creation?

> **KM: Answer (capitalizations are his):** If it exists, it is bound by some laws—of mathematics and logic, at least—though not necessarily all the laws which govern our Universe. There are aspects of our Universe (the specific speed of light, the ratios of certain particle sizes) which scientists have debated could be different in alternate Universes, so the question really is, what characteristics must persist in any Universe. And there we'll find what governs any Creator.

Physicists and others working in the natural sciences consider anything that exists, whether or not it is yet discovered, to exist in the *natural* world, which is comprised of physical matter, including subatomic particles so far identified in the Standard Model. That is, nothing exists that has no physical properties. For example, humans do not have a 'soul' apart from the biological processes occurring within the physical body. Similarly, 'consciousness' is nothing more than the subjective experience of bioelectrical processes within a living brain. When the brain ceases to function, as when the body that houses it dies, consciousness ceases. Consequently, there is no conscious afterlife and no soul that survives physical death. To be sure, the abiogenetic origin of life is a yet-to-be fully understood process, and is a subject of active research, but there is no scientific basis for thinking that life or consciousness is a *super*natural phenomenon that functions outside the laws of science.

My third question to Mr Mapson above asks whether pandeism holds that the creator deity was an entity composed of physical matter. Or, alternatively, do pandeists believe that the creator was *super*natural, having no physical properties? If the former, then the deity is part of the natural universe and therefore must be comprised of physical properties consistent with the Standard Model, and so is subject to research by the scientific method. If the latter, we must utterly reject the notion of a supernatural deity, since the evolving Standard Model describes and defines all that is natural.

The supposed creator deity is believed by adherents of pandeism to have possessed consciousness and intelligence. Absent physical properties, such attributes are scientifically impossible.

I shall close this critique with a brief rebuttal of three additional notions advanced by proponents of pandeism to support their creationist worldview.

Fortuities and the Fine-Tuned Universe

Apologists for pandeism, and for creationism more broadly, argue that certain improbable 'fortuities' constitute compelling evidence for the existence of a creator deity. Several examples are proffered[17] of 'fine-tuning' of the laws of physics and other cosmological conditions that, if significantly different from their existing values, would render the universe structurally dysfunctional and make carbon-based life impossible. These conditions include the ratio of the strength of electromagnetism to the strength of gravity and the ratio of dark energy to the density of the universe. Astrophysicist Martin Rees[18] cites these and other technical features of the physical structure of the universe as so improbable that a conscious and intentional creator must have designed it to allow life to appear. (Interestingly, Professor Rees has more recently stated, 'I've got no religious beliefs at all.'[19])

Although some scientists, such as Rees, support the fine-tuning hypothesis, most do not, arguing instead that the universe is not fine-tuned to us; rather, we are fine-tuned to the universe. That is, humans, and all other life forms, exist only in the conditions in which it is possible for us to exist. If our universe were fatally unaccommodating to life, then life would not exist here. We happen to reside where life is possible; hence we are here to ask these questions. There is no support for a cosmic mandate that life must exist, in our universe or in others.

Cosmologist Victor J. Stenger, author of *The Fallacy of Fine-Tuning: Why the Universe Is Not Designed for Us,*[20] explains how the "strong anthropic principle"[21] distorts perception by causing human observers to assume the universe exists for the special benefit of humans, when in fact the universe is simply the way it is. We humans happen to be compatible with the minuscule niche of space-time in which we find ourselves, where we were suited to evolve, to currently exist, to observe ourselves, and to reflect upon our own existence. This is quite a simple notion, actually, once we cease insisting that we are on the cosmic center stage.

Why Does the Universe Exist?

Pandeism attempts to answer this question by positing a conscious creator deity who had a desire or intention to create the universe.

It is human nature to wonder why. "Why did you say that?" "Why did that accident happen to me?" "Why was I born?" But asking 'why' is the wrong question in scientific inquiry, except in some social-psychological research. 'Why' presupposes an intention, which in turn presupposes a conscious entity that has a purpose for its actions. As Lawrence Krauss explains in *A Universe from Nothing,* the more useful question is how: "How did the universe come into existence?" "How will it end?"[22]

Cosmologists have yet to achieve consensus about how the universe will end. A Big Crunch, in which the universe collapses under force of gravity into a singularity (a zero-dimensional point of infinite density), was the leading contending theory until dark energy was discovered in the 1990s. Dark energy (an apparently repulsive gravitational force) accounts for the increasing rate of acceleration of expansion of the universe.[23] Eternal expansion is now considered more likely. Time, as a mathematically measurable dimension, might indeed end if the Big Crunch were to be our universe's fate, since presumably there would no longer be matter-in-motion, although current physics is inadequate to explain what happens at or near a singularity. But, infinite space-time would remain, possibly containing other universes, under either outcome.[24] Theology in general, and pandeism in particular, contributes nothing to our understanding of this question, nor to its answer.

So, the scientifically appropriate answer to "Why does the universe exist?" is: There is no reason, there is no purpose. No conscious creator deity had an intention that led to creating the universe.

Supernaturalism

Pandeism claims that the creator deity existed prior to creating the physical properties of the material universe, or at least appeared concurrently with it.

Supernaturalism is the mystical belief that entities exist beyond empirically observable reality, outside the laws of nature, specifically the Standard Model of particle physics.

Prior to the advent of modern science, generally ascribed to the work of Galileo in the early seventeenth century, humans had few observational and analytical tools for determining what is 'real.' The ancient Greeks made an attempt at empirical understanding of reality by proposing earth, water, air, and fire as the four elements of the natural world. Microscopes, telescopes, astral spectroscopes, the Large Hadron Collider, and a multitude of other data-gathering tools have since been developed that dramatically increase our ability to 'see' nature beyond the human scale.

Two obstacles impede popular acceptance of scientism as the most authoritative approach to acquisition of knowledge:

1. Insufficient science education among the global population;
2. The psychological propensity of humans to invent religions and other forms of mysticism.[25]

I recognize that scientism is controversial, criticized by some as *excessive* dependence on science and the scientific method.[26] To be sure, personally meaningful insights can and do occur through music, art, and other non-scientific endeavors. And the impacts of such endeavors on subjective human experience can be, and are, studied scientifically. But if one's goal is to understand *objective* reality, apart from human subjectivity, science represents the only valid approach to achieving it.

Religious believers who regard faith alone, without empirical evidence, as sufficient for belief in their particular creation story, gods, afterlife myth, spirits and other supernatural beings, conveniently ignore many settled scientific facts and, by logical necessity, refute scientism. I have long been baffled that reason and unquestioned faith can co-inhabit an intelligent, educated mind—perhaps an unrecognized sleight-of-mind bridges the dissonance.[27] Darrel Ray examines in *The God Virus: How Religion Infects Our Lives and Culture* how mystical beliefs propagate within a host culture and impair rational thought by means that are curiously analogous to viral infection in living organisms.[28] As with biological viruses, the 'God virus' can infect intelligent, well-educated people as it does those of us who aspire to the fiftieth percentile, although not as markedly.[29]

Pandeism, in positing a creator deity, is a form of supernaturalism, notwithstanding pandeists' belief that the creator became the natural world once the act of creation occurred. It follows that if the now-defunct deity is not describable by the physics that describes the universe we find today, as pandeists appear to acknowledge, the belief is incompatible with science.

My purpose in this article is to encourage science-based critical thinking among adherents of pandeism and of religion in general. I regard science and religion as inherently incompatible because they put forth mutually inconsistent theories of existence. I anticipate that as further scientific discoveries advance our knowledge of the natural world, religion will recede as a harmful presence in human affairs. I readily admit, however, that pandeism is perhaps the least harmful religion yet invented.

Notes

1 Wikipedia, retrieved 3 February 2016 from https://en.wikipedia.org/wiki/Pandeism.

2 Edward O. Wilson, *On Human Nature: With a New Preface*, Revised Edition (Harvard University Press, 2004).

3 In Wikipedia, retrieved 3 February 2016 from https://en.wikipedia.org/wiki/Religious_text.

4 In *Stanford Encyclopedia of Philosophy*, retrieved 3 February 2016 from http://plato.stanford.edu/entries/kant-religion/.

5 Stephen Hawking, *A Brief History of Time* (Bantam Dell, 1988).

6 In Wikipedia, retrieved 3 February 2016 from https://en.wikipedia.org/wiki/Tests_of_general_relativity.

7 Lawrence M. Krauss, *A Universe from Nothing: Why There Is Something Rather than Nothing* (Simon & Schuster, 2012). See also Keele University (UK) professor Coel Hellier, personal communication, 9 February 2016.

8 Coel Hellier, "How Many Big Bangs? A Philosophical Argument for a Multiverse," coelsblog, retrieved 3 February 2016 from https://coelsblog.wordpress.com/2015/12/30/how-many-big-bangs-a-philosophical-argument-for-a-multiverse/.

9 Sean M. Carroll, "Why (Almost All) Cosmologists Are Atheists," retrieved 7 February 2016 from http://preposterousuniverse.com/

writings/nd-paper/.

10 National Academy of Sciences, *Teaching about Evolution and the Nature of Science* (National Academy Press, Washington DC, 1998).

11 See note 7.

12 In Wikipedia, retrieved 3 February 2016 from https://en.wikipedia.org/wiki/Standard_Model.

13 In Wikipedia, retrieved 3 February 2016 from https://en.wikipedia.org/wiki/Dark_matter.

14 Ohio State University astrophysics professor Paul M. Sutter, personal communication, 6 February 2016.

15 In Wikipedia, retrieved 10 February 2016 from https://en.wikipedia.org/wiki/Multiverse.

16 See note 10.

17 Knujon Mapson, retrieved 3 February 2016 from http://everything2.com/title/For+atheists%252C+what+is+the+proof+for+pandeism%253F. See also, in Wikipedia, retrieved 3 February 2016 from https://en.wikipedia.org/wiki/Fine-tuned_Universe.

18 Martin Reese in Wikipedia, retrieved 3 February 2016 from https://en.wikipedia.org/wiki/Martin_Rees.

19 In *The Guardian*, retrieved 13 February 2016 from https://www.theguardian.com/science/2011/apr/06/astronomer-royal-martin-rees-interview.

20 Victor J. Stenger, *The Fallacy of Fine-Tuning: How the Universe Is Not Designed for Humanity* (Prometheus Books, 2011).

21 In Wikipedia, retrieved 3 February 2016 from https://en.wikipedia.org/wiki/Anthropic_principle.

22 See note 7.

23 In Wikipedia, retrieved 11 February 2016 from https://en.wikipedia.org/wiki/Dark_energy.

24 Ohio State University astrophysics professor Paul M. Sutter, personal communication, 11 February 2016.

25 See note 2.

26 In Wikipedia, retrieved 3 February 2016 from https://en.wikipedia.org/wiki/Scientism.

27 Dan Dana, *The Reason Revolution: Atheism, Secular Humanism, and the Collapse of Religion* (2014), retrieved 10 February 2016 from http://www.dandana.us/atheism/.

28 Darrel W. Ray, *The God Virus: How Religion Infects Our Lives and Culture* (IPC Press, December 2009); ISBN 978-0-9709505-1-2.

29 In Wikipedia, retrieved 31 March 2016 from https://en.wikipedia.org/wiki/Religiosity_and_intelligence.

Ode: Intimations of Immortality from Recollections of Early Childhood

William Wordsworth

Stanza V:

Our birth is but a sleep and a forgetting:
The Soul that rises with us, our life's Star,
Hath had elsewhere its setting,
And cometh from afar:
Not in entire forgetfulness,
And not in utter nakedness,
But trailing clouds of glory do we come
From God, who is our home:
Heaven lies about us in our infancy!
Shades of the prison-house begin to close
Upon the growing Boy,
But He beholds the light, and whence it flows,
He sees it in his joy;
The Youth, who daily farther from the east
Must travel, still is Nature's Priest,
And by the vision splendid
Is on his way attended;
At length the Man perceives it die away,
And fade into the light of common day.

BOOKS

Iff Books

ACADEMIC AND SPECIALIST

Iff Books publishes non-fiction. It aims to work with authors and titles that augment our understanding of the human condition, society and civilisation, and the world or universe in which we live.

If you have enjoyed this book, why not tell other readers by posting a review on your preferred book site. Recent bestsellers from Iff Books are:

Why Materialism Is Baloney

How True Skeptics Know There Is No Death and Fathom Answers to Life, the Universe, and Everything

Bernardo Kastrup

A hard-nosed, logical, and skeptic non-materialist metaphysics, according to which the body is in mind, not mind in the body.

Paperback: 978-1-78279-362-5 ebook: 978-1-78279-361-8

The Fall

Steve Taylor

The Fall discusses human achievement versus the issues of war, patriarchy and social inequality.

Paperback: 978-1-90504-720-8 ebook: 978-184694-633-2

Brief Peeks Beyond
Critical Essays on Metaphysics, Neuroscience, Free Will, Skepticism and Culture
Bernardo Kastrup
An incisive, original, compelling alternative to current mainstream cultural views and assumptions.
Paperback: 978-1-78535-018-4 ebook: 978-1-78535-019-1

Is There an Afterlife?
David Fontana
Is there an afterlife? If so what is it like? How do Western ideas of the afterlife compare with Eastern? David Fontana presents the historical and contemporary evidence for survival of physical death.
Paperback: 978-1-90381-690-5

Readers of ebooks can buy or view any of these bestsellers by clicking on the live link in the title. Most titles are published in paperback and as an ebook. Paperbacks are available in traditional bookshops. Both print and ebook formats are available online.

Find more titles and sign up to our readers' newsletter at http://www.johnhuntpublishing.com/non-fiction
Follow us on Facebook at https://www.facebook.com/JHPNonFiction
and Twitter at https://twitter.com/JHPNonFiction